TEXTILES

AT THE CUTTING EDGE

TEXTILES

AT THE CUTTING EDGE

LESLEY
CRESSWELL

FORBES PUBLICATIONS

Textiles at the Cutting Edge
(For the GCE A/S and A-Level Examination)

text by Lesley Cresswell

Edited by Tess Livingstone
© Forbes Publications 2001
Abbott House
1-2 Hanover Street
London
W1S 1YZ

Illustrations by Tony Barrett

Cover image fabrics were produced
by Winnie Wing Yan Au

Cover photograph by Abbas Nazari

Cover design by Jerry Goldie Graphic Design

ISBN 1899 527 176

Printed in Great Britain by Thanet Press
Margate, Kent

CONTENTS

Introduction 1

Unit 1 **INDUSTRIAL AND COMMERCIAL PRODUCTS AND PRACTICES** **5**

Preview 5

CHAPTER 1 Products and Applications 10

2 Materials and Components 20

3 Industrial and Commercial Practice 32

Exam Practice 54

Unit 3

Section A **MATERIALS, COMPONENTS AND SYSTEMS** **55**

Preview 55

CHAPTER 1 Classification of Materials and Components 58

2 Working Properties of Materials 91

3 Hand and Commercial Processes 94

4 Testing Materials 117

Exam Practice 122

Section B **DESIGN AND TECHNOLOGY IN SOCIETY** **123**

Preview 123

CHAPTER 1 The Physical and Social Consequences of Design and Technology on Society 126

2 Professional Designers at Work 155

3 Anthropometrics and Ergonomics 168

Exam Practice 172

Section B **CAD/CAM** **173**

Preview 173

CHAPTER 1 The Impact Computer-aided Design and Manufacture (CAD/CAM) on Industry 176

2 Computer-aided Design 185

3 Computer-aided Manufacture (CAM) 207

Exam Practice 214

Unit 4

Section A   **FURTHER STUDY OF MATERIALS,**
                  COMPONENTS AND SYSTEMS   215
                  Preview   215
CHAPTER 1   Selection of Materials   218
        2   New Technologies and the Creation of New Materials   225
        3   Values Issues   259
                  Exam Practice   262

Section B   **DESIGN AND TECHNOLOGY IN SOCIETY**   263
                  Preview   263
CHAPTER 1   Economics and Production   266
        2   Consumer Interests   280
        3   Advertising and Marketing   291
        4   Conservation and Resources   307
                  Exam Practice   320

Section B   **CAD/CAM**   321
                  Preview   321
CHAPTER 1   Computer-aided Design, Manufacture
                  and Testing (CAD/MAT)   323
        2   Robotics   339
        3   Uses of Information and Commications
                  Technology (ICT) in the Manufacture of Products   357
                  Exam Practice   373

Introduction

Textiles at the Cutting Edge is intended to support your work in Textiles Technology when you are following the Edexcel Advanced Subsidiary (AS) and Advanced GCE course in Product Design. If you are following another Advanced Level course you will also find the book invaluable in developing knowledge and understanding about Textiles Technology.

This student-friendly book follows the structure of the Edexcel Specification. It covers the content of the externally assessed units and helps you prepare for end-of-unit examinations. As with any Advanced level course you are advised to read around the subject to broaden your knowledge and understanding. Newspapers in particular are very useful for finding out about lifestyle and fashion trends and for keeping up with the latest developments in technology. The Internet is another source of information, although it is advisable to decide on a 'hit-list' of useful-looking sites before you begin any research.

Textiles at the Cutting Edge:
- guides you through the knowledge and understanding requirements of the Edexcel Specification
- provides tasks to help you understand the issues and improve your own learning
- provides a picture of cutting-edge developments in materials and product manufacturing
- covers subject knowledge related to product analysis, textile materials and components, industrial practices, CAD/CAM, quality, health and safety
- contains exam-type questions to help prepare you prepare for end-of-unit examinations.

USING THIS BOOK

SECTION 1

This explains how the Edexcel course is structured and gives an overview of the assessment requirements. You should read this section before starting your course.

SECTION 2

This section of the book provides unit-by-unit guidance on each of the following externally assessed units: AS Unit 1, AS Unit 3 Section A and

Section B; Advanced GCE (A2) Unit 4 Section A and Section B. Both Units 3B and 4B cover the options Design and Technology in Society and CAD/CAM.

All of these units will provide you with a great deal of background understanding to help you through your course. They will also help you prepare for external assessment and increase your chances of success. You should therefore refer to this section of the book for guidance as and when you need.

Each of the AS and A2 units uses similar headings and sub-headings to those found in the Edexcel Specification, so you can be sure that you are covering all the content of the Specification.

SECTION 2 STRUCTURE

The first page of each unit summarises:

- what you will learn or do in the unit
- how the unit is assessed
- what the examiner is looking for and / or exam tips.

The main body of each unit:

- covers the subject content in detail
- provides tasks and questions to help you improve your own learning.

The last page of each unit provides exam-style questions that:

- give you exam practise
- help you prepare for assessment
- help you to be successful.

In the A2 Unit 4 Section A and Section B you may find 'Signposts' to the AS units. These refer you to information or topics that have been discussed in the AS course.

TAKING RESPONSIBILITY FOR YOUR OWN LEARNING

Once you have a clear understanding of the course requirements, you can plan your time and your work. Taking responsibility for your own learning will enable you to be more independent and to manage your own learning. This may require you to use a wide range of support beyond your teacher or tutor.

Any work that you do during the course may provide opportunities for you to generate evidence for your Key Skills portfolio. It may be helpful to check out the Key Skills requirements for Communication, Application of Number and Information Technology at Level 3.

SECTION 1: HOW THE COURSE IS STRUCTURED

The AS course can be studied as a discrete course in order to achieve an AS qualification in Product Design (Textiles Technology). In this case you would study Units 1–3.

The AS course may also be studied as a foundation to the Advanced GCE course in order to achieve an Advanced Level qualification in Product Design (Textiles Technology). In this case you would study Units 1–3, followed by Units 4–6.

AS 50% of the Specification content		A2 50% of the Specification content	
Unit 1	Industrial and commercial products and practices	Unit 4	Further study of materials, components and systems with Options
Unit 2	Product Development I	Unit 5	Product Development II
Unit 3	Materials, components and systems with Options	Unit 6	Design and technology capability

THE AS UNITS

The three AS units combine to make the AS course. They:

- build on the knowledge, understanding and skills you developed in GCSE Design and Technology
- contribute 50% of the Specification content. You must follow the AS course before progressing to A2.

THE A2 UNITS

The A2 units combine with the three AS units to make the Advanced GCE course. They:

- build on the knowledge, understanding and skills developed in the AS course
- contribute the other 50% of the Specification content

ASSESSMENT OF THE AS UNITS

AS 50% of the Specification content		Assessment	% of AS course	% of A2 course
Unit 1	Industrial and commercial products and practices	External 1 ½ hour examination	30%	15%
Unit 2	Product Development I	Internal Coursework Project	40%	20%
Unit 3	Materials, components and and systems with Options	External 1 ½ hour examination	30%	15%

Unit 1 and Unit 3 are externally assessed by examination. These units are covered in this book.

Unit 2 is the coursework unit, which is assessed by internal marking and external moderation by the Edexcel Moderator.

ASSESSMENT OF THE A2 UNITS

A2 50% of the Specification content		Assessment	% of AS coure
Unit 4	Further study of materials, components and systems with Options	External 1 ½ hour examination	15%
Unit 5	Product Development I	Internal Coursework Project	20%
Unit 6	Design and technology capability	External 3 hour examination	15%

Unit 4 and Unit 6 are externally assessed by examination. Unit 4 is covered in this book. Unit 6 has no content. It is assessed by a Design Exam.

Unit 5 is the coursework unit, which is assessed by internal marking and external moderation by the Edexcel Moderator.

Preview

WHAT YOU WILL LEARN IN THE UNIT

Unit 1 will help you to develop your understanding of industrial and commercial practices through the process of product analysis. During the unit you should investigate the design, manufacture, use and disposal of a variety of textile products. The product analysis you undertake must include knowledge and understanding of the following areas:

Chapter 1   Products and Applications
- The processes involved in the development of a range of manufactured products

Chapter 2   Materials and components
- The range of materials and their potential application
- Working characteristics of materials

Chapter 3   Industrial and Commercial Practice
- Manufacturing systems, including one-off, batch and high volume production
- Stages of production
- Detailed manufacturing methods, when combining or processing material
- The use of ICT in the design and manufacture of products
- Quality
- Health & Safety
- The appeal of textile products

WHAT YOU WILL DO IN THE UNIT

During the unit you should undertake a variety of activities to develop your understanding of the unit content. You may be asked to:

- work collaboratively with others on some activities such as the analysis of a variety of products
- work individually on some activities, like recording the analysis of products
- work individually on the detailed analysis of some products
- work individually on some theoretical aspects of the unit content
- work individually on exam-style product analysis questions

CHOOSING PRODUCTS FOR PRODUCT ANALYSIS

The products that you analyse must enable coverage of the unit content and provide the opportunity for you to meet assessment requirements. In order to cover the subject content, the range of products should include those manufactured by one-off, batch and mass-production. The suggestions below are for the kind of products that may fall into these categories. You do not have to analyse all the products suggested, but should investigate a selection. Products that fall into one category are often made following similar principles. For example:

- One-off products are often made to a client's specification and may be made from more expensive or unusual materials
- Batch-produced products may be indistinguishable from mass-produced ones, because they are made following the same quality requirements, but they may differ in style or colour from mass-produced ones, since short runs are possible. These may follow the required style changes as dictated by fashion – Quick Response manufacturing is often used for batch-production
- Mass-produced garments are made to fit a range of standard measurements. They may follow trends that are seen to be popular, so that they sell well for a period of time. For example, socks or tights will need to follow colour and styling trends but these trends may well last for more than a season. Mass-produced fashion goods are often at the lower cost end of the market – lower- cost, sell fast.

ANALYSING AND EVALUATING PRODUCTS AND PROCESSES

Most people undertake product analysis quite regularly, only they don't realise that they are doing it! Think about the last time that you bought a new pair of trousers or a T-shirt. When you shop for products such as these, you evaluate the style, the look, the value for money and the image that the product might give you. What you also do is to make value judgements about the quality of design and manufacture of the product. This means that you are already well practised in judging the worth of a product from a personal point of view. In order to carry out the analysis of a variety of products required by this unit, you will now need to apply your analytical skills in a more formal way.

PRACTISING PRODUCT ANALYSIS

In order to improve your product analysis skills you need to undertake a wide range of product analysis activities. Try to include the analysis of actual products and ones in photographs and drawings. The unit includes information about product design and manufacture to help you understand the issues that are relevant to the development of different products. For example, quality and fitness for purpose are important issues for all products, but safety in relation to children's nightwear is quite different from safety in relation to protective clothing for the chemical industry.

The key to developing your ability to analyse products and to increase your understanding of product design and manufacture is to look, examine and question.

- Looking at products will involve examining them by eye and may involve taking them apart.
- Asking questions about products should enable you to target what you need to find out.

DEVELOPING A STRATEGY FOR ANALYSING PRODUCTS

If you are to analyse a range of products such as those manufactured by one-off, batch and mass-production, you will need to develop a strategy to help you with the process. This is best achieved by practice and by using the framework set out in the Product Analysis Assessment Grid shown in Table 1.1 below. Not only will this provide you with a strategy to use during the unit itself, but also it means that you will be familiar with the Product Analysis Assessment Grid when you sit the examination.

a) Outline the product design specification for this textile product.	7
b) Justify the use of: (i) material or component (ii) material or component.	 3 3
c) Give FOUR reasons why this textile product is one-off or batch or mass-produced.	4
d) Describe the stages of production for this textile product. Include references to industrial manufacturing methods.	16
e) Discuss quality issues for this textile product	8
f) Discuss product safety issues associated with this textile product and its production.	8
g) Discuss the appeal of this textile product.	8
Quality of written communication.	3
Total marks	60

Table 1.1

The Product Analysis Assessment Grid.

UNIT 1 ASSESSMENT: THE PRODUCT ANALYSIS EXAM

Unit 1 is externally assessed through a 1½ hour Product Analysis exam, which assesses your understanding of the unit content. The exam question will always follow the same format – only the product to be analysed will be different. This means that you will know what to expect in the exam. If you practise working through a complete 1 ½ hour exam, you will also learn how to allocate the time available to you.

The information provided about the product will always include: an illustration or drawing, with written information about materials, components and aesthetics and limited construction details. Figure 1 shows the kind of information you will be given in the exam.

Figure 1

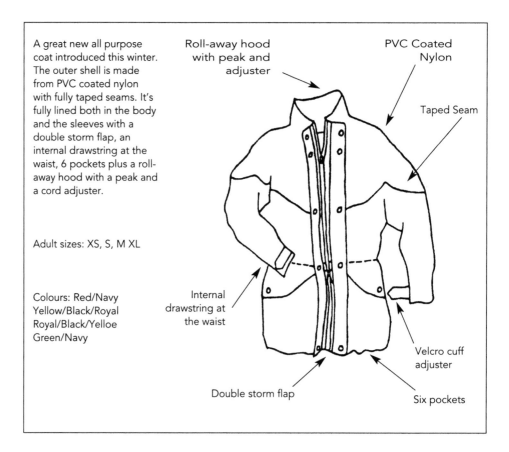

A great new all purpose coat introduced this winter. The outer shell is made from PVC coated nylon with fully taped seams. It's fully lined both in the body and the sleeves with a double storm flap, an internal drawstring at the waist, 6 pockets plus a roll-away hood with a peak and a cord adjuster.

Adult sizes: XS, S, M XL

Colours: Red/Navy Yellow/Black/Royal Royal/Black/Yelloe Green/Navy

Roll-away hood with peak and adjuster

PVC Coated Nylon

Taped Seam

Internal drawstring at the waist

Double storm flap

Velcro cuff adjuster

Six pockets

The Product Analysis Assessment Grid shown in Table 1.1 shows how the examination questions will be set out. Notice where the marks are awarded and work hardest on areas with the most marks. Within the exam paper, three marks are awarded for quality of written communication. This includes the use of appropriate technical vocabulary and correct spelling, punctuation and grammar

WHAT THE EXAMINER IS LOOKING FOR

The paper is designed to give you the opportunity to demonstrate your capability.

- Always include function, purpose, performance, market requirements, aesthetics, quality standards and safety criteria in the product design specification
- When justifying the use of materials and components always apply your knowledge of properties and characteristics to the product in the exam question. This could include references to the appropriate use of materials and environmental issues.
- The level of production influences many design decisions, the cost and quality of the product.
- Stages of production should include preparation, processing, assembly and finishing. Reference to industrial methods will depend on the product in question. You may need to refer to manufacturing systems such as Quick Response, 'Just in time', concurrent manufacture, the use of ICT and environmental issues.
- Quality issues relate to quality control, the fitness for purpose of the product and quality standards.
- The appeal of the product is about why the product looks as it does, its form and function, the influence of trends, style and cultural issues on its design, image and appeal to the consumer.
- Don't forget that quality of communication is important. Any sketches should be annotated. Use the appropriate technical terms. Write legibly and use the correct spelling, punctuation and grammar.

EXAM TIPS

- Analyse the *product in question*.
- Apply your knowledge to the product – marks will not be awarded for comments that do not address the product in question.
- Answer the questions in the assessment grid. Don't write everything you know about a topic if it's irrelevant to the question!
- Target the marks. Use bullet points where appropriate and use clearly written sentences.

Chapter 1

Products and Applications

The study of Products and Applications will provide you with information and tasks to develop your understanding of product design and development. It will help you understand how ideas for textile products are conceived and developed. It will also help you develop strategies for understanding, analysing and evaluating products and processes.

THE PROCESSES INVOLVED IN THE DEVELOPMENT OF A RANGE OF MANUFACTURED PRODUCTS

The design of products is a complex process that depends on a range of different factors. The various issues related to the need for the product, what it looks like, why it looks like it does, its function, its performance, how it's designed and manufactured and how it's promoted and sold are all interconnected.

Design development is therefore a complex activity, with many processes in industry being undertaken concurrently. This means that design teams develop products at the same time as developing the manufacturing process. It is also very common in industry for a design team to work in one country and for manufacturing to take place in another. The development of concurrent manufacture and of designing and manufacturing in different locations are increasingly possible through the use of Information and Communications Technology (ICT). You will learn more about concurrent design and manufacture later in the unit.

Wherever and whoever is involved in product development, all commercial products are designed and developed for specific target market groups, that have specific user requirements. Designers must take careful account of these needs. It is often said that product development starts and ends with the consumer and that for business to make a profit, design must be market led, market driven and market justified. The emphasis here as you can see is on the word 'market'. In order for a company to make a profit, it is best that product development takes place *after* establishing and justifying the size, needs and demand of the intended market. This is the case for both existing and new companies.

Another major factor influencing the design of products is the level or scale of production – the number of products to be manufactured. In this unit we will be concerned with the development of one-off, batch production and mass (high volume) production. In Figure 1.1 you will see some of the processes involved in the production of a designer dress from the drawing board to the

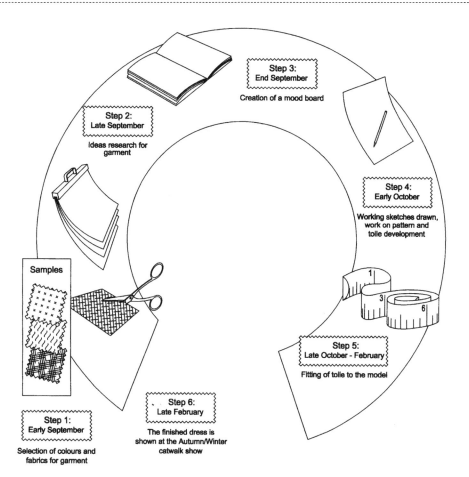

Figure 1.1
How a designer dress is created

catwalk. Such a dress may be batch or mass-produced. Whatever the level of production, all products must be manufactured efficiently in order that the company makes a profit. Without profits any company will fail and the people employed by it will very quickly become unemployed!

THE PRODUCT DESIGN CYCLE

In general the design and manufacturing processes that form the product design cycle follow the same pattern. A design cycle for mass-produced garments is shown is Figure 1.2. This is similar to the one that you use in Design and Technology. The key difference is that you work independently to research, design, manufacture and evaluate a product, whereas in industry a textile product designer generally works as part of a design and production team.

Although the design cycle shown in Figure 1.2 is linear, many activities tend to take place at the same time and there is feedback from any stage in the process to any other stage. For example, feedback from manufacturing may be based initially on a test batch of products, but is then continuous throughout the life of the product. Similarly feedback from the marketplace may be based on test marketing but is also continuous throughout the product life. Product development does not finish until the last product is made and sold!

Figure 1.2

A typical design cycle for mass-produced garments.

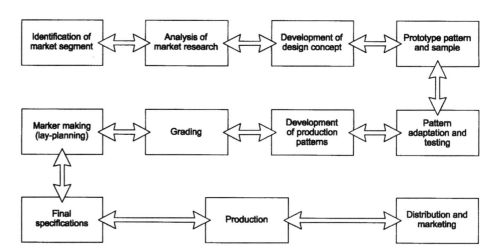

1 Identification of market segment and the development of a design brief
2 Analysis of market research and the development of a product design specification
3 Conceptual design – generating, developing and testing the feasibility of alternative ideas against specifications
4 Production of prototype patterns, toiles and samples to test the design concept
5 Pattern adaptation and testing
6 Production planning – development of manufacturing specifications and resources planning
7 Development of production patterns and templates, grading, marker-making (lay planning) and final specifications
8 Processing, assembly and finishing
9 Labelling, packaging, distribution and marketing.

A variety of aesthetic, technological and financial factors that include legislation, government policy and the interests of shareholders, influence the management of product development. In the clothing industry the situation is further complicated by the strength of retail organisations, such as chain stores. Often these retail organisations carry out their own design, then pass the design concept to an external product development company. Sample products and costings are then sent back to the retailer for approval, after which the product goes into production. As the competitive aspects of garment and other textile product manufacture become more critical, even more product development companies are becoming separated from the design of the product. This has resulted in the location of design in one country and production overseas where labour costs are lower.

By the time products reach the final stages of the design cycle, distribution and marketing, other factors come into play. Through promotion and advertising consumers are encouraged to buy new products.

TASK

Compare the product design cycle in figure 1.2 with the design and make process that you use to develop your coursework project.

STARTING POINTS FOR PRODUCT IDEAS

Designers constantly need to find starting points for developing ideas about new products. Most design teams use a logical process of market research, analysis and discussion, which allows them to identify new market opportunities. A design brief can then be developed. Successful product development needs a clear target market, which is often decided by market segmentation. This divides consumers into groups, which can be attracted to buy specific products. There are many ways of dividing up consumers into market segments, such as by age groups, gender, disposable income, lifestyle or by the end-use of the product – manufacturing for sportswear or corporate wear, for example.

There is a complex relationship between products and consumers. Companies need to develop new products or improve existing ones, in order to be competitive and to increase their market share. There are thought to be two main concepts relating to why and how products are developed – market pull and technology push, or a combination of both.

- Market pull refers to the requirements of the marketplace 'pulling' companies to produce what the market wants. One example of this is the requirement for 'easy care', where consumers demand textile products that are comfortable and easy to look after.
- In contrast, the development of new technologies leads to new products being 'pushed' into the market. Technology push is a strong driving force in the development of new textile materials, processes and technologies. Examples of technology push are new fibres such as Tencel and new processes such as biostoning.

TASK

Investigate two textile products that were developed through market pull and two that were developed through technology push. For each product explain the influences that contributed to its development.

PRODUCT ANALYSIS

Product analysis is also a good starting point for design, because it provides useful information about the design and manufacture of existing products. Product analysis is widely used by designers in many fields. It includes analysing existing products and collecting data from catalogues and trade literature. There are many reasons why designers undertake product analysis, mainly because it helps them to:

- evaluate the properties of materials used in an existing product
- examine the quality of design and manufacture of the product
- check the fitness-for-purpose of the product for a specific market segment
- find out why an existing product is selling/not selling or performing as well as predicted
- see how and why a competitor's product is successful.
- find out how well a product meets user requirements
- develop new product designs based on changed or new British or International Standards
- develop product design specifications and design ideas for new products.

PRODUCT DESIGN SPECIFICATIONS

The product design specification is an essential document that sets out the criteria for the design and development of a product and against which its performance can be measured.

Product design specifications often start as outline specifications, which are modified during design and development, in response to changes in materials, processes or other issues that affect design decisions. All product design specifications vary according to the type of product and its end-use. For example, the specification for a mid-market school jacket would be different from that of an up-market fashion garment.

Product design specifications are usually based on a set of generic criteria, such as those outlined below. These are the criteria that you should use during the unit when you develop a product design specification for an existing product. You should also use the same criteria to develop a product design specification in the end of unit Product Analysis examination.

1 Purpose – the aim of the product.
2 Function – how the product will be used or what it should do.
3 Performance requirements of the product, materials and components.
4 Market and user requirements, including ergonomics.
5 Aesthetic characteristics – relating to the appearance of the product.
6 Quality standards – appropriate to the performance, function and cost of the product.
7 Safety requirements – the safe production, use and disposal of the product cannot be compromised.

It must be remembered that the consideration of the scale of production is an extremely important aspect when developing a product design specification, because it has an impact on all design and manufacturing decisions. For example:

- a one-off product will need to meet the requirements of a single user and may use more expensive materials and more complex manufacturing processes

• whereas a batch or mass-produced product will need to meet the requirements of a range of users in a target market group and may use less expensive materials and simpler manufacturing processes.

During the unit you should have plenty of practice in developing product design specifications for a variety of one-off, batch and mass-produced products. This means that you will be well prepared when you are asked to develop a product design specification for a specified product in the Product Analysis exam.

Developing a product design specification for an existing product

One way to develop a product design specification is to ask a series of questions about the product. It is a good strategy to base these questions on the generic product design specification criteria shown above.

The actual questions you ask may vary slightly, depending on the product type. If you undertake this questioning process regularly, you should, with practice, be able to develop a product design specification for most types of textile products. This is a very useful skill to have – it will be invaluable when you have to develop a product design specification for your Unit 2 coursework project.

Developing a product design specification for a high visibility workwear jacket

The following product design specification is for the high visibility workwear jacket shown in Figure 1.3 Each of the specification criteria for the jacket was developed by asking questions based on purpose, function, performance requirements, market and user requirements, aesthetic characteristics, quality and safety.

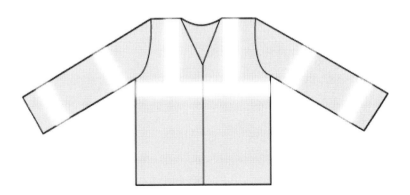

Figure 1.3
High visibility workwear jacket

Purpose
• *To design and make a high visibility jacket suitable for workwear, that provides a modern corporate image and storage for essential small tools.*

Function

- To be used by building construction workers in winter, to ensure clear visibility and protection on site at all times.

Performance requirements. The jacket should:

- Be easy to move in, smart, reflective, warm, rugged, waterproof and easy care
- Use reliable, strong, stable, colour fast, durable, tear proof, stain resist, breathable and safe materials with lifelong performance
- Use reliable, strong, durable, easy to use and safe fastenings to BS7271, BS3084

Market and user requirements, including ergonomics

- To meet a gap in the market for smart, modern workwear
- To meet the need for improving the image of construction workers
- To meet the visibility needs of building construction workers
- To meet the needs of a range of standard sizes to fit as many people as possible in the target market group.

Aesthetic characteristics

- Be attractive to construction workers and their companies
- Provide a masculine image in an attractive colour range
- Attractive design features to include corporate image and reflective strip
- Easy to use pockets.

Quality standards. The jacket should:

- Meet critical dimensions and tolerances, relating to the size range
- Conform to specifications.

Safety requirements. The jacket should:

- Meet safety requirements relating to the European CE mark.

TASK

Read each of the specification criteria for the high visibility workwear. List the questions you would need to ask in order to develop the product design specification for the workwear.

TASK: DEVELOPING A PRODUCT DESIGN SPECIFICATION

Choose a product with which you are familiar, such as your school bag or a product that you use at home. Use the following questions as a guide for developing a product design specification for your chosen product. Can you think of any other questions that might need to be asked about the product?

Purpose
- What is the aim of this product?
- What is the need that it solves?
- What is the end-use of this product?

Function
- Where and when will it be used?
- How will it be used?
- What benefits does it bring to users?
- Is it fit for its purpose?

Performance requirements
- What are the performance requirements of the product?
- What are the performance requirements of the materials and components?

Market and user requirements
- What is the target market group?
- What are the user requirements?
- Does the product need to take into account standard sizes or dimensions?
- What are the market requirements for this product?
- Does it need to be classic, traditional, modern or avant-garde?
- How well does the product meet these needs?

Aesthetic characteristics
- What are the aesthetic requirements of this product?
- What are its design features?

Quality standards
- Is the product well designed and well made?
- Does the product have to conform to any sizes, dimensions or tolerances?
- Is the quality appropriate to the performance, function and cost of the product?
- How would the manufacturer make sure that the product meets user requirements?

Safety requirements
- Does the product need to comply with any safety regulations, such as British Standards?
- Does the product carry any labels relating to the safety of the product?
- Is the product safe to use and safe to dispose of?

TASK

Figure 1.4

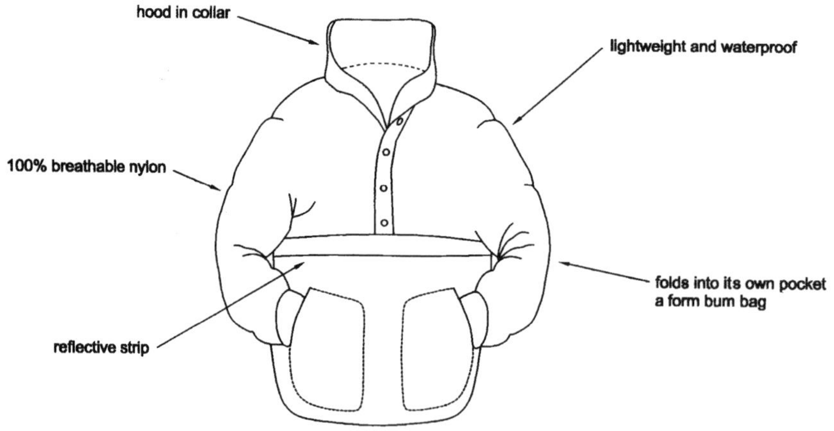

hood in collar

lightweight and waterproof

100% breathable nylon

folds into its own pocket
a form bum bag

reflective strip

Figure 1.4 shows a jacket

a)   Outline the product design specification for this jacket   (7)

GENERATING, DEVELOPING AND TESTING THE FEASIBILITY OF ALTERNATIVE IDEAS AGAINST SPECIFICATIONS

The development of a design concept is usually done by two dimensional (2D) modelling – drawing and sketching ideas by hand or by using computer aided design (CAD) software. This enables designers to refine ideas about the shape, colour and surface decoration of the product. 2D modelling is a key industrial practice because it enables designers to test the feasibility of alternative ideas against the product design specification. Once the final design proposal is decided, it can be taken forward for modelling and prototyping.

MODELLING AND THE PRODUCTION OF PROTOTYPES, TOILES AND SAMPLES FOR TESTING PRODUCTS BEFORE MANUFACTURE

Modelling and prototyping of products is a key industrial process, because it enables designers to test the feasibility of a design before putting the product into production. The further any product gets towards production, the more expensive it gets to makes changes to the design, so prototyping can actually save costs in the long run.

The production of prototype patterns, toiles and samples is a common method of testing products before manufacture. Prototype patterns for garments, accessories or for other non-garment products are developed either from a manufacturer's own block patterns or from a database of existing patterns. A toile, made from inexpensive calico, may be used to test the drape, fit and construction of a prototype garment on a stand model. A sample garment, made from the intended production fabric not only tests materials but also enables the planning and costing of the manufacturing process.

DESIGNING FOR MANUFACTURE

Designing for manufacture includes the development of a manufacturing specification and the management of the manufacturing process itself. All designers therefore need to have an understanding of manufacture in order to develop a cost-effective product that can be manufactured to a price-point. This means making the product in the least time and at the lowest cost. Many garment manufacturers use their own block patterns that are based on standard body sizes. This often means that a 'standard' size 12 varies between manufacturers. Even the reduction of a few pence per metre of fabric can make an enormous cost saving when scaled up for high volume. Designing for manufacture can involve:

- production planning – the development of manufacturing specifications that detail all the information needed to manufacture the product
- sourcing and the selection of materials and components to meet cost and quality requirements.

TASK

Explain and justify the processes of modelling and prototyping before the manufacture of a ready-to-wear coat.

Chapter 2
Materials and Components

FABRICS CHOICE

Choosing the best fabric to suit a product end use is one of the most important aspects of product development. The best fabric for the job is not necessarily the most expensive, because in many cases there needs to be a compromise between quality and cost. What is required in any high volume manufacture, though, is a supply of fabric of known performance and of an acceptable quality in use – the chosen fabric must be fit for its purpose.

The ability to make informed decisions when analysing textile products or when choosing fabrics for your own product development relies on an understanding of the relationship between fibre properties, fabric structure and any finishing processes that are applied to the fabric during manufacture. Other decisions that influence fabric choice include:

- aesthetic characteristics such as drape or soft handle
- functional requirements, such as strength or water-resistant
- the scale of production – one-off products may require the use of special materials
- the cost of the fabric in relation to its quality
- the availability of a continuous supply for high volume production – each fabric needs to have the same quality, colour uniformity, width, weight, dimensional stability and sewability.

FINDING OUT ABOUT TEXTILE MATERIALS THROUGH PRODUCT ANALYSIS

All textile fibres have different properties that make them suitable for a range of different end-uses. Spinning fibres into yarns, then weaving or knitting them into fabrics can change these properties, although fibre and fabric properties are closely linked. The finishing of woven or knitted fabrics can further change and improve fabric properties to make them suitable for a wider variety of products.

When you analyse any textile product you should aim to identify the fibre content, the fabric structure, the properties and working characteristics of the fabrics and the suitability of any fastenings. Always ask questions about why this particular material is suitable for this product.

- What is the fibre content? Looking at labels is always helpful.

- What is the fabric structure ? Is it woven, knitted or non-woven?
- Has a finish been applied during manufacture to enhance the fabric's properties? Again looking at labels is helpful – the product may state that it's easy care or has a stain-resist or water-resist finish.

Investigating the suitability of materials and components will mainly involve examining them by sight and touch – this is a good way of investigating fabric properties. In some instances you may need to take a product apart to see each different component part, such as interlinings or fastenings.

TASK

In the Product Analysis examination, your understanding of materials should enable you to justify the use of a particular material or component in a specific product. For example, the jumper left is made from weft-knitted acrylic fabric.

- Look up the properties of acrylic fibre and the characteristics of weft-knitted fabric
- Explain why the properties and characteristics of this fabric make it suitable for this jumper.

Figure 1.5
An acrylic jumper

PROPERTIES AND WORKING CHARACTERISTICS OF NATURAL AND MANUFACTURED FIBRES

All fibres have different properties that make them suitable for a range of end-uses. It is the job of the design technologist to decide which properties and characteristics are essential to meet the end-use requirements. The aim is to provide an optimum level of product performance without an increase in costs or disadvantaging the aesthetic characteristics of the product. A designer therefore has to balance the following properties against the cost of the materials:

- aesthetic properties – related to the 'look', touch and style. For example, the aesthetic properties of a fashion garment could be that it requires a fabric with good drape, soft handle or trendy colours

- functional properties – related to the function and use. For example, the functional properties of industrial clothing could be strong, flexible, lightweight and fire-resistant.

- comfort properties – related to comfort-in-wear. For example, the comfort properties of blankets could be warm, absorbent and soft.

Natural Fibre	Warmth (C)	Absorbency (C)	Comfort (C)	Handle and drape (A)	Strength (F)	Elasticity (F)	After care (F)
Wool	Warm to wear.	Slow, can absorb $\frac{1}{3}$ its weight in water and not feel wet. Repels raindrops. Very slow drying.	Fine wool very comfortable. Coarse wool scratchy.	Very soft or coarse handle. Good drape	Medium strength, not durable.	Very good. Creases drop out.	Wash and iron with care, may shrink. dryclean
Silk	Cool, but good insulation so warm as well.	Fast, can absorb $\frac{1}{3}$ its weight in water	Very comfortable.	Soft handle and elegant drape.	Good strength.	Very good. Creases drop out.	Wash and iron with care, best dry cleaned
Cotton	Cool to wear unless brushed.	Highly absorbent. Slow drying.	Very comfortable, unless wet.	Soft handle. Good drape	Good strength, abrasion resistance and durability	Poor. Creases easily.	Wash, boil, iron damp may shrink.
Linen	Fresh and cool to wear.	Highly absorbent. Fast drying.	Stiffer and harder than cotton.	Firm handle. Smooth surface Good drape	Good strength and durability.	Poor. Creases very badly	Wash, boil, easily ironed.

Table 1.2

The aesthetic, functional and comfort properties of natural fibres.

The chart in Tables 1.2 and 1.3 provides an at-a-glance view of the aesthetic (A), functional (F) and comfort (C) properties of the natural and manufactured fibres shown in the classification map in Figure 3A.1. As we have seen previously, fibre and fabric properties are closely linked, so any product materials that you investigate will have similar properties to the ones described in the Table.

PROPERTIES OF YARNS

You will not be asked to analyse yarns but you should be aware of how they affect fabric properties.

• All staple yarns are spun from fibres into a variety of different yarns such as singles, plied, cabled, core or fancy yarns.
• The thickness of yarn (yarn count) and yarn twist affect a fabric's weight, flexibility, handle and end-use.
• Too much twist may make a yarn hard, whereas too little twist may result in a weak yarn. Soft knitting yarns usually have less twist, but warp yarns for

Natural Fibre	Warmth (C)	Absorbency (C)	Comfort (C)	Handle and drape (A)	Strength (F)	Elasticity (F)	After care (F)
Viscose	Low warmth.	More absorbent than cotton	Comfortable to wear.	Soft or firm handle. Good drape.	Lower strength than cotton.	Poor. Creases .easily	Washable. Easy to iron.
Acetate	Low warmth.	Low absorbency. Fast drying.	Comfortable but prone to static.	Soft handle and elegant drape.	Low strength Poor abrasion resistance	Higher than viscose, but creases.	Wash and iron with care. Thermo-plastic.
Polyester	Low warmth, unless textured.	Very low absorbency. Hydrophobic Fast drying.	Comfortable but prone to static. Micro fibres breathable.	Soft or firm handle.	Very strong and abrasion resistant.	Very good. Crease-resistant.	Machine washable. Iron with care. Thermo-plastic.
Polyamide (Nylon)	Low warmth, unless textured	Very low absorbency. Hydrophobic Fast drying.	Comfortable but prone to static. Micro fibres breathable.	Soft or firm handle.	Very strong and abrasion resistant.	Very good. Crease-resistant.	Machine washable. Iron with care. Thermo-plastic.
Elastane	Low % always used in blends.	Absorbent. Dyes well.	Adds stretch comfort.	Soft or firm handle.	Good strength.	Very high. Crease-resistant.	Machine washable. Thermo-plastic
Acrylic	Warm to wear.	Fast drying.	Comfortable to wear.	Very soft wool-like handle, good drape.	Good strength.	Very good. Crease-resistant.	Machine washable. iron with care, may shrink. Thermo-plastic.

weaving need a higher twist so they are strong enough to withstand the tension in the loom.

- Staple yarns are made from fibres such as cotton, flax, wool, spun silk or cut manufactured fibres.
- Filament yarns are made from continuous filaments of silk and manufactured synthetic fibres such as polyester or nylon.
- Blended fibres like acrylic/cotton can be made permanently bulky using heat to increase the volume of thermoplastic acrylic. This gives a warm soft handle, suitable for knitwear.
- Thermoplastic continuous filament synthetic yarns can be textured using a heat process. This gives an elastic, warm, soft handle, suitable for tights, swimwear, underwear, outerwear and carpets.

Table 1.3

The aesthetic, functional and comfort properties of manufactured fibres.

TASK: EXPLORING FIBRES.

1 Explore a range of children's leisurewear made from natural fibre blends.
  - Investigate the properties of these fibres and explain why they are suitable for their end-use.
  - Draw up a product design specification for one of these products.

2 Using magazines and catalogues, choose two products suitable for different sports.
  - Investigate the fibre types used in each product.
  - Match the fibre properties with the needs of users of these products.

LOOKING AT LABELS

Looking at **product sewn-in labels** is a good starting point for finding out about materials. Some labels are mandatory and are therefore a statutory requirement, such as those for flammability.

Labels may also include information about any special finishes that have been applied to the fabric, such as easy-care. Care labels provide helpful instructions about the product aftercare. The range of laundering instructions may cover temperature of the wash, the degree of agitation, the time and the washing medium, drying, bleaching, ironing and dry-cleaning.

All this information will give you vital clues about the suitability of the fabric for the product. For example, is it machine washable? Does it need dry-cleaning? What is the percentage fibre blend? What do you already know about the properties of these fibres? Is the fabric easy care? Has a special finish been applied to make it easy-care?

It is fairly apparent to see that a product made from one component material will be easier to care for than one made from different types of materials. Most garments that have interlinings and linings such as suits, must be dry cleaned, because one of the textiles may shrink or the interlining may become detached from the main fabric during washing.

BRITISH STANDARDS AND GARMENT LABELLING.

There are two British Standards that apply to garment labels:

- BS 5722, Flammability performance of fabrics and fabric assemblies used in sleepwear and in dressing gowns – mandatory for nightwear for children and the elderly. Flammability performance relates to the whole garment, including all threads, trimmings, decorations and labels
- BS EN 23758, the care labelling code. Care labels are voluntary and use

symbols that are consistent with those used on washing machines, irons and detergent packs.

Regulations require that most textile products be labelled with the type and quantity by percentage of different fibres use. The label must:

• Use the generic name of the fibre, such as acrylic, rather than a trade name like Dralon
• Give the percentage fibre composition, such as 60% cotton 40% polyester, with the highest quantity first.

TASK: LOOKING AT LABELS.

Collect a variety of commercial care labels and sort them into product types – try to include a wide range.

• Evaluate the information provided on the labels.
• Draw up a chart to show fibre types, properties and end-uses.

FINDING OUT ABOUT FABRIC STRUCTURE THROUGH PRODUCT ANALYSIS

When you analyse products you will come across the three most used fabric structures – woven, knitted or non-woven. Each of these fabric structures helps determine a fabric's quality, weight and handle, making it suitable for different types of products.

WOVEN FABRICS

The most common woven structures are plain, twill and satin weaves. You may also come across pile weaves in the form of corduroy or velvet fabrics. (See Figure 3A.10 on page 79.)

• Plain weave is the most used weave structure and is made from most fibre types. Plain weave fabrics are strong, firm, and hardwearing. They are used for many types of end-uses, including garments, household textiles and accessories.
• Twill weave produces fabric with diagonal lines, which generally run bottom left to top right of the fabric face. Weaving twills in different directions produces chevron or herringbone fabrics. Twills are made from many fibre types and drape well. They are used for a variety of end-uses including jackets, suits, trousers, jeans and curtains.
• Satin weave fabric is warp-faced, with a smooth, shiny face and a dull back. Satin fabric drapes well so it is used for curtain linings, evening wear,

upholstery, ribbons and trimmings, depending on the fibre used. Satin can be made from cotton, polyester/cotton, acetate, polyester or silk.

- Velvet has a cut warp-pile on the face of the fabric. This gives a smooth, rich, soft, dense and lustrous fabric. Velvet should be used in one direction only, so pattern pieces run along straight grain with the pile stroking downwards from head to toe. Cotton velvet is used for jackets or upholstery, wool velvet for suiting and silk velvet is used for luxury products, such as evening wear. Polyester velvet is used for upholstery.
- Needlecord has a cut weft-pile on the face of the fabric. The fine ribbed pile runs along the length of fabric, which may be brushed. Needlecord is usually made from cotton and is used for dress-weights.

TASK

Choose two woven structures that could be suitable for a man's winter jacket. Describe the characteristics of each fabric, then select one that you think would be the most appropriate. Justify your choice.

WARP AND WEFT-KNITTED FABRICS

Weft-knitted fabric is made from a single yarn, which is fed across the width of the fabric. Weft knits are stretchy, with a right and wrong side and may ladder. Weft knitting, done by hand is used to make one-off designer products, such as jumpers or cushions. Industrial computer-controlled knitting machines, using CAD/CAM systems produce around 90 per cent of jersey, rib and jacquard fabrics, used for T-shirts, underwear, socks and knitwear.

Warp-knitted fabrics are made on straight or circular knitting machines. Each loop of the fabric is fed by its own separate yarn. The loops interlock vertically, along the length of the fabric. Warp knits are stretchy but do not ladder and can't be unravelled. Warp knits such as velour and Terry are used for leisure and sportswear, furnishings and sheets.

Figure 1.6
Warp and weft-knitted fabrics

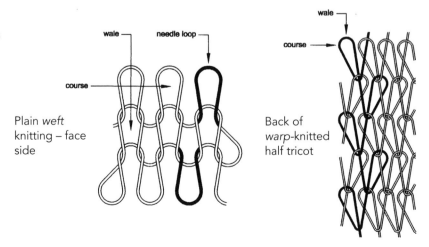

Plain *weft* knitting – face side

Back of *warp*-knitted half tricot

TASK

Compare the structure of a knitted jumper with that of a polyester fleece jacket. Describe the characteristics of each fabric.

Check it out! Unit 3A Making up knitted fabrics page 85

NON-WOVEN FABRICS

Non-woven fabrics are textile structures made directly from fibres rather than from yarn

- Felt is a non-woven fabric made from animal hair or wool fibres matted together by moisture, mechanical action and heat. Wool felt is expensive, but blends with acetate, nylon or acrylic reduce its price. Felt has no strength, drape or elasticity, does not fray and is warm and resilient. It retains its shape and can be made flame-retardant. It is used for blocking into hats, for slippers and toys.
- Bonded-fibre fabric is made from a web of fibres, bonded with adhesives, solvents or by the thermoplastic property of some or all of the fibres. Bonded-fibre fabrics are used mainly as fusible interlinings, which are air-permeable, dimensionally stable, crease-resistant, stable to washing and dry-cleaning and easy to use.

TASK

Examine the different types of fabrics used in the construction of a suit jacket. Explain how the structure of each component fabric affects the quality of the garment.

WORKING CHARACTERISTICS OF FABRICS

When selecting fabrics, design technologists need to be aware that there are different performance requirements where fabric characteristics are concerned. Manufacturing requirements relate mainly to quality versus cost, whereas users have other priorities as well. Table 1.4 compares the performance characteristics important when making up garments with the performance requirements of users.

- The characteristics important for making up will apply to most fabrics required for garments and other products. Fabrics need to be of known performance and with an acceptable quality in use.
- The characteristics important to the user are similar for many types of products, but some of characteristics may only apply to specific products. For example, most products require fabrics with good strength and durability, but only some need to be shower or rain resistant.

Fabric characteristics important in making up		Fabric characteristics important to the user	
• Freedom from visible faults • Uniformity of appearance • Uniformity of width • Dimensional stability • Accurate colouration for prints and dyes	• Good drape • Good sewability • Resistance to seam slippage • Good performance in pressing and fusing • Resistant to shrinkage	• Good strength and durability • Resistance to abrasion and pilling • Good seam strength • Colour fastness to light, washing, dry cleaning	• Easy care • Crease and flame resistance • Shower or rain resistance • Breathable • Good appearance in colour, texture and lustre

Table 1.4
Fabric characteristics

FOCUSED TASKS: EXPLORING FABRICS.

1 Using magazines and catalogues, explore a range of similar fashion products for the young career man or woman.
  • Compare the fabrics, styling and product prices.
  • For each product list the fabric characteristics required for making up and those required by the user.

2 In the Product Analysis examination, your understanding of materials should enable you to justify the use of a particular material or component used in a specific product.
  For example, think of a skirt or trousers made from a plain-woven viscose polyester fabric.
  • Look up the properties of viscose and polyester and the characteristics of plain-woven fabric.
  • Explain why the properties and characteristics of this fabric make it suitable for this product.
  • Describe the characteristics important for making up this fabric.
  • Explain why the product is suitable for the target market.

Finishing process	Example of how finishing benefits fabrics
Physical finishing processes use heat, pressure or steam and machine processes.	• Cotton or nylon is brushed (or 'raised') to give a soft, warm handle. • Wool fabrics are shrunk to make them compact and to reduce further shrinking.
Chemical finishing processes involve the use of chemicals, which can cause environmental damage.	• Viscose fabrics may be given an easy-care treatment. • Silk ties can be Teflon coated to make them stain-resistant.
Biological finishing processes involve the use of natural enzymes, such as those used in biostoning denim, which causes little environmental damage.	• Most denim produced in Europe is biostoned. This is less expensive than traditional stonewashing and reduces damage to the fabric.
Dyeing and printing involve the use of chemicals to enhance the aesthetic characteristics of textiles.	• Most fabrics are dyed to improve their aesthetic characteristics and to make them fashionable. • Printing makes fabrics attractive to the target market.
Decorative and stitch techniques.	• Appliqué and embroidery add to the style of the product.

FABRIC FINISHING

All fabrics used in products will have been 'finished' in some way to make them suitable for their end-use. When you analyse a textile product, it is often a good idea to examine its care label to see if any special laundering requirements are necessary. This may indicate a special finish has been applied to the fabric. Fabric finishes include both physical and chemical processes, such as those shown in Table 1.5. Good finishing can greatly improve the aesthetic and functional properties of fabrics, enhancing their handle, drape and aftercare properties.

Table 1.5

Fabric finishing

PRODUCT FINISHING

Textile products are also finished as part of a quality assurance process. Product finishing ensures that the product is fault-free, clean and matches specifications. Finishing improves the properties and quality of the product. and can be:

• aesthetic, like pressing to improve the ease of manufacture. Final pressing improves presentation of the product
• decorative, like applying logos, braid or fringing to add to the style or image of the product
• functional, like self-finishing seams by overlocking to improve the product quality.

TASK

Analyse a simple product such as a cushion.
- Look at the care label for clues about fabric finishes.
- Explain the aesthetic or functional finishes that were used during manufacture.
- Explain how additional fabric or product finishing could improve the quality of the product.

STANDARD FASTENINGS AND COMPONENTS

Textile products are made not only from fabrics but also from a variety of components and fastenings. The main purpose of these is to enhance the product's style and performance. Since most product manufacturers specialise in products for specific market segments (such as sportswear), they buy in fabrics and components according to the product needs. The use of any component or fasting adds to the cost of the product. Specialist manufacturers make fastenings such as buttons, zips, buckles, ribbons and braids – in fact all such fastenings follow fashion trends to match the products themselves.

All fabrics, including fusible interlinings and linings come in standard widths, which are appropriate for different types of product. Fastenings such as zips or buttons are also standardised items, which are suitable for different products. Table 1.6 below is a guide to the end-use of a range of fastenings.

Table 1.6

Typical end-uses of fastenings

Type of fastening	Typical end-use	Type of fastening	Typical end-use
Polyester button	Shirts, blouses and underwear.	Metal zip fastener	Sports goods.
Nylon buttons	Coats and jackets, sports and leisurewear.	Single and double-sided zips	Leisure and sports products.
Metal buttons	Blazers, jeans and knitted waistcoats.	Nylon Velcro	A range of fashion garments, sports and leisure goods.
Leather buttons	Sports jackets and knitted cardigans.	Metal hooks and eyes	Trousers and skirts.
Wooden buttons	Knitted and sports garments.	Metal or plastic press studs	A range of garments and household goods.
Mother of pearl buttons	Women's outerwear and underwear.	Metal, leather or plastic buckles	Belts. and clasps
Plastic zip fastener	Lightweight and fine fabrics used in garments and household products.		

TASKS

1 Analyse a garment or household product to see how many different kinds of fastenings are used. Explain how the aesthetic and functional characteristics of the fastenings make them suitable for the product.

2 Suggest the use of different types of fastenings and explain how these would improve the style and function of the product.

FINDING OUT ABOUT FIBRES, FABRICS, FASTENINGS AND FINISHES THROUGH PRODUCT ANALYSIS

The table below summarises what you need to do or find out when you analyse textile products. It suggests how you can find out the information you require. This information will help you understand the suitability and performance of textile materials in the products you analyse.

Table 1.7

Finding out about fibres, fabrics, fastenings and finishes through product analysis

What to do or find out	How to find out
• Identify the fibre content	• Examine product labels to find useful information about the fibre content. • Examine the yarns through a magnifying glass. Is the yarn rough, smooth or stretchy? What properties does it bring to the fabric?
• Identify the fabric structure	• Examine fabric through a magnifying glass to see the structure, pattern repeat, colour repeat. Is the fabric woven, knitted or non-woven? Is the fabric warp or weft knitted? Is it plain weave, twill, satin or a more complex weave? How much stretch is there in the fabric? Which direction has the most stretch?
• Investigate the properties and working characteristics of the fabric and component fabrics.	• Look up the expected properties for the fibre types. • Examine fabrics using sensory analysis, using feel, touch and sight. How do they feel? How do they handle? Do they crease? • Compare what you find out about the properties of these fabrics with their expected properties.
• Investigate the fabric performance and comparative costs.	• What properties do the fabrics have that enable them to meet performance requirements for making-up and in use? • Find out the cost of similar fabrics. Would the product perform better if more expensive materials were used?
• Think about the fabric finish	• What finish might have been given to the fabric / product? What does the finish do? Why was it used? Does it cause environmental damage?
• The suitability of fastenings.	• Examine the fastenings to see how well they are fixed and what they are made from. Explain their suitability for the product. • Suggest other fastenings that that would enhance the aesthetic or functional performance of the product.
• Examine the product finishing for quality of manufacture.	• Check the quality of the seam and hem finishing. Are the seams overlocked? What is the seam allowance? Are there any faults in the fabrics or stitching?
• Product aftercare requirements.	• Examine product labels to find useful information about the fabric's maintenance and aftercare. • How does the product perform in use?

Chapter 3
Industrial and Commercial Practice

MANUFACTURING SYSTEMS, INCLUDING ONE-OFF, BATCH AND HIGH VOLUME PRODUCTS

A number of manufacturing systems have been adopted by industry to manufacture textile products. The approach adopted by companies is related to the level or scale of production used to manufacture their products. Whether a product is to be made by one-off, batch or mass-production is extremely important, because the choice of manufacturing system will influence:

- which materials and fastenings are appropriate
- the manufacturing processes
- how the product is manufactured
- the eventual retail price.

ONE-OFF PRODUCTION (BESPOKE, MADE-TO-MEASURE, CUSTOM MADE OR JOBBING PRODUCTION)

This is where a one-off textile product is made by an individual designer-maker, a craftsperson or a company to meet an individual client's requirements. A textile made by one-off production may be made by one person, where quality is checked as the work progresses. The tools and equipment may be less automated than in mass production, but the end product is more individual and often made to a higher quality. Designing and making one-off textile products results in exclusive or specialist products, but at a high unit cost, because materials and labour costs are higher than for mass-produced goods.

Textiles made by one-off production can include:
- products designed and made by a designer-maker, such as garments, hats, bags, cushions, curtains and upholstery
- bespoke tailored garments made to a client's measurements by individual craftspeople. Nowadays bespoke garments are often made for people whose job requires perfect fit, such as airline pilots or army personnel
- haute couture garments and accessories designed for clients by mainstream couturiers worldwide.

The bag shown in Figure 1.7 was hand-made from 100% woven cotton. The bag has a hand-woven front panel, a Velcro fastening under the front flap and a bound edge, which continues to form the long strap. It can be worn comfortably over the shoulder. The selling price is £10.99.

When you undertake the product analysis of a one-off product such as the bag in Figure 1.7, you will need to consider how the level of production as a one-off affects its manufacture, the look of the product and its cost. The following analysis is not exhaustive, but will give a flavour of how to think through the benefits/disadvantages of one-off production.

Analysis of one-off woven bag:
- Unlike a mass-produced product the bag was not made to follow fashion trends.
- As a one-off product the bag is an individual / exclusive product. This is an attractive selling point.
- Although the bag is made from inexpensive cotton and has a fairly simple construction, the hand-woven fabric on the front panel adds to its cost. This may be a disadvantage to the manufacturer as it could reduce sales.
- The selling price of the bag is attractive, especially for an individual product, so there is good value for money of a high quality product. The disadvantage to the manufacturer of the high cost of the front panel may therefore be offset by high sales of an attractive product.
- Since the bag is hand-made, it may not meet British Standards requirements for colourfastness and there is no care label. The colour may run or it may shrink when washed and the colours may fade after exposure to sunlight. This is a disadvantage for the user and may compromise further sales for the manufacturer.

Figure 1.7
this 100% woven cotton bag was hand made in Peru.

TASK

One important aspect of lifestyle over the last generation has been the move to standardise the human body to a slimmer shape by dieting and exercise. This has resulted in a decline in the made-to-measure market, which is now limited to very highly priced garments.

1 Using one product example, list the benefits to the user and producer of making a one-off garment. Use the following criteria to help you:
- market and user requirements
- benefits of having an individual / exclusive product
- the complexity and cost of the manufacturing process
- economies of scale in costs of materials and components
- the selling price and value for money
- quality control and safety.

2 Using newspapers or magazines, collect images of designer products shown at catwalk shows.
- Give FOUR reasons why such products are made by one-off production.

BATCH PRODUCTION

This is where fixed quantities of products are manufactured, either for stock or to order. This manufacturing system can include both traditional 'make through' and Quick Response cellular methods of production for fashion products. In a 'make through' system an operator carries out the main construction operations while less skilled people do preparatory and finishing work such as overlocking or pressing. In a cellular Quick Response system a team of eight to ten skilled operators shares the responsibility for producing batches of complete products. This system is very motivating for the production teams and results in high quality products.

Batch production is planned for ease-of-manufacture, using standardised materials and components, standard production flat patterns, specialised equipment and production control to monitor production. Quality is planned, with quality control checks taking place throughout manufacture, to ensure that each product is identical and meets specifications. There are economies of scale in batch production because of standardisation of pre-manufactured materials and components and standardisation of production processes within batches. For example repeated orders for fabrics or buttons would reduce unit costs considerably.

Batch sizes can be increased or decreased according to demand. Sometimes repeated batches of garments are made over a longer period of time, to fulfil orders from retailers for specific sizes or colours. The use of cellular Quick Response systems enables companies to produce the garments the customer wants in the right place, at the right time and at the right cost.

Examples of batch produced products

Since batch produced products are made to the same quality requirements as mass-produced ones, it is not always easy to distinguish them. However they are sometimes made in batches of different styles or colours, to meet the fast turn round of fashion products. Batch produced products may include:

a) Ready-to-wear products and accessories designed and made by manufacturers for a range of different retailers or companies. These must be cost-effective to manufacture and could be fashion items, more up-market products or corporate products.

b) Batch produced products designed and made by designer-makers. These could include items such as a set of cushions or a set number of garments or accessories. These must be cost-effective to manufacture and must make use of a quality control system to ensure consistency.

TASKS

A cushion is made from cotton velvet and wool felt, both expensive fabrics. The cushion is one of a batch, which is sold to an individual client through a craft fair. The designer-maker also sells batches of cushions that are made to a client's individual colour requirements.

1 Read the information about batch production and about the batch produced cushion described above.
2 Explain the benefits to the designer-maker and to the client of making batch produced cushions.
3 Find a picture of a batch-produced product.
   • Give FOUR reasons why this product is batch produced.

HIGH VOLUME PRODUCTION (MASS PRODUCTION)

This is where a high volume of textile products is manufactured to fit a range of standard sizes or dimensions, for stock or to order. High volume production is a cost-effective method of making products for specific target market sectors that don't change quickly with fashion, such as menswear, underwear or household products. Quick response methods are also used to make a wide range of high volume fashion products.

Volume production is achieved through the use of different manufacturing systems that can include the traditional Progressive Bundle Unit and the quick response Unit Production System (UPS). In the Progressive Bundle Unit operations are laid out to follow the sequence of manufacturing for one garment style. UPS uses computer technology to control a powered rail which transports work in progress from operator to operator. The system keeps track of orders, sequence of operations and production performance to meet delivery dates. The use of UPS can reduce work in progress from up to three weeks to eight hours. This means that decisions about orders from store buyers can be made later, thus increasing the potential for making correct decisions related to fashion products.

High volume production is planned for cost-effective manufacture, using standardised materials and components, standard production patterns, specialised equipment and production planning and control to monitor production. Quality is planned, with quality control checks taking place throughout manufacture, to ensure that each product is identical and meets specifications. There are economies of scale in high volume production because of standardisation of pre-manufactured materials and components and standardisation of production processes. For example in a manufacturing company making styles which carry over from one season to another, there is usually an opportunity to use fabrics and components purchased for the previous season.

Examples of high-volume products can include:
- A wide range of textiles such as fibres, yarns and fabrics that are made by continuous production.
- Ready-to-wear products designed and made by manufacturers for a range of different retailers. These could include fashion products that are more classic in style or more standard items like shirts or underwear.
- Ready-to-wear products designed and made by manufacturers for more up-market retailers and boutiques.
- Sportswear, activewear, all-weather wear or leisurewear designed and made by manufacturers for a range of retail outlets.
- Other products designed and made by manufacturers for household uses, outdoor uses, sport, interiors, the theatre, protection or transport.

TASK

Investigate the materials, components and construction processes used to manufacture jeans.
- Give FOUR reasons why jeans are mass-produced.

STAGES OF PRODUCTION AND MANUFACTURING METHODS

The stages of production for textile products follow a sequence that is common to many 'sewn' goods. Within the stages of production there will be a number of processes that are specific to different products. Most sewn products require the development of flat patterns and production patterns, but it is the production of garments that also requires patterns to be graded. When you think through the stages of production for any product it is the actual product and not the production of the fabric that you need to be concerned with.

Although the stages of production may vary slightly for different products, one aspect – the use of feedback – is common to all. Feedback from quality control and from the market place is vital throughout the whole production process.

FINDING OUT ABOUT THE STAGES OF PRODUCTION THROUGH PRODUCT ANALYSIS

In the Product Analysis examination you will be asked to:

- 'Describe the stages of production for a given product.'
- 'Include references to industrial manufacturing methods.'

STAGES OF PRODUCTION

As we have seen at the start of this section, many sewn products follow similar processes and it is only if you are asked to analyse a garment that you will need to refer to pattern grading. A product like a cushion or a bag may be sold in different sizes but would generally be manufactured in large batches all of the same size product to ensure efficient fabric utilisation. As a general rule the main stages of production for most products include preparation, processing, assembly and finishing. These are described below, together with references to one-off, batch or mass production where it is relevant to the process.

References to industrial manufacturing methods

Any references to industrial manufacturing methods in the stages of production may include some discussion of:

- the use of CAD/CAM
- the use of cost-effective processes and minimising waste. References here could relate to marker making and ensuring the efficient utilisation of fabrics in a lay plan.

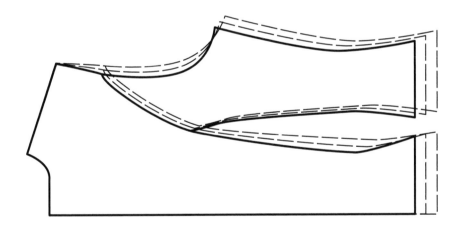

Figure 1.8

Pattern grading may be developed from a production pattern based on a manufacturer's own block patterns. The result is that a standard size 12 often varies between different manufacturers.

PREPARATION

In one-off production a pattern is developed for an individual client. This may involve the use of basic blocks or adapting a commercial pattern. One-off production often uses expensive fabric and may involve further modifications of the pattern to ensure accurate fit.

In batch and high volume manufacture, preparation before manufacture is more complex. It involves the development of production patterns and templates, grading and marker making.

- Production patterns include all the seams, hems, grain lines and pattern information required to make up the product.
- Templates make batch and mass production faster and more accurate, i.e. making a template for jobs such as buttonhole marking.
- Grading a production pattern creates all the sizes in the required range of the target market – the use of computer systems make this process faster and more accurate. (See Figure 1.8)
- Designing the lay plan – called marker making – works out the amount of fabric required to make a specific number of products in a range of sizes. Lay planning is also important in one-off production in order to cost the product.
- The lay plan provides a cutting marker, which goes on top of the fabric plies to be cut. With modern CAD systems it is not necessary to make a physical cutting marker. Cutting instructions are sent electronically to the fully automatic cutting machines.

TASKS

1 The orientation of the pattern pieces in a marker needs to take account of the fabric grain, nap or pile. Explain how the pattern pieces would be placed for a needlecord fabric.

2 Draw up a chart to compare the processes involved in preparation before manufacture of a one-off and batch-produced product.

PROCESSING

In the section on processing you will need to discuss fabric preparation, spreading and cutting for the product in question. The process is similar for many products. Fabric is checked for faults, spread in a single-ply or a multiple-ply (a number of layers) ready for cutting. A cutting marker may be laid on the top to guide the cutting of all the individual fabric pieces. The type of spreading and cutting system used depends mainly on the level of production. One-off production tends to use simpler, manual systems, whereas mass production can afford to use high cost computer-controlled systems. As computer systems gradually get less expensive, this may change. However for the purposes of this course you should follow the guidelines below.

Manual and semi-automatic systems:

- In manual spreading, the fabric is pulled from a fabric roll by hand and cut to the required length, then smoothed by hand. It is used for short length fabric lays needing frequent changes of fabrics and colours – often used in small companies for bespoke or batch production. A small business run by a designer-maker may use this system or may simply spread the fabric in a single ply on a large table.
- In semi-automatic spreading the cloth is unwound from the roll and spread automatically using a manually driven carriage to lay the fabric and smooth the plies. This is very efficient and is used for long, wide lays, suitable for large batches for large orders.
- In manual and semi-automatic systems fabric cutting may use circular cutters or straight knives, which are pushed by hand. Fabric layers may also be guided by hand against band knives. A small business run by a designer-maker may use cutters or knives or power shears to cut by hand.
- After cutting is done using manual and semi-automatic systems, notches and sewing guides are marked onto each garment piece. Pieces are numbered, labelled and bundled ready for assembly.

Automatic systems:

Many medium and large companies now use computer-controlled systems which:

- integrate the development of production patterns, grading, marker making, spreading and the labelling of each individual fabric piece before cutting. Modern labelling systems provide bar codes to aid production control.
- match patterns, stripes and checks, cutting accurately through the plies of fabric.
- mark notches and sewing guides automatically. The function of these is to guide the product assembly.

Although computerised systems are very high cost, they are becoming the norm in medium and large companies for mass and batch production. Computer systems control costs and reduce waste. They speed up the whole manufacturing process, giving companies the advantage of faster shorter production cycles.

TASK

Draw up a chart to compare the processes involved in fabric spreading and cutting for a one-off and high volume product.

ASSEMBLY

The assembly of sewn products usually involves fusing, joining and pressing. These processes require continuous feedback from manufacturing to ensure that products meet specifications.

Fusing

For some types of garments the process of fusing an interlining to selected cut parts is as important as the sewing operation. A fused interlining reinforces the outer fabric, enables it to keep its shape and reduces creasing. Fusing is used on areas such as jacket fronts, collars, cuffs and waistbands. The use of fusible interlinings shortens the manufacturing time, needs less skill and produces more consistent quality than the use of sewn-in interlinings. In one-off production fusing may be done by hand using an iron. Fusing with a flat-bed press is used for batch runs or small garment parts. Fusing with a conveyor press is suitable for long fabric runs in high volume production.

TASK

Fusibles are the most common types of interlinings used in textile product manufacture. Compare similar products that are made by different levels of production. Do any of the products used sewn interlinings? What kind of products are they? Explain the popularity of fusible interlinings.

THE ORDER OF ASSEMBLY

The order of assembly varies for different products but often involves processes such as:

- assembly of fabric pieces (fused as appropriate)
- addition of working parts such as zips or other fastenings
- assembly of principal product pieces
- decoration using top stitching or trimmings
- lining
- addition of decorative / functional pockets (at an appropriate point in the order of assembly, depending on pocket type).

It is important in all levels of production that the order of assembly is thoroughly worked out so that the product is made in the most efficient manner. In batch and mass production the work content for each product is broken down into separate operations. These have to be 'balanced' so that each operator takes the same time to perform an operation, before the assembly moves on to the next operator. Balanced operations result in a continuous flow of products through the sewing room. The total assembly time will be different for each product depending on its complexity. The assembly time is likely to be short for underwear but long for a man's jacket.

Sewing and joining

When you undertake the analysis of a range of sewn products you will come across a number of different joining techniques. The most common ones are stitching and heat-sealing.

- A plain seam is the most commonly used method of joining woven fabrics. (See Figure 1.9)
- An overlock seam stitches, cuts and finishes the seam in one process. This is used for a range of products including underwear and knitwear.
- A flat seam (seam cover) is made using twin needles to create a stitch on top and an overlock stitch below. This binds the cut edges of straps, belt loops or the hems of fabrics that fray, e.g. for T-shirts or belt loops on jeans.
- A cup seam is used for the seams of knitted fabrics.
- A lap seam is commonly used on the seams of jeans and shirts, providing a very strong seam with two rows of stitching. (See Figure 1.9)
- Heat-sealed joins are applied to fabrics made from thermoplastic fibres, like polyester and polyamide (nylon). Heat-sealing is often used in combination with taped seams to help waterproof products such as all-weather wear or tents.

Figure 1.9
Seam types

'Plain seam' with edges separately overlocked

'Plain seam' with edges overlocked together

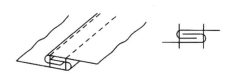

Lap felled seam

TASK

Examine the joining techniques used in two different products that vary in price. Measure the seam allowances. Decide if the cost of each product has any impact on their quality of manufacture.

TASK

Find two similar products – one simple, one more complex – to compare and contrast. The product could be a jacket. For each of the products work out the order of assembly.

a) Produce annotated sketches to show construction details, seam types, fastenings, linings and interlinings.

b) Draw the pattern pieces

c) Work out the order of assembly for the product.

d) Compare the number and length of the assembly processes required for each product.

Finishing

Pressing is a labour intensive craft skill, which has a critical impact on product quality. Some garments such as wadded jackets need minimal finishing. Products such as suit jackets, skirts or trousers may need under pressing, moulding and top pressing.

During manufacture under pressing:

- relaxes the fabric and reduces shrinkage
- removes wrinkles and creases before cutting or sewing
- improves the ease and quality of sewing, such as flattening seams or hems before hemming.

Moulding is used on tailored garments to mould the garment to the contours of the body. It involves stretching and pressing darts, collars and rounded shapes such as sleeve heads, shoulders and armholes.

Top pressing is the final finishing process for a garment to make it ready for sale. It refinishes the fabric after manufacture and improves the aesthetic properties and quality of the product.

TASK

Investigate the manufacture of a one-off product.

- Describe the stages of production for this product. Include references to industrial manufacturing methods.
- Explain how the product could be adapted or redesigned to reduce costs and increase efficiency of production.

Labelling and packaging

Product labelling requirements are discussed on page 24.

Any packaging used for textile products needs to be suitable for the purpose of protecting and presenting the product. Packaging is a key environmental concern and some retailers are encouraging the use of recycled packaging.

THE USE OF ICT BY INDUSTRY IN THE DESIGN AND MANUFACTURE OF PRODUCTS

Computer-based Information and Communications Technology (ICT) has a key role to play in the integration and control of manufacturing and distribution. The use of ICT provides a means of improving decision making in an increasingly complex and fast-changing manufacturing environment. ICT enables business partners to communicate via electronic links and to manufacture on a global scale.

COMPUTERS IN THE DESIGN PROCESS

Computer systems are increasingly used for creative design, product illustration, sample production and product costing. CAD is a standard tool for designing and modelling ideas in 2D or 3D. Specialist software such as Product Data Management (PDM) is used to input design information, simulate virtual products on screen, manage product costing and to plan all the technical data required for manufacture. PDM systems reduce the product time to market through the fast communication of product data between all members of a design and production team.

COMPUTERS IN PRODUCTION

The use of computers in production provides greater flexibility, increased productivity, greater efficiency and a reduction in labour costs. Computer systems are used in flat pattern making, grading, marker making, fabric spreading and cutting. The only area of sewn product manufacture to have been fully automated is fabric cutting. However, computer systems are also used to control the retrieval of fabrics from store, load it on the laying-up carriage and remove cut material. Within assembly computer systems control overhead conveyors that speed the work round a factory, balance the workflow and monitor the quality of individual products through the use of bar codes. The use of computer systems results in the throughput of a greater range of different styles per season.

QUICK RESPONSE MANUFACTURE

Quick Response (QR) has evolved through the rapid transfer of information among all parts of the production chain (fibre producers, fabric manufacturers, clothing manufacturers and retail stores). QR depends on the use of electronic point of sale (EPOS) tills. These send product sales inform-ation to the garment manufacturer, to allow quick response to changes in product demand. Batches of products in the required sizes or colours can then be delivered from stock or made to order in a very short time.

Batch production using Quick Response is a way of achieving more flexibility of production and a faster time to market. The benefits to manufacturers of using QR include:

- reducing the cost of keeping stock
- faster productivity and efficiency
- retained orders from retailers, through product reliability and improved delivery performance
- fast changeover for new styles, to reflect the needs of the target market group.

TASKS

- Explain the benefits of using a computer system to aid the design and manufacture of one-off, batch and high volume products.
- Describe how computer systems are used in product manufacture.
- Discuss the reasons why fabric cutting is the only area of sewn product manufacture that has been fully automated by computer control.

QUALITY

Quality issues are related to the concept of 'fitness for purpose'. Quality is about the relationship between performance, price, aesthetic appeal, saleability and customer satisfaction. Quality issues are different for the consumer and the manufacturer:

- Quality for the consumer means a product's fitness-for-purpose. This can be evaluated through its performance, price and aesthetic appeal.
- Quality for a manufacturer means meeting specifications (including British Standards) and finding a balance between profitable manufacture and the needs and expectations of the consumer and the environment.

QUALITY ASSURANCE

All the above quality issues are aspects of a quality assurance (QA) system, which monitors every stage of design and manufacture through to delivery to the customer. There is a saying that 'Quality cannot be inspected into a product, it must be manufactured into it.'

1 Quality assurance involves the use of a company's internal quality system in which:

- quality control monitors and achieves agreed standards through inspection and testing
- defects are traced back to the production process and eliminated
- sustained levels of quality performance involve all areas of an organisation and its suppliers.

Total Quality management (TQM) is the aim of every company that wants to achieve sustained levels of quality performance. TQM is achieved by using a Quality Management System and successful companies might comply with British Standard (BS) 5750 – where the need to specify quality requirements extends throughout the company and its suppliers. Successful companies can be awarded the international standard of quality, ISO 9000.

2 Quality assurance involves the use of external quality standards, which may include the use of:

- standard working processes and practices to BS standards
- BS testing procedures for materials, components, processes and products
- BS such as for care labelling, zip fasteners, test methods for colourfastness of textiles, for the determination of dimensional change in washing and ironing, for crease resistance or for safe ironing temperatures.

3 Quality assurance may also involve the appropriate use of materials and technologies:

- materials that are non-toxic, safe for the environment and that suit the end use – bleaching, dyeing, printing and finishing involve environmental issues
- manufacturing processes that are suitable and safe for employees, users and the environment.

HOW TO RECOGNISE QUALITY ASSURANCE

Table 1.8 shows the factors involved in achieving quality assurance through a job being well done. With all these factors present and in operation, quality is assured.

Table 1.8

For a job to be well done, everyone must:	This involves:
1. Know what to do	Specifications and drawings
2. Know how to do it	Training and agreed procedures
3. Be able to do it	Equipment and materials
4. Know how well it has been done	Inspection and testing
5. Be able to influence it	Controlled action and involvement in decisions
6. Want to do it	Being motivated

TASK

Investigate two similar products made by different manufacturers, such as two pairs of denim jeans or two shirts. Try to get products that are the same size.
- Measure the two products. Are they the same size or do some measurements differ? Why do you think this is?
- Examine the quality of the products. Is one better made than the other?
- Discuss the quality issues for both of these products.

QUALITY CONTROL

Quality control (QC) is part of a company's quality assurance system, which uses inspection and testing to monitor quality against agreed standards. QC makes use of:

- detailed specifications
- standard systems to prevent faults
- standard sizes and tolerance
- inspection to check quality at critical control points in manufacture
- BS tests to monitor quality.

NACERAP

NACERAP is a quality assurance term, used in garment manufacturing. It provides a standard system for identifying faults, analysing them and putting them right. NACERAP provides a system for training everyone in the same company to use the same words to describe, record, repair or prevent faults.

NACERAP stands for:
N   =   Name of the fault
A   =   Appearance of the fault
C   =   Cause of the fault
E   =   Effect the fault has on the overall quality of the garment
R   =   Repair of the fault or equipment
A   =   Action, to be taken to correct the fault / inform other departments about the fault
P   =   Prevention, to prevent the fault happening again.

TOLERANCE

With all the factors involved in manufacturing sewn products, it is very difficult to achieve perfectly accurate dimensions. Consequently a defined amount of tolerance is usually specified. Tolerance is the acceptable level of variation allowed in the sizing of the product, for it to fit together accurately. Since a tolerance of +/- 1cm in the seams of a garment could result in under sizing, a safer tolerance would be positive (+1cm) which would produce a product which is half a tolerance too big. Too many variations in tolerance could result in too many faults, which could mean a textile would not fit together properly. This would cause the rejection of the textile by quality control.

INSPECTION

Inspection is the examination of the product to see if specified standards and tolerances have been met. It takes place at critical control points in manufacture such as preparation, processing, assembly and finishing, together with a final inspection of the product against a sealed sample. Inspection involves monitoring:

- quality of materials
- accuracy of sizing and fit
- quality of appearance and finish.

Quality and reliability in garment manufacture depends on variables or attributes.

- Variables are factors that are measurable such as stitches per cm, seam turnings, seam strength, the amount of elasticity and so on.
- Attributes cannot be measured. This aspect of quality is concerned with judgmental factors like appearance, symmetry, drape or how much a garment enhances the wearer's personality or social status – the image it gives the wearer. It is always the attributes that sell a product.

TESTING

For sewn products testing is concerned with performance standards and wash/care requirements. Performance standards will vary with the product – swimwear is tested for chlorine, salt water and sunlight, whereas school wear must be rugged, hardwearing, durable and easy-care. Tests are regularly reviewed by British Standards.

TASK

Use the following checklist when you analyse a product for quality:
- Is the product creased?
- Is there a label with fibre content and care instructions?
- Are the components or trims rusting, tarnishing or broken?
- Are the zips/fastenings faulty?
- Are the seams secure, puckered, grinning or twisting?
- Is there needle damage?
- Have the threads been trimmed?
- Are the collars, pockets, zips or darts sewn correctly?
- Are buttons, buttonholes or studs misaligned or miss-stitched?
- Are the cuffs, pleats, fronts, hem, vents stitched correctly?
- Are there any faults in printing/dyeing, the fabric or lining?
- Is the garment measurement correct?

A high quality coat for example is an expensive purchase that needs to combine practicality, comfort, warmth and durability with aspects that reflect what is happening in fashion.

Table 1.9 shows some of the processes used by one company to achieve the manufacture of well-designed and well-made coats. Fabric preparation to packaging takes one hundred minutes.

Table 1.9

Stage of production	Quality control
Fabric preparation	• Each roll of fabric checked for flaws • Computer linked to cutting adjusted to avoid flaws
Cutting	• Each whole pattern cut from one ply to ensure colour consistency
Labelling and fusing	• Swatch kept for reference, stray threads trimmed
Materials handling	• All coat pieces on mover in correct order, cover with satin to keep clean
Pockets sewn on coat body	• Guide/feel fabric to ensure no pulls at corners
Front/back assembly and lining	• Coat on automatic moving hanger
Buttonholes, top-stitching	• Hand stitching
Steaming and pressing	• Expert presser also makes shoulder moulds
Final checking	• Coat turned inside out, check seaming, damage to fabric, hems, lapels, final steaming
Packing	• Coat in plastic on moving rail

HEALTH AND SAFETY

HEALTH AND SAFETY ISSUES RELATED TO PRODUCTS

Health and safety (H&S) issues for products are related to the protection of the consumer.

General safety requirements mean that products need to comply with BS and International Standards. Products must be made from safe materials that are non-toxic for people and the environment and must be safe to use. Specific safety issues are related to toxicity, metal contamination, flammability, fastenings and trim components and children's clothing. Table 1.10 gives examples of various H&S requirements

Table 1.10

Regulation	Example of application
The Trade Descriptions Act 1988	Can't say a product is waterproof if it's not. A fabric can be waterproof.
The Textile Products (Indication of Fibre Content) Regulation 1986	Fibre content must be accurate, but there is a tolerance of 3 per cent.
The Weight & Measures Act 1985 & 1987	Stated sizing must be accurate
The Consumer Protection Act 1987	The onus of proof of a fault is on the consumer
The General Product Safety Regulations Act 1994	Product must have correct labelling description. In normal use children's wear must not give any risk or potential risk.

HEALTH AND SAFETY ISSUES RELATED TO PRODUCTION

Health and safety at work is the responsibility of employers and employees. Manufacturers are required to follow strict rules and regulations, based on the Health and Safety at Work Act 1974. Employees are required to follow safety procedures to reduce risks in using materials, machinery and manufacturing processes.

RISK ASSESSMENT

Risk assessment means identifying the risks to the health and safety of people and to the environment. In practice, this means using safe designing and manufacturing processes, and making textile products that are safe to use and safe to dispose of.

Manufacturers use risk assessment techniques to look for possible hazards in their products. They use British Standards to test and monitor textile production. All possible health hazards to employees have to be eliminated and safety procedures have to be followed to ensure the safety of people at work. Some manufacturers use Life Cycle Assessment (LCA) to assess a product's impact from cradle (raw materials) to grave (disposal).

One of the risks associated with production is contamination with needles and pins. In order to control this risk, machinists are only allowed one needle in the machine at a time. A supervisor will dispose of the old needle and replace it with a new one. If a needle breaks there is a search for the bits. If they are not found, a metal detector is used. If the needle is still not found the product does not enter the supply chain.

The Risk Assessment Code of Practice BS 1996 sets out safety requirements for the design and manufacture of children's clothing. For example:

- no cords and ribbons accessible to a child's mouth (choking hazard)
- no cords in hoods (strangulation hazard)
- no zips in trousers of boys under 5 years old (ouch!)
- nightwear must comply with BS 5722 relating to flammability.

TASK

Draw up a chart to show the key stages of manufacture for a product. For each stage list the risk assessment procedures required to make the product as safe as possible.

THE APPEAL OF TEXTILE PRODUCTS

In this section you need to consider the appeal of textiles products for the consumer. In the exam you will be asked about a specific product. In your answer you should include references to the product's quality of design – its form and function as well as the trend, style and cultural influences on the product.

FORM AND FUNCTION OF DIFFERENT PRODUCTS

These days we buy products for all sorts of different reasons. We buy fashion products partly because of the image that they give us, as well as for other more practical reasons, such as the product's quality in relation to its cost – its value for money. Modern products are increasingly developed and marketed through styling and image for specific target market groups. These days a product is thought to have three basic functions:

- its practical and technical function – does it 'work' efficiently? Does it fit a range of sizes?
- its aesthetic function – how it looks, its styling.
- its symbolic function – or the image it gives the user.

THE INFLUENCE OF TRENDS AND STYLE ON THE DESIGN, PRODUCTION AND SALE OF PRODUCTS

For a company to make a profit, product design must be market led and market driven. Product design must therefore take into account the needs of the target market group and the various influences on product development such as trends, colour, style and cultural influences.

TRENDS AND STYLE

The influence of trends on textile and product design is very important, especially for fashion products. Trend forecasting is an essential activity for designers of fibres, yarns, fabrics, accessories, garments and interiors. They use market research techniques to research colour, style and fashion trends, so they can predict what people will buy.

TASKS

1 Discuss what you think is meant by 'good design' and 'style'. The following questions may help you:
   • Well-designed but badly made – does it sell?
   • Badly designed but well made – does it sell?
   • Is style the 'in' thing – a fashion statement?
   • Does style come naturally?
   • Is it necessary to have money to have style?
   • What does style do?
   • Is it important?
2 The work of other designers and artists has always been used as a starting point for colour and style ideas. Find and discuss some pictures which illustrate such influences on product style.

COLOUR

Colour is an essential characteristic of textiles products and it is a powerful marketing tool, which can encourage consumers to buy.

- In fashion textiles colours gradually change with each spring/summer and autumn/winter season. Wearing the 'right' colour can be important if you want to look 'fashionable'.
- In interior design different colour combinations can change the mood of a room, creating stimulating or calming effects.
- In performance or safety wear bright colours can help identify people at risk and those who can help them.

CULTURAL AND SOCIAL INFLUENCES

Cultural and social influences are related to the way in which aspects such as fashion and lifestyle affect design. Cultural influences include traditional textiles as well as the influence of exhibitions or artists. Social influences from the media such as film, television and music also influence design.

TASKS

1 Explain why designers use the inspiration of other cultures when developing ideas of their own. Do we exploit these cultures by making use of traditional design styles?

2 Consumer magazines use attribute tables to compare the key features of different products. They identify the important features or attributes that can be used as a basis for judging the products. Then a table of the analysis and results is drawn up, with the product given a score out of ten for each attribute.

Use attribute analysis to analyse a range of winter jackets. For each product identify:
  • how well it performs – qualities such as warmth, waterproof or durability
  • aesthetic characteristics and design features
  • target market and user requirements.

3 Select a product that is a popular seller at present and discuss its appeal.

DEVELOPING PRODUCT ANALYSIS SKILLS

By the time you get to the end of this unit you will have had a lot of practice doing tasks that are similar to the questions in the Product Analysis exam.

• A further way of developing your skills is to practice doing timed tasks (using the product in Figure 1.10) so that you will learn how to allocate your time during the exam itself.

TASK

An attractive and colourful handmade bag, with one compartment. It has a woven front panel, a Velcro fastening under the front flap and a bound edge, which carries on to form the long strap. Made from 100% woven cotton. The main body of the bag is navy blue. The front panel is woven in vertical stripes with patterning in red, orange, turquoise, pink, purple and green.

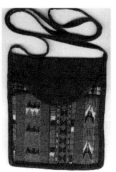

a) Outline the product design specification for this bag.
b) Justify the use of:
  (i) woven cotton fabric
  (ii) Velcro fastening.
c) Give FOUR reasons why this bag is hand-made.
d) Describe the stages of production for this bag. Include references to industrial manufacturing methods.
e) Discuss quality issues for this bag.
f) Discuss product safety issues associated with this bag and its production.
g) Discuss the appeal of this bag.

Figure 1.10

- Revising and reviewing what you have learned during this unit will also help you prepare you for the exam.

This unit is also a good way to develop a range of skills that you can use in coursework. You can use product analysis as a 'jumping-off point' for developing ideas for new products and for learning how to develop product specifications. It is also useful for developing 2D and 3D drawing and modelling skills. The task below can be applied to any product and will give you practise in developing these skills.

TASK

For a one-off, batch or high volume product:

- Develop a product design specification for the product.
- Examine the working properties of the materials, components and fastenings.
- Draw, sketch and model the product in 2D to demonstrate your knowledge of the product assembly, showing construction details, materials, components and fastenings.
- Model the product in 3D – draw the pattern, mock-up the product in paper and work out the order of assembly.
- Develop a new product design specification, by changing the design context and target market group.
- Generate a range of ideas for the new product.
- Produce a new product using rapid prototyping. You could use inexpensive materials such as paper, card, plastics, wire, recycled materials, inexpensive fabrics. Use fast techniques such joining by glue, staples or stitching to enable the production of a creative product.

PRODUCT ANALYSIS QUESTIONS

You should also practice doing a complete product analysis question, working to the same time and under the same conditions as the Unit 1 Product Analysis Exam. Below is a specimen examination question. You have 1½ hours to complete it.

EXAM PRACTICE

- An easy wear and care casual outfit, suitable for those long summer days.

- The top has a tie neckline, patch pockets, sleeve binding and is finished with topstitching. Made from 60% cotton, 40% viscose.

- The printed trousers have an elasticised waistline. Made from 60% cotton and 40% viscose.

- The outfit comes in a range of small, medium and large sizes, suitable for ages 4-6, 7-9, 10-12.

- Colours:
  White, apple green, turquoise, orange
  White, mint green, lilac, pink
  White, bottle green, ochre, rust.

Figure 1.11

a) Outline the product design specification for this outfit.   7

b) Justify the use of:
   (i) cotton/viscose fabric.   3
   (ii) an elasticated waistline.   3

c) Give FOUR reasons why this outfit is batch produced.   4

d) Describe the stages of production for the trousers. Include references to industrial manufacturing methods.   16

e) Discuss quality issues for these trousers.   8

f) Discuss product safety issues associated with the trousers and their production.   8

g) Discuss the appeal of this outfit.   8

   Quality of written communication.   3

   Total marks   60

Preview

Unit	Level	Components	Areas of study
3	AS	Section A: Materials, Components and Systems	• Classification of materials and components. • Working properties and processes • Testing materials
		Section B: Options	• Design and Technology in Society OR • CAD/CAM

Unit 3 has two sections, both of which must be studied. Section A includes subject content related to textile materials, components and systems. Section B has two options, each with subject content. You must study ONE Option from Section B.

WHAT YOU WILL LEARN IN THE UNIT

The content of Unit 3 Section A enables you to develop your understanding of textile materials, components and systems. The work you undertake include knowledge and understanding of the following areas:

Chapter 1   Classification of materials and components
- Natural and manufactured fibres
- Yarns
- Woven fabrics
- Knitted fabrics
- Non-woven fabrics
- Fastenings and components

Chapter 2   Working properties of materials and components.

Chapter 3   Hand and commercial processes
- Preparing, processing, manipulating and combining materials and components
- Finishing processes
- Product manufacture

Chapter 4   Testing materials

WHAT YOU WILL DO IN THE UNIT

During the unit you should undertake a variety of tasks to enable you to understand the subject content. You may be asked to:

- work individually on some theoretical aspects of the unit content – for example you could research information about a specific fibre type and share your information with the group.
- work individually on some tasks – for example you could undertake practical tasks to develop understanding of working properties and processes.
- work collaboratively with others on some activities – for example you could undertake the comparative testing of fabrics for quality, performance and aftercare.
- work individually on exam-style questions.

UNIT 3 ASSESSMENT

Unit 3 is assessed externally through a $1\frac{1}{2}$ hour written exam, which assesses your understanding of the unit subject content. There is one question paper with two sections:

- Section A: Materials, Components and Systems
- Section B: Options

UNIT 3 SECTION A ASSESSMENT

The work that you do in Materials, Components and Systems will be assessed through Section A of the Unit 3 examination paper.

- It consists of six short-answer knowledge-based questions, each worth five marks
- You are advised to spend 45 minutes on this section of the exam.
- This section together with the option is worth 15 per cent of the full Advanced GCE.

WHAT THE EXAMINER IS LOOKING FOR

The examination paper is designed to give you the opportunity to demonstrate your understanding of what you have learned in the unit. Examiners will look for concise answers, often a description, explanation or annotated sketch showing an understanding of the topic or process.

EXAM TIPS

- Make brief notes about the topics covered in this unit.
- Summarise the key points on one or two sheets of paper.
- Learn these key points.
- Practise working through a complete exam so you will learn how to allocate the time available to you.
- In the exam, read the questions through, and then read them again, to make sure you understand what you are being asked to do.
- Plan your answer briefly, then check the question again to make sure that you have covered it fully.
- Work through your answer making sure that you address each point in your plan.
- Don't write everything you know about a topic if it's irrelevant to the question!
- Use clearly written sentences and bullet points to make your answer clear.
- Use specialist technical terms and clear sketches to illustrate your answer where appropriate.
- Read through your answer then move on to the next question.

Chapter 1

Classification of Materials and Components

IN A fast moving industry, new materials, processes and finishes are continually being developed to meet new needs and situations. As a result, designers and technologists have to regularly update their materials knowledge and understanding, if they are to design products that meet changing market requirements. This unit gives you the opportunity to develop your understanding of the range of natural and manufactured fibres shown in Figure 3A.1. This classification is not exhaustive, but provides knowledge and understanding of a good range of fibres, from which you can extend your knowledge in the A2 course and beyond. The unit further enables you to develop knowledge related to fibre properties, fabric structure, finishing processes and product manufacture. The final section goes on to discuss the principles and techniques of testing before manufacture.

Throughout this unit you will come across a number of textile terms, which are defined at intervals through the unit. It would be a good start to discuss a few basic terms, related to polymers and fibres.

POLYMERS

Textile materials are made from natural or synthetic fibre-forming polymers. A polymer is the generic name for a combination of large molecules, made from a chain of smaller repeating chemical units called monomers.

1. Natural polymers exist as short fibres, which need to be combed, lined up and twisted to make longer, usable lengths.
   - Vegetable fibres, such as cotton and linen, are composed of the glucose polymer cellulose.
   - The animal fibre wool, from the fleece of the sheep, is composed of the protein polymer keratin.
   - Hair fibres, such as cashmere and mohair, are also based on the protein polymer keratin.

2. 'Regenerated' natural fibres, such as viscose and modal are manufactured from the cellulose in wood pulp. This is dissolved in chemicals and extruded through the tiny holes in a spinneret into an acid bath, to produce fine continuous filaments of pure regenerated cellulose.

3. **Most synthetic polymers are manufactured from petrochemicals, using**

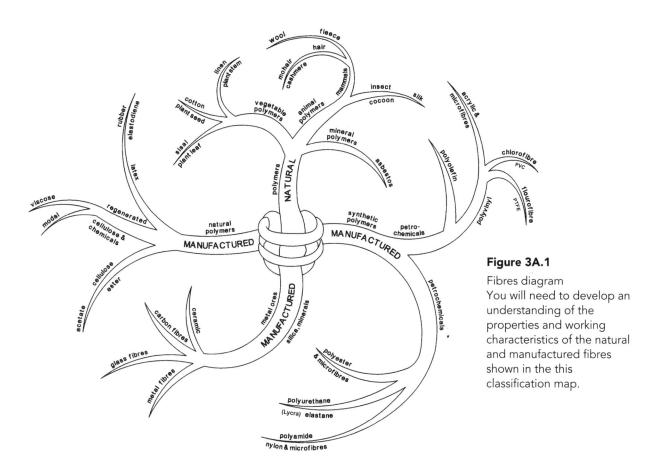

Figure 3A.1

Fibres diagram
You will need to develop an understanding of the properties and working characteristics of the natural and manufactured fibres shown in the this classification map.

the process of polymerisation to produce long chains of fibre-forming linear polymers. These are converted by solution or melted and extruded through spinnerets to form continuous filaments of synthetic fibres. There are two main methods of polymerisation, called addition polymerisation and condensation polymerisation.

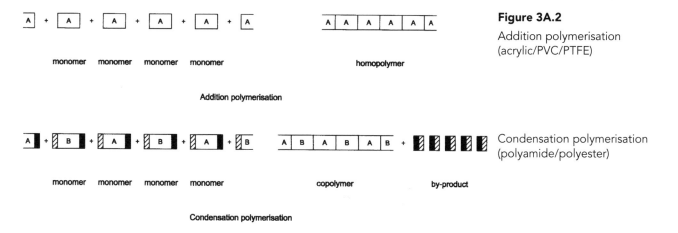

Figure 3A.2

Addition polymerisation (acrylic/PVC/PTFE)

Condensation polymerisation (polyamide/polyester)

- Acrylic, PVC and PTFE are made by addition polymerisation – in which similar monomers are added to each other to form long chains, called homopolymers.

- Polyamide and polyester are made by condensation polymerisation – in which two different monomers are added together to form long chains, called copolymers.
- Elastane is made by block polymerisation – in which two different monomers are pre-formed into blocks and then added together, to form block copolymers.

Grouping polymers
Polymers can be put into three groups, according to their structure.

Elastomers	Thermosetting polymers	Thermoplastic polymers
Elastomers can be stretched and return to their original shape, such as the branded elastane fibre Lycra.	Thermosetting polymers have cross-links between the long chain molecules. They set with heat and cannot be softened when re-heated. They are not used for textiles.	Thermoplastic polymers have long chain molecules that are not cross-linked. They soften when heated and become hard again when cool. Acetate, acrylic, polyamide and polyester are all thermoplastic and should be ironed with care.
Elastomers	thermosetting polymers	Thermoplastic polymers

Table 3A.1

FIBRE

A fibre is a fine and flexible textile raw material, which has a high ratio of length to thickness. All fibres can be classified as natural or manufactured, each with a number of sub-groups. Fibres can be short or very long, depending on where they come from and how they are manufactured.

- Staple fibres are relatively short in length. Natural staple fibres can range in length from a few millimetres (such as cotton linters) to around a metre (as in some linen, jute or ramie fibres).
- All synthetic fibres are manufactured as continuous filaments of indefinite length, which run the whole length of the yarn. Some synthetic continuous filaments are cut into staple lengths.

- Silk is the only natural continuous filament fibre. It can be as long as one kilometre, when it is taken from the silk cocoon.

MICROFIBRE

Microfibre technology combines a high number of very fine fibres into one yarn of one decitex or less. This means that 10 kilometres of the filament weigh one gram or less. In every day terms, a microfibre is around 60 to 100 times finer than a human hair! Microfibres can be:

- manufactured from polyester, polyamide or acrylic.
- blended with other synthetic fibres or with natural fibres.
- used in fabrics that have an enormous variety of appearances and end-uses.
- used in smart and technical fabrics for activewear, all weather wear and for a range of industrial uses.

TASKS

1 Discuss the processes involved in the production of natural, regenerated and synthetic fibres.

2 Explain what is meant by the following terms:
  - polymer
  - fibre
  - microfibre.

NATURAL FIBRES

Vegetable fibres (cellulose)		Animal fibres (protein)		Mineral fibres	
seed	cotton	wool	wool	silicate	asbestos
stem (bast)	linen (flax)	fine hair	cashmere mohair		
leaf	sisal	silk	cultivated wild		

Table 3A.2

VEGETABLE FIBRES

Cotton

Figure 3A.3
Cotton fibre.

longitudinal view

immature   mature   dead   mercerised

Source	Properties	Improved performance through finishing	Typical blends
Natural cellulose from the seed of the cotton plant. • Produced as staple fibre 	• Absorbs up to 65% of own weight without dripping. • Non-static because it always contains some moisture. • Naturally breathable. • Soft handle, good drape, dries slowly. • Good strength, abrasion resistance and durability. • Poor elasticity, so creases easily. • Biodegradable and recyclable.	• Mercerising – for higher strength and lustre. • Synthetic resin treatment – for non-iron / crease-resist finish (dries faster, but gives reduced strength and absorption). • Stain-resist finishes using Teflon or silicone • Flame-retardant finish – using the Proban process.	• Polyester • Polyamide • Viscose • Modal • Elastane • Common blend ratios – 50/50, 60/40, 70/30.

Typical cotton fabrics	End-uses	Aftercare
Calico, corduroy, denim, gingham, drill, terry towelling	• Household linen, curtains, towels. • Shirts, underwear, trousers, jeans. • Workwear, tents, awnings, sewing thread.	Washable, can be boiled and bleached, dries slowly, best ironed damp, can be dry-cleaned and tumble dried (may shrink)

Table 3A.3

Linen

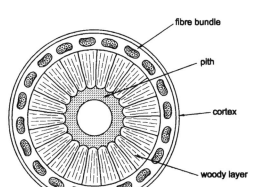

Source	Properties	Improved performance through finishing	Typical blends
Natural cellulose from the stem of the flax plant. • Produced as staple fibres MASTERS OF LINEN	• Strong, durable, long lasting, smooth surface, good drape. • Highly absorbent, fast drying, fresh and cool to wear. • Non-static because it always contains some moisture. • Crisp, firm handle, stiffer and harder than cotton. • Shrink-proof, washes, irons and dyes well • Low elasticity, so creases very badly. • Dirt-repellent, anti-microbial. • Biodegradable and recyclable.	• Synthetic resin treatment – for crease-resist finish. • Stain-resist finishes using Teflon or silicone	Linen 50% Cotton 50% Linen 70% Nylon 25% Elastane 5% Linen 70% Modal 30% Linen 50% Cotton 46% Acrylic 4% • Viscose • Tencel • Polyester • Silk

Typical linen fabrics	End-uses	Aftercare
Interlining, Holland (for window blinds), mattress ticking.	• Household linen, tablecloths, curtains, tea towels. • Shirts, skirts, suits. • Ropes, sewing thread, geotextiles.	Washable, can be boiled and bleached, quick drying, irons easily when damp, can be dry-cleaned and tumble dried.

Table 3A.4

Sisal

This is a natural sustainable fibre, produced from the leaves of the agave cactus. Sisal is high strength, durable, easy to dye, water resistant, has good abrasion resistance, good anti-static properties and is fairly easy to keep clean. It is used for agricultural twines, ropes, hairbrush bristles, baskets and natural floor coverings, which can be blended with wool to make them softer and warmer.

TASK

1 Make notes to compare the properties of cotton and linen.

2 Investigate the finishes that can be applied to fabrics made from each of these fibres.

3 Research the aftercare symbols for pure cotton and pure linen fabrics.

4 Find examples of 100% cotton and 100% linen fabrics and add them to your technical notebook.

5 Compare the known properties of cotton and linen with the characteristics of your own fabric swatches.

ANIMAL FIBRES

Wool

Source	Properties	Improved performance through finishing	Typical blends
Wool from the fleece of a sheep. • Produced as staple fibres	• Hydrophillic – can absorb 1/3 of its weight in water without feeling wet. • Naturally breathable, rapidly absorbs moisture vapour. • Hydrophobic – repels raindrops. • Mostly non-static, because it always contains some moisture. • Very soft or coarse handle, depending on fineness. Good drape. • Medium strength, not durable. • Smooth worsteds can be cool, bulky woollens are warm to wear. • Inbuilt UV protection and fire-resistant. • At least 40% inbuilt natural stretch and elasticity – good crease-resistance, creases drop out. • Bio-degradable and recyclable	• Machine Washable Wool – for wovens and knitwear at 40°C, using the wool cycle and approved detergents. • Total Easy Care wool – for wovens and knitwear at 40°C, using the wool cycle and approved detergents, followed by tumble-drying on low heat setting. • Silicon treatment – for weatherproofing knitting yarns. • Mothproofing – especially for uniforms.	• Polyester • Polyamide • Acrylic • Tactel • Elastane • Silk • Cotton • Cashmere • Mohair • Common blend ratios – 50/50, 55/45, 60/40, 70/30. 'Sportwool' • 50% merino wool inside • 50% polyester outside

Typical wool fabrics	End-uses	Aftercare
'Cool Wool', felt, herringbone, flannel, 'Sportwool', tartan, tweed, Viyella	• Blankets, carpets, upholstery. • Suits, jumpers, overcoats, sports garments, ties, scarves, hats, socks. • Industrial felts, agricultural blankets, geotextiles	Washable (with care, unless easy care finish), do not bleach, very slow drying, steam iron under a cloth or fabric goes shiny. Can be dry-cleaned. Do not tumble dry, dry in direct sunlight or over direct heat.

Table 3A.5

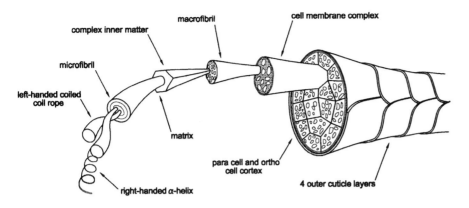

Figure 3A.5

The structure of wool fibre

Cashmere

Source	Properties	Typical blends	End-uses
The fine underhair of the Kel goat from India, Mongolia and Iran, shorn once a year. • Produced as staple fibres • One goat produces 200-250 grams per year – enough for a scarf. • Two goats produce enough yarn for a 1-ply sweater. • It takes 24 goats to produce enough cashmere for a coat.	• Soft, luxurious handle and appearance. • Light, lustrous • Good thermal insulation • Crease-resistant, dirt-repellent. • Non-static, fire-resistant. • Expensive due to limited supply.	• Wool • Silk • Polyester	• Expensive luxury fabric for coats and suits. • Luxury knitwear. • Luxury interior textiles for cars, planes, yachts.

Table 3A.6

Mohair

Source	Properties	Typical blends	End-uses
Hair of the angora goat, from Texas, South Africa, Turkey, shorn twice a year. • Produced as staple fibres	• Soft, silky, luxury handle and touch. • Good thermal insulation – 35% warmer than wool. • Durable, hardwearing – 10% stronger than wool, crease-resistant, dyes well. • Dust-repellent, fire-resistant. • Expensive due to limited supply.	• Wool • Cotton • Silk	• Expensive worsted fabric for suiting. • Eveningwear. • Scarves, knitwear.

Table 3A.7

TASK

1 Find examples of woollen, worsted and wool blend fabrics and add them to your technical notebook.

2 Compare the known properties of wool and other fibres with the characteristics of your own fabric swatches.

3 Investigate the finishes that can be applied to wool fabrics.

4 Research the aftercare symbols for fabrics made from Pure New Wool.

Cultivated silk

Source	Properties	Improved performance through finishing	Typical blends
Silk fibres from the cocoon of the Mulberry silkworm (Bombyx Mori). • Produced as filaments up to 1km in length and as spun silk.	• Fine, smooth, lustrous, soft handle, elegant drape. • Elastic, fairly crease-resistant, creases drop out. • Can absorb up to 1/3 of its weight in water without feeling wet. • Non-static because it always contains some moisture. • Strong, durable, light. • Cool, but a good insulator, so it also provides warmth.	• Polyurethane coating – to make silk fabric waterproof.	Filaments mainly produced as pure fibre. Staple fibre blends with most apparel fibres: • wool • mohair • cotton • polyamide

Typical cultivated silk fabrics	End-uses	Aftercare of cultivated and wild silk
• Chiffon, crepe, damask, satin, twill, voile.	• Luxury day and evening wear, underwear. • Wadding for performance skiwear. • Racing bike tyre reinforcement • Scarves, ties, hats, handbags, umbrellas. • Sewing and embroidery threads.	Can be affected by perspiration, causing it to rot. Wash carefully, do not bleach, iron on back of fabric, steam and water can leave stains, best to dry-clean, do not tumble dry or dry in direct sunlight.

Table 3A.8

Wild silk

Source	Properties	Typical wild silk fabrics	End-uses
Silk filament fibres from the cocoon of the wild Tussah silk moth. • Filaments and spun silk	• Coarse, 'rustic', uneven, thicker fibre. • Harsh handle, heavier than cultivated silk. • Absorbent and non-static because it always contains some moisture. • Dyes to dark, dull colours, dull lustre. • More sensitive than cultivated silk to perspiration – could stain.	• Tussah silk • Doupion • Shantung	• Curtains, wall coverings, lampshades • Evening wear, hats.

Table 3A.9

MINERAL FIBRES

Asbestos

There are many types of the mineral fibre asbestos, all of which are mined. Asbestos is non-flammable, resistant to most types of chemicals, insects and micro-organisms and can provide thermal insulation – very useful properties.

Traditionally, asbestos was used where heat resistance was required, in products like car brake linings, roof insulation, fire-resistant clothing, theatre safety curtains or on ironing boards. The fibre is no longer in use because it is a serious health hazard. It is occasionally found in buildings and has to be removed with great care by experts. These days, modern fibres such as Nomex can provide superior heat and flame resistance, combined with high-strength and easy-care.

TASK

1 Investigate the uses of silk fabrics for summer and winter wear.
2 Collect examples of cultivated and wild silk fabrics for your technical notebook.
3 Compare the known properties of silk fibres with the characteristics of your own fabric swatches.
4 Research the aftercare symbols for 100% silk fabrics.

MANUFACTURED FIBRES

Natural polymers		Synthetic polymers		Inorganics	
regenerated cellulose	viscose modal	polyvinyl	acrylic	carbon	carbon fibre
cellulose ester	acetate	chlorofibre	polyvinyl chloride (PVC)	glass	glass fibre
latex	rubber	polyurethane	elastane	metallic	metal fibres
		fluorofibre	Teflon	ceramic	ceramic fibres
		polyamide	nylon		
		polyester	polyester		

Table 3A.10

NATURAL POLYMERS

Regenerated cellulose: viscose

Source	Properties	Improved performance through finishing	Typical blends
Natural cellulose from wood pulp from pine or eucalyptus trees. • Produced as staple and filament yarns.	• More absorbent than cotton, non-static because it always contains some moisture. • Naturally breathable, absorbing 11-14% of water vapour. • Fine, with soft handle and good drape. • Low ability to trap air – low warmth. • Lower strength, abrasion resistance and durability than cotton, can tear when wet. • Poor elasticity, so creases easily. • Dyes and prints to bright colours, shrinks. • Biodegradable and recyclable, inexpensive to produce.	• Synthetic resin treatment – to reduce creasing and shrinkage, although absorbency is reduced. • Wide range of finishes can be applied – such as textured, crimped or moiré.	• Cotton • Linen • Wool • Polyester • Elastane

Typical viscose fabrics	End-uses	Aftercare
Filament viscose produces lustrous and crepe fabrics. Staple viscose produces cotton, linen and wool-type fabrics.	• Curtains, lining fabrics. • Shirts, dresses, lingerie. • Ribbons, trimmings.	Washable, do not bleach, easy to iron, can be dry-cleaned but not tumble dried.

Table 3A.11

Regenerated cellulose: modal

Source	Properties	Improved performance through finishing	Typical blends
Natural cellulose from wood pulp. • Produced mainly as staple fibre. • Mainly used in blends.	• Absorbs up to 50% more moisture than cotton, non-static because it always contains some moisture. • Naturally breathable. • Silky, smooth, very soft handle and good drape. • Low ability to trap air – low warmth. • Lower strength, abrasion resistance and durability than cotton. • Poor elasticity, so creases easily. • Dyes to brilliant colours, shrinks less than viscose. • Biodegradable and recyclable, inexpensive to produce.	• Synthetic resin treatment – to reduce creasing and shrinkage, although absorbency is reduced. • Wide range of finishes can be applied – such as textured, crimped or moiré.	• Cotton • Polyester • Wool • Silk • Elastane

Typical modal fabrics	End-uses	Aftercare
Lustrous fabrics, blended knitted and woven fabrics.	• Bed and table linen, terry towelling. • Shirts, jumpers, socks, nightwear, jackets, sports and active wear, soft denim.	Washable, do not bleach, easy to iron, can be dry-cleaned and tumble dried.

Table 3A.12

Cellulose ester: acetate

Source	Properties	End-uses	After-care	Typical blends
Cotton cellulose and acetic acid • 95% of the acetic acid can be recycled. • Produced as filaments and microfibres.	• Low absorbency, fast drying, prone to static. • Naturally breathable. • Subdued lustre, smooth, very soft handle with elegant drape • Low warmth, dyes well • More elastic than viscose, but creases easily. • Thermoplastic, sensitive to dry heat. • Biodegradable and recyclable, inexpensive to produce.	• Silk-type fabrics for dresses, blouses, linings. • Microfibre performance fabrics. • Embroidery yarns, ribbons and trimmings. • Trubenising collars and cuffs.	Wash and iron with care, do not bleach, can be dry-cleaned, and do not tumble dry.	• Wool or viscose for winter fabrics • Cotton, linen or silk for summer fabrics. • Polyester • Elastane

Table 3A.13

Latex: rubber

Natural rubber is made from latex, although synthetic rubber from petrochemicals is mainly used today. Its natural stretch and pliability have made rubber useful for flooring, waterproof coverings, tyres and Wellington boots. In the past, rubber yarns were used to provide stretch in swimwear and underwear. Rubber can be printed onto garments and accessories and can be used as moulded hoods or pockets. It can also be applied to specific areas of a product, such as the fingers of work gloves. Natural rubber is:

• warm, pliable and soft
• antistatic, antibacterial and anti-slip
• sensitive to light, oils, solvents or grease
• not breathable, so ventilation is needed
• joined by stitching or adhesives
• recyclable.

TASK

1 Investigate the uses of regenerated fibres and blends, explaining the suitability of each fibre or fibre blend.
2 Collect examples of viscose, modal and acetate fabrics for your technical notebook.
3 Compare the known properties of these fibres with the characteristics of your own fabric swatches.
4 Research the aftercare symbols for 100% viscose, modal and acetate fabrics.

SYNTHETIC POLYMERS

Polyvinyl: acrylic

Source	Properties	Typical blends	End-uses	After care
Petrochemicals • Inexpensive to manufacture. • Produced mainly as staple fibres. • Can be spun as microfibres.	• Low absorbency, fast drying, prone to static. • Good strength, crease-resistant • Soft wool-like handle with good drape. • Warm, easy care. • Thermoplastic, sensitive to steam and heat, can result in shrinkage. • Non-renewable resource.	• Wool or viscose for winter fabrics. • Cotton, linen or silk for summer fabrics. • Polyester. • Elastane.	• Blankets, curtains, furnishing fabrics, carpets. • Microfibre performance fabrics. • Lining fabrics, pile, fake-fur and fleece fabrics. • Fluffy knitting yarns.	Machine washable, iron with care, do not bleach, can be dry-cleaned, and do not tumble dry.

Table 3A.14

Chlorofibre: polyvinyl chloride (PVC)

Source	Properties	Typical blends	End-uses	After care
Petrochemicals • Manufacture uses chlorine and dioxins. • Can be manufactured as filament fibres or spun. • Can be manufactured as a coating.	• Strong, flexible, durable • Breathable, easy care and waterproof. • Provides good insulation. • Thermoplastic. • Non-renewable resource, although PVC bottles can be recycled.	Spun fibres always blended with other fibres: • Cotton • Linen • Viscose • Modal • Wool • Silk	• Weatherproof coatings, raincoats, shower curtains, floor coverings, and architectural textiles. • Underwear, jumpers, hats, scarves, socks. • Active sportswear, fleece.	Machine washable, fast drying, iron with care, do not bleach, can be dry-cleaned, do not tumble dry.

Table 3A.15

Polyurethane: elastane

Source	Properties	Typical blends	End-uses	After care
Petrochemicals • Made from segmented polyurethane. • Composed of soft, flexible segments bonded with hard, rigid segments. • Elastane yarn is always covered by another yarn.	• Inbuilt capacity to stretch up to 7 times original length, then recover when tension is released. • Provides lively, supple fabric with enhanced drape. • Adds comfort, softness, and crease-resistance. • Improves body-shaping and shape retention. • Can be engineered to provide precise combination of yarn thickness, texture, brightness and stretch performance to suit the end use of fabric or garment. • For example can provide chlorine resistance and comfort in swimwear, lasting fit in leather, washable and crease-resistant linen. • Absorbent, dyes well, easy care. • Non-renewable resource.	Elastane fibres are always combined with other fibres, natural or synthetic. Common blends: • Maximum 20% for swimwear • 15% for hosiery • 2-5% jersey fabrics • 2% for woven fabrics • 1% for flat knits.	• Body-hugging, comfortable garments. • Sportswear, skiwear, lingerie, hosiery, leisurewear, fashion products. • Medical products e.g. bandages, nappies. • Shoes.	Depending on majority fibre component: Hand, machine wash or dry-clean, can be boiled.

Table 3A.16

Fluorofibre: polytetrafluoroethylene (PTFE)   Table 3A.17

Source	Properties	End-uses
Petrochemicals • Synthetic polymer used mainly as a coating.	• Flexible, durable. • Breathable, easy care, hardly dyes. • Water repellent, oil, chemical and stain resistant, windproof. • Water-based, CFC-free, doesn't harm environment. • Non-renewable resource, degrades slowly.	• Used to protect all fibres and leather. • Garments, upholstery, curtains, sportswear, ties, mattresses, workwear, shoes.

TASK

1 Investigate the uses of acrylic, PVC and elastane fibres in activewear, explaining the suitability of each fibre or fibre blend.
2 Collect examples of acrylic fabrics and elastane blends for your technical notebook. Look out for PVC coated fabrics.
3 Compare the known properties of these fibres with the characteristics of your own fabric swatches.
4 Research the aftercare symbols for 100% acrylic.

Polyamide: nylon

Source	Properties	Improved performance through finishing	Typical blends
Petrochemicals. Inexpensive to manufacture and produced as: • textured filaments • staple fibres • microfibres. Can be engineered to provide a wide variety of properties and characteristics.	• Non-absorbent and prone to static; textured filaments transport moisture away from the body. • Fineness ranges from microfibres to coarse fibres – can be fine and soft or firm, depending on fibre fineness, fabric construction and finishing. • Flat filaments trap little air so are cool; textured filaments trap air so provide warmth. • Very strong, excellent abrasion resistance, tear resistance and durability. • Windproof, hydrophobic, water-repellent, easy-care, lightweight, flammable, soft, good drape. • Good elasticity, so good crease recovery. • Thermoplastic, can be textured and heat set, sensitive to dry heat. • Can be engineered to provide breathable comfort. • Dyes well, yellows and loses strength with long exposure to sunlight. • Resistant to alkalis, solvents, mildew and fungus, but degraded by concentrated acids. • Non-renewable source, non bio-degradable.	• Anti-static treatment. • Flame-resist treatment • Wide range of treatments to engineer specific properties.	Filaments mainly produced as pure fibre. Staple fibres blended with: • Wool • Cotton • Linen • Silk • Other synthetics

Typical polyamide fabrics	End-uses	Aftercare
• Textured filament fabrics. • Staple fibre fabrics. • Microfibre fabrics.	• Carpets, curtains, umbrellas, sewing yarns. • Tights, underwear, socks, ties, nightwear, linings, clothing. • Active sports wear, all weather wear, fleece garments. • Tents, ropes, sails, parachutes, tyre cords, seat belts.	Machine washable, do not bleach, fast drying, iron with care without steam, can be dry-cleaned and tumble dried with care.

Table 3A.18

TASK

Investigate the properties of the range of Tactel fibres produced by DuPont. You can do this by:
• reading the case study about Tactel on page 138 in Unit 3B Design and Technology in Society
• looking up nylon manufacture on page 152
• accessing the Tactel website at www.dupont.com/tactel.

Polyester

Source	Properties	Improved performance through finishing	Typical blends
Petrochemicals. The most used and versatile synthetic fibre. Inexpensive to manufacture. • About 60% produced as staple fibres. • also produced as textured filaments and microfibres. Can be engineered to provide a wide variety of properties and characteristics.	• Non-absorbent and very prone to static, textured filaments transport moisture away from the body. • Fineness ranges from microfibres to coarse fibres – can be fine and soft or firm, depending on fibre fineness, fabric construction and finishing. • Flat filaments trap little air so are cool; textured filaments trap air so provide warmth. • Very strong, excellent abrasion resistance, tear resistance and durability. • Windproof, hydrophobic, water-repellent, easy-care, lightweight, good heat resistance, soft, good drape. • Very good elasticity, so very good crease-resistance. • Thermoplastic, can be textured, bulked and heat set, sensitive to dry heat. • Can be engineered to provide breathable comfort. • Dyes well, yellows and loses strength with long exposure to sunlight • Resistant to acids, alkalis, solvents, mildew and fungus, but attacked by concentrated acids. • Non-renewable source, but can be recycled – 25 bottles to make one jumper.	• Anti-static treatments. • Flame- resist treatment for interiors end-use. • Wide range of treatments to engineer specific properties. • Some PET fabrics can be laser cut and heat welded.	Filament fibres usually textured. Staple fibres blended with: • Wool • Cotton • Viscose • Modal • Linen • Silk • Common blend ratios – 70/30, 65/35, 55/45, 50/50

Typical polyester fabrics	End-uses	Aftercare
• Staple fibre fabrics. • Textured filament fabrics. • Microfibre fabrics	• Furnishings, upholstery, carpets, hotel bedding, children's nightwear, transport textiles. • Garments, ties, scarves, rainwear, linings, net curtains. • Sports and leisure wear, all weather wear, microfibre fleece garments, work wear, bed linen, 100% staple yarn sewing threads, wadding for duvets and pillows. • Medical textiles such as artificial ligaments.	Machine washable, launders well at low temperatures, do not bleach, fast drying, iron with some care, can be dry-cleaned and tumble dried.

Table 3A.19

TASK

1 Compare the properties of polyamide and polyester, explaining why you think that polyester is the most versatile synthetic fibre.

2 Research aftercare symbols for 100% polyamide and 100% polyester fabrics.

3 Find examples of polyester and polyamide fabrics for a range of end-uses, including microfibres. Add them to your technical notebook.

4 Compare the known properties of polyamide and polyester with the characteristics of your own fabric swatches.

INORGANICS

Carbon fibre

Source	Properties	Typical blends	End-uses	Aftercare
Made by burning acrylic fibre to produce carbon. • First produced about 20 years ago. • Used to replace metals.	• Very strong, lightweight, abrasion-resistant, tear resistant. • Flame-resistant at very high temperatures. • Resistant to chemicals, low shrinkage in heat. • Non-renewable resource.	New blend developments are in the pipeline.	Transport upholstery, rocket motors, sports products, protective	Machine washable, can bleach, can be dry-cleaned and tumble dried.

Table 3A.20

Glass fibre

Source	Properties	Typical blends	End-uses	Aftercare
Powdered compounds of mineral origin. • Glass fibre reinforced polyester produced for over 40 years. • Glass fabric painted with silicon to keep it pliable.	• Durable, strong, shatterproof, but poor abrasion-resistance. • Heat and cold resistant, so does not soften or become brittle. • Good electrical properties. • Non-stick, non-toxic and reflective. • Resistant to chemicals, mildew and fungus.	• Anti-static treatment. • Surface finish to reduce skin irritation.	Aerospace and military industries, flame and heat barriers, light and UV filters, roof coverings, sterile hospital wall coverings, outerwear protective garments.	Machine washable, can bleach, can be dry-cleaned and tumble dried.

Table 3A.21

Metal fibre

Source	Properties	Typical blends	End-uses	Aftercare
Aluminium, copper and steel most commonly used. • Silver and gold used for more expensive end-uses. • Silver is the most effective anti-microbial material. • Thin sheet metal cut in strips or fine wire used as yarn. • Metal thread spun round core yarn. • A metallised polyester yarn called Lurex, used since the 1950s – often coated with fine plastic to prevent tarnishing.	• Strong, lightweight, abrasion-resistant. • Protects against electromagnetic pollution. • Conductive – detectable by radar; useful for wearable electronics; provides anti-static properties. • Protection for active sports.	• Silk • Wool • Polyester • Cotton • 1% metal, 99% polyester to produce shiny fabric. • 50% aluminium provides shape memory, protection against abrasion and wear.	Decorative textiles, active sportswear, work wear and protective industrial clothing, medical end-uses.	Can be washed and tumble dried.

Table 3A.22

Ceramic fibre

Source	Properties	conductivity.	Typical blends	Aftercare
Powdered compounds of metal oxide, metal carbide, metal nitride or their mixtures. • Becoming more widely incorporated into garment fabrics. • Ceramic content fabrics can regulate the body temperature – wearer is cooler in heat or warmer in cold.	• Resistant to very high temperatures. • Provide UV protection. • Good insulation. • Resistant to chemicals.j • Low thermal		• Polyester fibre coated or encapsulated with ceramic particles.	Machine washable, can bleach, can be dry-cleaned and tumble dried.

Table 3A.23

TASK

1 Explain the properties that carbon, glass, ceramic and glass fibres can bring to garment textiles.
2 Discuss the opportunities for using some of these fibres in protective clothing.

YARNS

Yarn

Yarn is defined as a fine continuous length of fibres or filament(s), with or without twist. To be useful, yarns need to be strong enough to be made into fabric. Generally, lengths of fibres are produced through the process of spinning into a variety of different yarn types, such as singles, ply, cabled, corespun or fancy yarns. The thickness of yarn (the yarn count) and the tightness of the yarn twist, affect a fabric's weight, flexibility, handle, texture, appearance and end-use.

Twist

Twist is put into yarns during spinning to make them stronger, so they are suitable for weaving or knitting. Yarns can be spun clockwise ('Z twist') or anti-clockwise ('S twist'). Fabrics made from spun yarn usually have 'Z twist' in the warp and may have 'S twist' in the weft. Light is reflected in opposite directions from the two types of yarn, so striped effects can be produced in fabrics by having alternate stripes of 'S' and 'Z' twist in the warp.

Figure 3A.6

Different effects can be given to fabric using S and Z yarns.

• The twist level is the number of turns per metre and twist is a deciding factor for the end-use of the yarn.

spun yarn

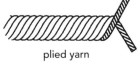

flat filament yarn

monofilament yarn

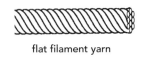

plied yarn

Figure 3A.7

Spun, filament, multi-filament, monofilament, plied yarns

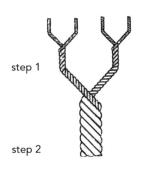

step 1

step 2

Figure 3A.8

Cabled yarns involve the twisting together of two or more plied yarns.

- Low twist yarns are softer, weaker and more bulky, making them more suitable for weft yarns or for knitting.
- High-twist yarns are strong and hard, making them suitable for weaving, where they need to withstand the tension in the loom.

Spun yarns

These are made by the mechanical assembly and twisting together (spinning) of staple fibres such as cotton, linen, wool, spun silk and cut manufactured fibres.

Filament yarns

Filament yarns are made from continuous filaments of silk or manufactured synthetic fibres such as polyester or polyamide.

- Monofilament yarn is made from a single continuous filament.
- Multi-filament yarn is made from multiple continuous filaments of silk or manufactured fibres, with or without twist.

Singles yarns and yarn ply

A single yarn is a continuous single thread of twisted staple or continuous filament fibres. The yarn can be made from one fibre or blended from two or more fibres, e.g. wool/acrylic. The plying of yarns involves:

- twisting together two or more singles (and/or plied) yarns together to make a thicker, stronger yarn, e.g. 2 ply, 3-ply yarn.
- twisting together yarns of the same or different types, to improve the strength, regularity, weight of yarns or to produce special effects, e.g. fancy yarns.

Core-spun yarns

Core-spun yarns are multi-component yarns, in which the core stays at the centre of the yarn, while other staple fibre yarns are spun around it to cover it, in a single spinning process. Stretch fabrics can be made from core-spun yarns, with the core being an elastane filament, covered by a non-elastic natural or man-made yarn, such as wool, cotton, nylon, linen or silk.

- Elastane filaments are always covered (or 'sheathed') by another yarn, because some weaving or knitting techniques cannot deal with elastic yarns.
- The elastane is temporarily stabilised by covering it with other yarns or fibres. The full elasticity of the stretch yarn is restored during finishing and dyeing processes.
- Core-spun yarns enhance fabrics, making them more comfortable and lively to wear.

- Covered core-spun yarns are used in a very wide variety of woven and knitted fabrics, for trousers, sportswear, uniforms, dresses and hosiery.

Strong sewing threads are often made with a filament polyester core, covered by a cotton yarn. The polyester provides high strength and the covering yarn prevents the sewing needle from overheating and melting the polyester during high-speed sewing operations.

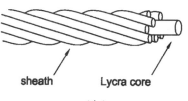

sheath   **Lycra core**

core-spun yarn with Lycra core

conventional spun yarn

Figure 3A.9
Conventional and core-spun yarn with Lycra core

Fancy yarn

Yarns are chosen primarily for their functional characteristics, such as strength or elasticity but also for their appearance. All yarns for weaving and knitting are formed by spinning staple or continuous filament fibres, into yarns that can be fancy or plain, thick or thin. Fancy yarns:

- are produced by special spinning processes to give irregularities in the construction. This can make the yarn textured, i.e. slub, loop, chenille or bouclé yarns.
- also provide colour effects, by mixing fibres of different colours during spinning or by plying two or more differently coloured yarns.
- can provide matt/lustre effects by mixing matt and bright fibres, i.e. using Lurex with polyester.
- are used to add value and improve the appearance of woven or knitted fabrics.
- are generally used in the weft, to add interest to a fabric, but they can make it more expensive.

Bulked and textured yarns

Yarn manufacturers can give extra properties to yarns by texturing and bulking.

- Bulked yarn is made by blending staple fibres of different shrinkage, which can be wet or heat- finished to make the resultant yarn thicker and softer. For example acrylic/cotton fibres can be bulked using a heat process to shrink the acrylic fibre and fluff up the cotton. This gives an inexpensive yarn that is warm, lightweight, easy-care, with a soft handle, suitable for knitwear.
- Textured yarn is made from thermoplastic synthetic filament yarn, such as polyester or nylon. This is finished using a heat process to have durable crimps, coils or loops along the length. Texturing adds bulk (thickness), makes the yarn warmer, more elastic, absorbent, increases the moisture transport and gives a softer handle. Textured yarns are suitable for tights, swimwear, underwear, outerwear, fleece jackets and carpets.

TASK

Examine the fabrics that you have collected for your technical notebook.
- For each fabric pull off a few of the warp and weft yarns.
- Cut two of the yarns to the same length and count the number of twists in each. Feel the yarns and describe their properties.
- Untwist the yarns and describe their structure. See if you can pull out a single fibre – is it a staple or filament fibre?
- Try to decide if any of the yarn is made from blended fibres. Do all the fibres look the same?

FABRICS

UNDERSTANDING FABRICS

Check it out! Unit 1 Materials and components pages 20-31

Textile product designers need to be both creative and have a good technical understanding of materials, so that their ideas can be translated into marketable products. Over the last few years, the development of innovative fabrics has been the driving force behind many areas of textile product development. At this stage in your course, you need to develop an understanding of standard woven, knitted and non-woven fabrics. You can do this by analysing fabrics – a magnifying glass is useful, together with squared paper to note down the weave. This will help you understand characteristics such as fabric construction, pattern repeat and colour sequence.

Plain weave
This is the most used weave construction, which can provide endless design variations though the use of plain, thick and thin, fancy and coloured yarns. Plain weave is strong, firm, and hardwearing and is used for many types of fabrics and end-uses, i.e. calico, gingham, muslin.

- Calico is a plain weave low-cost cotton fabric, made in different weights and widths, suitable for experimental textiles work. A fashion designer will often use calico to make a prototype garment (toile) to help in the development of the flat pattern for a new design. Interior designers sometimes use calico for making low-budget furnishings.
- Voile is a lightweight plain weave sheer fabric made from cotton, silk, rayon, nylon or worsted. It is used for blouses, dresses, children's wear, and curtains.
- Ripstop nylon is a high performance plain weave fabric, in which some of

1

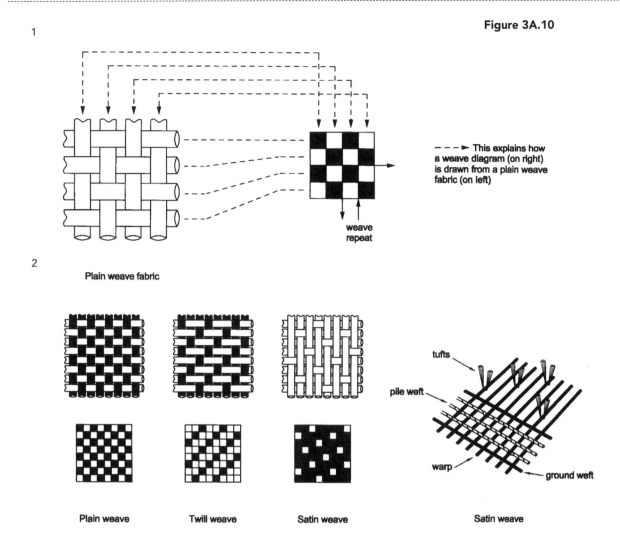

- - - ► This explains how
a weave diagram (on right)
is drawn from a plain weave
fabric (on left)

weave
repeat

2

Plain weave fabric

| Plain weave | Twill weave | Satin weave | Satin weave |

tufts

pile weft

warp

ground weft

the warp and weft yarns are doubled up at intervals in the warp and weft. This provides extra tear strength, useful for kites or performance sports-wear. These fabrics are lightweight, abrasion-resistant and sometimes have a fluorocarbon finish.

- Poplin is a plain weave warp-faced cotton-type fabric, which shows weft-way ribs on its surface. The warp is fine and the weft is coarser. Poplin is usually piece-dyed or printed, and is used for shirts, summer jackets, raincoats and children's wear. It can be given special finishes, such as being made water-repellent or fire-resistant.

- Seersucker fabrics are plain weave, with crinkled warp-way stripes. There are three ways of making seersucker fabrics:

    a) The fabric is woven in stripes, with alternate stripes under different tension in the loom. This results in a fabric with crinkled stripes, which can be used for dress fabrics or tablecloths.

    b) Linen or cotton fabrics can be treated with caustic soda, usually in stripes, to make the fabric crinkle.

    c) Seersucker can be made using yarns that have different shrinkage properties, resulting in crinkles in the warp and/or weft.

Figure 3A.11

Denim is a strong, firm, durable, hardwearing cotton fabric, made using a 3/1 warp-faced twill weave. Usually the warp is dyed yarn and the weft is white. Denim is used for jeans, jackets, accessories and upholstery. Drill fabrics are strong, dense, durable woven 2/1 or 3/1 twill fabrics used for work wear.

Figure 3A.12

In this herringbone twill the warp yarn lifts over two and under two wefts. The direction of the twill reverses at regular intervals. At the reversal the pattern is displaced by one or more cells, so the twill lines do not meet at a point. (A pointed twill is called a chevron)

Twill weave

Twill weave produces fabric with diagonal lines, which generally run bottom left to top right on the fabric face. Weaving twills in different directions produces weave variations, such as herringbone or chevron. Twill weave drapes well and is one of the most used weave constructions, making fabrics such as gabardine or denim. Twill is used for a wide range of products such as jackets, suits, trousers, and curtains.

- Viyella is a 2/2 twill fabric woven from wool/cotton blend fibres in the warp and weft. Viyella fabrics are 55%wool, 45% cotton and can have plain, checked or striped designs. They are used for products such as shirts, dresses and children's wear.

Satin weave

- A satin weave fabric is warp-faced, which makes it strong warpwise so it drapes well. Satin fabric has a smooth, shiny face and the weft shows only on the back. It is used for curtain linings, evening wear, upholstery, ribbons and trimmings, depending on the fibre used – such as cotton, polyester/ cotton, acetate, polyester or silk. (ss Fig 3A.10 p79)
- A sateen weave fabric is weft-faced, so that the warp shows only on the back. It is often used as a base for more complicated weave constructions, such as crepes.
- Damask fabrics are made from more expensive mercerised cotton, which is sometimes used for tablecloths. The design is made by interchanging satin and sateen weaves, so that the fabric alternates between being warp and weft-faced.

Crêpe fabric

Crêpe fabrics have a crinkled or puckered surface, with no definite pattern. Wool crêpe fabrics are used for high quality suits. Woven crêpe is produced by using:

a) S & Z high twist yarns
b) a crêpe weave construction
c) a chemical or thermal treatment to shrink the fabric differently.

Jacquard fabric

Jacquard fabric has a complicated patterned design in three or more colours. It is made by knitting or weaving on specialised Jacquard machinery.

a) Weft-knitted jacquard fabrics are used for jumpers, jackets or skirts.
b) Woven jacquard fabrics are made by interchanging satin, sateen, plain and twill weaves. They are mainly used for expensive upholstery fabrics or formal evening-type wear.

TASK

Examine plain, twill and satin weaves under a magnifying glass to see their structure.

- Using squared paper. plot out the weave construction. If a warp yarn is on top the square is filled in.
- If a weft yarn is on top leave the square blank.
- Once you have the weave plotted out you can work out the size of the weave repeat. You may need to work in pairs to undertake this task!

Pile weaves

A knitted or woven pile fabric has a raised surface effect, formed by tufts or loops that stand up from the fabric.

- Velvet and corduroy are pile fabrics, used for garments like jackets or trousers.
- Pile fabrics are also used for upholstery or carpets, which can have a surface pile that is cut, looped, sculptured, curled or textured.
- Pile upholstery fabrics that are a mixture of cut/uncut pile are the most hardwearing.

Needlecord and corduroy

- Corduroy is a ribbed cut weft-pile fabric that is brushed. The pile runs parallel to the selvedge and the cords may be medium or broad. Cotton

Corduroy   **Figure 3A.13**

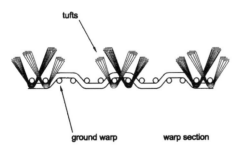

corduroy is used for trousers, skirts, jackets and upholstery.
- Needlecord is made in the same way as corduroy, but the cords are very fine.

Terry towelling

Woven terry towelling is a plain-woven cotton fabric made from two warps. The ground warp is highly tensioned and the pile warp is looser. When the weft yarns are beaten into the fabric the looser pile warp ends form loops, on one or both sides of the fabric. Towelling is usually made from cotton and this fibre in combination with the loops makes a very absorbent fabric, easy to wash and non-iron. It is used for bath mats, towels and dressing gowns.

Fabric mixture

A fabric mixture is made with the warp of one fibre, and the weft of a different fibre, e.g. cotton yarn in the warp, wool yarn in the weft. This is called a Union fabric, which can be cheaper than using all one fibre. When mixture fabrics are dyed, the different yarns can take up the dye at a different rate, so the fabric can look speckled – this can be used deliberately as a design effect.

Colour woven fabrics

- Colour and weave effects are used by woven fabric designers to create an endless variety of fabric designs. These effects are achieved by the way that coloured warp and weft yarns interact with the weave construction to produce different aesthetic effects. This can result in stripes, tartans, checks, hounds-tooth and many more designs.
- A chambray fabric has the warp in one colour and the weft in another, to give a shimmering, changeant, shot-silk effect.
- Gingham is a plain weave, lightweight, mainly checked cotton fabric, using white and coloured yarns. It was very popular in the 1950s and can be used for blouses, dresses and tablecloths. When used for shirts it is called Madras.
- Tartan was originally a woollen cloth woven in checks, using a 2/2 twill. It was used for shawls and kilts and each Highland clan in Scotland had its own tartan design. Tartan is now made using other fibres and weaves and is used in fashion clothing and for interiors.

TASK

Investigate the design, handle, properties and end-use of a range of woven fabrics, explaining why they are suitable for the end-use you have identified.

NON-WOVEN FABRICS

Non-woven fabrics are made directly from fibres (usually continuous filament

Figure 3A.14

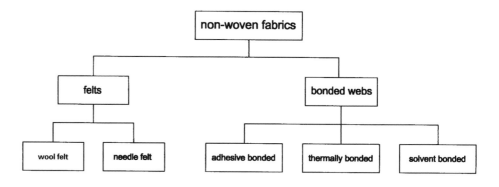

synthetic fibres) rather than by knitting or weaving yarns. As can be seen in Figure 3A.14, there are two main groups of non-woven fabrics – felts and bonded webs.

Felt

Felt is a non-woven fabric made by interlocking fibres so that they become matted. There are three classes of felt.

a) Pressed wool felt is made from animal hair or wool fibres matted together by moisture, mechanical action and heat.
   - Felt fabric is made from fibres containing at least 50% animal hair, usually wool, so wool felt is expensive.
   - The fibre web is squashed together in felting machine, then fulled (milled) using mechanical pressure, heat and moisture.
   - The fibres become entangled through repeated treatment until the required density of felt is achieved.

Felt has no strength, drape or elasticity, but does not fray and is warm and resilient. Acetate, nylon and acrylic can be blended with wool in felt, to improve the drape, reduce shrinkage and make it more economical to produce. Felt retains its shape and absorbs sound and can be made flame-retardant. It is used for blocking into hats, for slippers, toys, insulation materials and soundproofing in speakers. Felt made from animal hair, such as from rabbits is called fur felt – this is used for hats.

b) Woven or knitted felt is made from fabrics containing animal hair or wool, which are matted by moisture, mechanical action and heat in a milling machine. The original fabric construction is covered by a smooth surface, making the fabric warm and windproof. The woven fabric called Loden (used for overcoats) is produced in this way.

c) Needlefelt is made from fibres matted together by mechanical action using barbed needles to entangle the fibres. Almost any type of fibre can be used,

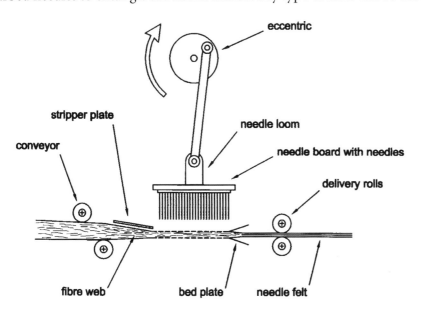

Figure 3A.15

The principle of needle felting

but in practice, synthetic fibres are generally used.

- In the mechanical process, a bulky web (batt) of fibres is repeatedly punched by a bank of barbed needles. Every needle drags fibres to the base of the web to form loops in the fibres. This entangles the fibres to form the fabric, which is usually given additional strength by a fibre-bonding technique.
- In hydro-entangled needle felt, staple fibres are entangled in a web with high-pressure water jets (also called spun laced fabric).
- Needle felts are elastic and lightweight and are used mainly for floor coverings, waddings, interlinings, upholstery materials, mattress covers and filters.

Bonded webs

Bonded webs are made from a web of fibres, bonded with adhesives, solvents or by the thermoplastic property of some or all of the fibres. Bonded webs for garments are layered in a carding machine, to build up a batt of the required thickness with the layers built either across or down or a combination of both. This kind of non-woven fabric is mainly used for fusible interlinings, which are air-permeable, dimensionally stable, crease-resistant, stable to washing and dry-cleaning and easy to use.

a) Adhesive bonded webs are made from a web of fibres, bonded together by the application of adhesive. The adhesive may be applied to the web by spraying, dipping or foam spreading, followed by pressing the web.

b) Thermally bonded webs are made from a web of fibres, bonded together through the thermoplastic property of some or all of fibres – under pressure and heat the fibre surfaces soften and fuse together permanently.

c) Solvent bonded webs are made from a web of fibres, bonded together using a solvent – the fibre surfaces soften and fuse together permanently at their touching points.

Tufted fabrics

Tufting is the most used manufacturing process for making carpets and rugs. They are made by machines that insert pile yarns into a backing fabric. The pile, which can be looped or cut, is fixed into the backing with an adhesive coating.

Open-work fabrics

These fabrics include lace, braid and crochet, all of which are minor textile techniques in comparison with knitting and weaving.

- Lace is a fine, open fabric of mesh or net, which can be patterned. Bobbin lace is traditionally produced by hand, using pins on a pillow, around which the lace bobbins work the lace. Embroidery lace is made by hand or machine, by working an embroidered pattern onto a ground fabric. The ground is removed by cutting it away or by using a burnt-out technique. Raschel lace is made on a warp-knitting machine. Lace is used for curtains, bedspreads, and as decorative edgings on garments.

- Braid is made by the diagonal interlacing of at least two sets of warp yarns. It is used for trimmings and ribbons.
- Crochet is a hand-made chain of loops, produced from a single thread using a hook. The chains of loops can be linked to make crochet fabric. When crochet is in fashion, it is generally machine-made and used to make accessories, like bags.

TASK

Research the use of non-woven and openwork fabrics. You could try experimenting with the production of hand-made felt.

KNITTED FABRICS

Check it out! Unit 1 page 20

Weft knitting

Weft-knitted fabric is made from continuous lengths of yarn, which is fed across the width of the fabric by a series of needles. Weft knits can be unravelled and if a stitch is dropped it will run down the length of the fabric, so weft-knitted fabric cannot be cut like woven fabric. This kind of knitting produces soft, comfortable fabric that has variable stretch, depending on the structure.

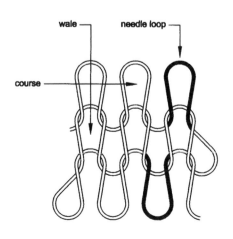

- A course is a horizontal row of loops formed by the needles during one knitting cycle.
- A wale is a vertical column of loops formed by a single needle.
- The size of the loop and fineness of the yarn determines the density of the knit construction.
- The number of wales in the fabric equals the number of needles across the width of the fabric.
- The length of the fabric is determined by the number of courses.
- The combination of loop size, fineness of yarn, width and length determine the weight of the fabric.

Figure 3A.16

Single jersey

Hand-made weft knitting can be used to make one-off designer products, such as jumpers or cushions. Industrial computer-controlled knitting machines produce around 90 per cent of jersey, rib and jacquard fabrics. There are three main types of weft-knitting machines:

a) Straight-bar or fully-fashioned machines produce high quality knitwear using natural fibres, especially wool.

b) Single or double flatbed machines are used to knit rectangular shaped panels for garments. They are very versatile for designing using CAD/CAM. Domestic knitting machines are similar to these.

c) Circular knitting machines vary in size, depending on what they make, such as socks or T-shirts. These machines use CAD/CAM systems for continuous production, making single or double jersey fabrics.

- In single jersey (see Fig 3A.16) the front is smooth, the back shows loops and the fabric has a tendency to 'curl' at the edges. It was first made by hand in Jersey for fishermen's clothing – in hand-knitted single jersey, the front is called 'plain' and the back is called 'purl'. Single jersey is made industrially using a single set of needles, to produce fabric that is generally plain without any rib. It has relatively low stretch in the width and can be made from cotton, cotton blends, acrylic, polyester, modal, viscose or wool. 2-5% elastane blends provide added comfort, crease-resistance, enhanced drape and better shape retention. Single jersey is generally used for T-shirts, jumpers and underwear.

- Double jersey fabric is made on two sets of needle beds, in which the needles are opposite each other and work alternately. It takes two courses to produce one row of loops on the face and back, which look identical. Double jersey fabrics are compact, stable, durable and retain their shape, although they are not very elastic. They can be cut like woven fabrics and can be used for T-

Figure 3A.17

Double jersey is made on two sets of needle beds.

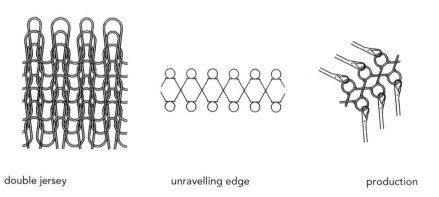

double jersey   unravelling edge   production

shirts, underwear, polo shirts, sportswear, skirts and leggings.

- Rib fabrics are made on two sets of needles, which are staggered. Alternate loops are knitted in opposite directions, to form vertical lines in the fabric. The most popular form of knitted rib is 2x2, in which both sides of the fabric look the same. The fabric is very elastic widthways,

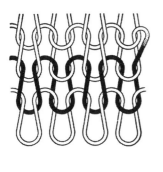 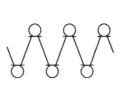 

Figure 3A.18
Rib fabric is used for cuffs and welts of sweaters.

rib fabric   unravelling edge   production

making it suitable for jumpers, waistcoats, underwear and socks.

- Jacquard fabric has a patterned design in three or more colours. It is made by selecting needles to knit coloured yarns in a specified pattern, using CAD/CAM systems. In each succeeding course, the pattern is built up and if the colour is not required on the face, it floats at the back. There is a limit to the length of float and the fabric is not very elastic. Jacquard knits go in and out of fashion for winter knitwear.

Warp knitting

Warp-knitted fabrics are made on straight or circular CAD/CAM knitting machines. Each loop of the fabric is fed by its own separate yarn, which is fed into the knitting zone parallel to the fabric selvedge. These loops interlock vertically, along the length of the fabric. Warp knits have some elasticity, do not ladder and can't be unravelled. Although they can be cut like woven fabrics, warp knits have a limited application for clothing, being mainly used for swimwear, leisure and underwear, linings, laces, ribbons and trimmings. They are also used for net curtains, furnishings and bed linen. Warp knits are

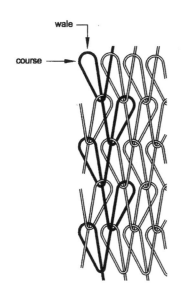

wale

course

- a course is a row of loops running across the fabric width
- a wale is a column of loops in the fabric

Figure 3A.19

mainly used in industrial end-uses, including geotextiles.

- Tricot (see Figure 1.6) is industrially produced warp-knitted fabric, mostly using synthetic yarns, with each yarn working in a zigzag fashion. It is used for gloves, lingerie and lightweight furnishing.

- Locknit is a combination of tricot and 2x1 plain knit stitches, made from filament yarns. The resulting lustrous fabric is used for linings and underwear. The face of the fabric has vertical wales of small loops, whilst the back shows a zigzag stitch formation.

- A knitted pile fabric ('velour'), made from continuous filament fibres, has a raised fleecy surface effect, formed from cut loops that stand up from the fabric.

- Modern manufactured polar fleece, made from acrylic, nylon or polyester, is a type of double bouclé knit, densely raised on one face or both, producing a fleece effect. Polar fleece is a lightweight, high bulk, breathable and warm fabric used as insulation in leisure and sportswear. This modern fleece should not be confused with natural fleece, the entire wool coat of the sheep, which is shorn off in one piece.

TASK

1 Make a collection of knitted fabrics used for a range of end-uses. Examine each fabric and identify its construction – if it is warp or weft knitted, the number of colours and the type of yarn used.

2 Add your fabric swatches to your technical notebook, sketch the construction and add notes to explain their suitability for purpose.

FASTENINGS AND COMPONENTS

Check it out! Unit 1 Fastenings and components page 30

Fastenings and components are vitally important for the manufacture of many products. In fact, a whole industry surrounds their manufacture, with trends and colour playing a key role in enabling product designers to choose fastenings and components that enhance the product's style and performance. Since most product manufacturers specialise in products for specific market segments (such as sportswear), they buy in fabrics and components according to the product needs. The use of any component or fasting adds to the cost of the product. On a domestic level, fastenings and components, such as zips, buttons, threads, bias binding or Velcro can be found in the haberdashery department of some stores.

Fusible interlinings, linings

As we have seen earlier in this unit, non-woven bonded webs are mainly used for fusible interlinings. These are air-permeable, dimensionally stable, crease-resistant, stable to washing and dry-cleaning and easy to use. They can be laminated to other fabrics by the use of adhesives, by stitching or by the fabric's own thermoplastic properties.

Fusible interlinings such as Vilene, often have adhesive on one side, which melts between 120 – 180°C. The use of fusible interlinings is a very important part of the product manufacturing process, because they:

- give body and shape control to the top fabric.
- reinforce and provide strength in areas of strain or wear.
- prevent stretching and sagging.
- give support to areas that have to withstand pulling and stretching in wear.
- are air permeable, breathable and comfortable.
- stabilise the top fabric, prevent then from fraying.
- aid crease recovery of top fabrics.
- are stable to washing and dry-cleaning.

Lining

A lining is a separate fabric used in the making-up of textile products. Linings provide warmth and give a 'finished' inside to the product. Lined textile products usually cost more than unlined ones. When used in a jacket, for example, lining would improve or add value to the product by:

- improving its appearance, performance and warmth.
- improving the drape of the outer fabric.
- protecting the outer fabric from perspiration, rubbing or staining.
- keeping the shape better, making it easier to put on and take off.
- neatly covering the seams and outer pocket stitching.

TASK

1 Investigate a range of fastenings and components, such as ribbons, braid, piping, Petersham and fringing. Describe the purpose, cost-effectiveness and end-use of each of these components. Use the notes below on bias binding to help you.

Bias binding is a narrow strip of fabric, cut from a large piece of woven fabric at 45 degrees to the selvedge. Bias binding is stretchy and is used to bind the seams or the edges of fabric to stop it fraying, such as binding the edges of a pocket or wallet. Bias binding is made commercially in different colours and widths, but it can be cut from scrap fabric to provide a more economical co-ordinated edging for a textile product.

2 Research the latest trends in fastenings design, using magazines and shop surveys. Explain your findings, using sketches and notes.
3 Sketch some quick ideas for using buttons, zips, clips, buckles, clasps, poppers, D-rings and hooks & eyes in exciting and innovative ways in product design.

Chapter 2
Working Properties of Materials

Check it out! Unit 1 Properties and working characteristics of natural and manufactured fibres page 21

All textile fibres have different properties that make them suitable for a range of different end-uses. Spinning fibres into yarns, then weaving or knitting them into fabrics can change these properties, although fibre and fabric properties are closely linked. The finishing of woven or knitted fabrics can further change and improve fabric properties to make fabrics suitable for a wider variety of products.

- Aesthetic properties are those that relate to appearance, touch and style, such as handle, drape, colour, lustre, pattern scale and repeat.
- Functional properties are those that relate to the function and practical use of the product, such as strength, elasticity, weight; resistance to chemicals, heat, stains and abrasion; wind-proof and water-proof, durability and aftercare.
- Comfort properties are those that relate to comfort-in-wear-or -use, such as warmth, absorbency, breathability, non-static, textured, soft or harsh.

When selecting fabrics, design technologists needs to be aware that there are different performance requirements where fabric characteristics are concerned. What properties and characteristics are essential to meet these requirements? For example, most products require fabrics with good strength and durability, but only some need to be shower or rain resistant. In industry, the aim is to provide an optimum level of product performance without an increase in costs or disadvantaging the aesthetic characteristics of the product. A designer therefore has to balance fabric properties against the cost of the materials and choose fabrics of known performance and with an acceptable quality in use.

TASK

The following working characteristics are important in product manufacture. Choose the characteristics from the list that would be appropriate to the manufacture of all weather wear, printed cotton T-shirts, a man's suit, silk curtains and denim made from modal.

- Good drape, handle, weight.
- Good appearance in colour, texture and lustre.
- Good strength and durability.
- Resistance to abrasion and pilling.
- Absorbent, breathable and anti-static.
- Uniform appearance and width.
- Fault-free with dimensional stability.
- Accurate colouration for prints and dyes.
- Colour fastness to light, washing, dry cleaning.
- Good sewability with good seam strength and resistance to seam slippage.
- Good performance in pressing and fusing with resistance to shrinkage.
- Easy care, with crease resistance.
- Flame, shower or rain resistant.

PROPERTIES

Properties are the characteristics of a material that make it what it is. For example, cotton fabric is absorbent, strong and dyes well. It is important to match the properties of a material with the requirements of the product, so that the product's performance matches consumer needs. For example, a football kit made from Coolmax fabric is breathable and wicks away perspiration from the body, so it is suitable for high-activity sports.

Fibre and fabric properties are closely linked. Fibres have inbuilt properties that transfer to the fabrics that they make, e.g. strength, elasticity, durability, resilience, warmth, absorbency. Manufacturers use fabric-finishing processes to give enhanced properties to fabrics. For example, cotton fibre is absorbent and strong. Cotton fabric is also absorbent and strong, but may be given an added property such as a crease-resistant finish.

The properties or performance characteristics of a fabric depend on the fibre content, the yarns used, the fabric construction, how the fabric is finished and the intended end-use of the fabric.

AESTHETIC PROPERTIES

- Drape is the supple and flexible character of a fabric, how a fabric falls when it hangs and how it behaves when folded, pleated or gathered. A fabric needs to drape well, so that it is not stiff – if it is too stiff the fabric won't take darts for shaping, can't be gathered or stitched with success. For example, curtains and clothes need to hang in an attractive way and be flexible when moved. (Curtains used to be called drapes).

- Handle is the way a fabric feels, its touch, a most important property. A fabric can be soft, flexible, smooth, rough, textured, cool or warm to the touch. Fabric handle depends on the way the fabric is constructed, the yarns and the finishing process used.

FUNCTIONAL PROPERTIES

- Abrasion is the rubbing of textiles in everyday use. This may cause a textile's surface to pill or wear, affecting its future performance and usefulness. Abrasion-resistant fibres such as nylon or polyester are often used in fibre blends to improve a textile's performance.
- Absorbency is the ability of a textile fibre to take up moisture. Different fibres have different levels of absorbency: Wool is a high-absorbency natural fibre which can absorb up to a third of its own weight in water, making wool comfortable to wear. Cotton is a medium-absorbency natural fibre, which can be comfortable and cool to wear, although it may get damp from perspiration in hot conditions. Nylon and polyester are low-absorbency synthetic fibres, which can be uncomfortable to wear next to the skin, because they do not easily allow perspiration to escape. However, the use of textured filaments and microfibres have revolutionised the breathability of synthetic fibres.
- Breathable fabrics allow perspiration to evaporate, making synthetic fabrics comfortable to wear. They 'wick' moisture away from the body but don't allow rain to be absorbed back. Breathable fabrics have the properties of the microfibres of polyester, nylon or acrylic, from which they are made.
- Durability means tough, hardwearing and resistant to abrasion. The durability of a fabric depends on the raw materials, how the fabric is constructed and finished.
- Elasticity is the ability of a material to be stretched and then return to its original shape. Wool fabrics are naturally elastic and crease-resistant, with the ability to resist and/or recover from creases. Fabrics made from cellulose fibres like cotton or linen have poor elasticity, so crease badly. They need a crease-resistant finish to make them easy-care.
- Fabric weight is important, because it is a measure of a fabric's quality. The weight of a fabric is determined by the yarn count, the numbers of warp ends and weft picks per cm and the fabric construction. Fabrics known as top weights are suitable for jackets or coats, while bottom weights are used for trousers or skirts.

Chapter 3
Hand and Commercial Processes

PREPARING, PROCESSING, MANIPULATING AND COMBINING MATERIALS AND COMPONENTS

COTTON PRODUCTION

Cotton is the most widely produced and used natural fibre, so its cultivation is an important agricultural crop. Cotton plants need a tropical climate and wet soil for good growth. The cotton emerges from the ripe seed boll as a bundle of soft fibres.

- Cotton is harvested by hand or by picking machines and may need to be dried if harvested wet.
- The fibres are separated from the seeds by a process called ginning. The separated fibres are called lint, with a staple length between 20 and 50mm. Some types of seed have very short fibres called linters, which are used in the production of regenerated fibres. Around 100kg of clean seed-cotton produces about 35kg of fibre.

Cotton spinning

Figure 3A.20

The cotton process

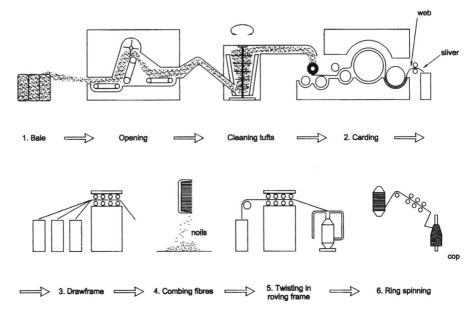

1 Compressed bales of cotton are opened into tufts and cleaned.
2 Cotton is transported to a carding machine for further cleaning, orientation of the fibres and formation into 'slivers'.
3 Slivers are cross-mixed to blend fibres in a drawframe.
4 Fibres are combed to remove short fibres (up to 25%)
5 Fibres are slightly twisted into a 'roving'.
6 Ring spinning is used to convert the roving into yarn by drafting to the required fineness, twisting and winding onto a spinning 'cop'.

Cotton growing accounts for around 25 per cent of total global pesticide use and half a kilo of chemicals is needed to produce the one and a half kilos of cotton needed to make a pair of jeans and a T-shirt. Although there is now more commercial interest in growing organic cotton, the use of conventional methods of production is likely to continue, in order to meet the worldwide demand for cotton.

WOOL PRODUCTION

The whole fleece is shorn from the sheep using electric shears, then graded into qualities according to fineness, crimp, length, impurities and colour. About 40 per cent of the weight of the fleece is grease (lanolin), dirt and burs, most of which is removed by gentle scouring. Any vegetable matter is removed by carbonising with sulphuric acid. The wool fibres are then spun into fine, smooth yarns using the worsted process or into coarser, more bulky yarns using the woollen process.

- Woollen yarns have a coarse, hairy, irregular, rustic appearance because they are made from shorter, sometimes coarse staple fibres, which are rubbed during manufacture. Woollen fabrics are finished to give a felted, hairy surface, suitable for blankets, jackets or overcoats.
- Worsted yarns are smooth, uniform, regular, fine and lustrous because they are made from longer types of staple wool fibres, which are combed, doubled and drafted smooth and fine during manufacture. Worsted fabrics are finished to give a smooth-faced fabric, which shows the yarn colours clearly. They are used for suits, trousers and skirts.

Figure 3A.21
Woollen spinning

The woollen system

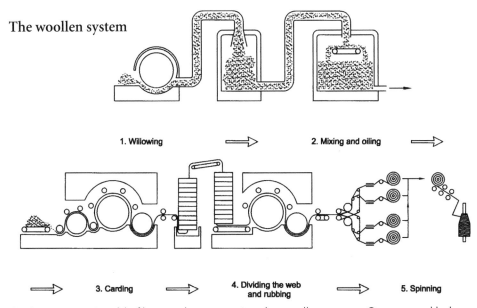

1. Willowing   2. Mixing and oiling

3. Carding   4. Dividing the web and rubbing   5. Spinning

1 Almost any spinnable fibre can be spun using the woollen system. Compressed bales of washed and sorted raw wool, recovered wool or other fibres are fed into a willowing machine for opening and cleaning the loose fibres.
2 Different fibre and colour types are mixed and oiled to improve spinning capability.
3 Fibre portions are fed into a carding machine for orientation and cleaning.
4 A fibre web is divided into ribbons and rubbed to form the slubbing, which is drafted to the required fineness, twisted and wound.

Figure 3A.22

The worsted system

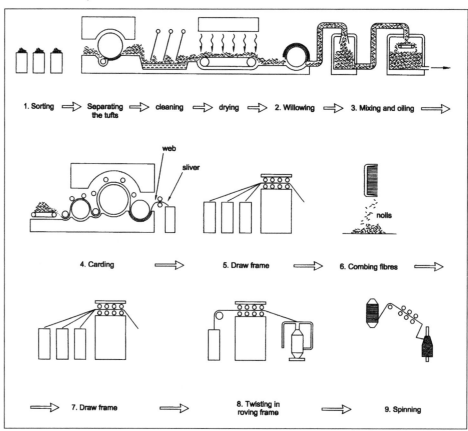

1 The fleece wool is sorted according to quality, separated into tufts, cleaned and dried.
2 These are fed into a willowing machine for opening and cleaning the loose fibres.
3 Different fibre and colour types are mixed and oiled to improve spinning capability.
4 Fibre portions are fed into a carding machine for orientation and cleaning.
5 Fibres are doubled, drafted and mixed to improve their regularity.
6–9 The short fibres are combed, drafted and twisted into a roving of the required fineness, twisted and wound.

REGENERATED FIBRE PRODUCTION

Viscose

The long, century-old viscose process uses chemicals that cannot be recovered or re-used. The raw material for viscose is cellulose extracted from eucalyptus, pine or beech wood chips. The cellulose is purified, bleached, pressed into sheets and dissolved in sodium hydroxide. It is then pressed again, shredded and aged. The addition of carbon disulphide converts the cellulose into a fluid honey-like liquid, which is extruded through the holes of a spinneret in a spinning bath. This is called wet spinning. The cellulose solidifies and is drawn into filaments, washed to remove chemicals, lubricated for suppleness, dried and wound onto spools as filament viscose. Staple viscose in made by cutting the filaments into a given length.

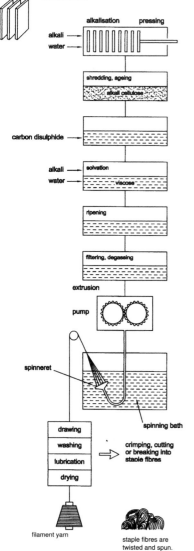

Figure 3A.23

The viscose process

SYNTHETIC FIBRE PRODUCTION

There are three similar types of synthetic fibre production, which all use a reservoir to hold the synthetic polymer, a metering pump, a spinneret, a fluid in which the filaments are formed and a take-up mechanism which draws the filaments ready for winding. The spinneret size and shape, together with the spinning and drawing processes, determine the diameter of the filament.

Table 3A.24

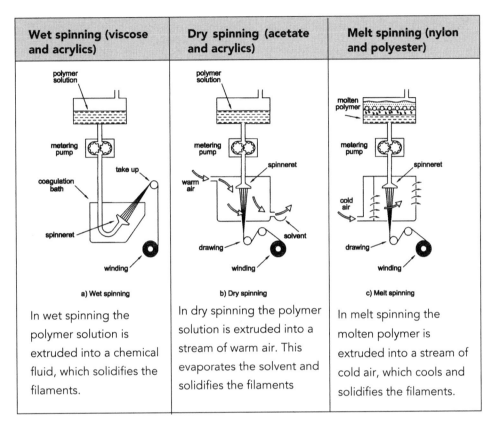

Wet spinning (viscose and acrylics)	Dry spinning (acetate and acrylics)	Melt spinning (nylon and polyester)
a) Wet spinning	b) Dry spinning	c) Melt spinning
In wet spinning the polymer solution is extruded into a chemical fluid, which solidifies the filaments.	In dry spinning the polymer solution is extruded into a stream of warm air. This evaporates the solvent and solidifies the filaments	In melt spinning the molten polymer is extruded into a stream of cold air, which cools and solidifies the filaments.

TASK

1 Compare the manufacture of natural, regenerated and synthetic fibres, noting any similarities and differences.
2 Explain why woollen and worsted yarns have different properties.

BLENDED FIBRES

Yarns can be made from one fibre type alone or be made from blends of two or more different fibres. Fibre blending is used to improve the properties and appearance of a given fibre type, making it more cost-effective to manufacture. For example, it can make a more expensive fibre, like linen, more economical to produce if it is blended with cotton. Blends have the combined properties of each component fibre. For example, in a polyester/cotton fibre blend the polyester provides crease-resistance and the cotton is absorbent. Elastane is used frequently in fibre blends with all types of natural and synthetic fibres to give fabrics added comfort and fit.

Table 3A.25

REASONS FOR FIBRE BLENDING		
Quality	**Appearance**	**Cost efficiency**
• Improved performance in use, such as abrasion resistance, crease resistance, strength and durability. • Improved finishing options. • Improved comfort, such as absorbency, stretch, or thermal insulation. • Improved aftercare performance, such as washing, drying, shrinkage, ironing.	• Improved appearance, colour, texture, handle or lustre. • Aesthetics can be engineered into a fabric.	• Improved ease of manufacture and cost efficiency. • Improved fibre supply, yarn count and uniformity of yarns.

TASK

1 Suggest two different fibre blends suitable for workwear, justifying your choice.
2 Discuss the benefits for a suiting fabric, of using a polyester/elastane/wool blend.

WORKING PROPERTIES OF YARNS

One of the easiest ways to find out about the working properties of yarns is to examine their use in woven and knitted fabrics. Making yarns is highly skilled work.

• The thickness of yarn (yarn count) and the amount of yarn twist affect a fabric's weight, flexibility, handle and end-use.
• Yarn count is expressed as a numbering system, which relates the weight of yarn to its length. For example in the international Tex numbering system, the yarn count is defined as the weight in grams of 1000 metres of yarn. The term 'denier' was originally used for silk yarn numbering but is now applied to all filament yarns.

The selection and choice of yarn depends on its strength, extensibility, elasticity, appearance and the intended fabric construction. For example, knitting yarns usually have less twist to make them soft and voluminous. Weaving yarns are spun with more twist to make them strong and smooth, so they withstand the tension they are under in the weaving process.

Continuous filament and spun yarns produce fabrics with clearly defined properties and end-uses. Some of these are shown in the Table 3A.26 opposite.

Fabric type	Smoothness	Handle	Lustre	End-use
Woven worsted gabardine Cool Wool	Fine, smooth and regular.	Smooth and soft	Some lustre	High quality smart suits
Woven woollen tweed	Rough, irregular and hairy	Coarser, with fuller handle	Matt	Bulky jacket and and coat fabrics
Woven cotton calico	Less fine and regular	Coarser and harder and less smooth	Matt	Workwear and furnishings
Fine knitted cotton	Fine, smooth and regular	Soft, with elastic fabric structure		T-shirts
Woven raw silk	Very fine,smooth and regular	Lightweight and soft	Very lustrous	Dress fabrics, ties
Knitted acrylic	Bulky, voluminous with crimps and loops	Soft, warm with elastic structure		Jumpers

Table 3A.26

TASK

1 Examine a knitted cotton T-shirt and an acrylic jumper. Are these fabrics matt or lustrous? Explain why these fabrics are elastic.

2 All of the fabrics in Table 3A.26 are made from either continuous filament or spun yarns. Explain which is which and give reasons for your choice.

3 Choose a different set of fabrics that are used in different products. Draw up a similar table to show the properties of yarns.

WOVEN FABRIC MANUFACTURE

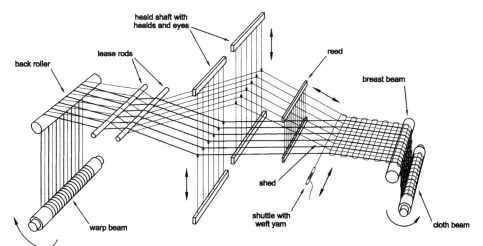

heald shaft with
heald and eyes
lease rods
back roller
reed
breast beam
shed
shuttle with
weft yarn
cloth beam
warp beam

Figure 3A.24

Woven fabrics are made by interlacing two sets of yarns at right angles to each other. The yarns along the fabric length are called warp yarns (warp ends), while the weft yarns (picks) run across the fabric. The lengthways edges of the fabric are the selvedges.

MANUFACTURE OF WEFT KNITS INTO GARMENTS

There are various methods for manufacturing garments from weft knitted fabrics, depending on how the fabric is manufactured.

Figure 3A.25

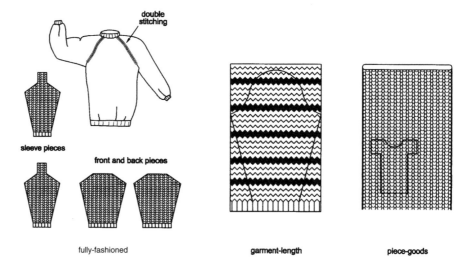

- Fully-fashioned knitting is where the individual components are knitted to shape so they can be sewn to make the product, without cutting the fabric. This reduces fabric waste.
- Garment length knitting (panel knitting) is where fabric is knitted in individual panels of a width to suit the end product. The start of the knitting is secured with a ribbed edge. This type of knitting produces some fabric waste.
- Cut-and-sew blanket knitting (piece goods) is where long lengths of knitted fabric are produced in the form of a tube on a circular knitting machine. The fabric can be processed in tubular form or cut open (usually after dyeing). It is then cut to shape and sewn to make the product. Although this type of knitting produces higher levels of fabric waste, this is kept to a minimum through the use of CAD lay-planning systems.
- 3D knitting is where whole products are knitted in one piece, incorporating all the garment shaping. There is minimal sewing necessary and no fabric waste.

FINISHING PROCESSES FOR FUNCTION AND DECORATION

Table 3A.27

FINISHING PROCESSES						
Preparation	**Colouration**		**Finishing**			**Coating and laminating**
	Dyeing	Printing	Modify the handle, drape and wear properties	Modify the appearance	Modify the aftercare properties	

All fabrics used in products have to be 'finished' in some way to make them suitable for their end-use. Good finishing can greatly improve the aesthetic and functional properties of fabrics, enhancing their handle, drape and aftercare properties. Finishing is part of a quality assurance system to ensure that textiles:

- meet quality requirements
- are fault-free and clean
- match the manufacturing specification
- are safe for user
- are fit for the intended purpose.

Manufacturers use finishing techniques to give fabrics quality and added value. Physical (mechanical) finishes provide aesthetic characteristics such as handle or drape, while chemical finishes enhance functional or performance characteristics, such as waterproof. There are four classes of finishing:

- permanent, often a chemical finish, like flame resistance
- durable, lasting the life of the product, like permanent pleating
- semi-durable, lasting several launderings, like shower proof
- temporary, removed by laundering, like pressing or calendering.

PREPARATION
Preparation means getting the fabric ready for dyeing, printing or finishing, by removing any spinning, weaving or knitting oils, lubricants, waxes, size or any other impurities.

- Cotton fabrics can be singed by heat to remove any short fibres protruding from the fabric. This process makes the fabric surface smoother and reduce pilling.
- Scouring is a washing treatment to remove natural fats and waxes, dirt, oils and other impurities, which may occur naturally or may have been applied during spinning, weaving or knitting. Washing also relaxes the fabric.
- Shrinking is a mechanical treatment, used to achieve dimensional stability, so that fabric will not shrink during later processing or in use. After washing, cellulose fabrics are steamed and allowed to relax on a vibrating table under no tension. This causes the fibres to swell and the fabric to shrink in length and width. After washing, dimensional stability is achieved in synthetic fabrics by the use of heat setting.
- Bleaching cellulose fabrics is a chemical process, using hydrogen peroxide to destroy the natural colour, to make fabric pure white. This makes it easier to dye to pastel shades in natural fibres and enhances the whiteness of synthetics.
- Mercerising is a chemical process, used for cotton yarn or fabric, which is held under tension in a solution of caustic soda. This causes the fibres to swell and become rounder, which makes cotton textiles stronger, more lustrous and take up dye solution more effectively.

COLOURATION
Dyeing

Natural dyes have been used for thousands of years, using mineral pigments such as red ochre, or vegetable dyes like indigo, madder or saffron. Synthetic dyes were first introduced in the 19th century and are now used almost exclusively. Modern dyestuffs use chemical dyes in solution and require large amounts of water. Dyeing can cause pollution when wastewater is released into rivers, although environmental legislation is now tackling this problem.

Textiles can be dyed at the fibre, yarn, fabric or product stage of manufacture. For example:

- Jacquard patterned socks use dyed yarns, but plain socks can be dyed after manufacture. They are dyed in batches of 2000 in a dye solution and fixer chemicals. The dyed socks are dried in a tumble drier and samples taken from every batch are tested on a spectrometer for colour consistency. Any failures are re-dyed.
- Fabrics are often produced in a greige (un-dyed) state and then piece dyed to meet the colour requirements of the maker-up and the selling season. The open-width fabric is passed through a bath of dyestuff and then squeezed between rubber rollers to ensure even and consistent dyeing across the fabric. Continuous fixation machinery fixes the dye in the fabric. This process not only enables continuous dyeing but also reduces costs of setting up machines for producing colour woven fabrics.
- Over-dyeing is used on fabrics made from different fibre types to produce colour effects, depending on the dyestuff used. For example, a fabric with a cotton warp and cotton/acrylic blend in the weft, dyed with direct dyes would produce a speckled effect. Different dyes are suitable for different fibres and need to form a physical or chemical bond with the fibre.
- Garment dyeing enables colours to be chosen late in the manufacturing cycle, as dictated by fashion. This is desirable and cost-effective for some manufacturers, because colour decisions can be made close to the selling season. Garment dyeing is often used for fashion products.

Colourfastness

Colourfastness is the resistance to colour loss during the manufacturing process and in use. A wide range of colourfastness exists for different fibre types and blends. Fastness depends on the type of dyestuff and fabric and there is no universal colour that has the same level of fastness on all types of fibres. Also, different end-uses, for example, underwear and upholstery, have different fastness requirements – underwear needs to be fast to perspiration and upholstery needs to be fast to rubbing and wear.

The International Standard ISO 105 evaluates different types of fastness in relation to rubbing, washing, ironing, perspiration, light, weather and seawater.

- Resistance of the colour to rubbing. The dye should be fast to wet or dry rubbing even for dark shades.

- Resistance to washing determines the wash program that can be used. Dyes are expected to be fast to the vigorous wash programmes at 60°C.
- Resistance to perspiration is very important in underwear, outerwear and sportswear.

Tie-dyeing

There are various methods of producing tie-dyed fabric, which goes in and out of fashion. It is worth experimenting with tie-dyeing in combination with other decorative techniques, such as machine embroidery. Some tie-dye methods are shown below.

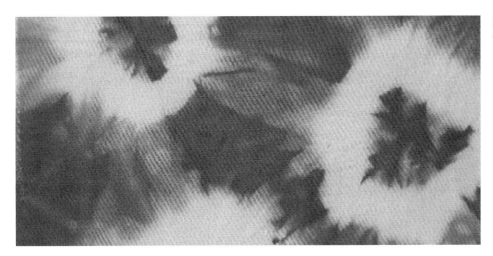

Figure 3A.26
Tie-dying

Method	Effect
Twist the fabric tightly and bind tightly at intervals	Stripes
Tie knots in the fabric	Stripes
Tie a button or other object into the fabric	Circles in the fabric
Tie objects into the fabric in lines or large circles	More complex patterns
Pick up points of the fabric and knot them, at regular / irregular intervals	Striped or all-over effect
Crumple up fabric and bind tightly	Complex all-over or random effect
Gather fabric with stitching, pull up the gathers	Simple or complex stripes and zigzags

Table 3A.28

Batik

Batik is a traditional technique produced all over the Far East. The process is done by hand to produce beautiful, expensive fabrics and by machine for mass-produced fashion fabrics.

Hand-produced batik

- Draw the design with melted wax, (or paste) onto white or un-dyed fabric, using a brush or tjanting, to cover areas of fabric to be left white or un-dyed. Wooden or metal blocks can also be used.

- When the wax is hard, crackle it, brush with coldwater dye or dip-dye, then rinse off the surplus dye.
- Repeat the waxing and dyeing process to produce more complex patterns by over-dyeing.
- Dry the fabric, then iron between absorbent paper to remove the wax and heat-set the dye.

Industrially produced batik

Mass-produced batik fabrics incorporate the use of machinery for fast, automated production, which reduces costs. This can be done using various methods.

- Print gum or wax-resist paste onto the fabric surface from hot rollers, to form a resist. Dye the fabric and use heat finishing to remove surplus gum or wax and fix the dye.
- Print resin onto white or coloured fabric, as a resist. Dye the fabric and use heat finishing to remove resin and fix the dye.
- Print a batik-style design onto the fabric from engraved rollers, using photographic methods or CAD/CAM. Apply finishing to fix the dye.

TASK

1 Investigate different methods of applying dye to fabric, such as tie-dye, dip-dye and silk painting.
2 Put your experimental work in a technical notebook, together with notes to explain each technique.

Printing

Printing is the controlled placement of defined areas of colour onto a fabric. The printing paste is brought to the surface of the fabric by different methods, such as direct, discharge, resist or transfer printing. Block printing, using engraved wooden blocks, is the oldest method of printing, dating back to around 2000BC. Since then, printing techniques have developed considerably and today, nearly two-thirds of the world's prints are done using rotary screen-printing.

- In rotary screen-printing the dye is applied to the fabric from within a roller. It is a fast method of printing, well suited to continuous production. The printing paste is pumped from reservoirs to the inside of rollers, from where it is squeezed onto the moving fabric. The new type of rollers are engraved with the printing pattern by laser to give a much more precise print.
- In machine screen-printing very detailed patterns suitable for top-of-the-range fabrics, can be printed with large motifs and a fairly large number of

colours. The fabric is held firm on a conveyor blanket and moved along the printing table. The screens are lowered onto the fabric and squeegees force the printing paste through the screens. This method prints around 20 per cent of the printing market.

- In transfer printing, the pattern is first printed onto special paper and transferred to the fabric using a pressurised, heated calender machine. The temperature of the calender is high enough for the dyestuff to pass into vapour and onto the fabric, diffusing into the fibres. This process is well suited to synthetic fabrics, but is still little used worldwide, printing only around four per cent of the printing market.
- In direct printing, the printing paste is applied directly to a light coloured fabric.
- In discharge printing a plain dyed fabric is printed with a discharge paste, which removes the ground colour.
- In resist (batik) printing a white fabric is printed with a resist paste, and then dyed.
- Digital printing uses ink jet printers to print CAD designs directly onto fabric, using special printing inks. Although this is a very flexible form of printing, it is currently reserved for short runs and for producing fabric samples for modelling products.

TASK

Analysing printed fabrics can provide a starting point for finding out about dyes, printing techniques and pattern repeats.

1 Ask your self the following questions:
- What fibre type and fabric construction is used for the base fabric?
- What type of printing process was used? (For example block, screen or resist printed?)
- How many colours are used?
- What end-use is the fabric suitable for? Explain.

2 Use the printed fabric to give you ideas for your own design work.
- Work out and sketch the pattern repeat, then re-colour the design in a new colourway.
- Choose one of the pattern motifs. Photocopy and enlarge it. Cut the motif or parts of the motif out and re-assemble into a new design. Trace a line drawing of this new design, photocopy and put into repeat. Produce three colourways for your design.
- Scan your design into CAD software. Change the scale, proportion and colour. Copy, rotate, make a mirror image and put into repeat. Print your design onto iron-on transfer paper (called freezer paper, from quilting suppliers, or use photocopy wrapping paper). Iron the design onto fabric and make a sample product.

PHYSICAL FINISHING (MECHANICAL)

Physical finishing is achieved through the use of mechanical processes, such as raising, calendaring or embossing.

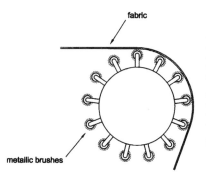

Figure 3A.27

Raising

Raising

Raising (brushing) is a mechanical finishing process that uses no chemicals. The fabric is passed over rollers covered with fine flexible wire brushes, which lift the fibres from the fabric to form a soft fibrous surface called a 'nap'. Raising provides a warm fabric that has a soft, fleecy handle, suitable for such as cotton pyjamas and other products.

Calendering

Calendering is a mechanical finishing process in which fabric is passed between heated heavy rollers under pressure (the industrial equivalent of ironing). It is used to:

- smooth the surface and compact the fabric by pressure
- improve lustre or shine and to provide various surface effects
- produce firm, lustrous Chintz furnishing fabrics (a durable finish using synthetic resin)
- produce moiré fabrics with a watermarked surface pattern, made by engraved rollers (a durable finish for fashion/furnishings)
- produce embossed fabrics with a relief surface pattern from heated rollers (fixation by resin for cotton fabrics or by heat setting for thermoplastic synthetic fabrics).

Figure 3A.28

Calendering

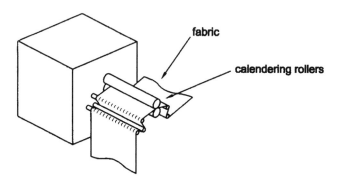

CHEMICAL FINISHING

Finish	Brand	Process	Applications
Easy-care		Apply and cure by heat a resin finish to make fabrics dry fast and smooth and need little or no ironing. Reduces tear strength and abrasion resistance.	Cotton and viscose.
Flame-resist	Proban	Apply and fix a chlorine / phosphorus finish, to reduce flammability to a low level. Increases fabric stiffness, reduces tear strength, adds to cost and degrades with laundering. Students can use a flame-retardant spray like Rosco Flamex to make fabrics fire-resistant.	All fibres, but especially children's nightwear and furnishings made from cotton and viscose.
Moth-proofing	Mitin	Apply and fix chemicals that make the fibres inedible to moth grubs. Conkers from the Horse Chestnut tree are said to repel moths!	Wool products, especially those stored for long periods, such as uniforms.
Permanent pleating		1 Heat set thermoplastic fibres. 2 Apply resin to cotton / viscose fabric, press and cure by heat in oven, to produce durable pleats and flat seams. 3 Heat set blends.	1 Polyester, nylon and acrylic 2 Cotton and viscose 3 55/45% polyester / wool 67/33% polyester / cotton 67/33% polyester / viscose.
Stain-resist	• Teflon • Scotchgard	Apply fluorochemical resin to make fabrics stain resistant. Environmentally-friendly process with no chlorine or CFCs. Biodegrades slowly.	All fibres, used in garments, ties, all weather wear, upholstery, curtains, carpets, garden furniture.
Water-repellent	• Teflon • Scotchgard	Apply fluorochemical resin to face or back of fabrics to make them water and windproof. Traditional methods use a waxed finish, but these are not breathable.	All fibres, used in all weather wear, leisurewear, bags and accessories, shoes, tents.

Table 3A.29

Coating

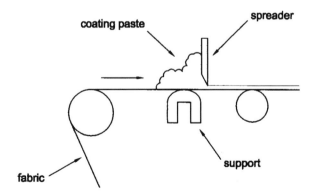

Figure 3A.29

Many chemical processes involve the application of polymer resins to either the face or the back of the fabric, to provide enhanced properties like easy-care or flame-resist. The coating polymer can be applied directly onto the fabric or carried on transfer paper. This is followed by fixing in a curing oven.

Laminating

Laminated fabrics combine two or more layers of different materials (at least one of which is a textile fabric), which are bonded together by adhesive or by the thermoplastic quality of one or both materials.

Figure 3A.30

Laminating fabric using adhesive

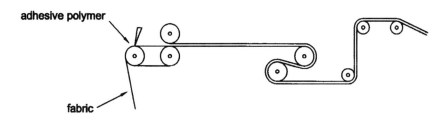

- Iron-on Vilene can be bonded to another fabric to stiffen and strengthen it.
- The waterproof membrane Gore-Tex can be laminated to any other fabric for use in all-weather wear.
- Foam can be laminated to upholstery fabrics for added strength and softness. Upholstery fabrics must be given a fire-resistant finish.

TASK

1 Give three reasons why it is important to finish fabrics.
2 Explain the difference between physical and chemical finishing, with examples of how and why they are used.

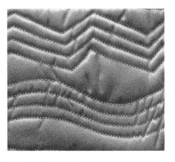

Decorative and stitch techniques

During this unit you should develop your own skills with textile techniques such as appliqué, batik, silk painting, tie-dyeing, printing, embroidery, quilting or patchwork. It is a good idea to develop your skills in a small number of techniques, rather than trying to explore every possible one. This will enable you to explore your chosen techniques in depth and experiment with combining, layering and embellishing fabrics to enhance their aesthetic properties.

Figure 3A.31

Experimental work with quilting.

TASK

1 Investigate and experiment with a small number of textile techniques to improve your skills and inspire your coursework project.
2 Using annotated sketches, give a step-by-step explanation of how to work each technique you use.
3 Present your experimental work to the group, sharing your findings and technical expertise.
4 Create a new image for denim jeans, using different decorative effects.

PRODUCT MANUFACTURE

Check it out Unit 1 Manufacturing systems page 32

Whether a product is to be made by one-off, batch or mass production is extremely important, because the choice of manufacturing system will influence:

- which materials and fastenings are appropriate
- the manufacturing processes
- how the product is manufactured
- the eventual retail price.

Designing and making one-off textile products results in exclusive or specialist products, but at a high unit cost, because materials and labour costs are higher than for mass-produced goods.

Batch production is planned for ease-of-manufacture, using standardised materials and components, standard production flat patterns, specialised equipment and production control to monitor production. There are economies of scale in batch production because of standardisation of pre-manufactured materials and components and standardisation of production processes within batches.

Textile products are manufactured in high volume to fit a range of standard sizes or dimensions, for stock or to order. High volume production is planned for cost-effective manufacture, using standardised materials and components, standard production patterns, specialised equipment and production planning and control to monitor production. There are economies of scale in high volume production because of standardisation of pre-manufactured materials and components and standardisation of production processes.

PRODUCTION PATTERNS

Check it out Unit 1 Preparation page 37

Flat patterns cutting is widely used because of it enables accurate sizing and the fast production of complicated styles. Pattern cutting (pattern-drafting) is a method of producing a shaped garment that fits a three-dimensional body shape. Flat patterns are cut for each part of the garment and the pieces are assembled to make the required 3D shape. Garment manufacturers use the basic block for pattern cutting, to make a pattern that fits an average figure. The measurements for basic blocks are based on British Standards BS 3666 (Specification for women's wear sizes) and BS 6185 (Specification for men's wear sizes). Production patterns are developed from basic blocks and working patterns.

1 *Basic block pattern*
   - This is used to develop every type of garment style.
   - It enables the quality control of garment sizes.
   - It is traced or 'wheeled' onto pattern paper, to produce a working pattern.

2 *Working pattern*
   - This is used for marking out basic styles and design features.
   - It can be adapted further.
   - It is used to trial the garment style.

3 *Production pattern*
   - This includes all the seams, hems, grain lines and pattern information required to make up the product.
   - It is used to cut the fabric for high-volume garments.

PATTERN GRADING

Grading a production pattern means increasing or decreasing flat pattern pieces, to create a limited range of sizes to meet the needs of the target market. Patterns are sometimes graded to small, medium or large, which is more cost-effective than making a wide range of sizes. Grading alters the overall size of a design, but not its general shape or appearance. Producing and grading patterns by hand is time-consuming, so manufacturers often use computer systems to make the process fast and accurate. There are two types of pattern grading:

1 Individual size grading for bespoke or one-off designs, adapting a basic block to fit the client's body measurements. This takes account of individual size variations.
2 Standard size grading for mass production, to fit a range of average body sizes. This is based on either:
   - British Standards size charts of body measurements
   - A manufacturer's own garment specifications or nest of patterns stored in a database

Pattern cutting in industry makes use of computer software to develop new garment paper patterns from existing basic blocks:

- The basic block must first be digitised and stored in a database. Digitising converts an existing flat pattern (laid out on a digitising table) into a series of number co-ordinates that are electronically transferred into a computer programme.
- The digitised block can then be displayed on screen and modified to develop a new garment style.

- Darts can be altered and parts can be moved, rotated and resized very quickly.
- The new pattern is then graded to make larger or smaller sizes.
- A lay plan (or marker) is produced and stored in the computer.

MODELLING AND PROTOTYPING

Check it out ! Unit 1 Modelling page 18

Testing a working pattern prior to developing the production pattern is essential in order to test the pattern draft, try out construction processes and to work out costs.

- In high volume manufacturing, a working pattern is generally adapted by computer from a basic block. The new pattern is cut and sent to the sample room. A sample garment is made up in a medium size, from the intended fabric, using production-type machinery. Once the sample garment has been agreed by the client, a production pattern is finalised. This goes to the production department, where samples are made and costed in a range of sizes, before the garment is put into production.

- In more exclusive one-off production, made-to-measure or haute couture, garments are made for individual clients. The prototyping process can be more complex, because the design is made to the client's measurements and may be more unusual. The garment design is developed from a basic pattern block, and a toile is made from inexpensive calico, in a similar weight to the intended fabric. The toile is trialled on a stand model, to test the drape, fit and construction of the garment. This process is sometimes called 'stand modelling'. Once the designer is happy with the design, the final production pattern is drafted. The garment pieces are cut, often from expensive fabric, so the pattern must be accurate. The client may go for 'fittings' as the garment is made, to make sure that it fits properly.

TASK

1 Explain what is meant by pattern drafting.
2 Describe the advantages of using computer software to aid pattern grading.
3 Explain why testing before manufacture is a key manufacturing process.

FABRIC SPREADING, LAY PLANNING AND CUTTING

Check it out! Processing Unit 1 page 38

Lay planning is important because it enables all of the templates for all of the individual components of a garment to be laid out together so they fit the fabric rectangle as closely and efficiently as possible in order to minimise waste. Designing the lay plan – called marker making – works out the amount of fabric required to make a specific number of products in a range of sizes. Lay planning is also important in one-off production in order to cost the product.

Figure 3A.32

Marker making has to take account of the fabric grain, nap or pile.

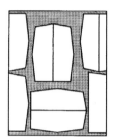

Nonwoven fabric

Plain weave fabric

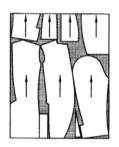

Corduroy or printed fabric

- The lay plan provides a cutting marker, which goes on top of the fabric plies to be cut. With modern CAD systems it is not necessary to make a physical cutting marker. Cutting instructions are sent electronically to the fully automatic cutting machines.

The positions of the pattern pieces on the fabric have to take account of the width, length and type of fabric, to minimise waste. Fabrics that have a direction, grain, nap or pile increase costs, because the pattern may have to be laid in one direction. Stripes, checks or fabric designs have to be carefully matched, which takes more fabric and more time, which adds to the cost of the product. For example:

- Non-woven fabric, such as Vilene has no thread direction, grain, nap, pile, pattern design, so the flat pattern pieces can be random-laid in any direction along or across fabric. This can produce an economic layplan with little waste
- Plain-woven fabric such as calico, lining fabric or laminated fabric has a thread direction and the grain direction is parallel to selvedge. Since this type of fabric has no pattern design, nap or pile, the flat pattern pieces can be laid in either direction along the length of the fabric. There must be careful pattern placement to reduce waste.
- Fabric such as corduroy, velvet or knitted fabrics have a thread direction and a nap or pile. The flat pattern pieces must be placed along the fabric length parallel to selvedge in one direction only. It is more difficult to

produce an economic layplan so there may be more waste, which makes the product more expensive.

In high volume manufacturing, the pattern cutter works out the marker (the pattern utilisation lay) to find out the amount of fabric needed for the garment in a ratio of x small, y medium, z large sizes for 20 garments, then does a costing based on the number of metres required per dozen (12) garments. Marker making may involve further modifications of the pattern, such as reducing the hem allowance, in order to reduce the amount of fabric used.

CONSTRUCTION AND JOINING TECHNIQUES

Check it out! Unit 1 Sewing and joining page 41

The assembly of sewn products usually involves fusing, joining and pressing. These processes require continuous feedback from manufacturing to ensure that products meet specifications.

Fusing
Fusing means permanently joining two fabrics together, by melting an adhesive resin, which is applied to one of the fabrics. For some types of garments the process of fusing an interlining to selected cut parts is as important as the sewing operation. Fusing is used on areas such as jacket fronts, collars, cuffs and waistbands. Fusing shortens the manufacturing time, needs less skill and produces more consistent quality than the use of sewn-in interlinings.

a) Fusing by hand, using an iron, can be used for:
  • joining a fusible interlining the outer fabric, to make it stable, strong, keep its shape and reduce creasing.
  • reinforcing and strengthening fabrics for accessories.
  • turning up hems without stitching.
b) Fusing with a flat-bed press is suitable for fusing short fabric runs or small garment parts.
c) Fusing with a conveyor press is suitable for long fabric runs in high volume production.

Joining
The joining techniques used for textile materials, depends on the type of fabrics to be joined, the processes available and the end-use of the product. The most common joining techniques are stitching and heat-sealing, but whichever technique is used, quality and a professional-looking result are essential.

Figure 3A.33

Lockstitch, overlock and seamcover.

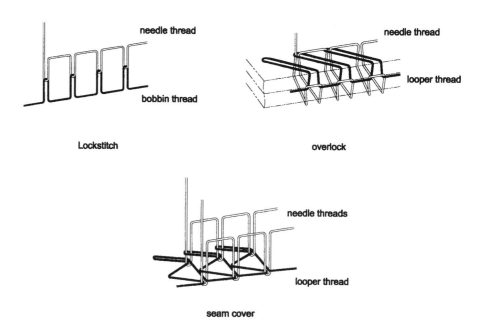

1 Stitching is a way of joining two fabrics, to produce an unfinished seam. The raw edges may need to be finished. This is done to prevent fraying and to produce a hardwearing, neat finish that adds comfort, effect and style.

a) Stitching by hand is called tacking and produces a temporary join for :
   • holding together parts of a product before permanent joining.
   • holding hems or pleats in place before pressing.

b) Stitching by machine produces a strong join, such as:
   • a plain (straight) seam, stitched with the right sides of the fabric together. This is the most commonly used method of joining woven fabrics, produced by a lockstitch machine. (See figure 1.9.)
   • a French seam. This double stitched plain seam, adds strength and stops fraying.
   • an overlock seam, made to stitch, cut and finish the seam in one process. This is used for a range of textiles, including underwear and knitwear.
   • a flat seam is made using twin needles to create a stitch on top and an overlock stitch below, sometimes called seamcover. This is made by a flat seam machine, which binds the cut edges of straps or the hems of fabrics that fray, eg. for T-shirts, belt loops on jeans or swimwear.
   • a cup seam, made by a linking machine. This links together the selvedges of knitted fabrics.
   • a lap seam is commonly used on the seams of jeans and shirts, providing a very strong seam with two rows of stitching. (See figure 1.9.)

2 Heat-sealing can be applied to fabrics made from thermoplastic fibres, like polyester and polyamide (nylon), which can be melted by heat. Heat-sealing is often used in combination with taped seams, to help waterproof all-weather wear, tents and groundsheets.

1 Discuss the implications for producing a marker for gingham, poplin, needlecord and felt fabrics.

2 Collect examples of a range of seam types and add to your technical notebook, using notes to describe their construction and end-use.

AESTHETIC AND FUNCTIONAL FINISHING

Check it out! Unit 1 Finishing page 29

Textile products are finished as part of a quality assurance process, to make sure that the fabric, seams and stitching are fault-free and that the product is clean and matches specifications. Finishing improves the properties and quality of the product and can be:

- Aesthetic, like pressing, to improve the ease of manufacture. Final pressing improves presentation of the product.
- Decorative, like applying logos, embroidery, braid or fringing to add to the style or image of the product.
- Functional, like self-finishing seams by overlocking to improve the product quality.

Pressing

Pressing means shaping, stabilising and setting a textile material, using dry heat or steam. In the clothing industry pressing can be done by hand or by using specialist equipment:

- Workstations for manual pressing are designed for specific types of pressing, i.e. for flat work or garments. The unit uses an electric steam iron, connected to a holding device and a pressing area provided with suction. Air is drawn through or blown onto the fabric, to absorb heat and moisture.
- A steam dolly is used for finishing whole garments, which are placed on a form. This is inflated by blowing with steam and air for a few minutes. Small parts such as collars or cuffs may have to be pre-pressed. Steam dollies are suitable for garments made from fabrics that are dimensionally stable, i.e. fabrics that have been pre-shrunk.
- A tunnel finisher is used for finishing whole garments on hangers or frames. The garments are conveyed through a chamber in which they are steamed and dried. Again, small parts such as cuffs may need to be pre-pressed. It is important to adjust the time, temperature and amount of steam to suit the fabric being processed. For example, thermoplastic synthetics fabrics would need different finishing conditions to a natural fibre such as cotton.

Pressing operations take place at different stages of garment manufacture:

1 Flat pressing removes creases and wrinkles before cutting, sewing or on the finished product.
2 Steaming is carried out to relax the fabric, which avoids shrinkage during later pressing processes.
3 Under pressing is the first stage of pressing a garment and means pressing seams and darts into their correct position on the wrong side of the fabric, before they are crossed by other seams or before hems are turned up. They make use of flat pressing and steam to improve the ease of accuracy of sewing.
4 Moulding is most effective on wool fabrics. It is used to create and fix 3D shapes in a garment, by stretching and pressing rounded shapes, like tops of sleeves, using ironing cushions or moulds.
5 Top pressing is the final finishing process for a garment, to make it ready for sale. It involves pressing hems, collar edges, necklines and facings into their correct position. This means pressing the right side of the garment, so a damp or dry pressing cloth is essential to stop iron marks showing on the fabric. Top pressing improves the aesthetic properties and quality of the product.

TASK

Make notes to explain how the use of high volume production techniques can reduce the costs of garment manufacture, relating to:
- flat pattern making and grading
- modelling before manufacture
- lay planning and cutting
- construction and joining techniques
- finishing.

Chapter 4

Testing Materials

British and International Standards

The British Standards Institute (BSI) helps develop British, European and International Standards, which are used to ensure the safety and quality of a wide range of products. Standard tests are often set at the request of individual manufacturers and retailers and form an essential part of a quality assurance system. Testing of materials and components, processes and prototypes prior to manufacture requires the use of standard tests under controlled conditions.

TESTING BEFORE MANUFACTURE

Testing before manufacture ensures the production of quality textile products, avoids costly mistakes and protects the consumer against faulty or unsafe goods. Tests make use of:

- manufacturing specifications.
- fibre testing processes, to identify fibre content and to avoid counterfeiting of expensive fibres.
- fabric testing processes, to identify properties such as abrasion resistance, aftercare, colourfastness, crease resistance, drape, durability, elasticity, flammability, pilling, shrinkage, stain-resistance, strength, thermal insulation, water and wind resistance.
- manufacturing prototypes, to test for performance, ease of manufacture, aftercare and fitness-for-purpose. Quality control is the standard method of putting quality assurance into practice. It can involve a statistical system of sampling (BS6001), to inspect a sample of garments across a colour and size range – for example in a box of 50 garments, five to ten may be sampled against an acceptable percentage level of quality.
- consumer testing, to test for performance in wear and acceptability of the product.

Testing textiles under controlled conditions

Tests on textiles need to be carried out under controlled conditions, to make sure that they are fit-for-purpose – in other words, that they meet the quality and safety requirements of the specification.

Product specifications are only of use if there are appropriate methods available for testing properties. Performance properties can be measured by a number of test methods. For example, for fluorochemicals, standard tests exist for oil and water repellence and stain release. Performance durability can be measured by testing after repeated laundering, dry cleaning or abrasion cycles.

Testing under controlled conditions means:

- using tests that can be repeated time and time again.
- taking into account physical and chemical properties, yarn and fabric construction, fabric finish and the end-use of the textile.
- controlling variables.
- being objective about results.
- taking account of the scale and dimension – for example, small fabric swatches may not behave in the same way as fabrics used in a product.

Comparative testing

It is very difficult to carry out objective testing outside a textiles laboratory, although two methods are appropriate – testing against specifications and testing against known properties. Table 3A.30 gives examples of simple tests that can be made to compare properties of different textile samples.

Test	Simple method	British Standard test for light woven fabrics
Tensile strength	Snap yarns by hand to judge the strongest.	BS 2576 Withstands 12kg in warp and weft
Seam strength	Pull the seam apart to see if it opens ('grins') either because the sewing thread or the fabric threads break.	BS 3320 Withstands 10kg
Tear strength	Make small nick in fabric square, into warp, weft and. bias. Tear sample along nick. Compare cotton and polyester/cotton blend.	BS 3356 Withstands 750g
Crease resistance	Using fabric samples 40x15mm, fold in half with paper between. Place a one kg weight on crease, for five minutes under weight and five minutes to recover. Can also screw up fabric square in hand.	BS 22313
Drape	Place a measured circle of fabric over a tube placed on graph paper. Shine a light over the fabric to cast a shadow. Draw round shadow on the graph paper. Good drape casts the least shadow.	BS 5058

Table 3A.30

Fire testing

General safety requirements mean that products must be made from safe materials that are non-toxic for people and the environment. Fire safety is an important consideration, as domestic fires kill 600 people a year.

- Textiles used in the home, for transport, for leisure and sports equipment, for fire-resistant products and for industrial textiles need to be tested to British Standards specifications.
- Some modern textiles and plastics give off toxic gases when burning, so special grades of upholstery foam must be used for furniture and bedding and special finishes are used to improve resistance to fire.
- Nightwear for children aged from three months to 13 years of age, must comply with BS 5722, relating to flammability. They must carry a permanent label to show they meet the flammability standard.

THE USE OF INFORMATION AND COMMUNICATIONS TECHNOLOGY (ICT) IN TESTING

Testing is increasingly carried out using computer modelling to test products before manufacture. Testing can involve the use of computer software to test ideas in 2D and 3D, to work out exact dye recipes, to develop virtual products and to design lay plans that enable the most efficient fabric utilisation. The benefits of computer modelling include that it:

- enables manufacturers to test and modify a prototype product before putting it into production.
- saves time by ensuring the product is 'right first time', so changes are not necessary when the product is in production.
- reduces the cost of re-working the product – modelling reduces the incidence of faults occurring.

Virtual products

Virtual products can be developed on screen, using computer software. This type of product development is called Electronic Product Definition (EPD). It uses CAD software to design and texture map, or 'lay' a fabric design onto a textile product. Designing virtual products can save a manufacturer time and money, because it reduces the need to produce actual product samples. Instead, the client can see a simulated product, which can be shown on screen, on a storyboard, or in a virtual reality catwalk show, produced using multimedia.

- Garments, furniture and accessories can all be texture mapped, with different fabric ideas. The resulting virtual products can be printed and used on a product storyboard.
- One sample product in plain fabric is made, in the same weight and quality as the intended design. This enables the client to evaluate the fabric handle, quality, garment style and fit.

- The client selects a design from the storyboard and a sample of that is made. Once the 'first fit' sample has been approved by the client, production can begin.

TASKS

1 Texture mapping is a good way to try out your design ideas, although it needs practice to get the images you want.
- A simple draw or paint programme can be used to produce design ideas on screen
- A scanner or digital camera can also be used to import images.

2 You could try the following:
- Draw or scan in a drawing of a textile product, such as a rucksack.
- Edit the rucksack design, if necessary.
- Draw or scan in a simple design motif and change its scale, if necessary.
- Use the select, copy and paste tools to paste (texture map) your design motif onto the rucksack.
- Experiment with different placements of the design motif.
- Experiment with different colourways.

Marker making

The use of computer software enables pattern technologists to design complex lay plans in the most cost-effective way. A lay plan is important for calculating fabric requirements and costs and for organising the production cutting of fabric for a range of different sizes of garments. Using a computer system saves time and costs, because all the flat pattern information can be stored on a database. When a new style needs to be planned, the closest design can be accessed and adapted to meet the new specification. Marker making using computer systems is specialised work:

1 A manufacturing specification sheet provides information about the style and construction of a new garment. The new pattern can be drafted by hand and put on a digitising table, to plot each pattern piece into the computer database.
2 Alternatively, the pattern cutter can choose an existing basic block in a medium size from the database, and adapt it to match the specification.
3 The pattern cutter produces a marker (pattern utilisation lay), to cost the garment at the sampling stage. A ratio of small, medium and large sizes is costed and at least 80 per cent utilisation of the fabric expected.

4 When the garment is put into production, the cutting instructions for the
   lay plan can be sent directly to an automatic cutting machine.

TASK

1 Explain the benefits of testing before manufacture.
2 Describe the criteria you would use to test a range of fabrics for seam
   strength.
   Compare your results with known properties of fibres and record your
   results.

EXAM PRACTICE

The questions below are similar in style to the ones you will find in the examination paper for this unit. Before attempting to answer the questions read the relevant sections in the unit. Make notes using key words or spider diagrams about the topic.

1 a) Explain the meaning of the following textile terms, giving ONE example of each:

(i)   fibre blend
(ii)   fabric mixture
(2)

b) Outline THREE benefits of blending fibres.   (3)

2 a) Describe the difference in appearance between woollen and worsted yarns.
(2)

b) Describe how thermoplastic properties aid the manufacture of trousers and shirts.
(3)

3 a) Using diagrams, describe the technique of producing batik by hand.   (3)

b) Explain the changes to the technique you described in (a), that would be required to mass-produce batik-style fabrics.   (2)

4 a) Stitching is a way of joining two fabrics. Describe TWO other ways of joining fabrics.
(2)

b) What is a basic block and how is it used?   (3)

5 a) Explain the terms cut-and-sew, shape knitting and 3D knitting.   (3)

b) State the meaning of the following textile terms:

(i)   course
(ii)   wale   (2)

6 Modelling and prototyping textile products is a key industrial process.

a) Give ONE example of using CAD as a testing aid before manufacture.   (1)

b)   Describe the process of 3D modelling by hand in garment production.   (2)

c) Explain the benefits to manufacturers of modelling a garment before manufacture.   (2)

Preview

Unit	Level	Components	Areas of study
3	AS	Section B: Options	• Design and Technology in Society OR • CAD/CAM

Design and Technology in Society is one of two options in Unit 3. You only have to study ONE of these options.

WHAT YOU WILL LEARN IN THE UNIT

The content of Design and Technology in Society explores the development of products, the work of professional designers and the effects of design and technological changes on society. The work you undertake must include knowledge and understanding of the following areas:

Chapter 1   The physical and social consequences of design and technology on society

• The effects of design and technological changes on society
• Influences on the development of products.

Chapter 2   Professional designers at work

• The relationship between designers and clients, manufacturers, users and society
• Professional practice relating to design management, technology, marketing, business, ICT
• The work of professional designers and professional bodies.

Chapter 3   Anthropometrics and ergonomics

• The basic principles and applications of anthropometrics and ergonomics
• British and International Standards.

WHAT YOU WILL DO IN THE UNIT

During the unit you should undertake a variety of tasks to enable you to understand the subject content. You may be asked to:

- work individually on some theoretical aspects of the unit content – for example, you could use this book to research information about new materials, processes and technology, then share your findings with the group
- work collaboratively with others on some activities – for example, investigating the role of design and production teams or the work of professional designers
- work individually on exam-style questions.

UNIT 3 ASSESSMENT

Unit 3 is externally assessed through a $1\frac{1}{2}$ hour written exam, which assesses your understanding of the unit subject content. There is one question paper, with two sections:

- Section A: Materials, Components and Systems
- Section B: Options

UNIT 3 SECTION B ASSESSMENT

The work that you do in Design and Technology in Society will be assessed through Section B of the Unit 3 examination paper.
- It consists of two compulsory long answer questions, each worth 15 marks.
- Your answers should be from the viewpoint of Textiles Technology unless you are taught this option through another materials area.
- You are advised to spend 45 minutes on this section of the exam paper.
- This section together with Section A is worth 15 per cent of the full Advanced GCE.

WHAT THE EXAMINER IS LOOKING FOR

The examination paper is designed to give you the opportunity to demonstrate your understanding of what you have learned in the unit. Examiners will look for your ability to apply your knowledge and understanding to open-ended contexts related to products, influences on design and the consequences of design and technology on individuals and society.

EXAM TIPS

- Make brief notes about the topics covered in this unit.
- Summarise the key points on one or two sheets of paper.
- Learn these key points.
- Practise working through a complete exam so you will learn how to allocate the time available to you.
- In the exam read the questions through and then read them again to make sure you understand what you are being asked to do.
- Plan your answer briefly then check the question again to make sure that you have covered it fully.
- Work through your answer making sure that you address each point in your plan.
- Don't write everything you know about a topic if it's irrelevant to the question!
- Use clearly written sentences and bullet points to make your answer clear.
- Use specialist technical terms and clear sketches to illustrate your answer where appropriate.
- Read through your answer, then move on to the next question.
- If you have time read through your answers to both questions – check to see if you can add anything – and check your spelling!

Chapter 1

The Physical and Social Consequences of Design and Technology on Society

THE EFFECTS OF DESIGN AND TECHNOLOGICAL CHANGES ON SOCIETY

For many people today, the world has changed beyond all recognition in just a few years. A short time ago the Internet was unheard of, faxes were smart and even computers were rare in schools, homes and offices. Nowadays, life would be unimaginable without electricity, television or personal computers (PCs)! Your parents probably grew up with black and white television, your grandparents without television at all and possibly even without electricity. Imagine also life without easy-care clothes that we just throw in the washing machine. In fact, developments in modern textile materials are providing solutions not only for fashion items, but also for a wide range of performance, industrial and technical products worldwide. Developments in technology have improved the lives of millions of people and will continue to do so. Its impact on society and how people live and work has been enormous, the pace of change extraordinary and accelerating all the time.

However, the technological revolution is not just a result of clever inventions and technological breakthroughs. We are able to take products like the PC for granted not only because of technical wizardry, but also because of developments in mass production and the economies of scale that mass production brings. As with any form of progress, there are benefits and disadvantages, such as the loss of employment by some less skilled workers. Changes in technology have also brought about the disappearance of entire industries and trades such as printers who specialised in 'hot-metal' printing techniques and bank employees whose roles have been changed by the development of cash dispensing machines. Other concerns about the use of technology relate to the impact of violent computer games on children. On a larger scale, developments in mass production have led to the over-use of the world's natural resources, some of them non-renewable. This has left a legacy of pollution, toxic rivers, acid rain and the Greenhouse effect, which all pose serious threats to our quality of life and to the future of the planet.

TASK

Make a list of the products that you use every day to make your life easier, more comfortable or fun. Talk to your parents or older people about their lifestyle when they were young. How did people manage without our so-called labour-saving devices? How did people enjoy themselves? What kinds of products were available to them?

MASS PRODUCTION AND THE CONSUMER SOCIETY

The history of design in the 20th century could be said to have begun with the invention of the steam engine in the UK in the 1760s and the resulting industrial revolution. Many inventions came about at this time, a lot of which were related to textile machinery. Inventions such as the Spinning Jenny and the Water Frame totally changed the manufacture of textiles. The revolution also dramatically transformed the working conditions of people living in cities. Whereas craftspeople, such as weavers, had previously worked from home or in small workshops, the manufacture of textiles now moved to factories. This set the scene for the development of industrial mass-production.

Clothing production

Before the industrial revolution most clothing was produced outside factories by craftspeople working for the well off. Working class women also worked in clothing manufacture in so-called 'cottage industries'. They had few options by which to subsidise their husbands' low wages. They could either become maids or work from home for terrible pay for 'middlemen' who received orders from the clothing manufacturers. At this time what we call ready-to-wear (RTW) clothing had just started to become available, but it was mostly produced by women at home.

One important invention had an enormous impact on women's lives – the invention of the sewing machine in 1851. Singer was one of the first entrepreneurs to offer payments over time to ordinary households, which enabled many women to but their first sewing machine. Although it was not directly responsible for the growth of RTW, the sewing machine contributed to its rapid development. Many women bought sewing machines on instalment, driving themselves into debt and isolating them further in their own homes. It was not until some years into the 20th century that ordinary women had the opportunity to work outside the home.

Factories

The alternative for unmarried women was to work for a tailor or in a textile factory. Textile manufacture became highly industrialised in the 19th century. The newly invented knitting machines enabled the production of elastic textiles, which could be used for stockings or gloves. These products still had to be cut and sewn because the circular knitting machine, which could produce seamless stockings, was not invented until the 20th century. Children also helped women in their work and were employed in factories in 'sweat shops', where there was a reduced requirement for skills. Unfortunately, this image of the textile and clothing industry is still prevalent today. Nowadays, employment in the industry has radically changed and people with technical skills are highly prized. In the 19th century, however, the poorly paid workers in factories could hardly keep their heads above water, let alone afford the expensive clothes they produced.

Another occupation for a young, unmarried woman was to be a saleswoman in the clothing section of one of the then-new department stores. A typical working day was at least twelve hours, six days a week and women in the cottage industry and the factories worked even longer. Not surprisingly, the poor living conditions, poverty and general dissatisfaction with the industrial sweatshops of the 19th century gave rise to the trade union movement, which attempted to harness the collective bargaining power of large groups of workers and bring about improved working conditions and wages.

The development of fashion

In wealthy Victorian families, women did not work and were sometimes seen to be status symbols for their husbands because they wore expensive and extravagant clothing that only the wealthy could afford. Their clothing allowed little movement and was very restrictive. As a result, high fashion became even more extravagant as women tried to outdo each other in the fashion stakes. Many middle class women hired 'advisers' to decorate their homes or advise on fashionable clothing. This eventually gave rise to the profession of the 'couturier', who created original fashion ideas for the wealthy, although most ordinary women still made their own clothes. Gradually, successful couturiers became household names and wealthy women's clothing began to be designed and made by men's tailors, rather than by seamstresses or milliners. This was the beginning of what we now call 'Haute Couture'. Women at home were still employed to make these clothes, but under the direction of the couturier.

The development of women's fashion in the 19th century became more lavish and exemplified the male view of the ideal figure – tiny waists and very wide skirts. This fashion depended on two items – the crinoline and the corset, both horrendously restricting. In the late 19th century, women had to lace themselves up mercilessly in corsets in order to achieve the fashionable tiny waist, often causing serious harm to their health. Fortunately, the modern day corsets, such as those shown on the catwalk for spring/summer 2001, are less restricting. Corsets should always be comfortable – many are worn to go clubbing in. Towards the end of the century, daring women began to wear 'bloomers', ankle length knickerbockers for bicycle riding. By the beginning of the 20th century more women were taking part in sports, travelling and working. This led to the gradual change in the concept of women's fashions and of the female form. Clothing became more functional and more form fitting, with simple lines. The corset eventually disappeared. This was due to a number of factors:

- change in the taste for 'artistic' dress made popular by William Morris and the anti-industrial Arts and Crafts movement. This dress reform movement argued that the corset and crinoline were unhealthy and cumbersome. They advocated loose flowing garments and flowing fabrics that ignored the waistline
- entry of women into the worlds of work, sports and travel
- The onset of World War I, during which women had to take on men's work, so they had to wear more functional clothing.

TASK

Describe the changes in the society during the late 19th century and early 20th century that led to the disappearance of the corset.

THE CHARACTERISTICS OF MASS PRODUCTION

The industrial revolution brought with it increasing specialisation. The traditional craftsperson, who was able to perform all aspects of garment manufacture and the cottage industry was superseded by factory workers. Factory work divided up manufacture into a series of smaller operations and each worker performed one specific small task repeatedly. The worker often did not know what the final product would be, let alone be able to afford it! This specialisation in small repetitive tasks characterises all modern industrial manufacturing. In the 19th century industrial manufacturing may have offered ordinary people opportunities to find work and be able to buy some consumer goods, but the reality for many people was a very miserable life. After all, compare the satisfaction of designing and making a dress from start to finish, with the drudgery of stitching hems for 12 or 14 hours a day for six or even seven days a week – and all for minuscule wages.

Technical advances

While the United Kingdom was the home of the industrial revolution, it was clear by the middle of the 19th century that the enterprise, business acumen and ingenuity of American entrepreneurs had taken mass production to an important new stage with the introduction of the moving assembly line. The first assembly lines were in use in the USA by 1850. Initially, they were used in slaughterhouses, then later in sewing machine manufacture and later in the all-important automobile industry. The use of assembly lines enabled products to be made easier, faster and more cheaply than ever before. The factory floor would never be the same again, although it was almost another century before robots began taking their places as 'workers' on the automobile assembly line.

Gradually, the emergence of mass production and assembly lines gave rise to new types of work and opportunities and new types of consumer products. In Victorian times, there was no tradition for the design of mass-produced household products. Factories turned out poor quality products that were decorated to imitate the traditional styles of over-decorated, hand-made products. The prevailing concept was that mass-produced goods were 'tasteless' and needed to be disguised beneath heavy decoration. For example furniture shown at London's Great Exhibition of 1851 typified the excessive use of decoration in Victorian times. The ball gowns of wealthy women at around the same time were also over-decorated with flounces, ribbons and lace, in line with the prevailing view of women at the time – they were seen as decorative objects.

Developments in product design

By the second half of the 19th century, a combination of market forces and the demands of the trade unions led to a recognition by entrepreneurs of the need for the design and production of simple, inexpensive household products. The mass-produced furniture currently being produced was a throwback to an era of grandeur that was inappropriate to the lives of many ordinary people. The furniture was poor quality, over-sized and over-decorated – totally inappropriate for the cramped housing conditions in which most factory workers lived. There gradually emerged a new field of design for simple, pared-down furniture, which was suitable for the urban homes of factory workers. This change in the concept of design was partly due to the influence of the William Morris and the Arts and Crafts movement. This movement advocated the manufacture of simple, well-designed consumer products and began the move towards the understanding of form and function – what a product looks like in relation to what it has to do. This understanding of form and function was a turning point in the history of product design and is the basis of all the work that we do today in design and technology.

It is interesting to note how the development of fashion design through history mirrors changes in lifestyle, social conditions and developments in technology. While the earliest ready-to-wear garments were geared to the needs of the newly emerging middle classes (such as the wives and daughters of factory owners), it was not long before mass production of affordable clothing was to emerge as a major industry. The less well off were eventually no longer to be dependent on home-dressmaking.

The development of functional product design

In contrast to Europe, design in the United States took a more functional and progressive turn. New democracies like the USA, were less hide-bound by the class tradition than in Europe. The development of mass production and mechanisation extended way beyond production methods and into the products themselves, products that meant that the world would never be the same again. The sewing machine, the microphone, the telephone and the mechanical typewriter were invented in the late 19th century and began to be mass-produced, fanning the flames of workplace change. For one thing, they led to opportunities for new kinds of employment outside the home. When such products were first invented, they were totally functional and lacked any kind of decoration, unlike the contemporary Victorian products in the UK. In the late 19th century the concept of adding styling to products was unheard of, mainly because there was no competition in the market place from similar products.

THE BEGINNINGS OF THE CONSUMER SOCIETY

The early years of the 20th century were decades of great uncertainty. In Europe, the Great War (1914-1918) devastated an entire generation of young men in England, France and Germany. The Russian Revolution of 1917 brought about Communism and with it the tight control on the lives of its citizens, in stark contrast to the new democratic freedoms emerging elsewhere.

Sheltered from the worst of these crises, the first thirty years of the 20th century in the USA laid down the foundations of what we now call the consumer society. In the roaring 20s, jazz, swing and the Charleston flourished in the USA. Popular culture and Hollywood played a key role in changing people's lifestyles, morality and spending patterns. Hollywood in particular focused on the elements of glamour and couture that were traditionally associated with the wealthy. The sheath dress of the 1920s and 1930s is said to be the fashion equivalent of the modern tubular steel chair, which was developed at around the same time. Both the dress and the chair represented minimalism, modernism and purity of form and line. The sheath dress was made from skin tight shiny satin fabric cut on the bias and it clung to the body outline, giving an impression of near nudity – very shocking!

TASK

- Find a photograph of Jean Harlow in the famous sheath dress described on pafe 130. Possible sources include the internet or books such as *Design, a concise History*, Thomas Hauffe, Laurence King Publishing 1998. ISBN 1 85669.
- Again, using similar sources, compare and contrast early Chanel designs with those of today.

The 1920s and 1930s

In France, the designer Coco Chanel epitomised the modern woman. She designed comfortable, loose blouses, chemise dresses and clothes that were sporty, relaxed, wearable and well suited to the outdoor lifestyle that was being promoted as healthy in the 1920s. These clothes were designed to be worn without corsets and were made with fewer linings to make them lighter and more flexible. Chanel believed that fashion must meet the needs of modern lifestyles and give women freedom of movement. In 1916 she began using knitted jersey fabrics, a relatively cheap fabric previously used for underwear and by 1918 was producing cardigans and twinsets. Chanel was one of the most influential designers of the 20th century. Her clothes broke away from the fussy over decorated clothing of the 19th century. She adapted men's tailoring and produced classic suits with short skirts, always relying on good cut, finish and high quality fabric. What we now consider to be a normal part of women's clothing – trousers, tweeds, pea jackets, berets, blazers, raincoats, the little black dress, slingback shoes and accessories were all introduced by Chanel.

In the 1920s, fashion clothing became more widely available as clothing by designers like Chanel was copied for RTW. Clothing that once had been only for the wealthy suddenly became available to the woman on the street. This was a dramatic change for ordinary people who had previously only had everyday and 'best' clothes that had to last for years. Of course designer clothing was still unaffordable for most people, but its very exclusivity increased its desirability. The production and distribution of affordable RTW fashion was an important turning point in the democratisation of fashion. The very styling of the clothes themselves, together with lower prices meant that social class was not immediately discernible through what you wore.

TASK

Supermarkets sometimes sell branded 'designer' clothing at low prices, making it available to all. What does this do to the concept of exclusivity? Does it still make these products desirable? Are designer products any better designed or made than cheaper products? Explain your views.

By the late 1930s, the gradual spread of electricity meant designers were able to design a whole new range of products using new technology. By the time of the outbreak of World War II in 1939, most middle class American homes had consumer durables such as radios, refrigerators, toasters and washing machines. As living standards improved across the world and demand for new products increased, advertising became an important new industry. Suddenly, marketing, packaging and product styling were all part of the business of selling the new products. Why buy that red lipstick when you could have this one, which promises so much more.allure, success, and happiness.

Advertising also played an important role after the Wall Street Crash of 1929, when product styling was used to motivate people to begin spending again. One aspect of product styling was called 'streamlining' which was used to give products the image of progress and dynamism. These products were often made from new materials such as plywood, plastics and sheet metal.

The 1940s and 1950s

World War II (1939-1945) slowed down the development of the consumer society in the United States. In Europe, the war meant sheer devastation and eventually, a rebuilding process that extended well into the 1950s, when rationing in Britain was finally phased out. The materials shortages caused by the war meant that fashion took a back seat, as women did many of the traditional men's jobs. In order to do these jobs, women needed to wear functional work clothes, which they were reluctant to give up after the war. It was now acceptable for women to wear trousers and men's style jackets, rather than the formal kind of clothing worn pre-war.

After the war there was not much money around and manufacturers of mass-produced goods once again had to encourage people to buy. This resulted in the introduction in the USA of the concept of 'planned obsolescence'. In terms of the world's scarce resources, this rather wasteful strategy involved making small but very visible changes to the style of a product each year, making it clear who had the latest model car, toaster or radio. Backed up by enticing advertising, this perpetuated, so the theory went, a perpetual cycle of demand. In fashion terms the cycle of spring/summer and autumn/winter performs a similar role. For example: 'Mum, I can't wear these shoes. They've got square toes. All the new shoes have got pointy toes.' The fact that the first pair is barely worn becomes irrelevant. Suddenly, pointy toes – or cars – or longer skirts or metallic eye shadow as opposed to matt shades are 'must haves'. Designers are kept busy, cash registers ring, and jobs are created. A later and far more controversial development in the USA was the idea of designing products which would physically wear out after a short period of time, thereby increasing demand for new products. By the end of 1950s the 'throw-away' society was upon us.

TASKS

1 Sales of fashion products depend on keeping consumers interested through changes in colour and styling. This means that we are encouraged to buy new products and throw away perfectly wearable clothes just because they are out of fashion. Is this ethical or moral? Explain your view on this issue.

2 Explain how Dior's 'New Look' of 1947 inspired the rock and roll skirts worn by teenagers in the 1950s. (see page 134)

3 Who was James Dean and what did his clothing style say about 1950's casual fashion?

After the austerity of World War II the theme of glamour returned with a vengeance, in the form of the 'New Look' in 1947 by Christian Dior. Full skirts and tight bodices were a revelation to a society used to coupons, rationing and functional clothing. The New Look style provided women with a bit of extravagance, but many people thought that it was inappropriate for most women's lifestyles and there were riots after it was shown on the catwalk. Some women were attacked for wearing the fashion, because it was also thought to be wasteful in an era of re-building after the war. The style was important though, because it inspired the look of the fifties, with full skirts and narrow waists. Teenagers in Europe and the USA took it up.

The 1950s

By the late 1950s and 1960s, on both sides of Atlantic, the so-called 'baby boomers', who were born just after the war, were growing up into a powerful and highly impressionable group of consumers – teenagers. This new group of consumers was (and still is) an important target market group. What was new in the 1950s was that teenagers had not existed before – not, that is, as a consumer group! Previously teenagers wore what their parents wore – there was no teenage fashion. One of the most visible aspects of teenage culture was to be seen in 'teddy boys', wearing American-style hair cuts, long drape jackets, narrow trousers and thick-soled shoes. Girls wore tight blouses and full skirts (à la Dior New Look) with wide belts and flat shoes – perfect for rocking and rolling! While the global village was still some years away, we were entering what social commentator Marshall McLuhan called 'the medium is the message' era. Television, in particular, with its heady mix of aspirational programming and advertising, was touching people's lives all over the world, creating new wants and helping dictate spending patterns.

TASK

Make notes to explain the changes in society and influences on lifestyles that led to the culture of teenage fashion. Compare the fashion of the 1950s and 1960s with what we wear today.

The 1960s and 1970s

The 1960s was another huge turning point in fashion. It was a time when young people rebelled against the ideas and fashions of their parents, the time of liberal reform movements such as the civil rights movement, anti-Vietnam War demonstrations and the 1968 student revolution on Paris. It was the age of 'flower power' and hippies and experimentation. It was also the age of the mini-skirt, Op-Art, space travel, the designer Mary Quant and unisex trouser suits. The real change that came about in the sixties was that youth culture became the role model for fashion – and 'street' fashion became the inspiration for Haute Couture. The Hippie movement in particular was closely linked with the interest in ethnic and Indian clothing and the culture of the East – which continue to influence designers today. This revolution in fashion led to the development of new young markets for designers – most Haute Couture houses developed RTW lines in the 1960s and 1970s – all fuelled by the media, pop culture and advertising.

Dramatic change was to happen again in the 1970s, with the development of three very different aspects of fashion – the work of the Japanese designer Issey Miyake and UK designer Vivienne Westwood. (See page 166)

THE 'NEW' INDUSTRIAL AGE OF HIGH-TECHNOLOGY PRODUCTION

Growth in 'high-technology' manufacturing has taken place since the mid 1980's. It has led to the use of many new types of materials and production methods and the development of new products. Many of the most exciting product developments bring together the fields of art, design, science and engineering. Textile materials these days are said to be 'engineered' – that is, they are developed to have specific characteristics that target fashion, industrial, technical and medical end-uses. Not only are textiles such as Kevlar and carbon fibres being used to replace traditional materials like steel, but also textile constructions are being used in high-tech engineered products. Some of the most exciting engineering developments include:

- the use of woven glass fibres in the manufacture of nose cones for the Tornado F3 fighter
- silicon carbon knitted parts for a Rolls-Royce jet engine
- the use of braided fibres in rocket motors.

MICRO-ELECTRONICS

Many new developments combine textile materials and micro-electronics to produce what are often called 'smart textiles'. These 'wearable electronics' aim to improve our ability to communicate or enable the wearer to survive in dangerous situations. The new generation of 'intelligent' clothing may also take sportswear into an entirely new dimension. Sportswear could soon be capable of monitoring heart rate, blood pressure, and body temperature and incorporate heating materials, radio transmitters and location monitors driven by global positioning systems (like those used in boats). These innovations could be potential lifesavers for skiers buried in an avalanche or climbers who are lost or injured. Such developments in intelligent sportswear will, in time, bring a number of benefits for consumers, such as:

- higher levels of comfort
- improved safety features for high-risk sports
- enhanced performance potential in a range of sports
- the potential for new feats of achievement
- the potential for ageing or disabled consumers to develop new sporting abilities.

DEVELOPMENTS IN MATERIALS

Often, developments in materials or products come about as a result of exploration or the need to work in dangerous situations. In space exploration, for example, the need to survive outside the earth's atmosphere resulted in the development of many high performance fabrics used in space suits.

Recent attempts to fly around the world by balloon also lead to the development of a range of technical innovations in balloon development and demonstrate the use of high-tech textile materials. The Breitling Orbitor balloon incorporated leading-edge innovations in the design to make it as safe as possible. The balloon consisted of four separate parts, all using high-tech textile materials:

- a helium-filled gas cell made from nylon, coated with a special gas-tight laminate
- a hot-air cone located directly above the burners made of nylon fitted with a nine-metre flame skirt of special heat-resistant Nomex fabric
- a heat reflective outer skin made from Mylar to reduce heat loss at night and minimise solar heating during the day
- a patented 'crown tent' above the gas cell, made from Mylar to further control unwanted solar heat gain. The tent was fitted with solar panels to power a cooling fan during hot daylight hours.

The bright yellow pressurised capsule in which the balloonists flew was made from a specially constructed composite of Kevlar and carbon fibre, which was stronger than metal alloys but half their finished weight. On-board equipment was made from a range of special fibres:

- sleeping bags made from Dacron polyester were filled with Hollowfil polyester fibre
- mattress covers, balloon bags and camera bags were made from hard-wearing, durable nylon Cordura
- all lines and thread were made from high strength Kevlar
- oxygen pipes were internally coated with Teflon
- protective clothing such as suits and gloves were made from heat-resistant Nomex.

TASK

Flexible textile materials are increasingly being used in combination with glass, metal, ceramic and carbon fibres or with micro-electronics to provide innovative new products. It almost seems as if Star Trek will be upon us sooner than we think.

1 What will life be like in the future? Will all these developments in interactive technology actually improve our lives? Will schools exist in the future, for example? What kind of textile products will we need or wear?

2 Brainstorm your ideas about the above issues and discuss with a partner. Produce some quick sketches of the most outlandish ideas you can think of for exciting new textile products. What will they do? What kind of materials will be used? Can you incorporate any of your ideas into your coursework project?

THE GLOBAL MARKET PLACE

These days, it would be unthinkable for any large company to be able to survive without the use of Information and Communications Technology (ICT). One of the key impacts of ICT is the growth of what is called the 'global market place' – designing, manufacturing, marketing and selling products on a global scale. To be successful at this level, a company has to develop products that have a global appeal. It is interesting to note how some products that have been around for a number of years sometimes change the name under which they are sold. Recently, for example, the kitchen cleaner sold in the UK as 'Jif' has changed its name to 'Cif' to bring it in line with what it is called in Europe.

Branding is a key marketing tool in the global economy and brands like Coca Cola and McDonalds are universal. The price of a Big Mac is even used as an international benchmark for judging consumer purchasing power! In the textiles and clothing sectors, several brands are global, including Woolmark, Gore-Tex, Lycra, Teflon, Tactel, Scotch-Gard, Nike and Adidas. Establishing a brand identity is vital for success in the global economy. To be successful a brand must:

- offer customers value that is over and above that of a non-branded product
- be backed by strong global marketing and promotion
- be supported by up-to-date production and distribution systems – so the product gets to the market
- be re-positioned in the market to take account of changing consumer needs.

CASE STUDY: THE CONTEMPORARY CONSUMER

The following case study shows how the textile company DuPont initiates a new advertising campaign to support the TACTEL® brand on a global scale.

The contemporary consumer

Lifestyle trends and consumer attitudes are radically changing the apparel market. The new 'contemporary consumer', defined by attitude not age, is someone who wears clothes to express their individuality and has a keen interest in new materials and ideas. Apparel retailers are working ever harder to attract disposable income in competition with technology products such as mobile phones and computers, and leisure and travel, which are increasingly appealing to the consumer with money to spend.

'ALL YOU CAN IMAGINE' advertising campaign

Awareness of TACTEL® has grown rapidly throughout Europe, from 8% in 1991 to 25% in 1999. Building on this success, DuPont is implementing a new, creative business and communications strategy – and an imaginative and dynamic new advertising campaign – to give a fresh element of emotional appeal to the brand across all its markets and at all levels of the textile chain.

This new direction for TACTEL® will reflect more closely the rapidly changing trends in both the apparel market and in consumer attitudes. The future of the business will be based on focusing both TACTEL® innovation and the TACTEL® brand communication on the needs of the 'contemporary consumer'.

The TACTEL® 'All you can imagine' consumer advertising campaign was launched in Spring 2001, and will appear primarily in mainstream fashion and sports titles, providing the focus for a wide range of consumer branding and retail promotional activities.

The new TACTEL® logo

As part of the new brand approach, the TACTEL® logo has evolved into a new, easier-to-read, fashion label look, creating a direct link to textiles through its 'woven' appearance. 'Benefit' swing tickets will carry the new logo and campaign slogan, conveying the consumer benefits throughout different garment categories. The 'Essential' swing ticket will also carry the new TACTEL® logo and slogan to further reinforce the overall TACTEL® vision and direction within the global textile and apparel industry.

MANUFACTURING IN THE GLOBAL MARKET PLACE

The emergence of multinational manufacturing companies has been closely linked to the international trade in minerals and mining and in products produced from food and cotton plantations. Many manufacturing companies became 'multinationals' during the boom in consumer spending in the 1950s, especially those making products such as cars and electrical goods.

At the outset of the 21st century, the trend towards global manufacturing is continuing at an increasing rate, driven largely by the forces of efficiency and competition and developments in Information and Communications Technology (ICT). Global industry covers a wide range of activities. Their brand names are recognised from one end of the earth to the other:

- DuPont, Nike, Reebok, Marks and Spencer (clothing)
- BP, Shell (petroleum)
- Ford, Toyota, General Motors (cars)
- Nokia, IBM, Philips, Sony, Panasonic (electronics)
- Barclays (finance),
- Coca Cola, Kellogg's (food)
- Sheraton, Hilton, Trust House Forte (hotels)

THE IMPACT OF ELECTRONIC COMMUNICATIONS OF GLOBAL MANUFACTURING

Globalisation and international competition will continue to be driven by the high-speed information revolution that has resulted in fast electronic communications. Competition for many companies means reducing labour and materials costs. It is global manufacturing that makes this possible, with manufacturing operations often moved from country to country to take advantage of lower labour costs. In clothing and textiles, for example, many European and American 'brand name' products are designed in the parent country but actually made in Asia or North Africa where labour costs are much lower. Likewise with cars and many other goods. Improved electronic communications, vital to the effective functioning of multinational companies, make it easier for designing to be done in one country, manufacturing in another, followed by global marketing and selling.

ECONOMIC, ENVIRONMENTAL, MORAL, POLITICAL AND SOCIAL ISSUES RELATED TO GLOBAL MANUFACTURING

Free trade and the emergence of the global economy are having a major impact on quality of life, employment and the environment across the world. While the head offices of most multinationals are located in the developed world (usually western Europe or north America), some multinationals are also based in newly industrialised countries (NICs), such as Singapore, Korea or Taiwan. These countries are becoming steadily more prosperous.

Developing countries in Africa or Asia have generally welcomed multinationals and the benefits that the location of manufacturing there brings, such as investment and regular employment for large numbers of people. Globalisation, like any other social change in history, has its drawbacks and its critics – witness the demonstrations in 1999 and 2000 outside World Economic Forum meetings in Seattle, London and Melbourne. Clearly, global manufacturing has advantages and disadvantages.

On the positive side, in newly industrialised countries (NICs) and the developing world, global manufacturing:

- provides employment and higher living standards
- may improve the expertise of the local workforce
- brings foreign currency into the country to improve their balance of payments
- widens a country's economic base
- enables the transfer of new technology to the developing country.

On the negative side, global manufacturing for NICs and developing countries:

- can cause environmental damage
- may provide mainly low-level skill jobs
- may mean that the top jobs are filled by executives from the developed world
- may mean company profits are exported back to the developed world
- may mean that multinationals cut corners on health and safety or pollution in a way they would not do in their 'home' country
- can mean political pressure is exerted by companies whose real interests lie outside that country
- may mean that raw materials are exported or not processed locally in the developing country
- may do little for local standards of living as many goods are exported and not for the local home market (where many people could not afford them anyway)
- may mean major decisions effecting people's lives are made tens of thousands of kilometres away with little regard for local conditions.

TASKS

The development of global manufacturing has given rise to many moral and ethical questions that are inherent in product design and manufacture. Global manufacturing will continue to have an effect on most people worldwide. It is a good idea to keep up with the latest happenings by reading newspapers, especially the financial ones.

The following topics are worth discussing to find out who are the winners and losers, in the race for jobs and quality of life, set against concerns about the environment and pollution:

1 The effects of the global economy on lifestyles in the developing world
   - the ethics of advertising products that many people cannot afford
   - the imposition of values of the developed world on traditional cultures.

2 The responsibility of multinationals for society and the environment
   - the effects of building new factories, transporting raw materials and products
   - the effects on energy demands in NICs and the developing world
   - the need for multinationals to follow sustainable manufacturing practices.

3 The need to conserve resources
   - the effects of deforestation
   - over-use of the world's natural resources
   - how to avoid the effects of global warming
   - how to avoid the loss of bio-diversity in many countries.

4 Problems associated with unemployment
   - moving manufacturing away from the developed world
   - the effect on NICs of relocating manufacturing where it's cheapest, i.e. from Hong Kong to China
   - how to overcome the threat of unemployment in a global economy.

5 Payment of debt by developing countries
   - the need to pay international debt to world financial institutions
   - the ethics of paying debt rather than spending money on food and development
   - the ethics of a developing country exporting food to pay debt during a famine.

INFLUENCES ON THE DEVELOPMENT OF PRODUCTS

THE IMPORTANCE OF DESIGN

Designing and making products is a complex activity, dependent of any number of factors. It is not always easy to know why some products are successful, but the way they are made, how they perform, how they are used and disposed of are issues that affect all consumers. Whether we realise it or not, every person who shops is part of the fascinating world of marketing. How do we choose which products to buy? Do we really need everything we spend our hard-earned money on? What is impulse buying? Are sales products good value? Do we recognise and go for quality products? Is good design important?

The answer to this last question is definitely yes. The Design Council recently surveyed 800 UK manufacturers about the importance of good design in the nation's overall economy. The results were extremely clear, since more than 92 per cent of businesses agreed that design helps to produce a competitive advantage. At the same time 87 per cent believed that good design can boost profits and pave the way to enter new markets.

When thinking about what we mean by good design it is interesting to know that in the 16th century the word 'design' meant a 'plan from which something is to be made'. This is similar to the term we use today, when we use the word design to mean the drafting and planning of industrial products. One important outcome of industrialisation has been the requirement for the profession of the 'designer', who drafts and plans everything from clothes and accessories to aircraft carriers and furniture.

Design as a means of self-expression

From small business to multinationals, companies are in business for one purpose – to make money for their owners, be they one person or millions of shareholders. If companies do not make money they go out of business and jobs are lost. For this reason, the design of products must be market driven. The vital link between market, profit and design also makes good designers highly valued (and well paid) members of any corporate team.

Design must also be market-led, taking into account the needs of the target market group and the various influences of market trends, such as colour and style. Many consumers these days see innovative design as an important means of self-expression. This is a relatively new trend, because for most of the 19th century clothes were a badge of social status or a way to keep warm. Ordinary people wore what was given to them or what others of the same class wore. The idea of style didn't exist for the masses and the idea that an individual could buy what she wanted based on personal taste was a revolutionary concept in the early years of the 20th century.

How different it is today when we can choose products not just for what they do, but also for what they tell the world about us. Products are no longer functional items bought purely for their usefulness and durability. For example, many people buy a Range Rover or other four wheel-drive vehicle not to go over rough country terrain but to drive themselves and their children around local city streets. Such high performance products have a sense of glamour; they impart the 'feel good' factor. We might buy a kitchen table not just as a functional product, but also because it can express a sense of tradition (country-style) or modernity (stainless steel top).

TASK

Image and style are all-important for many young people today. Even the 'tweens' – the 10–14 year olds are getting in on the act. Kids these days are bombarded with images and brands and have to put up with peer pressure about what they are wearing. For some it is essential to wear the right trainers, the right perfume, the right brands. What does this say about our society? Explain your views on image and style.

THE INFLUENCE OF AESTHETICS, FORM AND FUNCTION

AESTHETICS AND PRODUCT RELIABILITY

Today, for most products from mobile phones to cars, product reliability is no longer an issue. It is taken for granted. Most products these days carry guarantees and consumers are protected by legislation overseeing product quality and safety. Often, most leading brands in a given product category perform equally well. Does a Sony CD really play the music any differently from the Panasonic or Hitachi variety? In many product categories, therefore, the main reason for buying is how a product looks – its aesthetic qualities. This means that the primary purpose of many product designers is to inject a sense of personality in mass-produced objects – should the product look traditional, retro or high-tech?

What has also changed these days is that busy consumers also want to but products that are simple to operate and functional. Even in the clothing industry where image is all, busy, working people demand clothing that is easy-care and that requires minimal ironing. Sometimes, function even takes second place. For instance, does anyone buy platform shoes because they are durable, comfortable shoes?

FORM AND FUNCTION

For many years the connection between form and function has been one of the most controversial issues in design. Earlier, we learned that when mass-production first came about in Victorian times, goods were highly decorated – they were poor imitations of hand-made products. Whether the decoration was appropriate or not it was all-pervasive, from the ornate red roses on chamber pots to the vast carved frames of basic furniture.

Changes in design

The development of 'reform' groups such as the Arts and Crafts Movement gradually brought about long-overdue change in the concept of design. Products began to be functional and simplified and made from suitable materials. Why pay for oak kitchen fittings when functional polished pine is just as effective and often looks better? By the early years of the 20th century, many new products were coming on to the market. The earliest telephones or typewriters, for example, were the products of mechanical innovations – they were 'inventions'. Nobody had any pre-conceived ideas of what they should look like. As new products came on the markets, and competition hotted up between telephone manufacturers, for example, the appearance of the goods were an important point of difference. Coloured phones appeared, phones with antique trimmings, futuristic clear plastic phones and wall phones. Mobile phones today are a good example. The first ones on the mass market, about a decade ago, were invariably large, black and plain. While even more functional today, consumers often choose their phones on the basis of colour and style.

Mass production

From the early 20th century up to the1970s, the functional and technical requirements of mass production were the benchmarks for the form of industrial products – what they should look like. Mass produced products were standardised and their components simplified to make them easy and cheap to produce. The supporters of functionalism had won the day – product forms had to be functional and without excessive decoration.

The new concept of individualism

The 1980s, 90s and the early years of the new century, however, continue to see a new focus on creativity and style. Different influences have contributed to this, including concepts relating to individualism – and there is currently a move towards mass produced customisation of products, brought about by the increasing use of computers in manufacturing. There is a new emphasis on colour and form, as manufacturers strive to establish points of difference between themselves and their competitors. Such examples would include Apple's coloured computers or the distinctive appearance of Reebok trainers as opposed to Nike. Faced with ever-increasing competition, many manufacturers have to work harder in terms of design and marketing to attract and keep customer loyalties. Marks and Spencer, for example, are working hard to regain their once-strong hold on high street clothes spending, by paying far greater attention than before to design and marketing.

The function of products

The fundamental argument over form and function continues today in all its complexities. Student designers are often asked to simplify their designs for ease of manufacture. For any designer these days it is essential to realise that any successful product must have three basic functions:

- a practical and technical function – it must 'work' efficiently
- an aesthetic function – it must look good and be stylish
- a symbolic function – it must enhance its user's or wearer's image.

Today's products, especially clothes, furniture and cars are designed to communicate a message. They say if the owner has style, savvy – whether they are a winner. Image, of course, should not be confused with happiness (this idea could spark an entire psychology course). But the pragmatics of today's world are such that image and marketing matter a great deal to product designers and manufacturers.

TASK

Choose two products – fashion or household. Describe the target market for each product and the image that each gives the user. Make quick sketches to improve each product:
- for the same target market
- for a different target market.

Aesthetic and functional properties

While aesthetics and function are clearly important to the success of products, so, too, is consistency. It is for this reason that companies usually prefer to make changes in a product's colour and styling gradually rather than suddenly from one season to the next. Buyers of Doc Marten shoes, for instance, expect the latest ones to 'look likes Docs' – just a bit different/better than the last pair they bought. Building on already successful designs and marketing styles, leading companies tend to maintain their own style of 'handwriting'. Where the changes are gradual, an existing product design specification is often used to develop a new one.

- Aesthetic properties relate to the look of a textile product, matching its style with its end-use, e.g. matching aesthetic properties such as drape, soft handle or trendy colours with a fashion garment. As a student product designer you will need to develop an 'eye' for aesthetic characteristics, such as balance, line and shape, texture and surface pattern. Scale too is an important consideration, especially for fabric designers. It is a good idea to collect fabric swatches with different size patterns. Decide a suitable end-use for each fabric you collect.

- Colour is an essential characteristic of fashion products and it is a powerful marketing tool, which can encourage consumers to buy. Fashions in household products gradually change and at the time of writing the influence of the 1960's colours is strong.

- Functional properties relate to the technical performance of a textile product, matching its performance with its end-use, e.g. matching high-strength and lightweight fabrics with a bullet-proof vest.

DESIGN AND CULTURE

Industrial and commercial design as we know it started with the industrial revolution and the developing need for 'designers'. Since that time, designers have been increasingly influenced by what they see around them, by products already on the market and by the work of other designers and artists. Designers of any products these days need to be aware of market trends and of the values of the target market – those social, cultural and environmental influences that affect us all, whether we realise it or not. What these trends and influences do is to provide starting points for designers. In a commercial world no designer starts with a blank sheet. There is no time to start from scratch. Designers therefore need to develop an understanding of what has gone before and what is likely to happen in the future.

The next section discusses some of the design movements dating from the end of 19th century. It includes the influential Arts and Crafts movement, Art Nouveau, the Bauhaus, Art Deco and the 1980s movement called Memphis. It is impossible in a book such as this to examine every possible influence on design. Therefore, you should broaden your reading on the subject beyond this book.

If you have favourite designers, read about them in books, in magazines or on the Internet. Study their work and the factors that have influenced them and draw on this knowledge when you answer examination questions.

THE ARTS AND CRAFTS MOVEMENT

The Arts and Crafts movement is called a 'reform movement' because it was closely associated with the 'anti-industrial' movement that came about in the late 19th century. William Morris (1834–96) was the most influential thinker of the Arts and Crafts movement. His philosophy revolved around a love of simple design, inspired by the Middle Ages when art and production were closely connected in medieval craft 'guilds'. Morris saw the effects of industrialisation – environmental pollution, poverty for workers and the production of poor quality products – and proposed the reform of commercial art in order to manufacture well-designed and well-crafted consumer goods.

This was the start of a revolt against the over decorated products beloved by well-off Victorians. The Arts and Crafts movement promoted the idea of handcrafted products as being superior to industrial ones. William Morris started his company, Morris & Co., in 1861, to manufacture furniture, natural-dyed fabric, hand-woven rugs, wallpaper, painted tiles and stained glass. His company produced practical and comfortable wooden chairs, like the ladderback or Windsor. In the past this style of chair was used in working class cottages and now found a place in the homes of the wealthy. This type of simple undecorated furniture created a demand for simplicity of design and fitness for purpose. It had an important influence on Art Nouveau, the Bauhaus, on Scandinavian and UK design and can be said to form the basis of modern design in Europe.

The legacy of William Morris is still seen today. Working to his famous saying: 'Have nothing in your houses that you do not know to be useful or believe to be beautiful', Morris raised the design of everyday domestic accessories and fittings to an art form. He drew his inspiration from the flowing shapes of nature and interpreted them as repeat prints for wallpaper and textiles. These products represented the values of 'truth to materials and form'. Morris's style has been reproduced and reinterpreted throughout the 20th century, making him one of the UK's most influential textile designers. Today, manufacturers such as Liberty's and Sanderson are still producing textiles inspired by Morris. Check out your closest National Trust shop for textile accessories inspired by William Morris!

TASK

Modern manufacturers still sell machine-printed wallpaper and fabrics of William Morris's designs. Cite some modern examples of products inspired by William Morris.

ART NOUVEAU

Art Nouveau was an important reform movement that developed at the turn of the 19th century in France. It developed into an international movement between 1895 and the First World War. Art Nouveau styling was built around the use of:

- simple natural forms
- the curved lines and shapes of climbing plants
- geometric forms based on Japanese art.

Art Nouveau was an influential decorative style, which was used in architecture, wrought ironwork, glass, furniture, fabrics and wallpaper. The paintings of Gustav Klimt, often used as inspiration by textile designers, typify the Art Nouveau style.

In some ways Art Nouveau was similar to the Arts and Crafts movement. Art Nouveau designers:

- considered themselves to be artists rather than designers
- rejected industrial mass production
- produced design work that was only available to the wealthy.

Art Nouveau is sometimes described as being between art and industry, because it encouraged a return to handcrafted products. Some say that it delayed the development of modern industrial design.

TASK

Investigate domestic products that are inspired by the Art and Crafts movement and the Art Nouveau movement. Explain the similarities and differences between the products in terms of their form, decoration and styling.

THE BAUHAUS (1919 – 1933)

The Bauhaus school was founded by the architect Walter Gropius in 1919 and ran until the Nazis closed it in 1933, in an effort to stop modernism in design. In 1937 the 'new' Bauhaus was founded in the USA, where the Bauhaus style became known as the 'International Style'. Although this was mainly concerned with architecture, architects such as Le Corbusier and Alvar Alto also designed furniture, which followed the Bauhaus design style.

The place of the Bauhaus as the centre of modernism and functionalism is unchangeable, because it laid down basic principles of design that are still meaningful today. These design principles influence modern teaching about industrial design – many Bauhaus products still look modern today. The principal aims of the Bauhaus were to use modern materials and to combine the concepts of 'form and function'.

Design education in the Bauhaus school was centred on a preliminary apprenticeship in which students experimented with colour, form and modern materials. In some ways it had a similar philosophy to the reforming Art and Crafts movement, because it offered an education in artistic and handicraft skills. The Bauhaus art training was given by important artists of the day, such as Johannes Itten, Lyonel Feininger, Paul Klee, Georg Muche and Oscar Schlemmer. It was the first time that professional artists were involved in teaching future industrial designers.

The key difference from the Arts and Crafts movement was that the Bauhaus linked the design of products to their manufacture by industry. Students chose one of the commercial workshops for carpentry, pottery, metalwork, textiles, stage design, photography or commercial art. The longest running and most successful of all the Bauhaus workshops was textiles, which was run by and attended by women. Textiles, in the hierarchy of art and design, were seen as 'women's work' – a philosophy that still exists in some minds today. However the Bauhaus textile designers were talented designers who embraced technology and incorporated the use of new or unusual materials, such as cellophane, leather and early synthetics. The result was a rebirth of hand weaving and a new professionalism in designing textiles for mass production. The Bauhaus textile designers created fabrics that:

- had acoustic and light-reflecting properties
- were reversible
- were multi-layered, with some combining double and triple weaves
- were made by the Jacquard loom

In the metal workshop too, students were encouraged to use new materials – such as steel tubing, plywood and industrial glass. The aim here was also to produce economical mass-produced products, such as table lamps, metal teapots and chairs.

TASK

Choose an artist or designer whose work inspires you.
- Make sketches of aspects of the work that you like.
- Try to integrate these aspects into design work for your next project.

ART DECO

Art Deco was originally a French phenomenon that was influential in the early decades of the 20th century. Although the Art Deco style was thought to be highly modern and elegant, it was definitely anti mass production. It focused on one-off, expensive products made from precious materials like snakeskin, ivory, bronze, crystal and exotic woods. Later on materials like steel, glass and plastics were used, but the aim was to exploit their decorative characteristics rather than any functional properties.

The Art Deco style was influenced by Art Nouveau, Cubism, Futurism, African Art and Egyptian cultures. In furniture and other products the styling made use of geometric shapes and zigzag patterns or ornamental inlays imitating ivory or tortoiseshell. Although it was anti mass production, Art Deco did influence the design of many mass-produced products that were made from new materials such as aluminium and Bakelite – one of the first synthetic materials, invented in 1907. Bakelite was perfect for making into everyday products, such as radios, because it is a malleable, durable and inexpensive material.

The Art Deco style was used extensively in domestic interiors and architecture between 1920 and 1939. Examples include some remaining Odeon cinemas and railway stations. The great couturiers such as Poiret, Chanel, Lanvin and Schiaparelli were all influential designers of the Art Deco era.

TASK

Investigate the work of ONE couturier of the Art Deco era. Describe their work, using sketches and notes.

MEMPHIS

Memphis (no connection to the home of Elvis Presley in Tennessee) was the name of a group of designers who established themselves in Milan in Italy in 1981. The main figure in the group was the architect Ettore Sottass, a consulting product designer for the typewriter manufacturer Olivetti. The Memphis designers were interested in the practical objects of daily life, such as the Bel Air chair, the mass production of such objects and their promotion and marketing through advertising. Influenced by comic strips, films, punk music and different combinations of materials, their witty, stylistic designs typified the fast pace of interior fashion in the 1980s.

Memphis designers combined materials such as colourful plastic laminates (such as melamine and formica, used in 1950s and 60s bars and cafés), glass, steel, industrial sheet metal and aluminium. Some of their products resembled children's toys, so not surprisingly they were a huge hit with the 'born to shop' set. Emerging at exactly the right time, in the '80s, the Memphis group introduced a new understanding of design, the main purpose of which was decorative and witty, rather than functional. The group's sheer innovation and boldness influenced any number of bright, interesting ideas that emerged around that time. It sparked a chain reaction across Europe, most notably in Spain, Germany, France and the UK. Inspired by Memphis, designers shunned the purely functional in favour of the funky.

THE DEVELOPMENT OF MODERN DESIGN AND STYLING

In the 1980s, social, technical, ecological, cultural and style influences developed at a rapid pace. In the process, the status of design itself increased and took over a key role in product marketing and advertising and in the development of individual life styles. In fact the 1980s became known as the decade of design – and the decade of extravagance and consumption. It was also the decade of the 'body' when aerobics and the ability to shape the body according to the prevailing whims of fashion indicated an individual's level of self-discipline. Aerobics was the fashionable sport of the time, when women wore T-shirts, leg-warmers, trainers and headbands, whether they were athletic or not. The pop star Madonna became an icon of the 80s and contributed to the sporty element in fashion. The influence of sporty styling on fashion has been a recurring them throughout the 80s and 90s – especially in the use of modern 'breathable' materials and elastane in everyday garments.

TASK

Investigate one of the design movements described in the last section.

- Produce sketches and notes to show the style and colour of typical products made by designers in that movement.
- Explain how the materials used in the product influenced its design.

NEW MATERIALS, PROCESSES AND TECHNOLOGY

There are many reasons for the creation of new materials, most of which relate to keeping the consumer motivated to buy new products and in maximising sales and profits. In the decades after the Second World War there were many new developments in synthetic polymers – nylon, polyester, the aramids, elastane, polypropylene and viscose brought about unheard of benefits for consumers. Nylon and polyester fibres were easy-care, crease resistance and low-cost, with a good handle. Unfortunately the use of nylon in men's shirts in the 1950s was not successful. It was not breathable, so nylon itself had a poor image for a number of years. This has all changed now, of course, with the development of breathable microfibres – and the fibre is now sold under different brandnames, such as 'Tactel'. Viscose became popular because it was marketed as an artificial silk, that was cheaper and more easy-care than the real thing.

The development of foam materials and polypropylene (invented in 1952) revolutionised the furniture-making and carpet industries. Polypropylene, together with developments in other plastics, made it possible to produce chairs and other products in all possible shapes and sizes with the single action of a moulding machine.

Many recent developments in modern materials are based on fibre blending. This has long been used to develop new characteristics and properties in fabrics. Fibre blends can:

- lower the cost of an expensive fibre
- improve a fabric performance and aesthetics
- widen the option of using different types of finishes.

Many modern developments in materials used for everyday products have resulted in the consumer's interest in activewear – elastane, for example, is now used widely in fashion products because it allows a body-hugging form without any loss of movement.

TASK

Investigate the kind of fabrics that were used in fashion products between the 1950s and the 1970s – maybe you could talk to an older person about the clothes they wore. Compare these products with what is available today.

- What kinds of blends are used in fashion products today? What are their properties?
- How many modern fashion products make use of elastane or microfibres?
- Draw up a chart to explain your findings.

ENVIRONMENTAL ISSUES

Environmental issues are often the starting point for developments in textile technology. For example, cotton is still the most used fibre in the world, but it needs vast amounts of pesticide to help it grow. Technologists have developed natural bio-pesticides to provide a low cost, environmentally friendly alternative to chemical treatments. Other environmental concerns have led to the recycling of plastic bottles, which can be turned into fibres for knitting jumpers, socks or gloves!

TASKS

1 With changing environmental needs the whole process of design and manufacturing may change. Design for recycling or for a second use may be one of the most important requirements of designers in the future. Already textile technologists are developing ways of recycling materials, such as plastics. How many bottles do you think are needed to make a jumper?

2 'We live in a 'throw away' society, relying on convenience foods, cheap clothes and computer technology. We work at home and rarely go out even to buy food, because we order from the supermarket via electronic mail. We wear warm comfortable clothes and when we are tired of them they go out with the rubbish. Our dustbins need to be emptied three times a week. We don't know or care what happens to the rubbish – out of sight out of mind.'

- Explain what you think about this statement.
- Could this be the lifestyle in the future?
- What happens to our rubbish?
- Should we try and recycle rather than throw away?
- Come up with a range of designs for recycled textile products.
- Did you guess that 27 PVC bottles were recycled to make the jumper?

MINIATURISATION

One of the most interesting technological developments in recent years has been in the field of micro-electronics. Products are becoming smaller through advances in microchip technology and previously unimaginable products are now being developed. Star Trek here we come!!

It was as far back as the 1950s that the first transistor radios and televisions appeared and the colour video recorder for home use was developed in 1966. But by far the most influential product in the 1980s was the 'Walkman', which had a remarkable impact on people's lifestyles. Products such as portable CD players are now widely available and the inexpensive miniature 'watch' TV is said to be not far off.

Some people say that the product that has had the greatest influence on lifestyles in the 1990s is the mobile phone, the plaything of the 'yuppies' in the 1980s. It is hard to imagine life without the instant communication and safety aspects that the mobile phone brings.

Developments in miniaturisation have not passed textiles products by. In fact some of the most exciting developments in micro-electronics are expected to be in their integration with textile materials – so-called 'wearable electronics'. Some of these products will provide a new generation of 'intelligent' clothing, which will take sportswear to an entirely new dimension. Exercise kits of the future may incorporate bio-sensors that monitor body temperature and heart rate as well as providing a personal stereo/information system. These new products are expected to be made from a range of traditional fibres like cotton or wool and the garments will be completely washable. Some garments may be powered by batteries, but eventually it may be possible to harness the body's heat as a natural, renewable power supply.

SMART MATERIALS

In recent years a range of so-called 'smart' materials have been developed, which respond to the needs of the wearer. In the near future you could be wearing underwear that smells of roses – the manufacturing process locks in fragrance microcapsules into the fibre, which gradually releases its scent as the wearer moves. Other developments include a green jacket that turns blue according to the weather – liquid crystals in the fabric or thermochromic dyes allow colour changes according to the temperature.

TASK

Many new textile materials have been developed to meet the needs of performance products, such as activewear. Outdoor pursuits retailers also stock products that use innovative materials.
- either visit a local store or make a class collection of performance textiles
- make a list of the criteria by which you can evaluate the products and materials used in them
- use a chart to collate the information you have gathered.

Chapter 2

Professional Designers at Work

THE RELATIONSHIP BETWEEN DESIGNERS OF ONE-OFF, BATCH-PRODUCED AND HIGH-VOLUME PRODUCTS AND CLIENTS, MANUFACTURERS, USERS AND SOCIETY

All textile product designers have to work in advance of the intended selling season, so there is time to design, manufacture and sell the product. Although many textile and fashion designers produce collections for spring/summer and autumn/winter, the trend now is for companies to produce mini-collections within these two seasons. This has mainly come about through the use of ICT systems, which manage huge amounts of product data and enable a faster product time to market. It must also be realised that the textile and clothing industry is fiercely competitive and manufacturers have to target different market segments that are ever changing in their needs and aspirations.

The product design cycles for different segments of the textile product industry may be similar, but designers generally work to different deadlines. For example:

- Colourists may work up to 24 months ahead of the season.
- Fabric designers may work up to 18 months ahead of the season.
- Garment and other product designers may work up to 12 months ahead of the season.

These days, textile product designers need to be creative and innovative, but at the same time have an in-depth understanding of fabric and product technology. Product design incorporates aesthetics, ergonomics (applied to fit and fabric), the choice of construction methods (stitch and seam types and the chemistry of fusible resins) and target costs and selling prices. Design starts off as an open and creative planning process, but later develops into solving defined problems.

THE ROLE OF THE DESIGNER

Good designers need to take account of the design policy of the company for which they work. This means taking account of company resources, the customer profile and the company marketing objectives. For many sectors of

the textile product supply chain, effective marketing is about branding, image and developing a competitive edge. In order to develop products with a competitive edge a good garment designer needs to:

- understand the working characteristics of fabrics
- source and use modern fabrics
- adapt styles for different sizes
- develop a product to a price point – in other words design to a set budget.

In order to achieve the development of a product to a price point, designers undertake some or all of the following activities:

1 Forecasting:
- fabrics – mainly woven, knits or print
- colour, texture and pattern
- silhouette
- new design trends/themes.

2 Range planning, depending on the product type:
- Staple products like overalls, men's underwear or school uniforms are often made by continuous production runs, with styling unchanged from year to year.
- Classic products such as men's shirts or jeans often have minimal changes to styling and have long production runs. Variations may be introduced by variations in fit or simple changes to the collar or cuff shapes.
- Styled products are generally based on one type of garment, like skirts, jackets or coats and have production runs that are shorter than for staple or classic products. Styled products have frequent changes to fabric, colour and styling.
- Fashion products have very frequent and extreme changes in design and fabric from one style of product to another. Production runs are short and the manufacturer needs to produce repeat orders very quickly to meet customer demand.

3 Designing, including the use of CAD
- design briefs and initial concepts
- mood boards and story boards
- sketches of initial ideas
- further ideas
- testing the feasibility of ideas against specifications
- working drawings
- specification sheets.

4 Pattern making, including the use of CAD/CAM
- flat pattern cutting using blocks and style templates
- working pattern to trial the garment style
- draping/modelling/toiles to test the design concept

- pattern adaptation and testing
- final pattern drafting

5 Sample making
- work to the specification sheet
- produce a sample garment

The influences that come to bear on textile product designers depend at which level they are working. Designers of exclusive Haute Couture products set the trends in their twice-yearly cat walk shows, in which they often aim to 'shock' in order to get those column centimetres. Many of these leading fashion designers produce 'diffusion' lines and ready-to-wear ranges, which also project their brand image and style, although they target a slightly lower price range. Many designers also work with large retail stores to produce product ranges that aim for high quality and style at an affordable price. (see Table 3B.1)

Table 3B.1

Fashion level	Product	Influence on other fashion levels	Influenced by
Haute Couture	Very high cost, exclusive, made-to-measure, high quality, high fashion	Set garment styling and fabric trends	Fabric and colour trends, values issues, performance fabrics, new materials and technology, user needs
Designer diffusion lines	High cost, high quality, fashion RTW	Set and follow trends	Fabric, colour and market trends, values issues, performance fabrics, new materials and technology
Designer ready-to-wear (RTW)	Medium cost, high quality, fashion RTW	Set and follow trends	Fabric, colour and market trends, values issues, performance fabrics, new materials
Ready-to-wear for retailers	More affordable, high quality, fashion RTW	Follow trends	Fabric, colour and market trends, values issues, performance fabrics
Bespoke	High cost, exclusive, made-to-measure, high quality	Less trend orientated, often more traditional styling	Fabrics and styling related to user needs
Mass production	Reasonable cost, range of qualities, defined target markets, range of styles, RTW	Follow major marketable trends	Fabric, colour and market trends, values issues, performance fabrics

THE ROLE OF DESIGN AND PRODUCTION TEAMS

These days many designers work as part of product design teams, which need to include creative and open-minded thinkers, problem solvers, technicians and financial planners. A designer fulfils some of these roles but the responsibility for ensuring that the designs can be produced easily and economically is the role of the technologist. The technologist also has to make sure that customers are assured of quality garments in wear and washing/dry cleaning. The role of the technologist includes some or all of the following activities:

1 Initial costings of the product

2 Evaluation of prototypes

- analysis of assembly for production
- production costs
- quality
- fit
- production of a sample garment to mirror the way it would be made on the factory floor.

3 Pattern grading

- for range of sizes, working to grading increments and size charts
- use of tolerances and seam allowances
- evaluation of styling and garment fit
- development of production patterns.

4 Technical specifications

- specification sheets
- details of materials, including fibre content, shrinkage, colourfastness, pilling, wear, aftercare
- details of interlinings, fastenings and trimmings
- manufacturing processes such as embroidery or pleating.

5 Monitoring production

- quality checks during production
- visits to factory in the UK or overseas to monitor production.

TASK

Describe the role of the designer and technologist within a production team involved in the manufacture of:
- Haute Couture garments
- mass produced garments.

Take into account considerations of fitness for purpose, value for money, fabric limitations, and methods of manufacture and styling/design details.

PROFESSIONAL PRACTICE RELATING TO DESIGN MANAGEMENT, TECHNOLOGY, MARKETING, BUSINESS, ICT

DESIGN AND MARKETING

One of the key features of successful marketing is the development of a marketing plan, aimed at the needs and wants of the target market group. A successful business develops a competitive edge through:

- producing well designed, reliable, high quality products at a price customers can afford.
- lifestyle marketing – giving consumers products with a desirable image. For example, Rolex watches uses opera singer Kiri Te Kanawa to market its 'Flawless' watches. Consumers, in turn, feel good about themselves when they buy and wear these watches.

Successful product development needs a clear target market group, which is often decided by market segmentation. This divides consumers into market segments that can be attracted to buy specific products. There are many ways of dividing up consumers, including the following:

- age groups – using demographic information about population numbers to target a specific age group
- gender – specialising in market segments such as womenswear, menswear or childrenswear
- level of disposable income – targeting the available spending money of consumers
- lifestyle – targeting the taste, lifestyle, level of retail/brand loyalty of specific consumers and the level or degree of their fashion interest
- product end-use – targeting market specific products such as special occasion, sports, leisure, corporate wear.

A marketing plan can involve advertising and promotion of products and brands through retailers, newspapers and magazines, TV, radio, film and the Internet. A successful marketing plan often make use of market research to accurately gauge:

- consumer needs and demand
- the age, income, size and location of the target market group or segment
- the product type customers want and what they will pay
- trends affecting the market. For example, rising home mortgage rates may slow down sales of fashion or interiors products
- competitors' products and marketing style (is there a new, rival product due out on the market at the same time as yours?)
- the estimated time required developing and marketing the product. It is no good selling lightweight purple trousers in three months' time when the

fashion for purple has diminished and the colder winter weather has arrived. Any fashion item that has a short shelf life needs forward planning and speedy marketing to catch the market at just the right time.

TASK

Products such as childrenswear, golfing wear and nightclub wear were designed for specific market segments.

1 Describe the characteristics of three products and the lifestyle of the market segments for which they were designed.

2 Describe the factors that would encourage a consumer to buy these products.

Figure 3B.1

EFFICIENT MANUFACTURE AND PROFIT

For all manufacturing companies, the bottom line is to make a profit from the sale of their products after all manufacturing costs have been taken into account. Therefore, to maximise profits (or minimise losses in a very bad year), it is essential that products be produced as efficiently as possible. This means:

- making the best use of resources – such as labour and capital
- selecting the most appropriate inputs (materials), processing them via the most economical and effective manufacturing methods so as to maximise outputs (products and profit).

Efficient design management is an essential part of efficient manufacture. The aim is to produce profits that can be reinvested in research and development of new or improved products.

One aspect of efficient manufacture is making sure that the forecast demand for a product matches the production capacity of a company. The term capacity is defined as the maximum numbers of products that can be made in a specified time. If the demand is too great for the level of production capacity available, orders will not be met and potential customers will be lost. If capacity is greater than demand, there is spare production capacity and under-use of resources – production workers may even have to be laid off. Making the correct forecast of the demand for a product is therefore very important.

AESTHETICS, QUALITY AND VALUE FOR MONEY

Although industrial textile products, such as airbags, tyres or oil filters, are made solely to meet performance requirements, many of these products also need to take account of aesthetic criteria. In fact the impact of 'fashion' on the design of all kinds of industrial and technical products is increasing. In the car industry for example, colour and style forecasting is used to predict the future needs and wants of consumers. Colour forecasting is even being used to predict future trends in gardening! It is in the design of fashion products, though, that the impact of aesthetics is most keenly felt, where lifestyle marketing and branding are well-established marketing tools.

Quality and value for money

In a competitive, global market place no product will sell if it is of poor quality. These days, consumers expect to be able to buy reliable, good quality products at a price they can afford. Good quality for the consumer is often described as 'fitness-for-purpose' – which can be evaluated through a product's performance, price and aesthetic appeal. All of these criteria must meet consumer needs if products are seen to be 'value for money'. As the saying goes: value for money is in the eye of the beholder!

For manufacturers product development involves juggling the competing needs of function, appearance, materials and cost. In many cases, there needs to be a compromise between quality and cost. Quality is therefore an important issue, both for designers and those responsible for marketing the product. As consumers have different amounts of money to spend, there will always be a need for products which vary in quality and hence in cost. For example, a company like Burberry makes some of the most appealing, high quality and long-lasting trench coats available today. Since many consumers will never be able to afford (or even want to buy) a high-cost classic coat, there will always be a need for cheaper outlets to sell coats for the same purpose and with similar performance criteria – medium-weight warmth and waterproof for showery days.

TASK

Manufacturing companies must take account of consumer demand when planning production schedules.

1 Explain the importance to manufacturers of forecasting consumer demand.

2 Discuss the relationship between aesthetic, quality and value for money.

CULTURAL, ECONOMIC, ENVIRONMENTAL, ETHICAL, MORAL, POLITICAL, SOCIAL AND POLITICAL ISSUES RELATED TO DESIGN

The so-called 'values' issues are those that have an impact on our lives and on the products that we use. In some instances values issues are the 'driving force' behind product development. An example of this is the introduction of legislation related to the environment. The need to follow such legislation often drives the development of new products or processes.

In the design field values issues are very important because there is an understanding that products carry powerful messages about the people who use them. These messages can change with fashion, so that what is cool one minute can be next season's embarrassment. Designers therefore need to consider very carefully the values of the market into which a product is aimed. This means keeping up with current and future trends relating to artistic, cultural and social influences and understanding how economic, political, ethical, moral and environmental issues impact on the interests of consumers.

- Fabric and clothing design, interior design and even car design are all influenced by cultural and social trends and by lifestyle issues. Many fashion designers, for example travel to exotic countries where traditional textiles are still practised. The influence of all things 'eastern' has been a strong trend in fashion and interiors for a number of seasons. Social influences, spread via the media (especially film, television and music) also have an impact on design. Exhibitions also stimulate interest in particular influences, be it Art Nouveau or minimalism.

- The economics of the global marketplace mean that many companies are now manufacturing 'off-shore', where labour costs are lower. This often results in designing in one country and making in another, with a loss of manufacturing and unemployment in some economies. For example, much of the textile manufacturing in Hong Kong has now gone to China.

- Values issues can be very sensitive and companies need to approach moral and ethical issues with great care. For example, fashion products considered desirable in western democracies might be frowned upon and even outlawed in strict Moslem countries. Other sensitive issues include the use of children to make carpets/rugs, so-called 'sweat shop' labour and the impact on economies and people of the minimum wage.

- Companies trading in many parts of the world also have to be careful that their product names do not cause offence to religious or cultural groups. Consideration also needs to be given to the ethics of imposing values from traditional industrialised nations on those countries that do not have the same tradition. For example sugary soft drinks are advertised on television worldwide but are of limited nutritional value to people who lack the basic essentials of life such as clean water and enough food. Is it moral to advertise such products and to create a demand for them?

MAKING VALUE JUDGEMENTS

One way of making value judgements about textile products is to ask questions about the products themselves. The table below shows a variety of questions that you could ask about products.

Questions about products	
1 Your response to the product • Do you want to touch or use it? • Who it is intended for? • Why would they buy it? • Would you like to own it? • What would this say reveal about you?	**4 The product manufacture** • What materials and components are used and why? • Where do the materials come from? Will they run out? • What other resources are used to manufacture the product? • What impact could using these resources have on people or the environment? • What happens to any waste produced during manufacture? • What skills are needed? • What are the working conditions in the place of manufacturing like?
2 The need for the product • Is the product needed? • Whose needs were identified to produce it? • Who benefits from the manufacture of the product? • How will they benefit?	**5 Promotion and marketing** • How is the product promoted and packaged? • What is the target market? What are their needs? • Does the product have an identity or image? • How has this been achieved? • How and where is the product sold? • What is its cost in relation to the income of the target market?
3 Design of the product • Who made decisions about the design? • Is there a choice of designs? • How was the design developed? • What influences had an impact on the design?	**6 Use and disposal** • How is the product used? • Will it have any impact on people's lives or the environment? • How long will it last? How will it be disposed of? • What factors may limit or lengthen the product life? • How easily can it be recycled? Who would pay the cost of recycling?

Table 3B.2

TASK

Select one fashion product and one functional product. For each product:

1 List the values issues in order of importance to potential customers.

2 Explain how the order would change for people of different age, culture or lifestyle.

3 Put the values in order of importance for the manufacturer.

THE WORK OF PROFESSIONAL DESIGNERS AND PROFESSIONAL BODIES

It is impossible in a book of this nature to include detailed information about every influential textile or fashion designer. The following list of designers is therefore intended as a starting point. It is not necessary for you to study of every designer listed – a more sympathetic approach would be to study the work of two or three designers whose work you admire. Keep a sketchbook with a collection of images and notes about their work, including the kind of fabrics, colours and silhouette they use, their design themes and the market they design for. Do they design for their 'own label', for fashion houses or do they have their own 'diffusion lines', sold in department stores?

One of the best ways of finding out about these designers is to collect articles and pictures about them from newspapers, which have weekly sections related to fashion. Many libraries also have electronic versions of newspapers, going back over the previous year. Some designers also have their own websites.

Chalayan, Hussein (1970-)

Hussein Chalayan graduated from Central St Martin's College of Art and Design in London in 1993. His final-year collection was bought by London's leading designer store called Browns. Chalayan is mostly known for his minimalist tailoring, using soft, fluid, luxurious fabrics. His 1997 collection of evening wear featured fine matt jersey, decorated with gold chains, gold embroidery and jet beads. He designs for his own label and for TSE New York.

Galliano, John (1960-)

John Galliano was born in Gibraltar and graduated from Central St Martin's College of Art and Design in London. He sold his graduation collection to the London designer store Brown's in 1984. He is one of the most creative and original designers of the late 20th century, whose clothes are often shocking. His collections are sometimes based on themes such as 'Fallen Angels'. Galliano also bases his ideas on historical themes, using contexts such as the Highlands of Scotland, the Russian Steppes, and American gangsters, to produce kilts, frock coats and ball gowns. Although Galliano raids historical themes for his ideas, he uses modern fabrics and precision tailoring with bias fabric cutting to create clothes that influence many other designers. In 1995 Galliano was made chief designer for the French fashion house Givenchy haute couture and RTW, but left in 1996 to design for Dior. He also designs for his own label.

Gaultier, Jean-Paul (1952-)

Jean-Paul Gaultier was apprenticed to the French fashion designers Jean Patou and Pierre Cardin and launched his own label in 1977. Since then, Gaultier has become one of the most influential French RTW designers. His clothes are humorous and sometimes outlandish, but always underpinned by his technical knowledge and skills. Gaultier cleverly mixes old and new fabrics, such as mixing lace and satin. He was influenced by London street styles in the late 1970s and by Punk and he redesigned the outmoded corset as an undergarment and recreated it as outerwear. The pop star Madonna wore Gaultier clothes during her world tours of the 1980s and early 1990s. Gaultier designs for Gaultier Paris, Gaultier Classique and JPG Jeans.

McCartney, Stella (1972-)

Stella McCartney graduated from Central St Martin's College of Art and Design in London in 1997. After graduation, at the age of 24, she became chief designer at Chloe, the Parisian fashion house. McCartney's style – a mixture of girly glamour and rock n' roll – has established Chloe as the best selling label in Paris. It has also established McCartney as a major force in the fashion world and more noticeably on the high street, which copies her designs mercilessly. 'I like to explore the mechanics of the sexes through my work. …You can now wear a pretty, fragile chiffon dress and it doesn't mean you're not a foxy lady, it depends on what you accessorise it with. Fashion is a question of confidence, emotion and style – not rules.' McCartney is set to create her own label under the auspices of the fashion house Gucci.

McQueen, Alexander (1969-)

Alexander McQueen is one of the most influential and creative fashion designers around today. He learned his tailoring skills when working as a pattern cutter for a Savile Row men's tailor. He then trained as a theatre costume designer and worked for Romeo Gigli in Milan, before training at Central St Martin's College of Art and Design in London. In 1992 McQueen launched his own label and became the 'enfant terrible' of the fashion world. Despite the shock value of his designs McQueen is a highly creative designer with finely honed tailoring skills. He designs for his own label and was chief designer for the French fashion house Givenchy. McQueen uses cutting edge fabrics, such as laminated lace, vinyl with metal rivets, tartan PVC and synthetic fabric spattered with stainless steel.

Treacy, Philip (1967-)

Philip Treacy was born in Ireland and went to the Dublin National College of Art and Design, then studied fashion and millinery at the Royal College of Art in London. While still a student he worked for John Galliano and opened his own business in 1990. Treacy is one of the world's most creative and original milliners, who has enormous skill and technique. He is a master craftsman who often creates hats that are oversized, sometimes up to two feet high. Treacy often makes use of twisted, curled and singed feathers and creates fantastic shaped hats that resemble pieces of sculpture. He works for many of the most influential clothing designers.

Westwood, Vivienne (1941-)

Vivienne Westwood is one of the most influential designers of her time. She went to Harrow Art School for one term, before training as a teacher! In the late 1960s, Westwood opened a highly influential shop in the King's Road, London, selling leather and rubber clothes. In 1976 Westwood produced her 'bondage' collection of studded, strapped and buckled clothing. Although these clothes were thought to be shocking at the time, they have since influenced much of mainstream fashion and she is credited with setting off the Punk trend. Westwood's 'Pirate' and 'New Romanticism' themes of the 1980s set fashions that were ten years ahead of their time. These styles included huge swirling petticoats, buckles, ruffles and pirate hats. Her signature styles have also included underwear worn as over wear, corsets and crinolines and 'Grunge', using torn clothing and exposed seams. In 1991 Westwood began showing her collections in Paris, designing for Vivienne Westwood Gold Label and Vivienne Westwood Red Label.

The Crafts Council (www.craftscouncil.org.uk)

The Crafts Council is the UK's national organisation for the promotion of contemporary crafts. Established in 1971, it is an independent body funded by the Arts Council of England, responsible for promoting fine craftsmanship, encouraging high standards and increasing public awareness of contemporary crafts and applied arts.

- The Crafts Council's premises in London provide a craft gallery, reference library, photo library, shop and café.
- The Crafts Council Gallery, Britain's largest crafts gallery, hosts a continuous programme of major craft exhibitions, some of which tour nationally and internationally.

Students can access this information to research examples of contemporary design to help them develop their own ideas.

The Design Council

Founded in 1944, the Design Council has for over fifty years been striving to promote the effective use of design – and design thinking – in business, in education and in government. The purpose of the Design Council is 'to inspire the best use of design by the UK, in the world context, to improve prosperity and well-being.' The Design Council is independent of Government and run as an autonomous, non-profit making public body. It is funded through a grant from the Department of Trade and Industry.

The Design Council supports design education in schools and colleges through its publications. It supports professional designers by providing advice on the marketing of products and on how design can assist businesses. The Design Council also helps students by providing information and advice about its activities, such as the following:

- events and exhibitions
- case studies and stories of innovation
- design information
- news and publication
- business partnerships

The Textile Institute (www.texi.org)

The Textile Institute is a worldwide professional association people working with fibres and fabrics, clothing and footwear, interior and technical textiles. It is the only organisation that covers the entire global industry, from fibres to retailing, from engineering to fashion, from Australia to Zimbabwe. The TI provides a forum for informing the six thousand Textile Institute members and the world about textile activities. The Textile Institute:

- has special membership packages for students and teachers
- runs local events, special interest groups, conferences, seminars, training courses and factory visits
- is the world's leading publisher of a wide range of books and magazines covering the broad spectrum of the textile industry
- runs an information service relating to textiles.

Chapter 3

Anthropometrics and Ergonomics

THE BASIC PRINCIPLES AND APPLICATIONS OF ANTHROPOMETRICS AND ERGONOMICS

- Ergonomics is all about applying scientific data about human beings to the problems of design. It is about the art and science of matching the product to the user.
- Anthropometrics is a branch of ergonomics that deals with measurements of the physical characteristics of human beings – in particular their shapes and sizes.

The application of anthropometrical data is found in many areas of design, such as the design of furniture, tools or clothing. For many of these products, data is required about any number of critical dimensions relating to the human form. In general products are matched to a target population of users who come in a variety of shapes and sizes. Sometimes products are matched to a single user, such as happens in Haute Couture and bespoke tailoring where the product is customised to suit the measurements of one person.

When designing products a designer who matches the product to him/herself will only meet the needs of people who are of a similar shape or build. Size is therefore important to designers, manufacturers, retailers and consumers. In the clothing industry sizes are standardised, so that there is a means of assessing the size required.

APPLYING ANTHROPOMETRICAL DATA TO CLOTHING

In the clothing industry there is a series of standards that specify the sizes of clothes. These are:

BS 5511   Size designation of clothes – definitions and body measurements procedures
BS 3666   Size designations of women's wear
BS 6185   Size designations of men's wear
BS 3728   Size designations of children's and infants' wear.

The drawings opposite show in pictogram form the BS 5511 measurements that need to be taken into account when designing a garment. These are called the control measurements.

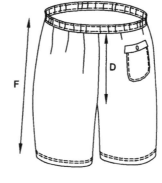

Figure 3B.2

The BS 3666 mentioned above gives a table of size codes for women's wear from size 8 – 20, with a range of measurements for each size. One problem that manufacturers find with British Standard measurements is that the anthropometrical data was collected a number of years ago and is now out of date. Consequently, many garment manufacturers use their own size charts, which can mean that a size 12 from one manufacturer is different to a size 12 from another. At the time of writing a new survey of sizes is being undertaken in the UK.

Points of measurement

A	Waist
B	Seat (18cm from waistband)
C	Front rise (excl. waistband)
D	Back rise (excl. waistband)
E	Inside leg
F	Outside leg (excl. waistband)
G	Fork
H	Thigh (5cm from crotch)
I	Bottoms

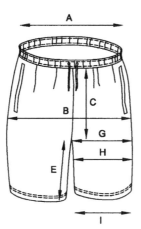

Figure 3B. 3

Typical points of measurement taken by a manufacturer for a pair of shorts.

TASK

Compare two pairs of shorts of the same size produced by different manufacturers.
- Measure each pair of shorts at the waist, seat, front rise, back rise, inside leg, outside leg, fork, thigh and bottoms.
- Draw up a chart to show the results.

BRITISH AND INTERNATIONAL STANDARDS

Founded in 1901, the British Standards Institution (BSI) is the world's leading standards and quality services organisation and the oldest national standards-making body in the world. BSI is independent of government, industry and trade associations, is non-profit-making and recognised globally as an independent and impartial body that serves both the private and public sectors.

Working with manufacturing and service industries, the BSI helps develop British, European and International standards. It operates in more than ninety countries across Europe, the USA, Canada, Mexico, South America, Russia, Singapore and China. Over the last ten years BSI has evolved from being simply a standards-setting organisation to one that has developed a commercial portfolio of global products and services in the quality sector. BSI's income is largely derived from its commercial activities, from subscriptions from its members and from the sale of standards. It also receives some Government support.

The BSI and other similar bodies belong to the International Organisation for Standardisation (ISO).

The joint European Standards Organisation goes by the rather long name of CEN/CENELEC/ETSI.

- CEN is the European Committee for Standardisation, which implements the voluntary technical harmonisation of standards in Europe.
- CENELEC is the European Committee for Electrotechnical Standardisation.
- ETSI is the European Telecommunications Standards Institute.

The need for standards

Why have set standards? Apart from the obvious answer 'for safety reasons', standards are often set not by government legislation, but at the request of industry itself.

British Standards sets standards, testing procedures and quality assurance processes to make sure that manufacturers make products that fulfil the safety and quality needs of their customers and the environment. Manufacturers of furnishing fabrics, for example, have to conform to established fire safety standards. The test procedures for checking fire safety have to comply with BS guidelines and must be carried out under controlled conditions. If a product meets the set standards and a quality assurance system is in place to ensure that every subsequent product meets the requirements, a manufacturer can apply for the BSI 'Kite Mark'.

There are hundreds of British Standards relating to textiles and fabrics. For example, these can include processes and tests that relate to:

- fibre, yarn and fabric testing
- appearance, handle, flexibility, creasing, shrinkage, strength, wear, stretch and recovery
- colour fastness, finishing and aftercare
- sewing machines and sewing thread.

Using Standards

Whatever project you are working on, there is probably a set standard to meet. These standards provide technical details and specific design constraints and can also provide a planning framework to follow if you have to devise your own test procedures. You can find information about fasteners, test methods for fabrics and labelling requirements in the 'Compendium of Essential Design and Technology Standards for Schools and Colleges'. The BSI website is on www.bsi.org.uk/education.

Ergonomic considerations for designs and models

It is clearly important to take size and dimensions into account when designing. This includes being very clear about the target market, because designing for the average user doesn't mean that a product will be suitable for everyone.

- It is a mistake to think that just because a product is the correct size for you it will be correct for everyone in the same age group
- The use of modelling is a key part of the manufacturing process. It is used to test a flat pattern and to try out construction processes. The use of seam allowance with agreed tolerance levels ensure that a product fits together correctly.

TASK

1 Define the following terms:
  - Ergonomics
  - Anthropometrics.
2 Describe the role of the British Standards Institute in relation to product quality and safety.

EXAM PRACTICE

The questions below are similar in style to the ones you will find in the examination paper for this unit. Before attempting to answer the questions read the relevant sections in the unit. Make note using key words or spider diagrams about the topic.

1 Aesthetic considerations have an important influence of the design of products. Identify two different products and compare their form and function. Give reasons for your views.

(15)

2 a) A number of different design movements have influenced design since 1900. Select two contrasting design movements and compare their influence on the design of products.

(8)

b) Describe the work of ONE designer from EITHER of the design movements you selected in part a)

(7)

3 a) Outline the importance of values issues in designing.   (7)

b) Describe how values issues have influenced the design and manufacture of two different products.

(8)

4 Products can be manufactured by one-off, batch or mass production. Describe how each of these levels of production impact upon the design and manufacture of products.

(15)

Preview

Unit	Level	Components	Areas of study
3	AS	Section B: Options	• Design and Technology in Society OR • CAD/CAM

CAD/CAM is one of two options in Unit 3. You only have to study ONE of these options.

WHAT YOU WILL LEARN IN THE UNIT

The content of the CAD/CAM option explores the impact of CAD/CAM on industry, computer-aided design (CAD) and computer-aided manufacture (CAM). The work you undertake must include knowledge and understanding of the following areas:

Chapter 1   The impact of CAD/CAM on industry
- Changes in production methods
- Global manufacturing
- Employment issues.

Chapter 2   Computer-aided design (CAD)
- Creating and modifying designs
- 2D/3D modelling and prototyping
- Constructing accurate drawings
- Creating complex products
- Creating virtual products
- Creating total design concepts
- Common input devices
- Common output devices.

Chapter 3   Computer-aided manufacture (CAM)
- CNC machines
- Using CAM for different levels of production
- Advantages/disadvantages of CAM.

WHAT YOU WILL DO IN THE UNIT

During the unit you should undertake a variety of tasks to enable you to understand the subject content. You may be asked to:

- work individually on some theoretical aspects of the unit content – for example you could research information about CAD techniques, then share your findings with the group
- work collaboratively with others on some activities – for example, developing your understanding of practical skills using CAD
- work individually on exam-style questions.

UNIT 3 ASSESSMENT

Unit 3 is externally assessed through a $1\frac{1}{2}$ hour written exam, which assesses your understanding of the unit subject content. There is one question paper, with two sections:

- Section A: Materials, Components and Systems
- Section B: Options.

UNIT 3 SECTION B ASSESSMENT

The work that you do in Design and Technology in Society will be assessed through Section B of the Unit 3 examination paper.

- It consists of two compulsory long answer questions, each worth 15 marks.
- Your answers should be from the viewpoint of Textiles Technology unless you are taught this option through another materials area.
- You are advised to spend 45 minutes on this section of the exam paper.
- This section together with Section A is worth 15 per cent of the full Advanced GCE.

WHAT THE EXAMINER IS LOOKING FOR

The examination paper is designed to give you the opportunity to demonstrate your understanding of what you have learned in the unit. Examiners will look for your ability to apply your knowledge and understanding to open-ended contexts related to computer-aided design and manufacture.

EXAM TIPS

- Make brief notes about the topics covered in this unit.
- Summarise the key points on one or two sheets of paper.
- Learn these key points.
- Practise working through a complete exam so you will learn how to allocate the time available to you.
- In the exam, *read the questions through and then read them again, to make sure you understand what you are being asked to do.*
- Plan your answer briefly on paper then check the question again to make sure that you have covered it fully.
- Work through your answer making sure that you address each point in your plan.
- Use clearly written sentences and bullet points to make your answer clear.
- Use specialist technical terms and clear sketches to illustrate your answer where appropriate.
- Read through your answer, then move on to the next question.

Chapter 1

The Impact of Computer-aided Design and Manufacture (CAD/CAM) on Industry

Textiles are a fast moving industry, which needs to produce quality products that consumers want. The right information is vital to sell the 'right' product at the 'right' time at the 'right' price. Companies that want to stay competitive need to manage this information so that product development is fast and effective. The use of computer systems is a key element in this design and production process.

Computer systems are used in many sectors of the industry for computer-aided design (CAD), production planning, data control and for computer-aided manufacturing (CAM). CAD/CAM is where the two systems are integrated. The degree of integration depends on the scale of production, the type of end product and commercial considerations.

RESPONDING TO CHANGES IN THE MARKET PLACE

The development of CAD/CAM technologies has not only created a driving force for change, but is providing a means of responding to changes in market place. For example, clothing products have always needed to have a fast time to market. This can be seen in the six monthly product development cycles for spring/summer and autumn/winter seasons. The impact of the use of CAD/CAM technologies, however, enables an even faster time to market and the production of five or six collections per season is now fairly common. It is apparent, therefore, that the use of computer systems has revolutionised the design and manufacture of textile products.

ADAPTING TO CHANGE

The manufacture of fibres, textiles and clothing is one of the driving forces of industrialisation throughout the developing world. In many of the developed countries, however, clothing industries are trying to maintain their market share of design, manufacture and distribution.

In the past it has been the older, established industries of Japan, Europe and the USA that have controlled developments in technology. Information and Communications Technology (ICT), however, has changed all that. Not only is ICT providing new opportunities for young industries in the developing

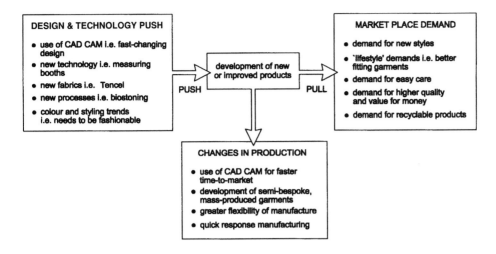

DESIGN & TECHNOLOGY PUSH
• use of CAD CAM i.e. fast-changing design
• new technology i.e. measuring booths
• new fabrics i.e. Tencel
• new processes i.e. biostoning
• colour and styling trends i.e. needs to be fashionable

PUSH → development of new or improved products ← PULL

MARKET PLACE DEMAND
• demand for new styles
• 'lifestyle' demands i.e. better fitting garments
• demand for easy care
• demand for higher quality and value for money
• demand for recyclable products

CHANGES IN PRODUCTION
• use of CAD CAM for faster time-to-market
• development of semi-bespoke, mass-produced garments
• greater flexibility of manufacture
• quick response manufacturing

Figure 3B.4

Changes in production methods are either pushed by new technologies or pulled by market place demand (or a combination or both).

world, but it is also providing a means for the older industries to locate manufacturing where labour costs are lower. This is having a profound social impact on the numbers of people employed worldwide and on the skills, training and management needs of different companies.

The pressure for change has never been greater. In order to maintain their market share, textile and clothing manufacturers worldwide have to take account of the market drivers – technology push and market pull. This may mean that companies in the future will have to put a greater emphasis on design, technical innovations, flexibility, quality and a quick response to the demands of the market place – individual consumers as well as retailers.

TASK

Select a fashionable textile product for the teenage market. Explain the aesthetic and functional needs of a person buying this product. Describe how the product meets these needs and how it could be improved to meet these needs more closely.

CHANGES IN DESIGN AND PRODUCTION METHODS

In the 1980s, the principal technical challenge for manufacturers in developed countries, was thought to be the automation of clothing manufacture. One research project centred on the design of sewing machines which could be programmed to work on fabric draped over three-dimensional forms, providing a flexible method for adapting to changes in style. Another project concentrated on using computers and robots to automate the setting in of sleeves, but the project was abandoned in favour of automatic seaming. None of these projects has been really successful and the automation of fabric handling and sewing operations has been much more difficult than originally thought.

In contrast, much progress was made in the use of computers and automatic systems for pattern grading and marker making, fabric cutting and materials transport between workstations. The rapid uptake of these technologies meant that there was a decrease in the cost of computer systems for industry. By the end of the 1980s, there was a lot of interest in the use of CAD as a creative design tool.

COMPUTER-AIDED DESIGN (CAD)

The development of CAD in textile, garment and product design has had a far-reaching impact on the efficiency of design, sample production and costing. Modern CAD systems provide the opportunity to communicate design ideas faster and better than ever before. CAD technology is used from creative design and styling right through to the preparation of flat pattern markers and cutting instructions.

High-resolution colour systems are widely used for two-dimensional (2D) design, with the ability to scan in images and adapt them. Digital cameras are also used to import images directly into design software. Modern CAD systems allow greater control over the quality of these images, usually through the use of an object or image browser. One of the key features is the ability of the software to create knit, print and woven fabrics and to drape these fabrics onto product sketches. The comparatively recent introduction of three-dimensional (3D) CAD systems allows the creation of virtual products and environments.

COMPUTER-AIDED MANUFACTURE (CAM)

CAM involves the use of computer systems to control manufacturing equipment, making it easier and quicker to produce cost-effective one-off, batch-produced and high volume textile products.

Textile and product manufacture uses computer systems and CAM mainly in:

- high volume and continuous production of fibres and yarns
- high volume woven, knitted and printed fabric manufacture
- batch and high volume product manufacture using CAD systems for flat pattern and marker making, fabric cutting, production planning and materials handling
- one-off, batch and high volume product manufacture, using CAM for fast, accurate and repeatable processes.

It is not expected that there will be a major breakthrough in computerised sewing in the foreseeable future and developments in CAM for sewn products currently fall into three categories:

- flexibility for quick-response, with the ability to adapt stitch sequences and machine settings for small orders
- semi-automation for the high-volume production of a few basic subassembly operations such as attaching pockets to jeans
- specialist sewing machines for specific tasks like bar-tacking, buttonholing or embroidery.

COMPUTER NUMERICALLY CONTROLLED (CNC) MACHINES

The use of CNC machines, controlled by computer software, is widespread in many industries. In textile manufacture, CNC equipment, such as spinning and knitting machines, looms, printing and dyeing equipment ensure the fast, reliable and cost-effective production of fibres, yarns and fabrics. In sewn goods product manufacture fabric cutting is the only operation to have been fully automated. Specialist sewing machines are used to automate specific tasks like bar-tacking, making buttonholes, sewing on buttons or producing embroidery. Modern computer-aided circular knitting machines enable the production of high volume and short runs for just-in-time production.

CNC machines are controlled by number values written in a sequence called a program. Each number or code is assigned to a particular operation or process. Computer programs, often called 'wizards' eliminate the need to learn elaborate CNC machining codes, making CNC machines easier to use.

Most modern systems generate NC machine codes from the digital data created from a drawing. The numbers or codes are easily changed from within the CAD software when required. Most CNC machines also have the capability to be programmed manually from an adjacent keypad.

CNC machines provide numerous benefits for manufacturers, because they can:

- do repetitive tasks accurately and repeatedly
- speed up production and increase efficiency
- bring higher and more reliable quality
- make it easier to control processes
- lead to increased flexibility of manufacturing, as production can be switched easily to different products
- lead to more cost-effective products, despite their high initial cost.

COMPUTER INTEGRATED MANUFACTURE (CIM)

Traditional methods of manufacturing have involved a linear approach, similar to the process by which you are assessed for your coursework. In industry, using this method extends the time taken to design, manufacture and market a product. As the use of computer systems within manufacturing have become more common, more efficient ways of operating have developed, through the use of CIM.

CIM systems integrate the use of all the different functions of computers, including CAD/CAM, to enable fast, efficient and cost-effective textile manufacturing. They enable the management of product design, development, production planning and control, quality assurance and control, materials and stock control and costs. CIM reduces the product time to market and enables manufacturers to use just in time methods of production and quick response manufacturing.

CIM makes use product data management (PDM) systems and ICT to organise and communicate information between the product development team, the manufacturing site and the customer – often a retailer. The following types of data can typically be managed by a PDM system:

- drawings
- materials and component information
- lay plan
- work orders
- costing
- wearer trials and testing

- fibre and yarn content
- labelling and care information
- suppliers
- barcode
- marketing information – the story, season, selling and range data.

TASK

Explain how CAD/CAM systems enable a faster time to market of cost-effective, high quality products.

CONCURRENT DESIGN AND MANUFACTURE

This term describes the integration of design and manufacture, in which a product development team shares the responsibility for designing and manufacturing products. The use of a computer system – CIM – is the enabling technology for this to take place. Specialist product data management software manages all the product data, which is easily communicated between the members of the product development team. Up-to-the-minute information keeps every team member current on style changes, conceptual and technical drawings, trim alterations, costing and measurements. All this 'real-time' (as it happens) design, business and manufacturing information means a faster product time to market.

FLEXIBLE MANUFACTURING SYSTEMS (FMS)

A central file server within a CAD/CAM system can process the production data from a network of computers, which are part of a flexible manufacturing system. The file server runs numerous operations such as a

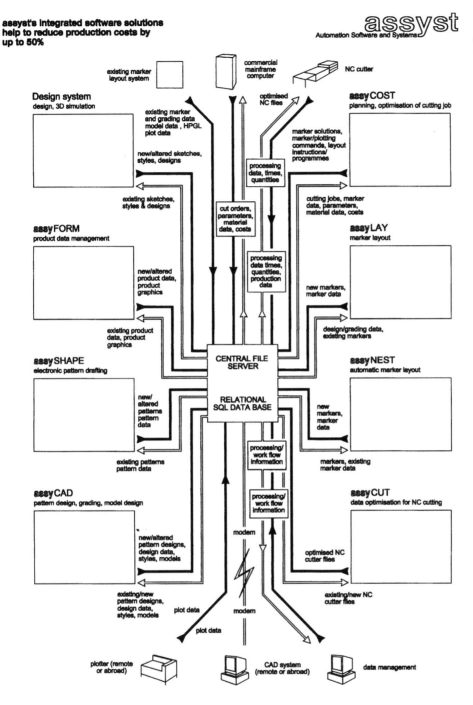

assyst's integrated software solutions help to reduce production costs by up to 50%

assyst
Automation Software and Systems

design system, product data management, electronic pattern drafting, pattern design and grading, costing cutting jobs, lay planning and cutting. Some integrated software solutions can help reduce production costs by up to 50 per cent.

The use of computer systems means that product quality is no longer the responsibility of one department in a company. All the digital data generated by a CAD/ CAM system is stored in a database. This provides clean, legible specification sheets containing the latest documentation from concept to costing and production. This enables quality to be built into the product right from the start and a concept of 'right first time' and Total Quality Management (TQM) – which aims at continuous improvement, always trying to make things better.

TASK

Discuss the impact that changes in design and production methods have had on the manufacture of products.

GLOBAL MANUFACTURING

The main driving force behind the established clothing industry in the 1980s was the need for industrialised countries to protect themselves against low-cost imports. They did this by improving productivity and reducing manufacturing costs. But towards the end of the 1980s, even newly industrialised countries such as Hong Kong or Taiwan, started to find themselves displaced by a new generation of developing countries, such as China and other Pacific Rim countries.

By the beginning of the 1990s, new technology had brought enhanced economies of scale to some of the preparatory stages of clothing manufacture, but had not changed the most labour intensive area of manufacturing on the sewing room floor. Since labour costs are a key component of garment costing, it made sense and still does for established companies to manufacture where labour costs are lower. The global revolution had begun! Even Marks and Spencer, the company that once prided itself on supporting British manufacturing has succumbed to manufacturing 'off-shore'.

The development of so-called global manufacturing would not be possible without the use of computer systems and Information and Communications Technology (ICT)

TASK

Investigate the textile products that you own. Examine their product labels to find out where they were manufactured. Draw up a chart to show the product type, the manufacturer and the country of origin.

EMPLOYMENT ISSUES

New technologies are continuing to change working patterns in textile and clothing manufacturing around the world, resulting in job losses in many countries. There are three major reasons for this:

* a lack of trained people
* developments in CAD/CAM
* the move to manufacture 'off-shore'.

For those people who are still involved manufacturing their jobs have changed significantly. As companies subscribe to the concept of flexibility, so must employees. There is also a need for industry and the workforce to keep up-to-date with the skills and technology for them to continue to compete. In the UK textiles and clothing may have already lost many jobs, but at the time of writing it is still larger than the car industry. Companies that compete sometimes tend to do so by concentrating on 'niche' or specialist markets. It is expected that the UK will be capable of retaining jobs in product development, technical and management skills, with much manufacturing going overseas.

TRENDS IN DESIGN

The growing uses of CAD systems in textiles and clothing means that many design jobs have changed. Sophisticated design software enables the design of fabrics, products, technical illustrations, logos, packaging and assembly drawings in one package. This means that the scope of the designer has expanded to include a high level of computer and visual literacy alongside creativity and problem solving skills. The increased use of CAD and CAM systems means that training is vitally important, especially in the technical area, such as flat pattern development.

TRENDS IN MANUFACTURING

The manufacture of sewn goods products is still a 'hands-on' process. The actual sewing usually accounts for only 10 – 30 per cent of the sewing time. Handling and positioning of fabric pieces take much more time and effort. The major obstacles to automation therefore come from the need to manipulate and stitch limp and distortable fabrics.

The major impetus in garment manufacture has been in the implementation of systems for management, materials handling and team working. In cellular manufacture, a production team of three to six machinists produce complete garments. Each team member moves from one machine to another and completes several manufacturing processes, before passing the garment on to the next team member for further processing. This has resulted in higher productivity and higher quality products. Team working is a feature of modern production systems and requires a skilled, trained and flexible workforce.

In the UK, there is a shortage of multi-skilled and technical personnel in clothing manufacture. When this is combined with developments in computers and electronic communications, many companies relocate their manufacturing overseas and take advantage of lower labour costs. Although product design and development is expected to remain in the UK, the loss of manufacturing has had a devastating impact on some local and regional employment prospects.

QUICK RESPONSE AND FUTURE INNOVATIONS

Quick Response (QR) was one of the first key strategies for survival against low-cost imports. It led to the development of technologies such as CADCAM, electronic point-of-sale (EPOS) and Electronic Data Interchange (EDI) systems. It has been shown that QR can save up to 25 per cent of the retail price of some garments.

Future investment in research and development will probably focus on developing a communications and computer network that will analyse consumer trends, meet demand better and provide bespoke mass-produced products by QR. Future innovations in manufacturing systems are expected to be built around the following:

- more sophisticated computer-based systems, including CIM. The use of multimedia for manipulating and communicating visual images, sound and data and to provide retailing outlets
- continuing use of EPOS and EDI to enable QR and 'Just-in-time' manufacturing, to speed up the flow of information between suppliers and customers and keep stock levels to a minimum
- use of expert systems such as 'Artificial Intelligence' (AI). This will allow the automation of quality assurance, using complex on-line inspection and the control of machines and processes
- enabling technologies, such as electronics, computing and mechatronics. These will have an impact on automated testing, machine monitoring and process control.

TASK

Global manufacturing has significant implications for employment prospects in many countries around the world. Explain your views on the contribution of CAD/CAM systems to this situation.

Chapter 2

Computer-aided Design

Computer aided design involves the use of computer hardware and design software to create the data that is required to design, manufacture and market sewn goods products. A CAD system speeds up the entire product design cycle and eliminates costly mistakes. It keeps track of all the design data, specifications, grading and marker making information, costing details and quality issues. The integration of CAD systems with electronic communications systems enables instant global communication between business partners worldwide.

CAD SYSTEMS

Powerful central processing units (CPUs) and large amounts of memory are essential for the effective functioning of CAD systems. Until the mid-1980s specially constructed 'dedicated' computers were used to operate CAD systems. Since then, however, the capacities of personal computers have improved so much that that professional quality CAD systems can be operated effectively on personal desktop and laptop computers (most efficient of all for designers on the move) through local area networks (LANs) and wide area networks (WANs).

CAD systems integrate the use of hardware and software, which communicate through a graphical user interface (GUI).

Hardware

The hardware of a CAD system consists of computers, data storage devices, input and output devices.

- Mainframe computers are suitable for large manufacturing companies because they have high processing speeds and vast memory to store large amounts of data. The mainframe controls a network of computer terminals comprising a local area network (LAN), intranet or wide area networks (WAN). It all depends on the size of the company and whether it is spread over a number of sites.
- Minicomputers are smaller versions of mainframe systems. They are used for networking in large organisations.
- Individual microcomputers, desktop or laptop personal computers (PCs) are used for individual computing needs or as Machine Control Units (MCUs) for controlling CNC machines.
- Hard and floppy disks, CD-ROMs, DVDs and zip drives are called data storage devices.

- Keyboards, mouse and tracker-balls, graphics tablets and styluses, digitisers, digital cameras, videos, and 2D and 3D scanners are called input devices.
- Monitors, printers, plotters, cutters and CNC machines are called output devices.

Software

All software applications programs are run from a central operating system (OS), which is used to manage both the software and computer files. The various operating systems available include Windows 95, 98, Millenium and NT 2000, Unix, MAC-OS (Apple Computers) and DOS (Disk Operating System).

- All CAD software, whatever the operating system, provides graphic display data and prepares data for export to output devices such as printers or plotters.
- Modern CAD programmes contain hundreds of functions that enable users to undertake a variety of drawing tasks. These tasks may range from drawing a product, editing an existing design, print previewing the design, printing or saving it.
- Software packages contain menus, commands and functions that enable users to specify exactly what they want to do and how they want to do it. Typically, good programs contain convenient drawing-aids, which enable basic faults to be easily corrected electronically, similar to spell and grammar checks.

Making connections

A graphical user interface (GUI) provides a link between the user and the computer, providing visual on-screen clues to help the user 'talk' to the computer. For example, the Windows GUI provides a consistent operating environment that is very easy to learn. If you learn to use one application and you can translate that learning to other applications. GUIs are essential tools that make computers easy and fun to use, even for children who are familiar with most on-screen icons before they enter primary school! (See Figure 3B.6 on page 190.)

GUIs are user-friendly devices that enable users to enter data through:
- commands or functions selected from menus
- the keyboard (e.g. Ctrl+S to save work)
- from toolbars buttons and on-screen icons (like the print icon)
- using text or dialogue boxes.

In the textile industry, GUIs provide an important flexibility for computer users – they allow users with different operational requirements to use various function keys to set up their own individual working environments. This may include for example, specifying text and dimensions that match industry standards from standards organisations such as BSI, ISO or ANSI.

Storing data

All CAD software applications store and file data either on the hard disk or on floppies. Computers running CAD systems need to have vast amounts of memory, because drawing files are huge. Some applications allow files to be zipped (compressed) to take up less room on the system – a little like the library microfilming old newspapers. For ease of access, files need to be managed in clearly marked directories and sub-directories (otherwise it's easy to forget where they are!)

Not all companies use the same operating system or applications software, so standard data translation formats, such as Data Exchange Format (DXF) are essential for reading and accessing data from other systems. These formats become recognised as standard when they have been approved by one of the standards organisations. Most CAD systems are designed for compatibility with other systems, using industry-standard file formats, which allow seamless integration with existing computer environments.

Some examples of standard formats include:

- Data exchange format (DXF)
- Hewlett-Packard Printer Control Language (PCL) for laser printers
- Post Script (PS) page description language for laser printers.

Some common formats for storing CAD data include:

- Tagged Image File format (TIF)
- Windows Metafile Format (WMF)
- PICT, the standard format for storing and exchanging graphics on Apple computers
- Hewlett Packard Graphics Language (HPGL)
- Virtual Reality Modelling Language (VRML).

TASK

1 Investigate the computer systems in use in your school or college, including the hardware, software and storage system.
2 Find out the meaning of the abbreviations BSI, ISO and ANSI and explain why the use of standard formats is essential in industry.

Computer-aided design techniques

All 2D and 3D CAD systems are enable the designer to work with a 'model' of a product. CAD graphics systems are classed as interactive because the user can control the image on screen; add, edit, modify and delete data. The generation of digital models and virtual products removes the need produce a model or sample early in the product development process. 2D and 3D models and virtual products become the designers' main means of communicating their ideas to others in the product design team.

Creating a digital product model requires graphics and specialist software that is capable of processing mathematical functions and making complex calculations in order to manipulate graphic images in 2D and 3D. These images are generated either by vector or raster graphics. CAD programs employ a combination of these two graphics, with a raster-to-vector conversion for easy interchange between the two.

Raster-based programmes
Raster graphics represent images as 'bit maps' and the image is composed of a pattern of dots or picture elements called pixels. Paint programs manipulate raster graphics, which are used for the rendering of surfaces and textures. Bit-mapped images always appear the same regardless of the resolution (picture quality) of a printer or a visual display unit (VDU) – the computer monitor.

Vector-based programmes
Vector graphics are used to draw lines and produce 3D shapes. Draw programs create and manipulate vector graphics, which are manipulated in the form of mathematical co-ordinates. Vectored images are more flexible because they can be resized and stretched. They often require less memory than bit-mapped images. Vector graphics are used for pattern cutting, grading, lay planning and for design and technical drawing.

CAD programs
CAD programs combine the characteristics of raster and vector graphics. The basic operating characteristics of CAD programs are:

- users can easily manipulate on-screen images
- displays can be split into two or more windows (sometimes called tiles or panes)
- each window can contain a different view of the product
- models can be repositioned or edited independently in each window
- when working with multiple windows, only one of the windows is active – the other windows are activated by clicking on them
- when editing, the effects of one action on the design affect all the different views of the same design
- pull down or pop up menus have commands that allow text and dimensions to be added
- line styles and colour schemes can be adjusted
- there are many keyboard shortcuts for drawing and other features. For

example Ctrl+G groups a collection of individual elements, Ctr+P (or icon) prints and Ctr+C copies
- pre-defined graphic elements are called primitives – 2D and 3D vectored objects that can be drawn, stretched and resized. Typical primitives are lines, arcs, circles, ellipses, splines, Bezier curves, and polygons.

CREATING AND MODIFYING DESIGNS

CAD modelling is a key part in the design process because it enables 2D ideas to be tested and modified and 3D product ideas to be simulated on screen. These 'virtual' 3D products can be shown to clients, who can then choose the one they would like to be sampled. Product modelling reduces the need for sampling a large range of products, saving time and costs.

CAD systems are therefore essential in helping design and production teams achieve productivity levels that were previously unattainable. They greatly speed up the design cycle, by reducing the time taken on non-creative and repetitive activities. This frees up valuable time for creative, 'thinking' tasks, leading to higher efficiently. CAD systems enable a wide range of functions such as the following:

Textile design:
- create and modify pattern motifs and repeats
- produce multiple views, repeat and undo changes
- re-colour and modify existing fabric designs
- create a range of colourways, matching colour palettes
- produce colour-separated artwork for printing, directly from the system.

Product design:
- sketch at any scale using lines and curves
- copy elements of a design, apply text and experiment with colourways
- 'map' textile designs over any drawing or photograph, for use on storyboards or in 'virtual' catwalk shows
- store designs and pattern motifs
- exchange data with customer and supplier systems.

TASK

1 Explain the difference between raster and vector graphics.
2 Investigate the capabilities of the CAD software available to you. Experiment with the use of CAD software for developing design ideas.

2D AND 3D MODELLING AND PROTOTYPING IN THE FASHION INDUSTRY

As well as being aware of the latest trends, designers working in the fashion industry need to be multi-skilled. At the start of the season, the designer and the retail client discuss the colour palette and style direction for a specific garment or range of clothing. Then the design development begins.

- A graphic workstation enables the designer to create garment sketches, illustrations, print, knit and weave designs.
- A digital camera is used to input information about fabric construction such as knit structures.
- A plain garment is made up in plain fabric in the same weight as the intended design. This enables a client to evaluate the fabric handle and quality and the garment style and fit.
- The plain garment is photographed by the digital camera, scanned into the software and used for garment mapping. This enables the designer to try out pattern ideas on the garment, which can be printed out or shown to the client on screen. Garment mapping minimises the need for actual sampling and reduces costs.
- Other style developments are generated, producing fabric and garment ideas, which are used for product concept boards. These can be produced practically or using DTP software. Concept boards enable the client to visualise and choose the product to be sampled.
- Multimedia is used to present a total design concept to the client using video and music. CAD can also be used to show how the products might look in the store.

Figure 3B.6

A workstation makes it easy to create the artwork required to design, manufacture and merchandise sewn goods products.

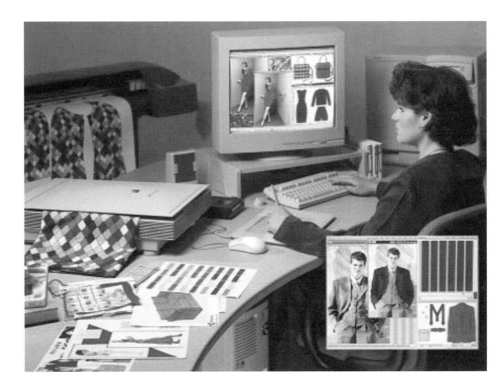

- The chosen fabric design is downloaded to a printer and a sample length printed. This can be used on concept boards or to make up a sample garment to show the client.
- The pattern cutter works with the designer's specification to produce a sample garment that mirrors the way it would be made on the factory floor.
- Once the design has been agreed and a 'first fit' sample has been approved by the client, production can begin.

TASK

1 Draw up a simple chart to show the main stages in the design process. Identify and justify how a computer can be used at each stage.

2 Produce a series of drawings to demonstrate your skills in using a CAD program.

Sharing design data

In modern CIM systems design data can be shared between designers, production teams, manufacturers and clients, so that design decisions can be made quickly and easily.

Product data can be used directly or converted into other file formats for a variety of uses, such as product and sales presentations, company reports, marketing materials and brochures that are made available at a company web site on the World Wide Web. The web sites often provide e-mail addresses to offer the possibility of a two-way communication with customers. Virtual Reality Modelling (VRM) and the use of 'knowledge based' expert systems via the Internet are growing in importance.

CONSTRUCTING ACCURATE DRAWINGS WITHIN A CAD SYSTEM

The drawing tools in CAD programmes enable the production of 2D technical drawings. These working drawings are included on a manufacturing specification sheet and communicate all the information necessary for the product to be made, such as:

- the front, back and side views of the product
- the design, styling and construction details
- dimensions, sizes and tolerances.

The information needs to be accurate enough for a pattern cutter to cut a flat pattern and a sample product to be made as the designer intends. An experienced pattern cutter is able to interpret the design by importing and adapting a similar flat pattern from the company's database.

TASK

Using a CAD program, generate line drawings to show the front, side and back views of a product, that are detailed enough for a flat pattern to be developed.

CREATING COMPLEX PRODUCTS

The creation of complex products combines the development of fabric designs with modelling 3D products.

Developing fabric designs
- Printed fabric designs can be created from scratch or scanned from existing fabric swatches, using CAD tools such as pens, pencils, paints and brushes in various sizes and shapes. Colours can be added, modified or changed completely. Once the design is finalised it is easy to create print repeat and colourways.
- Woven fabrics can also be designed from scratch, by designing the warp and weft sequences and other technical details. CAD packages can also create woven designs from a selected image, using a plain, twill, herringbone or other weave construction.
- Knitted fabrics or complete garments can be created, using a range of different stitches on a graph. Tools can create sweater bodies, sleeves, neck trim and knitted motifs in a selection of knit gauges.

Using CAD for knit designs
CAD is an essential tool for designers of knit fabrics

- Automatically convert a scanned design to a knit grid where each cell represents a stitch.
- Specify the grid size in wales and courses or by width and height.
- Use colourway, paint and texture mapping tools to develop the design.
- Specify and change the knit gauge size, without changing the overall design size or look.
- Insert, delete, copy, repeat and mirror specified design cells; add, alter or delete multiple wales/courses.
- Check yarn floats, or excessive colours in a course and correct errors.
- Apply stitches to the design to get a realistic simulation of the knitted sample on screen.
- Apply the knit design to photographs or drawings for use in marketing brochures.
- Put the design into production-ready repeat.
- Export digital information to a CNC knitting machine for production.

Developing 3D models

Geometric modelling describes an image mathematically (algorithm) in a form that a CAD or graphics program can display. These 3D wireframe models are represented as a collection of points, lines and arcs. They are used to produce what are called 'virtual' products, using 'texture mapping'.

Texture mapping (also known as 'digital draping') is a CAD tool that creates photo-realistic 3D rendering of designs, surfaces, colours, textures and patterns on to photographs, to produce virtual products. The process produces life-like representations of digital products, using scanned-in photographs of models, furniture or room-sets directly from a CAD system. Texture mapping enables the test marketing of a new product without the need to develop physical samples.

The texture mapping process involves identifying areas (called segments) on the photo where a pattern will be applied and creating a series of grid lines, that map the drape of the fabric across the segments. Once the grid has been created any number of fabrics, colourways or textures can be draped on the photo. This can be used to create a library of different styles. A proportional ruler enables the creation of images with real life measurements. This is useful when working with photographs of sketches.

The home furnishings sector was one of the first industries to make use of texture mapping. Interiors fashion silhouettes and styles do not change dramatically from season to season. Companies soon realised that texture mapping was an ideal way to develop a library of hundreds of product images cost effectively. With texture mapping a company can react quickly to changing market demands and show complete product ideas as they are created. By using texture mapping in place of sample development and the photography of new products for marketing purposes, home furnishings companies can make enormous savings. The costs of engraving screens, fabric yardage, strike-offs and sewing are completely eliminated.

TASK

Experiment with a CAD program to produce drawings and sketches on screen. You could:

- import images from a digital camera, CD-ROM or via the Internet
- develop your own library of design ideas
- adapt and modify design images through the use of scale and proportion, then work out design repeats and colourways
- map a fabric idea on a CAD drawing of your product, using copy and paste on selected areas
- print out your ideas to use on storyboards, to show to clients.

WORKING WITH VIRTUAL PRODUCTS

The ability to develop product ideas using 3D virtual products is a developing technology. In one CAD system, first marketed by Lectra, the design of a garment can be carried out in 3D on a 'virtual' mannequin. The mannequin is then 'undressed' and the pattern laid out in 2D for the detailed construction details to be applied – seam allowances, facings, dart shaping etc. The design is then viewed back on the mannequin to check the fit and accuracy.

Another 3D Virtual Pattern Design system, by PAD Systems, enables the 3D image to change automatically in 'real time' (as it happens) as the pattern maker develops the pattern in 2D. As changes take place they are replicated automatically on the related marker. The mannequin can be adjusted to a customer's measurements.

A co-operative project integrates the PAD System with cloth simulation software called Dressing Sim by Toyobo Ltd. This program produces garments using real cloth properties. Using CAD production patterns Dressing Sim 'sews' them together to create a realistic animation of the garment. Cloth property data is added through actual measurement and texture is mapped. The dressed dummy can move around on a virtual stage with wind and light effects added.

Gerber Technology has developed the Japanese APDS-3D pattern visualisation system on its own Accumark system. Pattern makers can select patterns from a library of 3D styles and drape them on a dress form. The user can define the viewing and lighting angles and can look at a vertical or horizontal cross-section of the style to check the fit ease. Style changes can be made and seen in 2D and 3D in real time.

Other features of virtual pattern design systems include the ability to:
* control the bending properties of fabrics on screen – silk for example drapes differently from cotton
* develop virtual 3D style catalogues – soon to be available on the Internet.

CREATING TOTAL DESIGN CONCEPTS, INCLUDING THE USE OF MULTI-MEDIA

Visual merchandising and store layout systems

It is already possible to use multimedia to present a total design concept to the client using video and music. Competition between retailers is now putting even more pressure on the clothing industry, which is increasingly turning to the use of visual merchandising and store layout systems to communicate their brand concepts. For several years, CAD packages have been used to design store layouts, providing 2D graphical representation of what the store will look like.

More recently, 3D visual merchandising and retail planning tools have been developed to enable manufacturers and retailers to plan, simulate, visualise and communicate merchandising ideas, brand concepts and store layout plans more efficiently. Design can be imported directly from any CAD package in the form of a sketch, photograph, scanned images or images downloaded from a digital camera. These can be placed on fixtures and fittings in a 'virtual' copy of a store. It is even possible to 'walk' round the store and view it from any angle!

E-merchandising

The developing texture mapping technology is expected to have an important impact on the marketing of products, through the use of Virtual Reality Modelling Language (VRML). This can be used to show simulated products on the World Wide Web using an Internet browser with a VRML plug-in. E-merchandising (electronic sales and marketing) uses online texture mapping that allows customers to play with a variety of mix and match options before purchasing. Using e-merchandising, potential customers will be able to download virtual products from anywhere in the world!

- Gerber Technology has recently announced the release of Artworks WebDraping™, a web enabled version of their Artworks Studio software. WebDraping uses Artworks Studio Draping to create thumbnails of all available colours and textures. Visitors to the site 'customise' their designs by dragging and dropping different combinations of colours and textures onto images.
- Lectra is offering LectraCatalog, which combines an Oracle-based database with texture mapping on a 2D or 3D image. Styles, fabrics and trims can be mixed and matched instantly and displayed photo-realistically. Lectra Catalogue can be used as a web-enabled catalogue.

The virtual dressing room

In an effort to promote sales and decrease the number of returns due to incorrect fit, some e-tailers (e-retailers) are implementing virtual fit technology on their websites. This 'virtual dressing room' enables users to get an idea of how a particular garment will fit or which will be the best size to buy. In a recent survey, 45 per cent of consumers said they would use virtual dressing room technology if offered. E-tailers are hoping this type of website will increase consumers' trust in the products they buy online, build brand loyalty, increase shopping efficiency and minimise returns.

In a few easy steps, the shopper answers prompts about measurements –

height, shoulders, bust, waist and hips – and selects from a group of general descriptions of hair colour and style, skin tone and face shape. From there, the cybershopper selects garments and tries them on the model in a single click of the computer mouse. The image revolves, enabling an outfit to be viewed from all angles.

A more accurate approach to measuring is body scanning.

Body scanning

Body scanning technology is new and developing. Its general aim is to accurately measure an individual customer, automatically develop flat patterns and mass customise a garment. Another application is the development of cyber mannequins that can be used to try on clothing for fit, size and look.

The body scanning technique uses a white light to capture a person's silhouette, from which measurement data can be extracted. Fast and painless, there is less chance of error in taking measurements, as long as the person is wearing a body suit or snug-fitting garment during the scanning process. The body scanning process offers the potential to:

- produce better fitting clothes
- exploit internet shopping
- increase sales
- reduce returns of wrong sized clothes
- automate measurement and pattern development of ready-to-wear clothing.

At present there are three types of body scanners, each with benefits and disadvantages:

- scanners that use structured white light – these are environmentally and psychologically acceptable to the public
- laser scanners – these are perfectly safe but not as acceptable to the public
- photographic scanners – these just take back and front views.

All these body scanners aim for accuracy within one millimetre and all but one record data in black and white. Most organisations that use them are interested in developing 'in-store' measuring booths and the potential for offering a made-to-measure service – in other words customised mass production.

Current body scanning technology works by exporting measurement data to a CAD system. This is used to grade a chosen design of the nearest size to the individual measurements, so that an accurately fitting custom tailored garment can be quickly manufactured. The measurement data can also be stored on a credit-type card, which can be swiped through an electronic card reader in a retail outlet for transmission to a manufacturer for customised tailoring.

At present, this automated pattern adaptation system represents the ultimate in rapid response clothing manufacture. The aim of future CAD developments is to overlay differently posed body scans to produce size and fit measurements that take account of ease and body movement. These data can then be used to produce flat patterns from scratch, rather than adapting existing patterns. Of the 3D scanners currently being used:

- One leading Japanese lingerie retailer is using a body scanner to help women choose the correct size bra.
- Another scanner type is in use in shops in Germany, Holland and Slovenia.
- The Triform 3D body scanner is probably the most tested system. It has been used, in combination with the Telmet 2D scanner in Marks and Spencer's latest women's sizing survey. In this survey, at different locations across the UK, around 3,000 women, ranging from sizes 6-30 were scanned The information from this survey will provide up-to-date accurate measurements for pattern drafting and provide the basis for developments in custom-made garments.

TASK

1 Discuss the impact that the development of 3D virtual products will have on shopping and leisure activities.
2 Investigate the potential for body scanning and the mass customisation of textile products.

COMMON INPUT DEVICES USED IN CAD SYSTEMS

In order to be both interactive and graphical, a CAD system needs a keyboard and a user interface, which acts as an input/output device. This allows maximum ease of use and flexibility in terms of graphic editing. The most common type of user interface is a graphical user interface (GUI), the most common type being Windows applications. Most GUIs use a Windows, Icons, Mice and Pull down/pop up menus (WIMP) operating environment. GUIs are simple and straightforward, and allow the user to:

- control the system by using set commands common to most word processing systems
- by selecting functions via a series of screen icons, windows, menus or by 'clicking and dragging' the mouse
- receive feedback about what the system is doing from the 'hourglass' icon
- enter data to be used in constructing a design on-screen
- highlight parts of the model for the system to manipulate.

INPUT DEVICES

Input devices position, locate, point or pick or combine these functions. The user presses a button or switch on the input device to show that an action has to take place. Input devices include the mouse, tracker-ball, digitiser, graphics tablet, digital camera and video and scanner.

The mouse

Invented in 1963, the pointing device called the mouse is the most common input device. A comfortable mouse can assist the user by reducing fatigue and minimising motion. The mouse operates mechanically and optically to control the movement of a cursor or a pointer on the screen. It allows the designer to 'point' to a function and 'click' to 'execute' it.

Mice contain up to three buttons, their functions depending on what software is used. Some also include a scroll wheel for moving through large documents rapidly.

In textile design, the major disadvantage of using a mouse is that a positional error will occur if the mouse is lifted from the surface on which it is running. It is also virtually impossible, using a mouse, to trace a drawing from a paper sketch or drawing (see digitiser).

The tracker-ball

A tracker-ball is a mouse lying on its back. It is often used when space is limited and can be manipulated by the thumb, fingers or the palm of the hand. Most tracker-balls have one to three buttons, which are used like mouse buttons. Trackballs can operate on any surface and are popular pointing devices for personal and laptop computers.

Digitisers

Digitising tables are used in flat pattern generation to input pattern information from existing paper or calico patterns. Digitisers therefore have a large working area, typically over A0 paper size. The input of pattern data must be accurate so the puck (cursor) has a window with cross hairs for pinpoint accurate placement. The digitising table is made of a reactive electronic surface, which may have a grid of embedded wires each carrying a coded signal. The puck has an electronic device that picks up these signals and translates them to give an exact fixed point on the screen.

Graphics Tablet

A Graphics Tablet is a tabletop digitiser. It consists of a board (tablet) and pen (stylus) electronically connected to a computer. The board's complex electronics detect movement of the pen. For designers, the advantage of this device is that the operator can use hand-drawing techniques in order to 'draw' ideas electronically, allowing for far greater precision and accuracy than with a simple mouse. The drawing can then be manipulated in the normal way by the CAD software.

Digital camera

Digital cameras are becoming very common in industry for tasks such as the input of design information and for monitoring quality on a production line. Digital cameras can store images digitally, as opposed to recording them on film. Once a picture or image has been 'captured', it can be downloaded as data into a computer system for manipulation within a CAD program or stored on a photo CD or printed on a digital printer.

Digital image quality is determined by the amount of the camera's memory, the optical resolution of the digitising mechanism and by the final output device's resolution. Established printer technologies have their limitations but three printer technologies, 'thermo autochrome', 'dye sublimation' and digital printers produce better images.

For designers, digital cameras are economical because they eliminate film-processing costs. They are also fast, and allow easy, flexible image manipulation and editing. A digital camera allows an image to be in a CAD system within minutes of shooting. Digitally enhanced images are now a standard part of a vast range of media from product presentations to Internet and print-based product catalogues. If a company needs to get images in electronic form as fast as possible, then a digital camera is the only way to go.

TASK

Produce a range of digital images for use in your coursework folder. Investigate ways of editing the image and how images are transferred from the camera to a computer.

Scanner

A scanner is a device for converting analogue data, into the digital data that a computer can read. Scanners allow graphic images and text to be captured electronically for imputing into design software, where it can be edited and stored in the same way as other material. Scanners are able to scan both 2D surfaces and 3D objects. They have become easier to operate and more effective in recent times. Many companies are developing scanners with 'one touch' operation for ease of use.

Scanners commonly used in CAD include:

- large drum scanners – expensive but capable of scanning both opaque documents and transparencies at high resolutions of over 400 dots per inch (dpi)
- dedicated photo/transparency scanners for high-resolution photographic images
- handheld scanners, low cost small capacity devices with restricted scanning widths
- flatbed scanners, the most versatile and popular devices
- body scanners – new technology used for taking accurate body measurements.

Using a flat bed scanner to develop print designs
- Scan in original artwork, line drawings or fabrics.
- Reduce the design to a specific number of colours based on the seasonal colour palette.
- Put the design into repeat by painting or modifying motifs.
- Place registration to exact specifications for half-drop, slides or straight repeats.
- Produce electronic strike-offs and colour proofs for storyboards.
- Texture map design onto photographs for photorealistic images for use in promotional materials.
- Perform colour separation of designs and send to film plotters, laser engravers or image setters.

3D Scanner
The 3D scanners currently being used for body scanning work by scanning or digitising a series of profile curves that define the characteristics and physical geometry of the person. Digital data is collected and recorded to develop a 3D model within the computer software. CAD can then used to add colour and texture to add realism to produce a virtual person on screen. Alternately, measurement data can be used by a CAD pattern system to grade individual flat patterns.

There are two different methods of scanning a 3D object – contact or non-contact scanning.

Contact Scanning Systems
Contact scanning systems make a physical contact with the surface of the object with a probe, that is machine driven or manually operated. Scanned data can be exported in 3D DXF or VRML format for use in other software.

- Manual systems often use a mechanical arm with digital sensors in each joint. The probe moves over the surface, clicking and recording positional data that generates the required profile curves.
- A machine driven contact scanning system common in UK schools and colleges is the Roland Model, which can operate as a low cost 3D scanner.

Non-contact scanning systems

Non-contact methods of 3D scanning are used for body scanning. (See page 196.) They generally use geometric triangulation to create the three dimensional shapes.

The laser scanners currently being used are expensive non-contact, high-speed devices. They scan either by directing beams at various points to create a profile curve or by generating a 'laser stripe profile' of the object. The beams or stripes are reflected back to a video camera or sensors. For body scanning, an accurate surface profile is generated by scanning from different angles and body positions and mathematically processing the digital data.

TASK

1 Evaluate the different input devices available for use with computer system and explain the benefits of each.

2 Experiment with the use of a scanner for importing images, line drawings or fabric swatches. Develop these images further to produce usable design ideas.

COMMON OUTPUT DEVICES USED IN CAD SYSTEMS

Output devices, such as monitors, printers or plotters, enable a computer to display and manipulate graphics, which can be printed as hard copy. While output devices are usually connected to the computer by cable, some printers can be operated by infra-red and are therefore, literally, 'wireless'. Look at the back of your PC. You will see that the various cables are connected into the computer by communication ports. These vary according to the make of the computer. Some manufacturers, for ease of assembly, use different coloured pins for different cables. CAD systems, like most graphics systems, use a combination of vector and raster graphics. Most output devices use raster devices.

THE MONITOR

A monitor (computer screen or visual display unit – VDU) is an output device that displays pictures. The visual, creative nature of design work means that the clarity and capability of the monitor are vitally important in any CAD system. Colour and screen size are key issues. Available choices include:

- monochrome monitors, the most basic kind. These display only two colours, one for the background and one for the foreground. The colour combination can be black and white, green and black, or amber and black. While such monitors are becoming rare as technology improves, they are still used in word processing and on CNC machines for tasks where colour is unimportant
- grey-scale monitors are slightly more sophisticated, displaying different shades of grey
- colour monitors can display up to one million different colours and are a vital part of textile and fashion design.

Screen size

Screen size or viewable area, is particularly important in any CAD system. Monitors measuring at least 400mm from corner to corner – known as full-page monitors – are most suitable for graphics work, with many designers using 450cm monitors. Large monitors can display two full pages, side by side. The screen's resolution indicates how many pixels (dots per inch) are on the screen. In general, the more pixels the sharper the image.

PRINTERS

A printer is an output device that can print text or graphics onto paper, card, film and fabric. Not all printers can produce high quality images. In this section we will consider the following printers:

1 Ink jet	4 Thermo autochrome
2 Laser	5 Digital.
3 Dye sublimation	

These printers are classified by quality, speed and their ability to create realistic images:

- Quality – ink-jet and laser printers produce letter-quality type, for example.
- Speed – printing speeds are measured in characters per second (cps) or pages per minute (ppm). The speed of printers within a particular type varies widely. Laser printers vary in speed from 4 to 20 pages per minute. In large, busy companies, it is a false economy to invest in printers that are too slow – the wastage of staff time where this problem exists can be extraordinary.
- Realistic images – techniques such as dithering, half toning and continuous tones produce printouts that most closely match what is on the screen and what a designer wants to produce.

Ink-jet printers

Ink-jet or non-contact printers (the kind found in many homes beside the family PC) produce low cost, high-quality text and graphics in colour by combining cyan, magenta, yellow and black. (CMYK) In a cost-conscious industry, their economy is a distinct advantage over more expensive laser printers. Using thermal technology, ink-jet printers produce heated bubbles of ink that burst, rapidly spraying ink on to the paper to form an image. As the ink nozzle cools, it creates a vacuum that draws in a fresh supply of ink and the process is repeated time and again. The print head prints in strips across the page, moving downwards to complete the full documents. Ink-jet printers, which work equally well in colour or black and white, are sometimes called 'Bubble Jet' printers – a very familiar commercial name, as it is the actual trade name of Canon ink printers.

While economical compared with laser printers, ink-jet printers, unfortunately, need their cartridges changed frequently. In the workplace, when high quality images are required, such printers will perform best when expensive, coated paper is used, increasing the cost per page. Images with large areas of colour can 'bleed' if used with cheaper absorbent paper of if too much ink has been used. Bleeding causes images to appear blurred as the colours run together. Ink-jet images can easily smudge, too, as they take some time to dry. Not a good look with which to impress potential customers.

Laser printers

Laser printers use the same technology as copying machines – often with price tags and service costs to match. Their modus operandi is: the printer receives data from the computer; this data is processed and controls the movement of a laser beam directing light at a large roller or drum. When the laser light hits the drum it creates an electrical discharge, which creates the required image. The drum then rotates through a powder called toner, which is attracted towards the electrically charged areas. The print is made when the toner is transferred onto the paper by a combination of heat and pressure. Laser printers produce very high quality text and graphics, suitable for presentations and sales brochures.

Dye Sublimation Printers

These are low speed devices that produce expensive, high quality graphic and photographic images. The four coloured inks or dyes – cyan, magenta, yellow black (CMYK) are stored on rolls of film. A heating element turns the ink on the film into a gas, with the amount of ink put on paper correlating to the temperature of the heating element. The temperature varies in relation to the image density of the original drawing or artwork. Dye Sublimation Printers produce high quality images because the ink is applied as a continuous tone rather than as a series of dots. Special paper is used to enhance the process to ensure precise, accurate colour reproductions – a major advantage when colour is a major selling point.

Thermo Auto Chrome (TA) printing

TA is used to print high quality images generated by a digital camera. The complex process involves the use of special TA paper, containing three layers of coloured pigment, cyan, magenta and yellow. The coloured pigment is sensitive to a particular temperature. The TA printer is equipped with both thermal and ultraviolet heads, which activate the colour in the paper. This is then 'fixed' by ultraviolet light.

Digital printers

1 Digital printers are used to produce photographic quality images from a digital camera without having to transfer data to a computer. The printers can also be connected to a monitor for viewing and editing images and layouts. Some digital camera manufacturers supply digital printers to match their cameras.

2 In the last few years, there has been a lot of interest from designers, manufacturers and retailers in the digital printing of fabrics. Although currently an expensive option, digital printing technology is expected to secure up to 15 per cent of the textile printing market in the near future. This is likely to be in niche markets and will be linked to mass customisation.

Digital printing

Digital printing uses inkjet technology to print designs, developed using a CAD system, directly onto a pre-treated fabric. Thermal inkjet printers use reactive dyes, but cannot print pigment dyes with built-in binder, due to the thermal nature of its drop head formation. The heat reacts with the binder causing the print head to fail. On the other hand, Piezo printers offer a distinct advantage – they run all available dyes, including the new pigment digital printing dyes. The higher resolution of Piezo printers and use of seven colours greatly reduces dither problems and they give photo-realistic reproduction of photographs. It is for this reason that they are expected to be the emerging technology.

- In digital printing systems ink-jet printers are used to print up to 1.60m width small run lengths of cotton, viscose or silk fabrics.
- This developing technology is already providing high-speed printing on-demand. This ink-jet technology can be linked to any CAD system to cut the pre-production process from weeks to days.
- There are no screens or paste to prepare, resulting in no machine down time.
- This system enables the printing of short lengths for sample making, the printing of side-by-side colourways and the production of short run lengths of exclusive designs at affordable prices.

Some digital printers have the capacity to plot pattern pieces, print and cut the fabric. With the rapid developments in digital printing, it is likely that printing and cutting in one operation will become the norm. The printing of single ply fabrics to order, to a pre-defined marker will mean that only the fabric that will become part of a garment will be printed. Stock holding of fabric would be reduced to a few greige fabrics printed on a just-in-time basis.

PLOTTERS

Plotters differ from printers in that they draw lines using a pen. As a result, they can produce continuous lines, whereas printers can only simulate lines by printing a closely spaced series of dots. A plotter draws images on paper or any other suitable surface via computer commands and can produce large, full-colour, high quality drawings.

There are two classes of plotter, vector and raster. Vector plotters produce an image as a set of straight lines, fill patterns are clearly visible and they operate comparatively slowly. All Raster Plotters generate an image as a series of points.

XY Plotter

The term XY simply refers to the axes along which the plotting pen can travel. Multi-colour plotters use different-coloured pens to draw different colours. Plotters are considerably more expensive than printers, but are essential where precision is required.

Plotter-cutters

Plotter-cutters can plot drawings in the same way as the XY plotter, but they can also produce cut shapes in card, vinyl and other sheet materials using thin blades. Plotter-cutters are used for cutting flat pattern card templates used in the garment industry. The cutting head operates two tools: a steel blade and a pen for annotation. Some flat bed cutters enable materials to be laid flat and held in place by magnetic strips.

TASK

Describe the difference between a printer and a plotter, giving examples of the end-use of each.

CNC MACHINES

CNC machines provide an interface between CAD and CAM. A jacquard loom is an early example of an NC machine. The jacquard loom was originally driven by instructions on a punched card system. Dobby looms had a system of linked wooden strips with holes for pegs to lift the selected loom shafts. However, computer programs now control the operation of many NC machines, which are now called Computer Numerically Controlled (CNC) machines. Knitting machines and looms, fabric cutting equipment, sewing and embroidery machines have all been computerised. Computerised digital printing systems enable the fast production of small runs lengths for exclusive designs. CNC laser devices now perform some operations, such as fabric cutting.

Chapter 3

Computer-aided Manufacture (CAM)

In the textile and sewn goods industry, CAD and its link into the manufacturing process (CAM) has had the greatest impact, so far, on creative fabric and product design, pattern generation and grading, marker-making and cutting. The use of CAD and CAM first appeared in the cutting room in the 1970s, led by Gerber in the USA. At that time the use of computer systems gave significant reductions in lead times, fabric utilisation and labour costs. By the early 1980s, around 50 per cent of companies in the USA used CAD systems. At present, it is used almost 100 per cent across all advanced sewn goods industries. Developments in software and hardware have brought down the price of CAD/CAM systems, so many small companies can now afford their own systems or use a bureau service.

CNC MACHINES

Computer-aided manufacturing relies on the use of computer software to control CNC machines. These enable the automated production of textiles, such as fibres, yarns and fabrics. Knitting machines and looms, fabric spreading and cutting machines, materials handling, retrieval and storage make use of CAM systems. Sewing machines make use of electronic control and programmable sequences and digital printing systems enable the fast production of small run lengths for exclusive designs. The following section examines the use of some CNC machines and related manufacturing technologies.

KNITTING TECHNOLOGY

The first true knitted sock was made around the 7th to 9th century, although knit-like structures (called 'sprang') were known in Peru around 1100 BC. Knitting remained, for centuries, the chief method for making footwear. Since that time, and especially over the last 100 years, there have been a number of key technological developments in knitting and knitting machine technology.

- These include the development of the latch needle, interlock, the double cylinder sock machine, automatic needle selection, the multi-feeder large diameter circular machine and early electronic selection devices.
- The revolutionary 4-feed seamless hosiery machine became the forerunner of today's all-electronic models.

- Further developments included, in 1969, the first electronic needle selection machine controlled by computer. This was followed in 1975 by a range of electronic selection and control V-bed flat machines, which sparked the electronic knitwear revolution.

FLAT KNITTING

Flat knitting is the only method for producing shaped 'fully-fashioned' textile goods. The evolution from cut-and-sew knitting to fully-fashioned has reduced the dependence on manual labour of cut-and-sew methods. However, fully-fashioned knitting has remained a very labour-intensive process, in which separately knitted pieces are linked and sewn together by hand or by manually-operated equipment.

In the 1990s, however, the Shima Seiki fully automatic, seamless glove knitting machines were developed using weft-knitting technology. These flatbed, narrow width machines could shape entire gloves with closed fingertips and required no post-stitching of the finger tubes. This technology enabled the development of 'WholeGarment' technology, in which an entire sweater could be knitted by machine without the need for any sewing or linking. The advantages of WholeGarment technology include:

- eliminates cut loss and waste
- lowers material costs per item
- reduces material consumption, leading to a more environmentally-friendly product
- makes on-demand production possible, because knitting a whole garment in one piece reduces lead time
- reduces the dependence on sewing and manual labour, providing an opportunity for bringing production back to the consumer market – rather than relying on cheaper labour overseas
- eliminates bulky seams to create a lightweight, comfortable garment with better drape and fit
- provides added value across the market from fashion garments to casual wear, sportswear and children's wear
- could enable the production of a new style garments that will attract the attention and purchasing power of a younger generation.

The most important advancement in improving WholeGarment technology has been the introduction of the next generation of 'FIRST' machines. (See 3BCC.2). The FIRST (Fully-fashioned, Intarsia, Rib transfer and Sinker) machine provides increased pattern capability, such as Milano rib, inlay, pleating and flared skirts. It enables improved 3D shaping, in which the front and back of the garment can be shaped independently of the other. This gives more flexibility for producing knitted-in pockets, collars, buttonholes and other trimmings, avoiding the need for sewing. In addition, the shoulder line for set-in sleeves can be positioned further back over the shoulder, resulting in a more comfortable garments which corresponds better to the shape of the body. Although WholeGarment technology may not totally replace more conventional forms of knit production, it may well be on its way to becoming the mainstream knit production method of the future.

CIRCULAR KNITTING

The main attraction of electronic circular weft-knitting machines is their high-speed production capability, which is five to ten times faster than flat machines. Circular machines have needles arranged in a circular formation, with a succession of yarns feeding the needles continuously in one direction. For example in a 24 multi-feed system there are 24 points at which knitting occurs at the same time, to produces tubular knitted fabric, composed of spirals of yarns. The rate of production for a 24 feed machine will be 24 times greater than for a single yarn feed machine.

Circular weft-knit manufacturers supply the clothing industry with a wide range of fabrics, including Polar fleece. These may be split open to their full width during finishing so that garments may be cut from flat single layers. If tubular fabrics are used for T-shirts and underwear, they are not split open, eliminating the need for side seams. Such garments are completed by cutting out and seaming the neck and armholes.

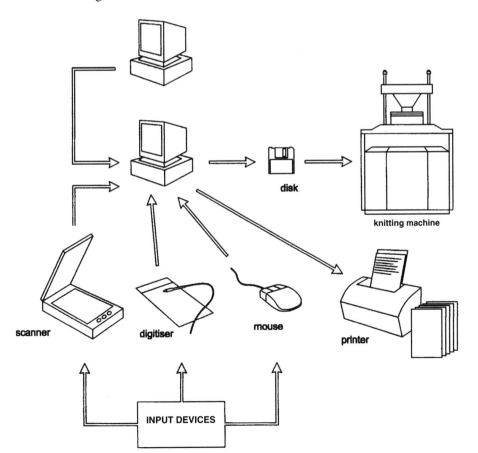

Figure 3B.7
Connecting a circular knitting machine to a computer system.

In circular knitting, high-tech pattern preparation systems deal not only with patterning, but also provide feedback about production. Work stations include a PC with screen, printer, scanner and graphics tablet. Pattern development programmes, data monitoring systems, programmable yarn feeders and precise tension control ensure speedy production.

Over the last 10 years the seamless bodywear concept has revolutionised circular knitting technology. This is expected to eventually capture as much as 40 per cent of the global clothing market for underwear and sportswear. The main advantages of these body-diameter circular machines is that they have unlimited pattern capacity, high productivity and reduce the need for garment assembly.

TASK

1 Investigate different uses of computer software for developing textile designs.

2 Examine a range of knitted products and explain which knitting technology was used in their manufacture.

WEAVING TECHNOLOGY

The basic concept of weaving fabric has always been the same – the interlacing of two sets of threads are right angles. In early Pre-Columbian times Peruvian weavers were able to construct complex woven fabrics using the most simple, backstrap looms. The industrial revolution, of course, brought about major changes in weaving technology, so that the production of textiles became an industry rather than a domestic activity. Since those times, developments in weaving machinery have been numerous, but it was in 1954 that weaving technology was revolutionised by the development of the projectile weaving machine, the first shuttleless loom. Today, there are more that 200,000 shuttleless looms in operation around the world. Most weaving developments these days are related to speed and weft insertion systems – for example, there are other sorts of shuttleless systems such as air-jet technology. These days high speed weaving systems are precision-controlled by microprocessors and monitored 100 per cent throughout production.

TASK

Describe the benefits that the use of CAM brings to fabric manufacture.

SEWN PRODUCT TECHNOLOGY

All the leading CAD/CAM companies supply automatic marker making software. The use of these systems results in fabric utilisation as good as that produced manually using CAD marker making packages.

- Fabric spreading and cutting are the only garment manufacturing operations to have been fully automated.
- Gerber's new automated plaid/stripe matching system uses an advance camera and optics system, which enables the user to zoom in on critical areas for added precision and thread-to-thread accuracy of cut parts.
- Sewing is still a hands-on process, although sewing machinery is becoming increasingly sophisticated and specialised. Around 5,000 different types of sewing machines have been designed for industrial sewing applications. Such machines use electronic and programmable control, or sequence functions to achieve the automation of some sewing processes and to obtain sewing quality. The basic principles of lockstitch and chainstitch, though, have not changed and probably will not for the forseeable future.

Using CADCAM for pattern cutting and sampling

Pattern cutting for garments is specialised and demanding work and all patterns were originally cut by hand. Now CAD/CAM pattern design systems make the work faster and cleaner. For example, a pattern making, grading and sampling system can print a fabric sample length, cut a pattern using digital information and make a sample garment in under eight hours, starting from the design development on screen. The sample garment then has to be accepted by the client before the pattern can be sent via a modem to the manufacturer. This is how a pattern cutter works to develop a new pattern:

- A standard specification sheet gives the garment construction and style.
- A new pattern can be drawn by hand and put on a digitising table to plot each pattern piece into the computer database.
- Usually a basic 'block' or template from the database, close to the chosen design can be adapted to match the specification. All sizes can be automatically graded to produce small, medium or large sizes.

The pattern goes to the sample room, which uses production type machinery to model production methods. The garment is made in a medium size and shown to the client for approval. At this stage adaptations can be made, then a 'first fit' is agreed and the pattern goes into production.

TASK

Use the Internet and other information sources to investigate modern CAD/CAM technology. Produce an information sheet to record your findings. Describe how you could use CAM in your own design work.

USING CAM FOR DIFFERENT LEVELS OF PRODUCTION

CAM involves the use of computer systems to control manufacturing equipment, making it easier and quicker to produce cost-effective one-off, batch produced and high volume textile products. The choice to use CAM will depend on the intended scale of production, the number of identical products to be produced and the cost benefits that it can bring.

One-off production (sometimes called bespoke)

Some textile end-products made using bespoke production require the development of different kinds of manufacturing technology. One example is the design and building of large architectural forms (such as the Millennium Dome) using tensioned textile structures. Such projects require the development of the most advanced materials and technologies. An Italian company called Cannobio designs and manufactures the textile components for such structures. These require the sewing of very strong seams. Cannobio worked with machine manufacturers to develop a computer-controlled sewing machine, operated by a rail-mounted system, that could both sew and weld Teflon-coated glass fibre fabrics. Since the design of these structures is done exclusively on computers, a digital cutting system capable of cutting the fabric for such large structures was required. The answer was to use a digital high-speed cutting system 12 feet wide and 105 feet long!

Batch production

Batch production requires the use of flexible systems and adaptable equipment, capable of managing the change over of styles required in a fast-moving industry. CNC machines are ideally suited to this kind of production, because they are easy to program to give a fast a turn round between batches.

High volume

CAM systems and the use of CNC machines are ideally suited to high volume production because they provide the capability of producing high quality identical products. Products like fibres and fabrics or even socks or underwear (that have a slower turn round of style or colour change) may be produced on a continuous basis. Future trends in high volume manufacturing will increasingly use CAD and CAM to enable quick response and 'customised' mass production to meet the needs of specific market sectors.

ADVANTAGES OF CAM

CAM systems provide numerous advantages for manufacturing industry, mostly related to time-to-market, reduced costs and waste management and the standardisation and reliability of products. The introduction of computer-controlled systems of manufacture such as Just in Time (JIT) means that:

- the level of production can be linked directly to the size of the order
- raw materials ordered 'just in time' reduce costly stock levels
- CNC machines can operate more flexibly to enable the development of quick response systems
- CNC machines can undertake repetitive tasks rapidly with fewer errors than human operators
- machines can operate 24 hours a day if necessary, do not need holidays and are not affected by other human constraints
- manufacturing time can be reduced from weeks to days or hours
- manufacturing costs can be estimated more accurately, as production rates are more consistent than with machines operated by humans
- high quality finished products can be distributed to order from retailers
- companies are more likely to manage sudden changes of demand in their particular market
- new technology that reduces the dependence on sewing and manual labour, may provide an opportunity for bringing production back to the consumer market
- companies have the opportunity to manufacture custom-made mass produced products.

DISADVANTAGES OF CAM

CAM does bring some disadvantages, mostly related to social issues and globalisation.

- The cost of buying and installing CAD/CAM systems and computerised machines is high, although costs of new technology fall in time.
- Manufacturers wanting to be competitive need to keep up with new technology – an expensive but necessary undertaking.
- With developments in automation, there may be less human involvement in the manufacturing process in the future – a pattern that may be repeated across the world.
- CAM can create social problems. The control of CNC machines by a central system reduces some jobs to 'machine minding', which can lead to poor job satisfaction and reduce productivity. This is balanced in some companies by the introduction of teamworking.

TASK

1 Explain what is meant by CNC.

2 Discuss the key issues relating to the introduction of computer-aided manufacturing.

EXAM PRACTICE

The questions below are similar in style to the ones you will find in the examination paper for this unit. Before attempting to answer the questions read the relevant sections in the unit. Make note using key words or spider diagrams about the topic.

1 a) The use of CAD has revolutionised the way designers work. Explain the following terms in relation to CAD:

    i) a digitiser   (2)

    ii) a 3D scanner   (2)

  b) Explain how computers are used in product design and manufacture.   (4)

  c) Using examples from your chosen materials area, explain the advantages of using CNC machines.   (7)

2 a) Define the following terms:

    i) Virtual product

    ii) Photorealistic image

    iii) Standard format   (6)

  b) Describe how a CAD system combines the use of raster and vector graphics.   (4)

  c) Discuss the impact of computer systems on the production processes in your chosen materials area.   (5)

3 a) Discuss how the choice of CAM as a manufacturing process depends on the scale of production.   (6)

  b) Explain the meaning of the term CIM. Discuss how CIM enables cost-effective manufacturing.   (9)

Unit 4 Section A
FURTHER STUDY OF MATERIALS, COMPONENTS AND SYSTEMS

Preview

Unit	Level	Components	Areas of study
4	A2	**Section A:** Further study of materials, Components and Systems	• Selection of materials • New Technologies and the creation of new materials • Values issues
		Section B: Options	• Design and Technology in Society OR • CAD/CAM

UNIT 4 STRUCTURE

Unit 4 has two sections, both of which must be studied. Section A includes further subject content related to textile materials, components and systems. Section B has two Options, each with subject content. You must study the same ONE Option from Section B that you studied in Unit 3.

WHAT YOU WILL LEARN IN THE UNIT

The content of Unit 4 Section A builds on what you studied at AS level and enables you to develop further your understanding of textile materials, components and systems. The work you undertake must include knowledge and understanding of the following areas:

Chapter 1   Selection of materials
• Understanding, devising and selecting appropriate methods of construction for textile materials and products
• The relationship between characteristics, properties and materials choice.

Chapter 2   New technologies and the creation of new materials
• The creation and use by industry of modern materials, smart fabrics and performance textiles
• The impact of modern technology and biotechnology on the development of innovative fibres, fabrics and finishing processes
• Modification of the properties of materials.

Chapter 3   Values issues
• The impact of values issues on textile product design, development and manufacture.

WHAT YOU WILL DO IN THE UNIT

During the unit you should undertake a variety of tasks to enable you to understand the subject content. You may be asked to:

- work individually on some practical tasks to develop understanding about materials properties.
- work individually on some theoretical aspects of the unit content – for example you could use the Internet to research information about new technologies and new materials, then share your findings with the group
- work collaboratively with others on some activities – for example you could investigate the influence that 'values' issues have on the design, development and manufacture
- work individually on exam-style questions.

UNIT 4 ASSESSMENT

Unit 4 is externally assessed through a $1\frac{1}{2}$ hour written exam, which assesses your understanding of the unit subject content. There is one paper, with two sections:

- Section A: Materials, Components and Systems
- Section B: Options

UNIT 4 SECTION A ASSESSMENT

The work that you do in Materials, Components and Systems will be assessed through Section A of the Unit 4 examination paper.

- Section A is similar in style to Unit 3.
- It consists of six short-answer knowledge-based questions, each worth five marks.
- You are advised to spend 45 minutes on this section of the exam paper.
- This section, together with the option, is worth 15 per cent of the full Advanced GCE.

WHAT THE EXAMINER IS LOOKING FOR

The examination paper is designed to give you the opportunity to demonstrate your understanding of what you have learned in the unit. Examiners will look for a more in-depth response, when describing or explaining topics or processes at the Advanced GCE level.

EXAM TIPS

- Make brief notes about the topics covered in this unit.
- Summarise the key points on one or two sheets of paper.
- Learn these key points.
- Practise working through a complete exam so you will learn how to allocate the time available to you.
- In the exam read the questions through and then read them again to make sure you understand what you are being asked to do.
- Plan your answer briefly then check the question again to make sure that you have covered it fully.
- Work through your answer making sure that you address each point in your plan.
- Don't write everything you know about a topic if it's irrelevant to the question!
- Use clearly written sentences and bullet points to make your answer clear.
- Use specialist technical terms and clear sketches to illustrate your answer where appropriate.
- Read through your answer, then move on to the next question.

Chapter 1
Selection of Materials

This section develops understanding of the relationship between the structure of materials, (i.e. yarns, woven, knitted and non-woven fabrics), their properties and their end-use in products. This will include knowledge and understanding related to your own use of materials and to commercial end uses. The section will help you understand the importance of selecting the right material for the job and introduce you to an exciting range of innovative fibres, fabrics and processes.

UNDERSTANDING, DEVISING AND SELECTING APPROPRIATE METHODS OF CONSTRUCTION FOR TEXTILE MATERIALS AND PRODUCTS

The ability to select and match the material to the end product is developed through knowledge and understanding of fibres, fabric structure (construction) and finishing processes. Each of these influences how a textile material looks, behaves and performs. Selecting an appropriate fabric construction that meets the requirements of the product is one of the basic decisions a product designer makes. The three most commonly used fabric constructions are woven, knitted and non-woven. Each of these constructions helps determine a fabric's quality, weight and handle – which in turn determine its suitability for different types of products.

THE RELATIONSHIP BETWEEN CHARACTERISTICS, PROPERTIES AND MATERIAL CHOICE

A basic knowledge and understanding of materials is essential for all designers, as well as the ability to keep up with developments in materials and processes. Designers need to use their creativity and technical knowledge to translate their ideas into saleable products that can be sold at a price consumers are prepared to pay. In order to make informed decisions when selecting the right material for the job, designers need to think about a range of different factors, including properties and characteristics, the cost of materials in relation to the required quality, the scale of production and life costs.

RAW MATERIALS

All textile product development begins with basic raw materials – fibres and fabrics. It is interesting to note that developments in raw materials have been the determining factor in most of the textile product innovation that has taken place over the last few years. This applies to developments in materials that we use everyday as well as those specially engineered fabrics used for a variety of products, ranging from sportswear to industrial end-uses.

- As consumers we expect that everyday textile materials perform well, both in use and in the long term. We expect them to be aesthetically pleasing, to perform to expectations, to be easy to care for and maintain and to last for as long as the product is required.
- Textile materials that are engineered for special end-uses have even higher expectations placed upon them. For example materials used for technical or industrial end-uses have to perform to the highest levels of safety, strength and durability. In an industrial product such as a car tyre, wear and deterioration are important factors that have to be taken in to consideration when choosing the materials to be used.

Properties and characteristics

Selecting the right material for the job is therefore of great importance. The ability to select and match the material to the end product is developed through knowledge and understanding of fibres, fabric structure and finishing processes. Developing an understanding of the relationship between the properties of fibres and the characteristics of fabrics is important for any textile product designer – even more so these days when the range of materials to choose from is ever widening.

For example, many industrial products make use of specially engineered textile raw materials. Ropes made of Kevlar®, fibre have been used to form the stay cables of a footbridge across the River Tay at Aberfeldy in the Scottish Highlands. The ropes provide the strength of steel without the drawbacks of weight and corrosion. In fact, Kevlar®, is five times stronger than steel of an equivalent weight!

TASK

Create a textile materials resource folder. This could include a collection of fabric swatches and/or magazine pictures of products made from innovative fabrics. Find out about the fabrics in your collection:
- Investigate the fibre content and fabric structure.
- Find out about the properties and characteristics of the fabrics.
- Suggest a range of end-uses for your fabrics.

MATERIALS CHOICE

A range of factors are involved in materials choice. A good starting point is to examine the property requirements of a product and to match those requirements with suitable materials. The characteristics of every textile raw material are built around a number of related factors:

- aesthetic and functional properties of fibres and fabrics
- fabric structure – is the fabric is woven, knitted or non-woven?
- the enhanced properties brought about through finishing processes.

It is helpful to look at the property requirements of a number of different products to see why a specific material was chosen for the job.

Looking at products

Motorcycle suits need to be made to the highest specification in order to provide protection against cuts and other injuries to the skin. The suits need to be abrasion-resistant, flexible, flame and heat-resistant as well as being breathable. Quite a tall order for the designer! Fortunately, the power of blends comes to the rescue. One such suit on the market today is made from a blend of Kevlar® Cordura®, (a high strength nylon fibre) and Lycra®. The suit is made from woven fabric that combines strength with elasticity, breathability and superior abrasion protection. It is flame and heat-resistant.

Geotextiles are permeable membranes made mainly from manufactured synthetic fibres. They are used in contact with soil or rocks in the construction of roads, rail track and buildings, for embankment reinforcement and to provide drainage in land reclamation. Geotextiles need to provide filtration for water but not for soil, so that land is stabilised. They need to be permeable, strong, bond with the soil and be very durable. For example, in road construction, rolls of geotextiles can be used on road embankments, holding together metres of soft muddy soils. Such geotextiles are made from warp-knitted 100% polyester and are required to be durable for 100 years. The strength requirements are calculated, with allowances made for chemical degradation. The rolls and roll lengths are custom made to eliminate overlaps or cutting. Look out for geotextiles next time you pass motorway roadworks!

Designers working at the fashion end of the market also have to make informed decisions about the right material for the job. Fashion fabrics need to combine quality with comfort and functionality and are usually knitted or woven. They need to provide good looks with the ability to fit in with modern lifestyles – easy care is expected. Look up some examples of clothing designed by Clements Ribiero using Tencel®, fibres. Tencel® provides a range of properties that include breathability, comfort, softness and aftercare performance. 'Tencel®, is the unique combination of natural luxury and high-tech performance', state Clements Ribiero.

Specifying fabrics

After looking at the property requirements of the different products shown above, it easy to understand why selecting the most suitable fibre and fabric for a product is one of the most important aspects of product development. There is the added complication that in sewn product manufacture fabric characteristics need to meet the requirements of efficient making up, as well as meeting the needs of users. Fabrics need to be fault-free, uniform in appearance, stable, shrink-resistant and provide good drape and performance in fusing and sewing. The fabric also needs to meet user requirements, which in clothing mainly relate to wear performance and easy care properties. Fabric requirements need to be very precisely specified so that the textile manufacturer knows what to produce and the product manufacturer gets what is required. A typical fabric specification for a woven fabric is shown in Table 4A.1. You will note that the specification refers to the fibre content and length / width requirements. It is important for manufacturers of any sewn product to have enough fabric to make the necessary number of products.

Table 4A.1

Fabric specification	
Fabric	Ten pieces of wool worsted/Lycra fabric
Fibre content / yarn	98 per cent wool / 2 per cent Lycra
Ends (warp ends)	36 per cm +/–1
Picks (weft picks)	24 per cm +/–1
Structure	2/2 twill
Length	50m x 10 pieces = 500m
Width	150cm +/–1cm
Weight	300g/m² +/–10g/m²
Shrinkage	1 per cent in warp and weft

These days, it is becoming more usual for fabrics to be bar-coded so that all the relevant details follow it right through the manufacturing process. For manufacturers of branded materials, issues related to fibre identification are vitally important. Imitation products labelled with false fibre identity cause problems for the whole product supply chain. Fibre, fabric and product manufacturers may lose the confidence of consumers if products do not live up to expectation. For example, there could be fatal consequences if branded materials used in high performance products are not correctly labelled. People undertaking high-risk sports or dangerous jobs have to be certain that protective wear will perform as required – whether the clothing is fire or chemical-resistant or all-weather wear, the user has to be able to rely on the product.

TASK

It is important to be aware of materials characteristics when selecting fabrics for products.

1 Collect magazine pictures of a range of different textile products.

2 For each product describe the requirements of the manufacturer and of the user.

3 Suggest suitable fabrics for each of the products, including the fibre content and structure.

Quality and materials

Quality is a very important factor when selecting materials. The selected material should have the most suitable properties for the job *and* be of an acceptable quality in use – all this adds up to fitness-for-purpose. It must be remembered that the most suitable material is not necessarily the most expensive, because in many cases there needs to be a compromise between quality and cost. For example, specifying a property on top of what is required – such as water-repellent or stain-resist – would add unnecessarily to the cost of a product and may require special or different making-up processes.

Fabric quality

The term quality has a special meaning in relation to textiles. Fabric 'quality' is a term used to describe technical details that result in the fabric having specific properties such as handle, drape and weight. The woven fabric is firstly based on the specified quality, then developed using coloured or textured yarns and weave variations. The fabric specification in Table 4A.1 gives the following technical details:

- Fabric – wool worsted/ Lycra®,
- Fibre content / yarn – 98 per cent wool / 2 per cent Lycra®,
- Ends – 36 per cm (how closely the yarns are set in the loom)
- Picks – 24 per cm (how closely the weft is beaten down into the fabric)
- Structure – 2/2 twill
- Weight – 300 grammes per square metre.

The technical details listed above enable the fabric to be made exactly to the quality required. The relationship between the ends and picks per centimetre, the yarn and the weave structure results in a fabric with a weight of 300 grammes per square metre. A fabric of this weight using wool worsted/ Lycra®, yarns will have the handle and drape required by the product manufacturer.

Figure 4A.1

A plain weave intersects over and under each thread, which is the tightest weave construction.

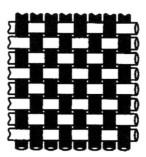

Plain weave

A plain weave intersects over and under each thread, which is the tightest weave construction.

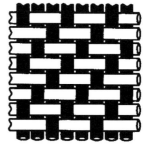

Twill weave

In a 2/2 twill weave the yarns intersect in pairs – over two threads and under two threads. The yarns slide over each other more easily, giving a looser construction. Twill weaves therefore need to have the warp yarns set closer together than plain weave.

- The fabric in Table 4A.1 is set at 36 ends per cm and 24 picks per cm, which means that there is a higher number of warp yarns than weft yarns per square cm. A higher proportion of warp yarns in a fabric give it good drape – which is why twill weave is used for garments and curtains – it hangs well.
- A twill weave fabric needs more ends per centimetre than a plain weave using the same yarn, because a twill structure has fewer intersections of warp and weft yarn. See Figure 4A.1.
- Most sewn product manufacturers buy fabrics of a specified weight in grammes per square metre, which is an indication of the quality of the cloth. Just for comparison, a chiffon fabric would weigh around 30g/m^2, shirt fabric around $100\text{-}150 \text{ g/m}^2$ and cotton denim around 400 g/m^2.

TASK

Compare the handle and drape of plain and twill weave fabrics.

1 Examine the fabrics through a magnifying glass to identify the weave structure.
2 Count the number of warp yarns and weft yarns per centimetre in the plain weave fabric. Are there the same number of warp and weft yarns per centimetre?
3 Count the number of warp yarns and weft yarns per centimetre in the twill weave fabric. Are there more warp yarns than weft yarns per centimetre?
4 Compare the handle and drape of each fabric. Explain which would you use for a shirt and which for a skirt and why.
5 Give two reasons why a 3/1 warp-faced twill is used for denim fabrics.

Manufacturing processes and materials limitations

The scale of production – if the product is to be a one-off, batch or mass-produced – also has an influence on the choice of materials.

- A one-off Haute-Couture product or a custom-made geotextile will need to use materials with specific properties and characteristics. This may add to the cost of the product.
- Batch and mass-produced sewn products are made to suit the requirements of target market groups. Although their needs are taken into account, there has to be a compromise between cost and quality. The materials and components selected must be fairly inexpensive and easy to process to enable cost-effective and efficient manufacture.

Life costs

Cost is an important factor in the manufacture of all sewn products. It has an impact on the choice and quality of materials and components and on the eventual retail price of the product. Costing involves producing an accurate price for the product, which will make it saleable and create a profit. The cost of materials and components is only a part of the total manufacturing cost of a product – advertising and marketing, packaging and distribution also have to be considered, together with 'hidden costs'. These are costs related to the effects that the production, use and disposal of products has on people and the environment. They are sometimes called 'life costs'.

Environmental costs are increasingly important for product manufacturers, because of increasing legislation related to the environment. Manufacturers are encouraged to select and use materials economically and to manufacture textiles carefully, so that pollution to land, air or water is minimized. One way that textiles companies can help the environment is to reduce materials waste, which also helps them to cut their own costs. The three key approaches to raw materials waste management are:

- reduce   - re-use   - recycle.

TASK

Consider the impact that textile materials have on the environment. Use the following questions to assess the environmental impact of a natural fibre such as cotton or a synthetic fibre like polyester.
- Is the raw material from a renewable source?
- Does cotton or polyester production cause risk to people or the environment?
- Is the material biodegradable?
- Can the material be recycled?

THE FINAL CHOICE

The final choice of materials is always a compromise between the requirements related to aesthetic and functional properties, quality and cost. Sometimes it is possible to meet all of these requirements, although for some products the choice of materials always comes down to cost. For some consumers, the one single factor that influences the choice of textile products is aesthetics – what the product looks like, especially if the product is a fashion or household item. Although aesthetic properties are important, these days consumers are more aware of the benefits of easy-care and materials such as breathable fabrics. This awareness has come about mainly through the development of sports products. One other important aspect that needs to be taken into account when selecting materials is safety, especially for childrenswear and performance products. For example, it is illegal to state that a product is waterproof if it's not, although the material itself may be waterproof. The legal framework surrounding Health and Safety is there to ensure that materials and components are non-toxic and safe for people and the environment.

Chapter 2

New Technologies and the Creation of New Materials

This section describes some of the modern materials, smart fabrics and performance textiles available today. You will be familiar with many of the fibres indicated in the diagram since you have studied these in Unit 1 and in Unit 3A.

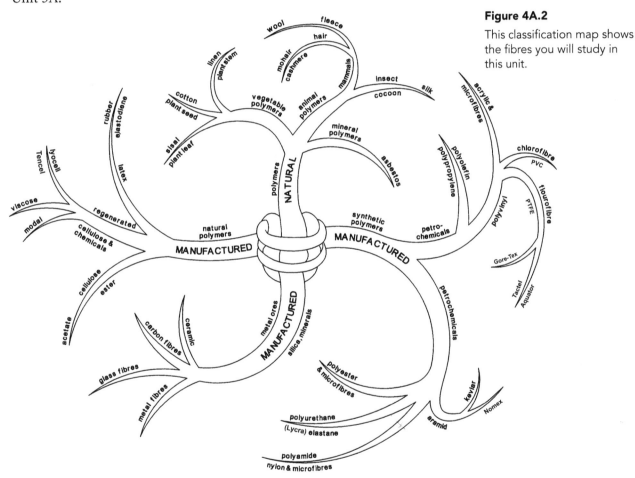

Figure 4A.2

This classification map shows the fibres you will study in this unit.

In textiles manufacture there is an ever-growing range of new fibres and processes being developed and used. It is neither possible nor desirable to cover all of these developments in this unit. Rather the unit provides an overview of some of the exciting developments in textiles that are currently being used for sportswear, fashion, technical and industrial products. You will be probably be familiar with some of the materials described in this unit – such as Tencel® – and may be less familiar with the aramid fibres Kevlar®, and Nomex®. Since many developments in textiles depend on blends, it is very difficult to avoid references to fibres such as Lycra®, which is used so extensively today.

The unit describes some of the developments in fabrics, fabric structures and composites. It gives examples of how such materials are used in products for industrial or technical textiles, including the use of smart fabrics. The section goes on to describe some of the ways in which modern technology and biotechnology are being used to develop new materials and processes.

The last section, 'Modification of properties of materials', challenges you to experiment with textile techniques and processes, including the use of unusual materials, in order to modify their properties.

Before progressing any further into the unit it would be a good starting point to define some of the terms that have been used in the preceding paragraphs. These terms include 'modern materials', 'smart fabrics', 'performance textiles', 'industrial textiles' and 'technical textiles'.

Modern materials

For the purposes of this unit modern materials include the regenerated cellulose fibres lyocell and Tencel®, the synthetic fibres Kevlar® and Nomex® as well as chlorofibre (PVC), fluorofibre (PTFE) and polyolefin (polypropylene). Not all of these fibres is entirely new, but many of them are engineered to produce fabrics with very special properties. Other ways of developing modern materials is through the use of blends.

Smart fabrics

Smart fabrics do more than make you look good and feel good. They provide added characteristics such as breathable, waterproof and windproof. Some smart fabrics are said to be 'intelligent' because they respond to the needs of the wearer and the environment. Smart fabrics often incorporate microelectronics.

Performance textiles

These are textiles that relate to a product's performance in a specific end-use. Performance textiles include products used for outdoor pursuits or sport.

Industrial textiles

These are textile materials manufactured to meet specific technical requirements. They are used for functional end-uses in industry, either as part of an industrial process or incorporated into industrial products.

Technical textiles

These are textiles manufactured mainly for their technical performance and functional properties rather than for aesthetic characteristics. They are used for protective clothing, upholstery, furnishings, buildings, civil engineering, sports products, leisure goods, agricultural products, medicine and health care.

TASK

Draw up a table with the headings 'modern, smart, performance, industrial and technical textiles'. Fill in the table to show end-use examples of each of these categories of textiles.

THE CREATION AND USE BY INDUSTRY OF MODERN MATERIALS, SMART FABRICS AND PERFORMANCE TEXTILES

There are many reasons for the creation of new materials, most of which relate to keeping the consumer motivated to buy new products and in maximising sales and profits. Fibre and fabric innovation have a key role to play. In this respect, the influence of performance textiles has been the driving force behind many exciting developments in fabrics in recent years.

The main areas in which fabric innovation occurs include:

- aesthetics – such as handle, drape, softness, lustre, weight, texture, pattern
- performance – such as easy-care, stretch, shape retention, durability, waterproof
- spinning and weaving – such as using blended yarns (like lyocell/Lycra®,) or microfibres
- finishing – such as bio-stoning denim, using resin treatments or producing peach skin effects
- garment finishing – such as non-iron or easy-care.

THE CREATION OF MODERN MATERIALS

The development of new materials is a difficult, expensive, complex and risky process. When developing modern materials, manufacturers need to meet a range of different demands depending on the end-use of the product. For example, when developing new fibres for garments, considerations of aesthetics, fibre versatility, fashion and performance-in-use characteristics need to be taken into account. In order to achieve commercial success in fibre/fabric innovation, the new material must offer consumers perceived benefits such as drape, handle, easy-care or crease-resistance. The benefits must provide consumers with a feeling of value-for-money.

Many developments in modern materials are based on fibre blending. This has long been used to develop new characteristics and properties in fabrics. Fibre blends are used for a number of reasons such as to:

- lower the cost of an expensive fibre
- produce a fabric to meet a price point – such as for the middle high-volume market
- improve the ease of manufacture of a yarn

Base Fibre	Added Fibre	Lower cost	Meet a price point	Easier to manufacture	Improve performance	Improve aesthetics	Widen finishes
Wool	Viscose		√	X		√	
Cotton	Modal		X		√	√	
Linen	Viscose	√ √			√	X	
Viscose	Polyester		√	√	√ √	X	
Polyester	Viscose		X	X			√
Modal	Nylon		√	X	√ √	X	
Cashmere	Wool	√ √				X	

Table 4A.2

- improve a fabric performance in use
- improve the aesthetics of a fabric
- widen the option of using different finishes.

Table 4A.2 shows the impact of blending a range of widely used fibres, using the criteria listed above. Benefits are shown by the use of a tick, whereas disadvantages are shown by the use of a cross. It can be seen that even the blending of widely used fibres results in changes in properties. It is this characteristic that enables textile manufacturers to produce such a wide variety of fabrics. It is easy to understand why the addition of even one single fibre (such as elastane) to the Table 4A.2 would have a far-reaching impact on the range of fabrics available to us today. Amazingly, the elastane fibre Lycra®, has been around for 40 years and was recently voted 14th out of 25 'Top fashion innovations of the 20th century! The addition of other modern fibres such as polyester microfibres, Tactel®, and Tencel®, also extend the possibilities for developing exciting new blends that provide aesthetic and performance characteristics in a range of different fabrics.

Meeting different demands

People working in high-risk environments need high quality protective clothing. This safety wear is made from knitted polyester for flexibility, strength and breathability. High visibility is achieved through the use of reflective bands. When developing modern materials, manufacturers need to meet a range of different demands depending on the end-use of the product. Many modern materials have been developed to meet the requirements of specific technological uses. For example in civil engineering or the emergency services, safety wear needs to meet the needs of both the user and the employer:

SPECIFICATION FOR SAFETY WEAR
For the user. The safety wear must be:

- highly visible, so the wearer can be easily seen
- flexible, so its easy to move in, not stiff or cumbersome
- comfortable to wear, breathable, cool in summer, warm in winter
- easy fastening, so nothing can get caught
- durable, waterproof, lightweight
- non-flammable for fire-fighters, provide protection

- resistant to real-life wear conditions, (e.g. soiling, storage in extreme heat of vehicle)
- attractive in style and colour.

For the employer. The product must:
- meet safety and performance requirements of British / European Legislation, carry the CE mark
- provide lifelong functional performance and be easy to maintain
- withstand industrial washing at extreme temperatures
- be a high quality, value-for-money product
- be available in a range of sizes
- provide a quality design that promotes a corporate image.

TASK

Discuss the reasons why fibre blending is often used as the basis for developing modern materials. Suggest two blends for each of the following textile products:
- a rucksack
- car upholstery
- a snow-boarding jacket

Justify your answer.

ENVIRONMENTALLY FRIENDLY FIBRES

Many of the fibres we use today are derived from oil, a precious commodity that took millions of years to create. As well as concerns relating to the over-use of non-renewable resources, many textile manufacturing processes also give rise to environmental problems. In response to such issues manufacturers

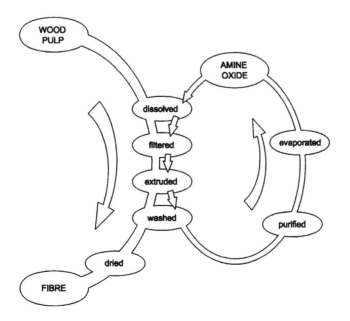

Figure 4A.3

The environmentally friendly lyocell process

are developing new methods of producing environmentally friendly fibres. The processes currently used for the production of regenerated cellulose fibres like viscose involve harmful chemicals that are costly to recycle. The new processes make use of renewable wood pulp cellulose which is processed using so-called 'clean technology' to produce a family of lyocell fibres.

Lyocell

Lyocell is the generic name for a high performance staple viscose fibre produced from renewable sources of wood pulp. It is made using an environmentally friendly process that recycles the non-toxic solvent amine oxide, used in its manufacture. Products made from lyocell can be recycled, incinerated, landfilled or digested in sewage. In anaerobic digestion (in a sewage farm) the fibre degrades completely in eight days to leave only water and carbon dioxide, which can be used to power the sewage plant itself. Characteristics of lyocell include:

- fibrillation – the ability for the fibres to split to give micro-fine surface hairs. Manufacturers of technical products can develop these microfibres to suit specific end-uses
- a variety of surface effects – finishing processes such as dyeing, milling, felting, sueding, sanding and brushing are used on woven fabrics, non-wovens and paper
- strength – lyocell is stronger than other cellulose fibres including cotton and out-performs many types of polyester
- absorbency – lyocell is easy-care, dyes well, has good 'wicking' properties so is breathable
- disposal – it is totally biodegradable and can be recycled.

Lyocell is an extremely versatile fibre, which can be used on its own or as a blend with cotton, or synthetic fibres. It is used for a variety of technical textiles, non-woven fabrics, special papers and fashion textiles, depending on the market needs.

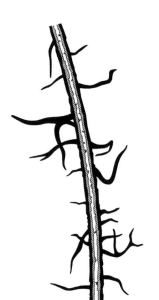

Figure 4A.4

Fibrillation of Tencel® and lyocell fibres is one of their most important characteristics. They can be manipulated during dyeing and finishing to give a wide range of surface properties.

Table 4A.3

Typical end-uses of lyocell

Technical textiles	Nonwovens	Special papers
• Protective clothing • Workwear • Coated fabrics • Sewing threads • Tents • Felts	• Medical wipes and dressings • Wet wipes • Leather substitutes • Filters • Interlinings	• Tea bags • Air/smoke/oil/ coffee filters • Map papers • Printing papers • High-strength Envelopes

Tencel®

Tencel® is the brand name for a high-performance viscose fibre, made from 100 per cent regenerated cellulose from trees in managed forests. It is made using a similar environmentally friendly process to lyocell. Tencel® is:

- stronger than cotton when wet and dry
- easy-care with very low shrinkage
- durable, luxurious yet practical
- very absorbent and breathable
- totally biodegradable and can be recycled.

When blended with other fibres such as wool, linen, cotton or elastane Tencel® provides enhanced softness, lustre and drape for clothing products. Tencel®, can be woven or knitted and is easily dyed and finished. The property of Tencel® to fibrillate (split) is one of its most important characteristics which is utilised in finishing to produce fabrics with variety of appearances. For example it can look like tough denim, but feel like velvet. Look out for denim jeans made from Tencel®!

TASK

1 Give three reasons for the development of modern materials.
2 Describe some of the benefits and disadvantages to textile manufacturers and to consumers of the development of modern materials.

HIGH SPECIFICATION ENGINEERED SYNTHETIC FIBRES

The development of new synthetic fibres and fibre blends provide textile product manufacturers with endless opportunities for marketing products with specific characteristics. It is worthwhile looking out for product swing tickets that may provide information about some of these fibres. Many high specification fibres that target specific end-uses are said to be 'engineered'. Not all of these fibres are new – for example, aramid fibres have been around since the 1970s. What is new for many high specification synthetic fibres is the wide range of end-uses to which they are now being put. One example is Kevlar®, which is now being used in blends for some leisure and fashion clothing.

Aramid

This is the generic name for a family of synthetic polymer fibres made from petro-chemicals. Expensive high-tech aramid fibres can be engineered to produce woven, knitted, non-woven or cabled technical textiles, which provide high strength and heat-resistance.

Kevlar®

This is the brand name for a family of aramid fibres are high strength, lightweight, flame and chemical-resistant, flexible and comfortable. Kevlar® is an important synthetic fibre because its unique properties make it suitable for a wide variety of industrial end-uses. It is five times stronger than steel of an equivalent weight which means that it can often replace more traditional resistant materials. As well as its uses in industry, the flexibility and comfort properties of Kevlar® make it suitable for a range of protective wear, such as chemical-resistant workwear. It has also been used for many years for bulletproof vests, because of its bullet-stopping power.

Other end-uses of Kevlar® include:

- equipment used for high-risk activities like hot-air ballooning
- high-tension cables and ropes for bridges, ships or space vehicles
- gloves that protect hands and fingers against cuts and other injuries
- strong, lightweight skis, helmets and tennis racquets
- industrial end-uses like tyres, car hoses, aircraft structures, and boats.

Nomex®

This is the brand name for a family of aramid fibres that are high temperature resistant. They have a unique combination of heat and flame resistance, durability, anti-static, low shrinkage, easy-care, comfort and aesthetic qualities. Nomex® is also resistant to most industrial oils, solvents and chemicals. The fibres can be dyed easily and are widely used for protection in industry, for the police and armed forces, for fire fighters and in high-risk sports. In motor racing, for example, Nomex® is used for protective overalls, head cover and underwear to protect drivers and mechanics from flames and heat caused by accidents.

Testing to meet safety requirements

All fibres used in protective wear have to be rigorously tested to meet safety requirements. The burns test manikin 'THERMO-MAN' is used by the textile company DuPont to evaluate the performance under simulated flash fire conditions of protective garments made from Nomex®. The manikin is dressed in the garment to be tested and exposed to flash fire for up to 10 seconds. The 122 sensors record the temperature rise on the surface of the manikin and computer programmes calculate the resulting area body burns and grades their severity. The protective capabilities of Nomex® were put to the test during the 1989 San Marino Grand Prix when the Austrian racing driver Gerhard Berger hit a wall at 270 km/h. His car immediately burst into flames but thanks to his protective clothing made from Nomex® and the rapid intervention by the rescue teams, Berger's injuries were limited and he was able to return to racing within a month.

Polyvinylchloride (PVC)

This is the generic name for a synthetic chlorofibre made from petro-chemicals. It is breathable, easy-care, non-flammable and can be blended with a range of other fibres like cotton, wool, silk or viscose to make fabrics that have a wide range of properties and end-uses. Chlorofibres can be recycled from

PVC plastic bottles and used in fibre blends for jumpers, socks, and gloves. It can be given a permanent anti-bacterial finish for use in medical textiles.

Polytetrafluoroethylene (PTFE)

This is the generic name for a synthetic fluorofibre, made from petro-chemicals. PTFE is hydrophobic (water-hating) and oleophobic (oil-hating) and is used in high-tech fabrics such as Gore-Tex®. (See page 235.)

Teflon®

This is the brand name for a high performance fabric-care product made from PTFE. It protects fabrics and leather against water, stains and oil-based spills. Teflon® works by surrounding each fibre with an invisible barrier so the fabric doesn't attract dry soiling or soak up wet stains. Teflon® is safe, gentle, effective, water-based and CFC free so it doesn't harm the environment. Teflon-coated fabrics are windproof, waterproof, stain-resistant, breathable and easy-care.

Originally Teflon® was developed as part of the American space programme and later used for non-stick saucepans – now you can wear it! Teflon® can be applied to all kinds of fabrics, from the finest silk to the hardest wearing cottons. It can be used for sportswear, streetwear, furnishing fabrics for the home, hotels or hospitals and for garden furniture, overalls and workwear. Even men's ties are now Teflon-coated. Look out for them at your local department store!

Polypropylene

This is the generic name for a synthetic fibre in the polyolefin family, made from petro-chemicals. Polypropylene fibres are:

- thermoplastic with a low melting point
- high strength
- resistant to chemicals
- non-absorbent
- very good wicking properties
- crease-resistant
- soft when finely spun
- good soil and stain release but not oil or grease
- non-allergenic.

Polypropylene can be engineered for use in a range of end-products and is extensively used is carpet backing, sacks, webbing, twine, fishing nets, vegetable bags and ropes. The fibre is also used for upholstery and for the pile of carpets because of its durability, soft touch and crush recovery. The good wicking properties of polypropylene enable it to be used in medical and hygiene products. Other end-uses include awnings, synthetic surfaces for sports, sportswear and geotextiles – where polypropylene has about 70% of the geotextile market.

TASK

Draw up a table to show the properties and end-uses of the following textile fibres:
- Nomex®
- Kevlar®
- PVC
- PTFE
- Polypropylene

LAMINATED FABRICS

In a laminated fabric, two or more different textile layers are joined to provide a fabric with enhanced technical properties. Laminated fabrics can be:

- engineered to be wind and waterproof, lightweight, durable, abrasion-resistant and breathable
- laminated by adhesive or by the thermoplastic quality of one of the constituent fabrics
- made breathable by the use of microporous membranes. These are often hidden between the outer fabric layer and the lining. In some laminated fabrics the membrane is designed to be visible in order to enhance the aesthetic properties of the fabric.

Breathability in a fabric works in two ways:

- in a microporous membrane, tiny holes allow water vapour to pass through the fabric but are too small for raindrops to penetrate.
- in a hydrophilic membrane, warm water vapour from perspiration 'wicks' through the fabric to the cooler outside of the garment. If the outside temperature is higher, outside wicking will not occur. The ability of a fabric to wick can be assessed by measuring the time taken for a drop of liquid to be absorbed. Fabrics that wick away moisture quickly are said to have a high moisture vapour transport (MVT).

Hydrophilic
This is a property of fibres that are water-attracting. For example:

- cotton is hydrophilic so it can absorb moisture both from perspiration and from rain – unfortunately, cotton takes a long time to dry so a wet cotton garment is very uncomfortable to wear
- wool is also hydrophilic and will absorb up to a third of its own weight in water without feeling uncomfortable
- both cotton and wool allow perspiration to wick through the fabric so they are both described as being comfortable to wear. Both fibres are used in blends with synthetic fibres to improve their hydrophilic properties.

Hydrophobic

Fibres such as acrylic, polyester, nylon and Nomex® are said to be hydrophobic or water-hating, because they don't absorb water. A drop of water on the surface of a pure nylon fabric just sits there until eventually, it evaporates.

- If a hydrophobic fabric is against the skin perspiration vapour has no place to go which is why garments made from hydrophobic fibres are uncomfortable to wear. They don't allow wicking to take place, so they are often blended with natural fibres to improve the comfort factor.
- In recent years, hydrophobic fibres have been coated with chemicals to make them work as moisture vapour transport systems. The chemicals work by surrounding the fibres with hydrophilic molecules, which draw moisture away to the surface of the fabric where it evaporates.

Gore-Tex®

This is the brand name for a 'smart' microporous membrane made from a composite of an oil-hating substance and PTFE, which is hydrophobic (water-hating). The membrane was originally developed for use in space missions and was the first breathable membrane ever developed. Gore-Tex® has nine billion microscopic holes per square 2.5 cm. These holes are big enough for perspiration to pass through, but too small for raindrops to penetrate. This makes Gore-Tex® breathable, waterproof and windproof. It is also durable and easy-care, so it can be machine washed, steam-ironed, dry-cleaned and tumble-dried.

Gore-Tex® can be laminated to any type of natural or synthetic fabric and is used by manufacturers of high-tech products for the most demanding electronic, industrial and medical end-uses. It is also used in protective wear for the police and armed services and by surgeons because it keeps out bacteria. The fabric is also used for all-weather wear in situations that demand the highest level of performance – such as in expeditions to the North Pole. In common with other manufacturers of specialist branded textiles, Gore-Tex® runs a quality system with strict criteria that product manufacturers have to meet. Any garment using the Gore-Tex® membrane has to have the seams heat-sealed to make the garment waterproof – a product that says it's waterproof must be just that.

Tactel Aquator®

Tactel Aquator® is one of a family of 'smart' high-tech fabrics made from microfibres. It is not laminated but rather is knitted as a two-sided fabric construction, with Tactel® on the inside and cotton on the outside. The inner layer of Tactel® is hydrophilic, so it wicks moisture away from the skin to the outer cotton layer, where it spreads and evaporates. This provides improved comfort, handle and breathability. Tactel Aquator® is also soft, strong, lightweight, supple, easy care and quick drying. The fabric is used in functional underwear, high activity sportswear, and socks and as a component fabric in garment layering systems.

TASK

Describe the difference between hydrophobic and hydrophilic properties of fibres. Describe, using fibre examples, how these properties benefit the consumer.

3D FABRIC STRUCTURES

Developments in textile engineering and construction techniques have led to new ways of producing three-dimensional (3D) textiles that may be knitted, woven or braided to form structures without any joins. These techniques can be used in products for engineering, furnishing and fashion end-uses. For example new 3D weaving systems are being developed, which enable fabrics to be shaped during the weaving process. This kind of system relies on computer technology, to give each fabric its own pattern and shape, which is designed on a jacquard software system. This technology is expected to be used for the production of composite fabrics for hats, helmets or even wheel rims. Knitting technology has, to date, provided the most commercially viable methods of producing 3D textile structures.

3D knitted upholstery

The UK company, Teknit, has developed a system for producing 3D knitted fabrics that can be used for office seat upholstery and technical textiles. The 3D knits combine the shaping possibilities of the V-bed flat weft-knitting machine, to include individual needle selection, loop transfers and the knitting of 3D wedge shapes. This new method of manufacturing makes use of Just in Time and Quick Response manufacture to knit to customer orders. Different sizes of 3D office seat upholstery can be produced without any cutting or sewing operations required. The fabric is simply attached to the under seat by staples. The major advantages are:

- faster time to market of a new product design – six months compared to the cut fabric route
- faster knitting time compared to knitting rolls of fabric – and no waste from cut fabric
- 30 minutes manufacturing lead time per seat cover, with less than 20 minutes set up time – a stockless system of production
- reduction of the number of individual seat fabric pieces to one piece
- easier application of the upholstery to the seat, using positioning guidance from the shaping and stitches
- jacquard designs can be located precisely on the seat cover and carried over the seat contours, extending the scope for chair design
- jacquard programming using CAD systems enables company to offer customers bespoke designs.

Total garment technology

WholeGarment™ knitwear technology has been developed by the knitting machine manufacturer, Shima Seiki. In this system parts of a knitted jumper, such as the front body, back body and sleeves (previously knitted separately and sewn together afterwards) can be weft knitted together in one 3D piece. Other products from hats, scarves, cardigans, jackets, dresses, skirts, tights, socks and gloves can also be knitted in 3D.

The system makes use of developments in computerised knitting technology, such as Digital Stitch Control, Four-Bed Technology and Compound Needles.

• The Digital Stitch Control System (DSCS) enables the yarn feed and tension to be automatically adjusted to allow knitting with consistent loop length. DSCS continuously monitors yarn consumption and any changes in humidity or temperature that may affect the loop size. It adjusts the yarn feed and tension through each course of knitting to produce a fabric with a tolerance of plus-or-minus one per cent.
• Four-Bed Technology enables the production of tubular knitting, which can knit ribs and purls and perform stitch transfers for narrowing and widening sleeves. Knitting with four-needle beds simulates the use of four needles when hand knitting tubular socks or gloves. A sweater body is separately knitted from the waist up and the two sleeves from the cuffs. These are knitted together at the lower armholes and the shoulders and neck are then knitted. The result is a completely reversible garment with no seams.
• Compound needles enable stitches to be knitted as closely together as possible.

Knitting a garment in one piece provides many benefits for garment manufacturers, because it:

• eliminates labour-intensive cutting and sewing processes, producing savings in time and cost
• eliminates waste from cutting knitted fabric
• reduces the manufacturing lead-time as garment are quicker to make
• enables Quick Response and on-demand knitted garment production.

By eliminating sewn seams, WholeGarment™ sweaters provide numerous benefits for the consumer, because it:

• eliminates bulkiness resulting from stitching at the shoulders and under-arms
• provides extra comfort, wearability with an easier fit
• garments have greater draping characteristics and a softer feel.

COMPOSITES

In industrial end-uses there is a growing need for cost-effective materials that combine strength and functional properties with lightness. In end-uses in the construction and automobile industries, for example, traditional heavier materials such as metals are increasingly being replaced by composite textile materials. These composites combine two or more materials that differ in appearance or composition and may be part textile and part glass, carbon, metal or ceramic. They are combined in a sandwich structure to make a new material with enhanced performance characteristics.

Glass fibres and carbon fibres

Check it out Unit 3A 74 page xxx

In the transport industries, composites are often used in car bodies, for boat hulls or in aircraft structures. They may combine a base reinforcement material like glass fibre with plastic resin. In fact, the first kind of reinforced plastics were made with glass-fibre strands and this is still the most common type of plastic composite in use today. More recently plastic composites include carbon fibres, which provide properties such as high strength with lightness. They are used in structural components for aircraft, in the aerospace industry and for sports equipment such as golf clubs, skis and tennis rackets. In fact, most professional tennis players now use composite tennis rackets made from carbon fibres in injection or compression mouldings. Many processes are used to manufacture composites.

- In the hand lay-up process, a woven mat of carbon fibres is placed by hand on to the surface of an open mould, and then combined with a liquid polyester resin. Brushes or rollers are used to remove trapped air.
- In the spray-up process, resin and cut carbon fibres are sprayed onto a mould. For both the hand lay-up and the spray process, additives may need to be added to the resin to make sure it 'cures' (goes off) at room temperature.
- In compression moulding the composite is compressed under hydraulic pressure in the required shape until the resin has cured.
- In injection moulding granular thermoplastic urethane or polyester resin is reinforced with chopped glass fibre. This is heated until it is semi-fluid, then injected into a mould.

Composites of Kevlar®

The inclusion of Kevlar® in composite materials is a major factor in the use of composites for bullet proof vests and cycling helmets. Kevlar is also used in as reinforcement in high-performance composites for protective wear such as motor cycle suits and chain saw chaps. These over trousers are made from five layers of fabric in a lightweight flexible sandwich, made up of the following layers:

- a top layer of tough durable Cordura nylon
- a layer of woven Kevlar

- two layers of Kevlar felt
- an inner layer of Cordura.

In any accident with a chain saw, the high-strength Kevlar fibres would be caught up in the chains of the saw causing it to clog and stop working, thus preventing a serious accident.

TASK

1 Explain how developments in 3D fabric technology benefit manufacturers and consumers.
2 Composite materials are increasingly used in industrial and technical products. Experiment with the use of thermoplastic fabrics and layering systems to develop new textile materials for use in your own products.

INDUSTRIAL TEXTILES

These are textile materials manufactured to meet specific technical requirements in a wide variety of industries. They are used for functional end-uses, either as part of an industrial process or incorporated into industrial products. Industrial textiles are often used in the aerospace and transport industries. They often replace existing traditional materials because they provide superior characteristics and properties such as strength, lightness, durability and resistance to heat or corrosion.

Examples of industrial textiles are:

- fire-resistant space suits, optical fibres
- seat belts, airbags, tyres, belts, carpet backing and upholstery
- conveyor belts, filters, cables and ropes
- hovercraft skirts, composite materials for the hulls of boats or aeroplanes.

The average car contains 13 to 14 kg of textiles. These are used not only in carpets, upholstery, seat belts and airbags but also as flexible reinforcements in the tyres, brake pipes, water hoses and belts. The bodywork may be made from glass-reinforced composites and insulation is achieved through the use of heat and sound absorbing textiles. Oil and petrol filters keep the car running smoothly.

Technical requirements relate to the functional performance of a textile, matching its properties and characteristics with its end-use.

- Technical requirements can relate to the way a textile performs, such as its strength, elasticity, breathability, durability or fire-resistance.

- For example, the technical requirements of a bouncy castle could be strong, hardwearing, waterproof, puncture proof and non-slip.

TECHNICAL TEXTILES

Technical textiles are manufactured mainly for their technical performance and functional properties rather than for aesthetic characteristics. Only a small proportion of technical textiles are manufactured from high-tech fibres like Kevlar®, Nomex® or carbon fibres. Most technical textiles are made from everyday fibres such as polyester, polypropylene, polyamide (nylon), acrylic, viscose or cotton.

- The properties and structures of technical textiles are usually modified to meet the requirements of specific end-uses. This may include the use of microfibres, which can be blended with other synthetic or natural fibres to make fabrics that are strong, lightweight, easy-care and weatherproof.
- Technical fabrics can be woven, knitted or non-woven, depending the end-use . Many geotextiles, for example, are warp knitted.
- Technical fabrics are often coated with Teflon® or PVC to give them enhanced properties, like stain-resistance.

End-users of technical textiles

Technical textiles are used in a wide range of applications including protective clothing, upholstery, furnishings, buildings, civil engineering, sports products, leisure goods, agricultural products, medicine and health care. They include products such as:

In industry, there is probably no tougher environment than an offshore drilling rig. Clothing needs to be hard wearing and protect against the risks of fire, chemicals and adverse weather conditions. The clothing also needs to be comfortable and easy to launder. Many oil companies specify the use of Nomex® 111 (a blend of Nomex® and Kevlar®) because of its high performance heat and flame protection, resistance to chemicals, comfort and easy-care properties.

Other end-users of technical textiles include:

- chemically-resistant workwear
- fire-protective wear
- all-weather clothing e.g. survival clothing for arctic expeditions.
- roofing felt, carpet backing and upholstery
- textile structures, e.g. the roof of the Millennium Dome
- geotextiles, used for reinforcing soil, e.g. embankments
- high-tech clothing for sports. e.g. breathable garments
- synthetic turf for tennis courts, fishing rods
- inflatable boats, bouncy castles and marquees
- agricultural bags and fishing nets
- medical textiles, bandages and hospital uniforms.

PERFORMANCE TEXTILES

Performance all-weather wear is designed to cope with extreme weather conditions while remaining versatile and comfortable. Performance textiles:

1 Transports moisture away from the skin for comfort. Highly breathable with some thermal insulation.
2 Breathable single fleece with high thermal insulation and moisture transportation.
3 Double fleece with high thermal insulation whilst maintaining breathability.
4 Tough woven outer fabric for total protection against extreme weather condition. Composite garment construction creates a breathable outer layer with high durability and thermal insulation.

Technical textiles that are used for more fashion-orientated products for outdoor pursuits or sport are sometimes called performance textiles. These are textiles that relate to a product's performance in a specific end-use.

Performance requirements relate to the functional and aesthetic performance of a textile, matching its properties and characteristics with its end-use. Performance requirements can relate to:

- the way a textile performs such as tensile strength, tear strength, abrasion resistance or shrink-resistance
- the way a textile looks such as its style, drape or comfort properties.

For example, the performance requirements of skiwear could be warm, breathable, waterproof, windproof, durable, easy-care and fashionable.

Performance textiles are developed from technical specifications that define how the product should perform, such as 'high-strength', 'breathable' or aerodynamic'. The look of these products is also important if they are to sell into a competitive market, so aesthetic properties are an important factor in their design. The development of performance textiles has been the driving force behind many innovations in clothing fabrics. Many of the benefits originally incorporated into performance wear such as 'breathable' are now seen to be indispensable in many fashion products. Similarly, the use of Lycra® is used extensively in fashion clothing to provide comfort properties.

Microfibres

Performance textiles manufactured for outdoor pursuits are often made from nylon or polyester microfibres. They are easy-care, quick drying and 'breathable', allowing the body to adapt to a variety of weather conditions and activities. Tactel® has created a layering system made from Tactel yarns. These are specially engineered to create high performance fabrics for winter wear. In the most extreme weather conditions and hostile environments – from the Arctic Circle to the mountain slopes – this garment layering system is versatile and tough enough to provide total protection.

TASK

1 Modern weatherproof clothing protects the body in extreme conditions. Describe the performance requirements of a garment needed for:
   - sailing in a hot climate
   - climbing in cold winter weather.

   Suggest a range of fabrics that would suitable for both activities.

2 Explain the difference between technical and performance requirements. Describe the properties of fabrics required for the following textile products:
   - an inflatable boat
   - a space suit
   - snow-boarding wear.

   Suggest a suitable fibre or fibre blend for each of these activities.

SMART TEXTILES

Fabrics are called smart when they provide added characteristics that do more than make you look and feel good. Smart fabrics can be 'engineered' to provide a whole range of properties such as breathable, waterproof and windproof, providing a micro-climate around the skin.

Many of these smart fabrics have been developed for specialist sports or outdoor pursuits end-uses and they are set to become even smarter as technology develops. For example, some smart fabrics are described as 'intelligent', because they respond to the needs of the wearer in an environment. The stimulus for some of these exciting textiles often comes from nature's responses to external stimuli, such as the way that pine cones open and close according to air pressure. This kind of design, which makes use of good ideas from nature, is called Biomimetics. The fabric called Stomatex, for example, allows the skin to breathe like a leaf surface transpires, but at the same time it acts as a barrier to rain water. The Stomatex system keeps the body at an even temperature so that perspiration does not occur – when the body is active, tiny pumps within the fabric remove perspiration vapour.

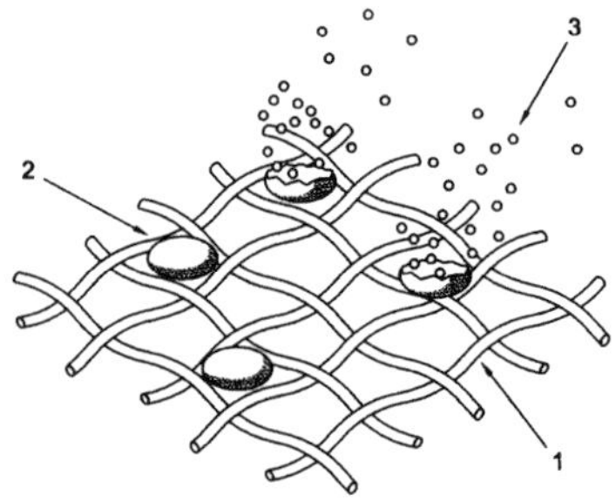

The demand for performance has already led to the development of textiles with moisture management, anti-bacterial and thermal properties. These performance properties are now incorporated into everyday textiles and manufacturers that want to stay ahead of the game are developing other benefits for fabrics, such as micro-encapsulation.

1 Fabric
2 Micro-capsule
3 Active agent

Figure 4A.5

Micro-encapsulation
Moisture management
and anti-bacterial
properties are familiar in
underwear and activewear.
Now, encapsulated fabrics
that release fragrances are
being used for underwear.

Micro-encapsulation

Some textiles now add the concept of 'well-being' in the form of micro-encapsulated fragrances. For example the UK company, Welbeck, offer around 40 encapsulated aromas based on fruits and florals, such as citrus, rose and lavender.

- The micro-encapsulation process can be applied to any finished fabric with an adhesive additive that is thermally fixed.
- The capsules release their fragrance during movement so the scent is not transferred to other garments in a drawer.
- The effect is semi-permanent and last up to 40 washes.
- Lingerie manufacturers are currently using these fabrics.

Sun protective clothing

Problems associated with sun bathing affect everyone. With the number of cases of skin cancer rising, especially in countries like Australia, there is a growing demand for clothing that protects the wearer from the sun's harmful ultraviolet (UV) rays. All clothing provides some degree of sun protection, of course, but research has shown that the UV protection of polyesters is often better than other synthetic fibres. The textile company DuPont has introduced a UV protection rating system for manufacturers using Coolmax® performance fabrics. The system is not the same as that used for sun-protective creams. Coolmax® fabrics can be tested for UV protection based on three Ultraviolet Protection Factor (UPF) ratings:

- UPF 15+ for good protection
- UPF 25+ for very good protection
- UPF 40+ for excellent protection.

It is estimated that in extreme temperatures outdoor workers should be protected with summer weight clothing with a UPF rating of 30+, and in Australia most employers aim to supply workers with UPF 50+ clothing.

WEARABLE ELECTRONICS

Smart fabrics are being developed to incorporate micro-electronics within the structure of the fabric and as devices get smaller they will be incorporated more and more into garments. This means that textiles are set to play an important role in developing technology that extends human performance. Some manufacturers are already producing prototypes for wearable electronics. Philips Laboratories, for example, have produced a business suit with a mobile phone built into the fabric and a child's anorak that has a tracking device. This enables parents to tell the exact location of children at any time of the day or night! Children who may object to being tracked are expected to enjoy wearing the anorak because the device will also act as a portable computer! (Some knitted fabric sports bras have, built in sensors to monitor the heart rate when exercising, while some new aerobics outfits have their own music system built into the pants section.) The effect is to make the clothing more involved in the activities of the wearer – in fact to become a kind of intelligent digital assistant.

Figure 4A.6
This metallicised elastane swimming costume by Zoggs incorporates Coolmax® fabric. It has a UPF rating of 50+, combining excellent protection with good design.

Other developments in wearable electronics from Philips include:

- disco wear which will change colour and even change shape in response to sound from the DJ's desk.
- golf jacket with sensors in the sleeve to monitor the performance of the golfer's swing when hitting the ball.

Soft switching

Some manufacturers are developing wearable electronics that are controlled by 'soft switches'. These textile-based switches and keypads are sewn into the product, using existing textile processes such as printing, coating and embroidery. The switches are washable and durable and perform just like conventional textiles. Fabric keypads are expected to be used to dial telephones, type pager messages and play music. Soft switching is also likely to be incorporated into interior textiles to control lighting, domestic appliances and audio-visual equipment.

TASK

Keep up to date with the latest happenings in textiles.
- Collect articles and images from newspapers and magazines.
- Use a search engine on the Internet to find information about textiles – or try using the Textiles Institute website on www.texi.org.uk where there is useful information and links to other sites.

DEVELOPMENTS IN COMPUTER TECHNOLOGY

It is sometimes said that in an age of mass production, individuality is the one thing that everyone wants. This concept is leading to a growing trend for customisation and the mass production of 'custom-fit' garments. Some manufacturers are even selling 'paint by numbers' style T-shirts or selling lengths of fabric with the pieces marked for making up yourself! Nike's new !D trainer customisation uses the Internet to revolutionise shopping – you go into their website and choose from a range of colours and designs to create your own perfect trainer. You can even write up to eight letters on the back of the trainers to customise them further! The new Levi's store offers a design-your-own jeans service to create a unique pair of jeans that may be embroidered, aged or trimmed. (see www.levi.com).

There are a number of reasons why there is this growing trend in what is coming to be called 'assembly line bespoke tailoring':

- the linking of computer-aided design and manufacture
- the ability to alter measurements easily within a production run
- technological breakthroughs in printing – especially in digital printing

- the versatility of modern embroidery machines
- the growing use of body-scanning to create accurate and individual flat patterns
- the development of on-line shopping on the Internet – which allows the manufacturer time to finish making a semi-complete product before delivery to the customer
- the development of fast electronic communications.

Benefits to consumers

These days, consumers want a greater variety of products without ordering in advance or waiting months for delivery. There are many benefits to the user in the customisation of the mass production process, such as:

- taking part in the design process
- taking part in the manufacturing process
- having an individual look to the product
- having a garment that fits perfectly
- only paying more for a more complex design
- having the satisfaction in getting a personalised product
- having the price advantage of a mass produced product.

Benefits to manufacturers

For manufacturers, on the other hand, customisation provides a number of benefits such as:

- making products more appealing to a wider customer base
- selling more products
- keeping the company in business and running to full capacity
- making higher profits.

Mass customisation can only work effectively through the use of CAD/CAM systems and easily adaptable processes, together with the use of team-based flexible manufacturing. The use of body scanners is expected to become more widespread as these systems develop. Some prototype systems map 300,000 points around the body and convert them into a virtual reality 3D image of the individual. Using virtual images customers will be able to see if specific styles or colours suit them. Virtual measuring tapes will offer greater accuracy and more reliability both for the customer and the manufacturer.

TASK

Choose three of the developments in technology in this section. For each draw up a table that shows the advantages and disadvantages of that technology to the user and the manufacturer.

THE IMPACT OF MODERN TECHNOLOGY AND BIOTECHNOLOGY ON THE DEVELOPMENT OF INNOVATIVE FIBRES, FABRICS AND FINISHING PROCESSES

Many of the textiles in use today are based on natural fibres, which are produced using a range of traditional dyeing and finishing processes. Many of these processes are now considered to be environmentally unfriendly because they involve the use of chemicals, which can cause pollution when wastewater is released into rivers. Manufacturers are increasingly under pressure from environmental legislation to reduce levels of pollution.

FABRIC FINISHING PROCESSES

Finishing processes can totally transform the handle, texture and performance of fabrics. Some finishes such as anti-static for synthetics and shrink resist for wool have been around for a number of years, but new ways of achieving these finishes are continually being developed, to improve fabric performance and to reduce pollution.

Shrink-resistant wool

Wool fibres shrink badly and felt (or 'compact') when washed, so they need to be made shrink-resistant by chemical or physical finishing processes.

* A physical 'wet' finishing process can be used for woven wool fabrics, which are then dried naturally without tension. This finishing process is called London Shrinking. Any subsequent washing will result in the fabric shrinking further and felting, so dry-cleaning is recommended for all wool fabrics finished by this environmentally friendly method.
* Chemical shrink-resistant finishes for wool have traditionally used chlorine, which is an environmental problem in wastewater, so new finishes continue to be developed.

New shrink-ristant finishes
* Newer finishes coat and surround the wool fibres with synthetic polymers to make the fibres resist felting. 'Soft Lustre' is a finishing process for worsted yarns using silicone which results in soft, smooth, lustrous yarns that dye well and that can be machine-washed. Machine-washable wool can also be finished using Teflon® coating, which doesn't affect the handle, drape or breathability of the wool fibre. Teflon® coating also provides wool fabrics with anti-pill properties.
* Another new chemical finish for wool is called 'inter-fibre bonding'. A soft polymer is applied, which sticks to the surface of the wool fibre to make polymer 'bridges' between the fibres. This process makes wool fabrics and garments machine-washable.
* You may see the term 'Superwash' wool applied to jumpers or socks, made from shrink-resistant worsted knitwear yarns. The term is not associated with any particular shrink-resistant process but means that the product can

be machine-washed. Any product called Superwash must achieve a high level of shrink-resistance, colourfastness and after-wash appearance.

Coated fabrics

Coating has been used for many years to provide finishes for fabrics. You may have come across PVC-coated cotton tablecloths for example. Many of the new finishes for high-performance synthetic fabrics make use of coatings to provide enhanced properties. The coatings can range from very thin films to heavy coatings, but generally the finer ones provide the best handle, as they are more flexible.

Coating can be applied using a layer of natural or synthetic polymer and normally only one side of the fabric is coated. Modern coatings use films of polyurethane, PVC, silicone or Teflon® to provide enhanced properties, which are a combination of the original fibre, the fabric construction and the coating itself. Coatings provide many exciting finishes for fabrics, giving reflective, iridescent, papery, high-gloss, neon or holographic effects.

- Transparent coatings on fine fabrics result in fragile yet strong and durable fabrics.
- Fabrics for high performance wear can be coated with polyurethane, which is either micro porous or hydrophilic – this results in a breathable fabric.
- Modern coated fabrics can be wiped clean, are scratchproof and breathable, as well as providing protection.

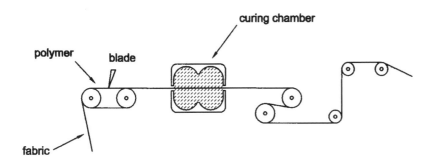

Figure 4A.7

The coating polymer can be applied directly onto the fabric or carried on transfer paper. This is followed by fixing in a curing oven.

Direct Coating

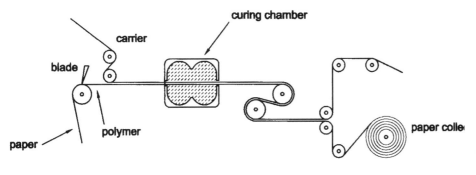

Indirect Coating

Coatings are used for many end-uses such as for:

- protective clothing
- high-visibility garments
- handbags and luggage
- furniture and car seat covers
- shower curtains and blinds
- floor and wall coverings
- industrial textiles such as conveyor belts or inflatable boats.

Anti-bacterial finishes

Anti-bacterial finishes copy the characteristics of a fibre that has been around for many years – linen. This fibre is non-allergenic so it does not provide an environment for germs to spread. Linen also releases dirt better than any other fibre and actually improves with washing – when the fibres are rubbed in the wash they provide a new clean surface. This is why linen was been used for many years in hospitals for sheets and bandages – until new methods of laundering and sterilisation were introduced.

Nowadays anti-bacterial finishes are extensively used for medical and active sportswear products. The finishes work by inhibiting the growth of microbes. They are mostly based on a small range of anti-microbial chemicals, such as Trilosan, which are applied to the surface of the fabric. Anti-bacterial properties can be further enhanced by the use of breathable fabrics because these reduce the presence of moisture in the body environment. Anti-bacterial finishes:

- are used to protect garments or shoes from a wide range of bacteria for the lifetime of the product
- must still demonstrate good anti-microbial performance after a minimum of 50 wash cycles.

Some anti-bacterial finishes are not simply applied to the surface of the fabric but are incorporated into the fibre itself – this means that it will not wash out. In this type of anti-bacterial finish the surface of the fabric can be rubbed in the wash but the finish returns, working in a similar way to linen fabrics.

The benefits of anti-bacterial finishes are as follows:

- They control odours that develop on warm sweaty garments such as socks or sportswear
- They reduce the risk of skin irritation or infection
- They reduce the risk of the fabric discolouring or deteriorating.

TASK

Choose two new finishing processes. Explain the benefits to the consumer and the environment of using these processes.

BIOTECHNOLOGY

Biotechnology has been defined as 'farming with bugs'. It actually involves the use of natural biological processes to aid manufacturing. You will probably be very familiar with some of these processes, especially those relating to food production. In the food industry biotechnology has been used for many years in fermentation processes to make bread, beer, cheese, wine, and yoghurt.

Using enzymes

Biotechnology has also been used for almost a century in the textile industry, where it makes use of enzymes to help in manufacturing processes. For example, the enzyme amylase is used to remove starch size from woven fabrics.

- Enzymes are naturally occurring chemicals that accelerate chemical processes without themselves being destroyed.
- Without enzymes life would be impossible because we all rely on them for digestion of food, growth and tissue repair and for the generation of energy.

Enzymes have also been used in 'biological' washing powders since the 1960's. These enzymes can degrade a wide range of stains and their use allows milder washing conditions at lower temperatures, saving energy and protecting the fabric.

Many new developments in biotechnology in the textile and clothing industries are expected to be based on the use of enzymes. These new biological processes will range from fibre preparation to fabric finishing and aftercare. The main benefits of using biotechnology in such processes are that they:

- require less energy
- speed up production
- are based on renewable raw materials
- reduce environmental pollution.

Modified textile materials

Other developments currently in the pipeline are new and modified textile raw materials based on improved plant varieties and biopolymers. These developments fall into two main categories:

- genetic modification of existing natural fibres such as cotton, wool, linen and silk
- the development of new sources of fibres based on microbes and fungi.

IMPROVED PLANT VARIETIES

Cotton

Cotton still accounts for a large proportion of all the textile fibres used in the world and is an important crop in many countries. The problem with cotton is that it uses vast amounts of pesticides in its cultivation. One way of reducing this pollution would be to grow organic cotton. Another approaches includes developing cotton plants with improved insect resistance so pesticides are not required.

Bio pesticides have already been developed to provide low cost and environmentally friendly alternatives to chemical pesticides. Work is also being done on insect resistant cotton plants. Genetic modification may lead to the development of high performance cottons. The target will be to modify cotton fibres so they have improved strength, length, appearance and thermal properties. It may even be possible to produce customised varieties of cotton specifically grown to meet customers' needs! Even more futuristic in concept is the possibility of introducing genes of the natural polyester PHB (see page 251) into the cotton plant. This could mean growing polyester-cotton! The aim would be to have a core of biodegradable polyester in the centre of the cotton fibre.

'Naturally' grown coloured cotton

Other research into the development of new cotton varieties has resulted in growing naturally coloured cotton. It is already possible to produce varieties of red, green, brown, grey, orange, yellow and mauve cottons using conventional techniques based on selection – these are the same techniques used by gardeners. Further development of this technology may be limited by difficulties in producing blue shades and more intense colours, although research into genetic modification is already taking place. The development of intensely coloured cottons could one day replace the need for bleaches and dyes.

Figure 4A.8

Work is currently being carried out in Australia on 'biological wool shearing'. An artificial growth factor injected into the sheep interrupts its hair growth. A month later, breaks appear in the wool fibre and the fleece can be pulled off whole in half the time it takes to shear a sheep!

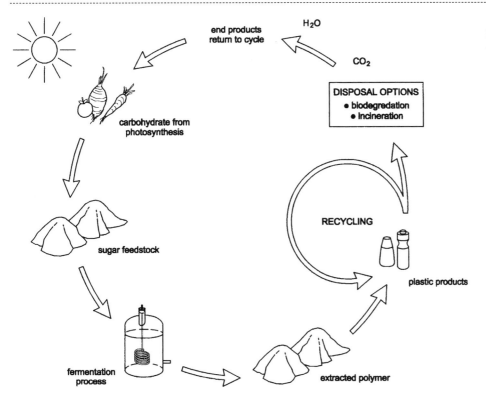

Biopolymers

Most recent developments in polymers have been in synthetic fibres, which are generally cheaper and easier to produce than natural fibres. Synthetic polymers also have the potential for producing engineered fibres with specific characteristics. Research over the last 40 years, however, has led to the production of Biopol, the first commercially viable biodegradable polymer. For example fishing nets made from Biopol would be environmentally friendly. If the net broke loose it would sink because it's heavier than water, then biodegrade, rather than cause a hazard to fish and boat propellers.

Biopol is a 'natural' polyester developed by the UK company, Zeneca, and produced by bacterial fermentation of a sugar feedstock. In this process glucose is converted into a thermoplastic polymer called polyhydroxybutyrate (PHB). The polymer is already present in the human body, which means it is biocompatible. This property will enable Biopol to be used for medical and surgical implants – it may even encourage the regrowth of nerves.

Biopol has a flexibility and tensile strength comparable with polypropylene. It can be:

- blow moulded, injection moulded and extruded as film or fibre
- used for shampoo bottles and paper coating (used for compostable garden bags)
- used to replace polyester (PET) bottles because of its good barrier properties
- recycled or made to biodegrade completely by composting, incineration or landfill.

Spider silk

Research into spider silk as a potential high performance material was started some years ago. The silk of the orb-weaving spider in particular is one of the world's strongest fibres and because the web is used for support, spider silk is very strong and elastic. Catching a fly in a spider web is the equivalent of stopping a jet plane with a net made from filaments 25mm thick! Spider silk is as strong as steel and it can be a mile in length – it is therefore a potential substitute for Kevlar®. The difficulty with spider silk is getting the spider to produce it to order!

The answer to the problem lies with genetic engineering. The textile company DuPont has been working on a project to manufacture biosilk by putting silk synthesis genes into yeast or bacteria. This process enables the manufacture silk proteins, which are dissolved in a solvent and then spun as biosilk fibres. This exciting new lightweight, high-strength fibre could be used in clothing to improve Lycra® or nylon and in engineering, satellites or aircraft. Research is also going on in the United States into the possibilities of 'milking' spiders for their silk, which could be used in bullet-proof vests. Take a good look at the next spider's web you see!

TASK

1 Explain the following terms:
   • Biotechnology
   • Enzyme
2 Describe the benefits to manufacturers of using biotechnology.
3 Discuss two ways in which biotechnology is used to develop new fibres.

THE USE OF BIOTECHNOLOGY IN DYEING AND FINISHING PROCESSES

One of the major environmental issues related to dyeing and finishing of textiles is the use of chemicals in these processes. Specific problems relate to the removal of:

• colour and pesticide from waste water
• toxic heavy metal compounds used in dyeing
• chemicals from finishing processes.

New biological production processes that are less polluting than the traditional ones are being developed. For example a new process for biological scouring and bleaching of fabric has recently been introduced in the UK. This new process uses a catalase enzyme to completely remove the hydrogen peroxide used in bleaching from wastewater.

Other new processes include those used for biostoning denim and biopolishing cotton and other cellulosic materials. Biotechnology is even able to solve the blue wash problem. This is one that we all know – leave a dyed item in with the white wash and the result is blotches on the whites or a miserable grey tinge all over. Biotechnology can provide two solutions to this problem:

- using naturally grown cotton that is permanently dyed so the colour won't run.
- using a colour-run system in which an enzyme acts to 'bleach' the dyes. The important thing is that this enzyme will only bleach the dye that has escaped into the wash water and not the dye in the offending item.

Biostoning

As recently as 1989 it was discovered that cellulase enzymes could replace the pumice stones used by industry to produce 'stone-washed' denim garments. In traditional stonewashed denim the pumice stones damaged the clothes – especially the hems and waistbands – and machinery. Most manufacturers are now using the enzyme treatment. This is suitable for denim fabrics because the indigo dye hardly penetrates the surface of the fibres, staying mostly on the surface where it can be removed by the cellulase. Biostoning provides a number of benefits for manufacturers:

- less damage to denim fabric and machinery
- reduced product variability – biostoning is a more controllable process
- 30-50% improved machine capacity – more denim can be processed in a shorter time
- reduced labour costs – no need to remove dust and stones from finished garments
- reduced environmental damage – no abrasive sludge left in waste water.

Biopolishing

Although cotton fabrics look smooth they are not – they are covered with tiny protruding fibres, which can go into 'bobbles' after a cotton product has been worn for a while. These annoying little bobbles reappear as fast as they are removed. This common problem has a name – 'pilling' – and it is one reason why cotton clothes are sometimes thrown away. A new biological process using cellulase enzymes has solved this problem. The Danish company Novo Nordisk has developed an enzyme treatment called Cellusoft which cuts off the protruding fibres, leaving a softer, shinier fabric. Only one treatment, before the fabric is dyed, is necessary for the cotton fabric to continue to look and feel new for the lifetime of the garment.

A similar process is used for other fibres:

- a protease enzyme treatment has been developed for wool
- biopolishing can be used to clean up the surface of Tencel® and lyocell fibres during peach skin treatments.

Biological security markers to aid fibre identification

The fraudulent labelling of country of origin and fibre content and the counterfeiting of branded products is a fast-growing crime. For example, a high value speciality fibre such as cashmere may be adulterated by cheaper fibres like wool or yak hair. Since this kind of fraud is difficult to find, yet alone prove, fraudulent labelling is one of the biggest barriers to free trade in the worldwide textile industry.

To combat this kind of fraud, the UK company, Biocode Ltd, has developed a technique for detecting the presence of 'markers' in fabric. The markers are highly sensitive monoclonal antibodies that can be applied to textiles at any stage of manufacture, processing or making up. These monoclonal antibodies can detect 'foreign' substances that should not be present. The mark is invisible and completely safe, but can be detected by customs or trading standards officers using special antibody kits. This technology has already been evaluated for use in the protection of denim fabrics and is expected to be used in the protection of brand names both for fibres and products.

TASK

Describe the use of enzymes in textile finishing processes. Evaluate the benefits of using biotechnology in this way.

RECYCLED TEXTILES

Concerns about the environmental damage caused by textile manufacturing have encouraged some companies to try to make changes to existing manufacturing processes. Pollution is caused not only by processes like bleaching, dyeing and finishing, but also by problems associated with the production of waste materials. It is a problem that involves each and every one of us – what to do with unwanted textile products. Recycling would seem to be an easy answer but it is not easy, especially considering that many textile materials are made from blended fibres. The recycling of 100% natural fibres is an easier proposition.

Natural fibres

The company called Evergreen produces yarns, fabrics and finished garments using a high proportion of recycled materials. These include cotton, man-made and cashmere fibres. Evergreen produces high quality, fashionable garments that require less energy to make than new products, cause less pollution and reduce the dumping of unwanted products in landfill sites. The company mainly buys its raw materials from charity shops, knitting factories and rag merchants. The waste products are sorted into single-colour materials in 40 standard shades, then torn into fibres called 'shoddy', using a 'rag-pulling' machine. The shoddy is then blended, carded, spun and knitted or woven into new fabrics.

The use of recycled fibres results in energy and cost savings and reduces pollution by eliminating the need for:

- transporting virgin wool from Australasia
- scouring – a washing process that removes dirt from the wool
- carbonising – an acid treatment to remove impurities from the wool
- dyeing – a process that causes water pollution.

Synthetic fibres

At the end of its useful life a product made from synthetic materials can take hundreds of years to break down or 'biodegrade'. As with natural fibres, there is a problem recycling synthetic blended fibres, but single-fibre materials have more potential for recycling. Polyester is the most frequently recycled synthetic material made from recycled soft drinks bottles. The majority of recycled polyester is used for fibres, but new processes enable the production of polyester resin suitable for recycling back into soft drink bottles and into food packaging.

The outdoor wear and equipment company, Patagonia, manufactures recycled and environmentally friendly products. It makes a polyester micro fleece called 'Synchilla' which is lightweight, breathable and warm. The company is so environmentally aware that it even uses scraps of Synchilla left over from making adult garments to make a range of tiny infant's clothing!

TASK

Recycling is an issue that affects everyone. Suggest three innovative ways that recycled materials could be used in textile products

MODIFICATION OF PROPERTIES OF MATERIALS

The modification of textile materials is an on-going activity in industry because it enables designers and technologists to develop products for specific technological end-uses. During this unit you should try to develop your own skills with textile techniques and processes in order to modify the properties of materials. This may involve experimenting with materials of known properties such as cotton, nylon or wool or using unconventional materials like plastics, polypropylene or recycled materials. The following sections provide some suggestions for experimental work.

TEXTILE CONSTRUCTION TECHNIQUES

One way of developing your creative skills is to use fabrics as a jumping off point for design ideas. It is good practice to collect fabric swatches and keep them in a notebook – you could add notes to explain why you like them and how they could be used. The work of other designers is also a constant inspiration for design, so collect images from newspapers, magazines and the Internet of fashion textiles – have a good look at the fabrics used by designers.

TASK 1: DEVELOPING FABRIC IDEAS THROUGH ANALYSING EXISTING WOVEN OR PRINTED FABRICS.

Figure 4A.11

Choose one woven and one printed fabric that use colour, pattern or texture in an interesting way.

1 Examine the woven fabric through a magnifying glass and map its colour repeat and construction on point paper.

2 Analyse the repeat of the printed fabric and sketch on paper.

3 If you have access to a scanner you could scan in both fabrics.

Then use the following ideas to develop design ideas based on each of your fabrics.

- Photocopy the pattern repeat or individual motifs either at the same scale or larger.
- Cut up the design or individual motifs and reassemble.
- Photocopy the new design and put it into repeat.
- Photocopy the resulting design three times and add colour to produce three different colourways.

The above process can be repeated any number of times – the use of scale is a very useful way of developing ideas.

If you scanned in your fabrics you could try using a CAD programme to copy, rotate, repeat, mirror, distort or resize your design idea.

Once you have developed a number of fabric design ideas try printing or painting them on fabric and embellishing them using decorative stitch techniques.

TASK 2: PRODUCING EXPERIMENTAL SAMPLES OF WOVEN, KNITTED OR CROCHET FABRICS.

There are all sorts of ways of developing fabric ideas. Try using some the following:

- Use coloured paper to trial weave constructions, then develop them using the ideas in Task 1.
- Use a simple frame loom to experiment with combinations of yarns, colours and textures.
- Try using knitting or crochet to develop fabric ideas – use a knitting machine if there is one around.
- Try developing quick print ideas using simple block printing – then embellish with decorative stitch techniques

USING UNCONVENTIONAL MATERIALS AND EXPERIMENTAL PROCESSES

You may not have access to many of the new or modern materials that have been discussed in this unit, but you can still experiment with unconventional materials. Some or all of the following materials may be used for experiments, depending on the effect required:

- wool – try shrinking and felting it.
- nylon or polyester – the thermoplastic fibres.
- polyester/cotton – a blend of thermoplastic and natural fibre – hot-washing a fabric blend will encourage each fibre to react in a different way.
- Vilene – cheap, can be dyed, printed on, embroidered.
- frozen food bags or polythene – can be melted, stitched – will not fray.
- polypropylene – often used for vegetable bags – is thermoplastic.
- old tea bags – dry them, dye them and stitch together or stitch onto a base fabric and paint.
- thermochromatic pigments that change colour at near-bodyheat – try using them for products.

Safety warning! Take care when handling hot liquids or equipment. Always follow safe working practices and consult your teacher or tutor when doing any kind of experimental work.

You can shrink, melt or felt fabrics depending on the type. Use physical processes like:

- washing in hot water and detergent or boiling in a saucepan (use an old one please)
- scrubbing with pan scourers or brushing with wire brushes to degrade the surface
- ironing thermoplastic fabrics between aluminium foil or sandwiched between grease proof paper or Teflon® baking paper
- applying dry heat from a hair-drier or oven (put fabric on tinfoil).

Don't forget that you can experiment with more traditional textile techniques to develop your skills. Combining and layering, distressing or embellishment techniques can enhance the properties, appearance, handle or performance of textile materials. Try combining layers of different weights of materials then quilting them. Experiment with painting, spraying, stencilling or printing to create enhanced aesthetic, functional or technical properties. It is a good idea to experiment with one or two processes so that you become skilled, rather than trying every technique suggested in this section! You can use your experimental work to inspire your coursework project.

Decorative and stitch techniques
In textiles, we are lucky to have the choice of many different techniques to enhance materials and products. Fashion designers often use traditional textiles from around the world to inspire their work. One way of improving your skills is to experiment with one or two techniques such as appliqué, machine embroidery or patchwork. Try combining different materials and techniques. All the experimental work you do in this unit will give you practice and experience that you can take forward into your Unit 5 coursework.

Chapter 3
Values Issues

As design technologists we have to make evaluative judgements about what to design and make, who the product is for and what kind of materials to use. When developing new materials and processes value judgements become even more of an issue. The development of new technologies has all kinds of impacts on people, society, economic, environmental and ethical issues. Currently, for example, there is great debate about the impact of global manufacturing on jobs and societies and about the impact of manufacturing on the environment – global warming, the greenhouse effect and pollution in general. There are also worries about the use of new technologies such as biotechnology or the use of genetic modification to improve plant varieties.

IMPACT OF VALUES ISSUES

Every human need is related to a values issue. For manufacturers needs are connected to wants – the requirement of the market for products. The main aim of manufacturing is to fulfil these market requirements and at the same time to make a profit. How manufacturers do this while taking account of values issues – especially those related to the environment and new technology – is a concern for everyone.

- Environmental issues are increasingly important for designers and manufacturers, mainly because of legislation that requires companies to dispose of waste in an environmentally responsible way. Many companies are also beginning to take recycling seriously, but should designers take this one step further and design for recycling? Initiatives like Envirowise (www.envirowise.gov.uk) and Biowise (dti.gov.uk/biowise) provide information and support for manufacturers wanting to become more sustainable.
- There is a continuous cycle of product development with many new textile materials coming on stream, including smart materials. How do these new products enhance lives? Should new product development make more use of environmentally friendly manufacturing processes? How can we as consumers encourage manufacturers to use these processes? Is 'fashion' necessary?
- Many people are unhappy at the thought of 'genetic engineering'. Why is this? What do you think about it? Could there be any long-term effects from the genetic modification of plants? Do the benefits outweigh any disadvantages?

RESPONSIBILITIES OF DEVELOPED COUNTRIES

Textile and clothing manufacturing are increasingly under economic pressure to manufacture 'off-shore' in countries where labour costs are lower. This 'global manufacturing' has an impact not only on jobs in developed countries such as those in Europe, but also on 'developing countries'. The criteria for deciding if a country is developing are based on socio-economic factors, related to manufacturing technologies – a country that has acquired modern manufacturing technology is deemed to be developed. There is pressure therefore on both sides – to manufacture where costs are lower and to acquire new manufacturing technology. The impact of global manufacturing will continue to have a major impact on many people and on the environment.

- The setting up costs of manufacturing off-shore are enormous, so the big companies may get bigger and small ones that can't fund global manufacturing are lightly to go to the wall. One way forward for small companies is to supply 'niche-markets' with high quality products.
- Although labour costs are lower when manufacturing offshore working conditions may not be to the same standard as in developed countries. Should manufacturers be responsible for Health & Safety? How can this problem be overcome?
- The development of industrial centres offshore provides many employment benefits but sometimes creates environmental problems. Rapid industrialisation is said to be part of the reason for 'global warming'. Yet how can developed countries deny people in developing countries the opportunity for employment and increasing economic benefits?
- Some developing countries cannot afford the technology needed to manage industrial or waste processes. Who should pay the costs of clean technology? How can we help developing countries to afford new processes? Should these processes be the responsibility of manufacturers or governments? Are we all prepared to pay the cost of cleaner technology?

Life cycle assessment

Any design and manufacturing decisions need to find a balance between cost and benefit. It is becoming increasingly difficult for manufacturers and society to find a balance in the development of new products and processes. One way of assessing the benefits and disadvantages of product development is the use of Life Cycle Assessment (LCA). This assesses the impact a product has on people or the environment for cradle to grave. LCA means investigating every aspect of a product's design, manufacture, use and disposal.

TASK

Prepare a list of questions that you could ask about a product in order to assess its impact on people or the environment. Try to relate your questions to materials, manufacturing processes, Health & Safety at work, the disposal of waste, safety of the product in use and recycling. Can you think of any more topics to ask questions about?

EXAM PRACTICE

The questions below are similar in style to the ones you will find in the examination paper for this unit. Before attempting to answer the questions read the relevant sections in the unit. Make note using key words or spider diagrams about the topic.

1 Choosing the right materials for the job is important for any designer.
   a) Describe the criteria that must be taken into account when selecting materials.   (3)
   b) Select and justify the use of one fibre that could be used for
        heat-resistant workwear.   (2)

2 New fibres are developed to meet specific market requirements.
   a) Comment on the stages involved in the manufacture of Tencel®
        fibre, using diagrams to explain the process.
        (3)
   b) Explain the benefits to the consumer of using Tencel® in garments.   (2)

3 Biotechnology is a developing technology.
   a) Give one example of how biotechnology is used to develop new
        textile materials.   (2)
   b) Describe the advantages to the manufacturer of using biotechnology to
        produce a stonewashed denim finish.   (3)

4 Textile materials are developed for specific technological end-uses.
   a) Explain what is meant by the term 'performance requirements'.   (2)
   b) Describe the properties of a fabric required for a skiwear.   (3)

5 Experimental techniques can be used to produce innovative textiles.
   a) Explain what is meant by the term thermoplastic.   (1)
   b) Describe how one experimental technique could be used to distress
        a nylon fabric to change its appearance or texture.   (4)

6 The environment is a growing concern.
   a) Describe one environmental problem associated with dyeing textiles.
        (2)
   b) Discuss how new technology can help overcome the problem you
        identified in a).   (3)

Preview

Unit	Level	Components	Areas of study
4	A2	Section B: Options	• Design and Technology in Society OR • CAD/CAM

Unit 4 Section B has two Options: Design and Technology in Society OR CAD/CAM. You must study the same ONE Option from Section B that you studied at AS.

WHAT YOU WILL LEARN IN THE UNIT

The content of the unit builds on what you studied at AS level and enables you to develop further your understanding of Design and Technology in Society. The work you undertake must include knowledge and understanding of the following areas:

Chapter 1   Economics and production
• Sources, availability and costs of materials
• Advantages of economies of scale of production
• The relationship between design, planning and production costs
• The manufacturing potential for a given design.

Chapter 2   Consumer interests
• Systems and organisations which provide guidance for consumers
• The purpose of British, European and International Standards
• Legislation and the rights of the consumer.

Chapter 3   Advertising and marketing
• Advertising and the role of the design agency
• The role of the media in marketing products
• Market research techniques
• Basic principles of marketing.

Chapter 4   Conservation and resources
• Environmental implications of the industrial age
• The management of waste, disposal of products and pollution control.

WHAT YOU WILL DO IN THE UNIT

During the unit you should undertake a variety of activities to develop your understanding of the unit content. You may be asked to:

- work individually on some tasks, e.g. when undertaking tasks to develop understanding of the relationship between sources, availability and costs of materials
- work individually on some activities, e.g. when using the Internet to research information about the rights of the consumer
- work collaboratively with others on some activities, e.g. when developing understanding of the impact that advertising and marketing have on product development.

UNIT 4 ASSESSMENT

Unit 4 is externally assessed through a $1\frac{1}{2}$ hour written exam, which assesses your understanding of the unit subject content. There is one question paper, with two sections:

- Section A: Materials, Components and Systems
- Section B: Options

UNIT 4 SECTION B ASSESSMENT

The work that you do in this option will be externally assessed through Section B of the Unit 4 examination paper.

- There will be two compulsory long-answer questions, each worth fifteen marks.
- You are advised to spend 45 minutes on this section of the exam paper.
- This option, with Section A, is worth 15 per cent of the full Advanced GCE.

WHAT THE EXAMINER IS LOOKING FOR

The examination paper is designed to give you the opportunity to demonstrate your understanding of what you have learned in the option. Examiners are looking for longer, more in detailed answers that show a greater depth of knowledge and understanding at the Advanced GCE level.

EXAM TIPS

- Make brief notes about the topics covered in this unit.
- Summarise the key points on one or two sheets of paper.
- Learn these key points.
- Practise working through a complete exam so you will learn how to allocate the time available to you.
- In the exam read the questions through and then read them again to make sure you understand what you are being asked to do.
- Plan your answer briefly on paper then check the question again to make sure that you have covered it fully.
- Work through your answer making sure that you address each point in your plan.
- Use clearly written sentences and bullet points to make your answer clear.
- Use specialist technical terms and clear sketches to illustrate your answer where appropriate.
- Read through your answer, then move on to the next question.

Chapter 1

Economics and Production

THE BUSINESS OF MANUFACTURING

The business of textile product manufacture has a number of stages that combine to form the product supply chain. Overall the supply chain includes three sectors:

Figure 4B.1

The business of manufacturing has a number of stages that form the product supply chain. The total time from fibre production to the consumer varies between six and eighteen months.

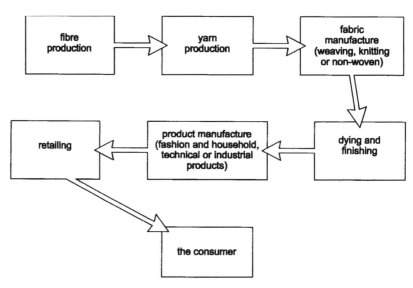

The primary sector

This includes, for example, the manufacture of chemicals used for fibre production and the preparation and maintenance of land for the grazing of sheep and growing of crops such as cotton.

The secondary sector

This involves the manufacture of textile fibres, yarns, fabrics, dyeing, finishing and product manufacture. This is a high export-earning sector both for developed and developing countries. However, as changes in technology and the global economy occur, the numbers of people employed in textiles and product manufacture in developed countries has continued to fall, mainly due to lower labour costs in developing countries.

The tertiary sector

This includes organisations related to textiles, such as retailing, advertising and marketing. The tertiary sector employs the greatest numbers of people in developed countries.

In your design and technology course you will mainly be concerned with the secondary and tertiary sectors.

ECONOMIC FACTORS IN THE PRODUCTION OF ONE-OFF, BATCH AND MASS-PRODUCED PRODUCTS

The term 'economic factors' sounds rather daunting, but it simply means the financial or cost aspects of designing and making products. When you design and manufacture your own coursework product, one of your concerns will be whether your product is cost-effective to manufacture – if it is 'viable'. For manufacturers in the secondary sector, product viability, in terms of the product's market potential and the profit it generates, is essential to the survival of the company and its workforce.

COSTS AND PROFIT

It is therefore the aim of all manufacturers in the product supply chain to make a profit, whether the company is involved in fibre, yarn or fabric production, weaving or knitting, dyeing or finishing or in product manufacture.

In order for a company to make a profit, it is usual these days to expect every function of the company to be profitable. This means that in many large companies:

- different departments are 'customers' to other departments within the same company
- each department has to work within a budget.

For all companies it is a simple fact of life that revenue from the sale of products minus manufacturing costs equals profit. In the same way that you must plan the cost-effective manufacture of your coursework product, a manufacturer must plan to achieve a certain level of sales and take into account planned costs in order to make a planned profit. As in your coursework, the key to success is planning. Planned costs generally include a combination of the following cost factors:

- direct (or variable) costs. These are the direct manufacturing costs, such as materials or labour;
- overhead (or fixed) costs. These are the overhead costs of manufacture, such as design and marketing or rent, rates and insurance.

TASK

Explain why producing an accurate product costing is important for manufacturers.

SALES REVENUE AND PRICE

The sales revenue from any product is the price per item multiplied by the number sold. Sales revenue may result from the sale of one haute couture garment sold to an individual client or from the sale of thousands of mass produced garments sold through high street retailers. Similarly, sales revenue may result from a bespoke geotextile designed for one large scale civil engineering project or from geotextiles made in high volume for use in motorway building to prevent the road surface cracking.

A haute couture garment generally attracts a higher price, because it is made to the requirements of fit and style of the consumer. Such a consumer has a perception that the 'value' of a haute couture garment is high – it is a unique product that provides 'special' qualities. A haute couture garment will always require a high selling price, because it has to absorb all of the variable and overhead costs. These costs are high because a one-off product takes longer to make, as there are no cost-savings to be made through the repetition of any processes.

On the other hand, the price of a mass produced garment will always be lower. This is partly due to the fact that the consumer has a different perception of the value of this type of product, which has the lower status of an 'everyday' item. In terms of manufacturing costs, a mass produced garment will always have a lower selling price, because there are more products to share the variable and fixed costs. Also cost savings can occur because processes can be repeated efficiently and quickly.

PRICING PRODUCTS

Pricing is a complex business. For manufacturers of high volume products the aim may be market penetration, so the product price may need to be set low enough to enable this to happen. On the other hand, many retailers will pay a higher price for fast delivery, for innovative or exclusive products or for the supply of small orders, because all of these considerations are valued by consumers. Sometimes, a higher product price will encourage the perception of higher value in the mind of consumers and this can even stimulate an increase in sales. Also, manufacturers or retailers often try to promote a range of products by offering a 'loss leader' at an artificially low price in order to promote sales of the entire range. Lastly, manufacturers and retailers have to allow for a percentage of 'mark-downs' – often sold in 'sales' – to sell off products at the end of a season.

A number of factors decide the eventual price of a product:

• how stylish, fashionable or functional the product is
• how innovative or exclusive the product is
• the value of the fabric and components – for example, is the product made from silk, polyester/cotton or Kevlar?
• the value of the work content – is the product lined or hand-stitched?
• the competition from other manufacturers.

TASK

Select two similar products, such as a hand-made cushion and a mass-produced one. For the two products compare the following:

- the materials and components
- the use of textile techniques
- the number and estimated length of assembly processes
- the selling price.

SOURCES, AVAILABILITY AND COSTS OF MATERIAL

The cost of materials depends on the type and quantity required. For fabrics the price per metre is based on the current price plus estimates of increases and reductions for large quantities. All sewn product manufacture requires a reliable and continuous supply of raw materials in the supply chain. This includes the supply of fibres, yarns, fabrics and components.

NATURAL FIBRES

The supply of raw materials for natural fibres comes from a variety of renewable and mostly reliable sources such as cotton or wool. Although there are fluctuations in the price of natural fibres, prices remain relatively stable. Cotton, for example, is grown in around 80 countries of the world. The price of some luxury fibres, such as mohair or cashmere, varies according to supply. Soft and lustrous cashmere, for example, comes from the Mongolian goat. It is harvested at the yearly coat change and is generally in short supply and therefore the most expensive hair fibre.

Cotton

Cotton represents 75 per cent of the total market share of all natural fibres. Prior to the 1980s cotton prices set the going rate in staple fibres but during the 1990s polyester took over. Australia is the lowest cost producer of cotton but even there it is not profitable to grow middle grade cotton for sale at a price to even match the price of staple polyester. Many countries therefore subsidise the growing of cotton.

Wool

Since 1990 wool has suffered a decline in consumption, even though Pure New wool remains a prestige product supported by the Woolmark label. Many consumers have moved away from suits towards less formal types of clothing. One other key event that lost wool its market share is the collapse of wool consumption in the former Soviet Union and much of Eastern Europe. The woolgrowers of Australia and New Zealand are expected to have to put big money behind marketing wool in order to hang on to the present market and prices.

Linen

Linen (flax) is now a niche market textile, having been forced out of its traditional markets – especially in medical and industrial textiles. Currently the linen market share is 90 per cent domestic and consumer goods and only 10 per cent industrial. The fibre is included in designer collections and recent improvements in finishing will improve its market pull, especially as it is superbly cool and comfortable to wear.

Silk

Although silk output is small in comparison with other natural fibres its production has survived and prospered, especially in India and China. The volume of silk production shows a slow but sure rate of increase and it holds a significant place in market share and price. Even though micro denier polyester filament fabrics are almost indistinguishable from real silk, consumers around the world still demand silk as a luxury fibre.

In the final analysis regarding sourcing and pricing of natural fibres human productivity is the deciding factor. On average, one person can just about produce two tons of natural fibres compared with around 22 tons of manufactured synthetic fibres!

REGENERATED FIBRES

Viscose, modal, Tencel and lyocell fibres are manufactured from a combination of chemicals and cellulose which is derived from softwood. The major sources of the world's supply of commercially grown softwood are the coniferous forests of the northern hemisphere, stretching across North America and Europe. Careful management of these forests ensures a consistent and controlled supply resulting in the production of relatively inexpensive fibres.

SYNTHETIC FIBRES

Synthetic fibres account for over 93 per cent of the world production of fibres, with polyester taking the greatest share. Although there is currently over production of polyester on a global scale, Europe consumes more than it produces and has to import polyester from Asia. The principle raw material for making all synthetic polymers and many other textile materials is crude oil, which also supplies much of the world's energy needs. In comparison with the use of oil for energy, synthetic polymer production takes up a relatively low percentage of the total world oil consumption. This means that synthetic fibres are inexpensive to produce and their supply is reliable.

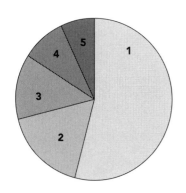

Figure 4B.2

1 polyester	54%
2 polyolefin	17%
3 nylon	13%
4 acrylic	9%
5 cellulosic	7%

The worldwide share of fibre production by fibre type.

The importance of oil

The development of many high-tech textiles would be impossible without oil. The world's largest oil-producing countries are not themselves major consumers and they are therefore able to export much of their oil. These countries form the Organisation of Petroleum Exporting Countries (OPEC), an international cartel which sets output quotas in order to control crude oil prices. OPEC's member states are the nations of Middle East and the oil producing countries of South America, Africa and Asia. However the USA, the Russian Federation, Australia and European oil producers such as the UK do not belong.

In the early 1970s, OPEC controlled 90 per cent of the world's supply of crude oil exports. Prices began to climb sharply around 1973, resulting in an international economic downturn.

These price increases, however, had the effect of breaking OPEC's stranglehold on oil production because the higher price made it worthwhile for more expensive fields such as the North Sea and Alaska to be brought into production. Oil costs continue to fluctuate, often producing a domino effect, resulting in higher petrol, energy and raw materials prices worldwide.

SUPPLY AND DEMAND

As a general rule the cost of raw materials is based on supply and demand:

- those in short supply cost more than raw materials that are plentiful
- raw materials that are difficult or more expensive to process cost more
- transporting raw materials adds to their costs.

ADVANTAGES OF ECONOMIES OF SCALE OF PRODUCTION

The level or scale of production is an important factor in predicting profitability, because it influences how a product is manufactured, where it is manufactured, the choice of products available and their selling price. In high volume production, manufacturers and retailers base their predictions of sales volume and price on a number of criteria:

- test selling of the product in selected retail outlets
- the actual sales of similar styles in previous seasons
- how the product matches current and future trends in colour, shape and design detail.

Economies of scale then, are factors that cause costs to be lower in high volume production than in one-off production. The unit price of a mass-produced product (the price of a single product) is lower, because raw materials can be used more efficiently. Economies of scale in mass production result from:

- spreading the costs of production and equipment between more products
- taking advantage of the lower capital costs charged by finance providers
- reduced materials costs because of bulk buying
- specialisation – dividing up the work processes between a workforce with specific skills that match the job
- an industry being concentrated in one area – this can attract a pool of labour that can be trained in specialist skills
- companies concentrated in one area – this can attract a supply network that can also lower costs because of their own economies of scale.

TASK

Draw up a chart that compares the costs of manufacturing a one-off product with a mass-produced one. Think about the range of materials, components and processes that are used.

Explain why mass-produced goods are cost-effective to manufacture.

THE RELATIONSHIP BETWEEN DESIGN, PLANNING AND PRODUCTION COSTS

Check it out! Efficient manufacture and profit Unit 3B page 160

These days it is more and more difficult for a company to remain profitable without developing new products, even when existing ones are selling well. Consumer demand can change and sales of even a best-selling product will fall off in time, as new or different styles appear on the market.

- The cost of product development can be very high, especially if it includes the cost of setting up a factory and equipment.
- New products require changes in production methods so that operators need to learn new skills – this involves training costs.
- Any changes in production methods needs planning and will need to overlap with existing production, in order to keep the company running and in profit.
- There is a constant need to reduce the time-to-market of new products. Some manufacturing companies have numerous product lines per season to keep up with fashion trends.
- Success comes through producing the right product at the right time, in the right quantity and at the right cost – consumers' perception of the product needs to be that it provides the right image as well as being 'value-for-money'.

COSTS OF PRODUCT DEVELOPMENT

The cost of product development includes both design and manufacturing costs. All of the following costs need to be included in the cost of the product:

- employing a designer
- developing design concepts
- modelling and prototyping
- employing a pattern cutter to produce a prototype pattern
- producing a sample – materials, labour and overhead costs
- producing a production pattern.

COSTS OF PRODUCTION

Development costs in a factory include those relating to adapting the manufacturing processes and the training of operators. If a company is to remain profitable total costs of production must be accurately calculated and a suitable selling price set. Target production costs need to be established at the design stage and their feasibility checked against existing or similar styles. The design team can then make sound decisions about costs early on.

All the production costs are therefore set up in the design stage, but it is in the manufacturing stage that the major costs are incurred. It is often said, therefore, that designing for manufacture (DFM) is all about designing for cost. The main aims of DFM are:

- to minimise assembly costs
- to minimise the product development cycle
- to manufacture high quality products efficiently.

Labour costs

The production of sewn products still relies heavily on labour, rather than on automation. The reason for this is that most textile products, such as garments, require complex construction processes that are difficult to automate. Processes such as cutting, sewing and pressing are classed as direct labour costs and they account for 20 to 25 per cent of the total direct costs of manufacturing sewn products. Of this 20 to 25 per cent, sewing and pressing are the most labour intensive processes, since fabric cutting now incorporates the use of CAD/CAM equipment and is the only part of sewn product manufacture to be truly automated.

Labour costs are related to productivity, which is measured by the efficiency of turning raw materials (production inputs) into products (manufactured outputs). Productivity is commonly measured through output per worker. The higher the level of productivity, the lower the labour costs per unit of production and therefore the higher the potential profit. Efficient companies with a high output per worker can keep the labour cost per unit of production as low as possible.

THE COST OF QUALITY

Check it out! Aesthetics, quality and value for money Unit 1 Industrial and Commercial Products and Practices page 33

The aim of all manufacturing is to produce a competitive product that finds a balance between quality and cost. The costs of quality are the same as any other costs, because like the cost of design or the cost of production they can be budgeted, measured and analysed. There are three types of costs related to quality:

- the costs of checking it is right
- the costs of making it right first time
- the costs of getting it wrong.

The costs of checking it is right

The costs of checking it is right are related to checking:

- materials, processes and products against specifications
- that the quality system is working well
- the accuracy of equipment.

The costs of making it right first time

There is only one way to get it right first time and this is 'prevention'. There are many costs related to prevention, such as those of designing, implementing and maintaining a quality assurance system. This has to be set up before production begins and results in costs relating to:

- setting the product quality requirements with the customer
- developing training programmes for employees so they know what to do
- the design, development or purchase of equipment for checking product quality
- developing specifications for materials, processes and products
- planning and using quality checks against specifications.

The costs of getting it wrong

There are two costs related to getting it wrong: internal failure costs and external failure costs.

Internal failure costs can occur when products do not reach the designed quality standards. They are detected before being sold to the consumer and include costs relating to:

- reworking the product or correcting faults
- scrapping products that cannot be reworked or sold
- inspecting reworked products

- products that still do not meet specifications but are sold as 'seconds'
- any product failures caused by errors, poor organisation or using the wrong materials.

External failure costs can occur when products fail to reach the designed quality standards but are not detected until after being sold to the retailer. They include costs relating to:

- customer service
- returned or replacing products
- investigating returned products
- product liability legislation and change of contract
- the damage to the company reputation relating to future potential sales.

TASKS

1 Discuss the reasons why manufacturers need to undertake the regular development of new products.
2 Explain why sewn product manufacture relies so heavily on labour rather than automation.
3 Describe and explain what is meant by the cost of quality.
4 Examine three similar sportswear products from different manufacturers or retailers. The products need to vary greatly in price and could be own label, branded or specialist. Compare the materials, quality of manufacture, styling and cost of the products. Try to describe why the prices differ so much and explain which product is the best value for money.

HOW TO COST A PRODUCT

Product costing is the process of producing an accurate price that will make the product saleable and create a profit. Setting the selling price too high may reduce sales below a profitable margin, while setting it too low won't allow a profit even if vast numbers of products are sold. Comparing the price of competitors' products is a frequent way to establish the potential price range of a new product, because it can give an indication of what the market can stand.

Accurate costing can be complex so computer systems are used widely for estimating costs and forecasting profits. Costing involves much more than adding on a set percentage to give a profit once all manufacturing expenses have been taken into account.

Cost and value

We will examine in more detail how to cost a product but firstly need to think about the concept of value, price and cost, from the point of view of the manufacturer and the consumer.

- Keeping a high level of stock is expensive, so for manufacturers the product 'in the hand' is of a lower value than the selling price of the product – the income from sales is required to generate a profit.
- Consumers, on the other hand, want the product more than the money in their hand. They see the product value as being higher than the selling price.

Figure 4B.3

The best price is one that generates the highest profit and not necessarily the one that sells the most products.

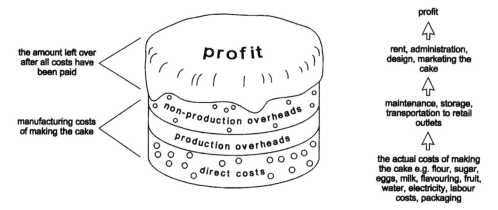

CALCULATING THE SELLING PRICE

Costing can be done in a number of set stages and needs to take account of the following:

1 *Direct costs* (also known as variable costs). These are the actual costs of manufacturing the product, such as materials, labour, energy used in production and packaging. Direct costs vary with the number of products made – the more that are made, the higher greater the direct costs. Direct costs may account for around 50–65 per cent of the total product-selling price (SP).

2 *Overhead costs* (also known as fixed or indirect costs)
These are the overhead costs of manufacture, such as design and marketing; administration and management; maintenance and repair of buildings and machinery; cleaning, security and safety; pattern cutting and sampling; quality costs; rent, rates and insurance; storage, lighting and heating; distribution costs; depreciation of plant and equipment.

Overhead costs are not directly related to the number of products made, so they remain the same, for one product or hundreds. Overhead costs are divided between the various product lines made by a company, so that each product carries its share. Marketing costs often account for 15–20 per cent of the total SP.

3 *Profit – gross or net*
This is the amount left after all costs have been paid. The gross profit is simply the revenue from sales minus the direct and overhead costs. Net profit is gross profit minus tax. Net profits pay dividends to shareholders, bonuses to employees and is used for reinvestment in new machinery or in new product development.

Direct materials costs can represent around 50 per cent of the total cost of a sewn product. Suggest ways that the selling price of the product could be lowered.

The break-even point

In order to cover their costs of manufacture, companies need to sell sufficient products at a high enough price. Working out how many goods must be sold in order to make a profit means preparing a 'break-even analysis'. In large companies accountants and financial controllers undertake this task. However, in many small businesses, the owners need to be able to do this for themselves. Getting it right, after all, is their key to success – and the survival of the business.

When working out the break-even point, the relationship between overhead costs, direct costs and the selling price is the basic starting point, For example, if a product-selling price is £10, how many need to be sold to cover costs and break even? The following formula can be used to work out the break-even point:

$$\text{Break-even point} = \frac{\text{overhead costs}}{\text{selling price} - \text{direct costs}}$$

Suppose that you work for a company that makes high quality knitwear. A new style in the autumn/winter range has been introduced. The direct cost of making one garment is £13 and it sells to the retailer for £20. The overhead costs for 1000 garments are £5000. The formula above can be used to calculate the break-even point.

$$\text{Break-even point} = \frac{5000}{20 - 13}$$

$$\text{Break-even point} = 714$$

This means that 714 products need to be sold to reach the break-even point.

1 The direct costs for a waistcoat are £6.90 and the overhead costs are 10 per cent of the direct costs. If the manufacturing profit is set at 15 per cent of manufacturing costs, work out the selling price of the waistcoat.
2 Calculate how many waistcoats you would have to make in a week to make a profit of £432.

THE MANUFACTURING POTENTIAL FOR A GIVEN DESIGN SOLUTION

As we have seen, when setting the selling price of products, manufacturers have to look at more than just the costs of making them. One of the key determining factors is consumer expectation – what consumers are willing to pay. This all depends on what customers see as value for money and what is on offer from others products in the market.

Figure 4B.4 illustrates some of the complex social, political, economic and technological issues that influence the pricing decisions of manufacturers. One of the key questions relating to the potential sales of a product is: will the demand for products fall if the price increases? Think about a range of different products that you buy regularly such as food items or tights. When there is a price rise their sales may drop for a while, but then return to the previous level because they are essential items.

Figure 4B.4

The selling price of products is determined by a range of complex issues.

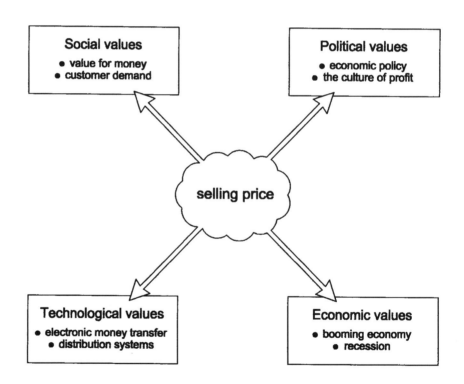

Cost and value

In other cases however, fashion items, luxury goods or trendy products can command high prices. Consumer 'crazes' for trendy products often mean that manufacturers can place a higher price on these products than would normally be the case. Increases in the cost of luxury goods can do one of two things – either reduce demand for a while or increase sales because the product is perceived by consumers to be of high value. There seems to be no right or wrong answer where cost and value is concerned!

The state of the general economy, too, has an impact on pricing policies. People have higher disposable incomes if the economy is booming and variables like the level of employment, taxes and interest rates are low – this results in high levels of consumer confidence, with more potential sales for products.

TASK

For some products it may seem that there is no direct connection between the manufacturing cost and the selling price. Manufacturers of popular products in limited supply (such as children's toys) can add huge mark-ups to the selling price. Give examples of products that prove or disprove this theory.

Chapter 2

Consumer Interests

The old saying: 'the customer is always right' is as relevant in the 21st century as ever it was. Consumers these days want to buy products that are fit for their purpose – in other words products that meet aesthetic and performance requirements and that provide value for money. In today's tough, competitive market it is vital that companies take note of consumer needs, values and tastes in order to provide the products they want. In the clothing and fashion market in particular, consumers can be very fickle and no retailer worth its salt can ignore consumer needs, even household names! To keep up-to-date with trends and changing lifestyles, companies use a range of market research techniques such as trend analysis or lifestyle marketing to establish a competitive edge.

Other organisations are also concerned with putting the customer first. The statutory rights of consumers when buying products are at the heart of consumer protection laws and fair trading legislation.

SYSTEMS AND ORGANISATIONS, THAT PROVIDE GUIDANCE, DISCRIMINATION AND APPROVAL FOR CONSUMERS

Consumers and their rights are protected and promoted by a range of organis-ations that provide guidance, discrimination and approval. These include:

- Consumer organisations
- British, European and International Standards organisations
- The Institute of Trading Standards Administration.

Consumers today are far more aware than they were in the past of new products and what they have to offer. The proliferation of 'style' sections in newspapers and magazines, for example, is one way that consumers are kept well informed. The development of these sections in the printed media itself is an example of how organisations respond to consumer (reader) demand – probably established through market research.

CONSUMER ORGANISATIONS

Apart from product evaluation in the media, consumer organisations and their specialist magazines also provide guidance and evaluation of new products. Often, these evaluations are picked up and run in the national press. To be really valuable, consumer organisations need to be independent of product manufacturers and provide objective reviewing and testing of the goods. The

Consumer Association, for example, publishes the magazine 'Which', providing reports of product testing and 'best buys'.

Its website, found at www.which.co.uk, is a good source of product information as the site is updated regularly with consumer news headlines and has links to electronic newspapers.

Consumers can also get advice and help with a wide variety of shopping issues from the Citizens Advice Bureau (CAB). The Citizens Advice Bureau web site will provide details of your local CAB and up-to-the-minute information about consumer issues: www.citizensadvicebureau.org.uk

TASK

Research textile products that are evaluated by two different media. This could include the printed media, electronic media or consumer organisations. Explain how such evaluations:
- encourage consumers to buy products
- guide consumer choice.

BRITISH, EUROPEAN AND INTERNATIONAL STANDARDS ORGANISATIONS

Check it out! British and International Standards Unit 3B D&T in Society pages 170

National and international standards, testing procedures and quality assurance (QA) measures are set by British, European and International Standards organisations. The purpose is to ensure that products fulfil the quality and safety requirements of consumers and the environment. Most of these standards are set at the request of industry or to implement legislation. Information about quality management systems, risk assessment, anthropometrics, textiles and packaging can be found in the 'Compendium of essential design and technology standards for schools and colleges'. This contains a collection of abridged British (BS), European (EN) and International Standards (ISO). Information about the compendium and the British Standards Organisation (BSI) can be found on the BSI website on www.bsi.org.uk

When you see a product that displays the Kite mark, you know that it has been independently tested under controlled conditions to confirm that it complies with a relevant British Standard. The manufacturer has to pay for this service and must have a quality system in place, because the product is tested and assessed at regular intervals. This means that every product is made to the same standard. The Kite mark symbol provides the customer with the assurance that the product meets the BS and is safe and reliable.

Figure 4B.5
The Kite Mark

Figure 4B.6

The CE mark.

The letters CE shown on a product means that a manufacturer meets essential safety requirements set up by a directive of the European Commission (EC). It is used on products sold across Europe that are required to meet common EC legal, technical and safety standards. For example it is illegal for any safety clothing or safety equipment marketed in Europe to be sold without the CE mark. This shows that the product has met specific performance, quality and safety requirements. Any manufacturer who claims that a product conforms to the relevant requirements may use the mark, but if the product does not conform, it can be seized and the manufacturer, importer or supplier prosecuted.

The Institute of Trading Standards Administration

The Institute of Trading Standards Administration (ITSA) was established in 1881 as the professional body of Trading Standards Officers in the UK. Trading Standards Officers are to be found in every local authority. They have the powers to enforce and advise of a wide range of legislation relating to consumer protection, the regulation of the consumer market and fair trading. Trading Standards Officers also have the powers to investigate complaints about:

- false or misleading descriptions of prices
- inaccurate weights and measures
- consumer credit
- the safety of consumer goods (except in Northern Ireland).

Some Trading Standards Departments run consumer advice centres that offer advice to shoppers and traders. Details of local authority Trading Standards departments can be found on the Trading Standards website at www.tradingstandards.gov.uk

THE RELATIONSHIP BETWEEN STANDARDS, TESTING PROCEDURES, QUALITY ASSURANCE, MANUFACTURERS AND CONSUMERS

One of the main concepts behind standards, testing procedures and quality assurance is the need to produce a quality product that meets consumer requirements. The two most common terms related to quality are quality control and quality assurance.

Quality control

Quality control (QC) has long been used in the clothing industry, where there are frequent changes of design. QC is characterised by inspection and repair and when used in isolation (i.e. without quality assurance), can be is very wasteful in terms of materials usage and time.

Quality assurance

On the other hand, quality assurance (QA) is characterised by the saying:

'Quality cannot be inspected into a garment, but has to be manufactured into it'. Many manufacturers apply QA on three levels:

- Using feedback to trace faults to the production process and eliminating the cause – possibly by adjusting existing machinery, by using more special equipment or by retraining a machinist to acquire a new skill.
- Using a Total Quality Management (TQM) system, to promotes sustained quality, based on British Standard 5750. In a TQM system all the areas of an organisation *and* its suppliers use agreed specifications and quality control methods.
- Making quality the responsibility of everybody in every department of a company, not just in production.

Using a TQM system

The aim of BS 5750 is to build quality into the design and manufacture of a garment, rather than relying on inspection and to reduce the need to inspect every garment. In other words TQM is pro-active rather than reactive. This type of TQM system is always capable of improvement, in order to meet the current and future needs of the customer.

ISO 9000

ISO 9000 is an internationally agreed set of standards for the development and operation of a Quality Management System (QMS). ISO 9001 and 9002 are the mandatory parts of the ISO 9000 series. They specify what standards manufacturers have to comply with, in order to be registered to the standard.

All industrial Quality Management Systems use structured procedures to manage the quality of the designing and making process. The procedures listed below explain the kind of the quality management processes at work in modern industry.

- Investigate the intended use of the product and the needs of the client (e.g. the retailer).
- Develop a design brief and initial product design specification.
- Use research and questionnaires to establish consumer preferences and market needs.
- Use product analysis to evaluate existing products.
- Generate a range of appropriate solutions and evaluate against the specification.
- Use modelling and prototyping to test that the product meets the design brief, specification and client needs.
- Plan manufacture, taking account of the need for safe working practices.
- Manufacture the product to specification.
- Critically evaluate the product against specifications and client needs.
- Undertake detailed product testing and produce proposals for further development, modifications or improvements.

TASK

Compare the designing and making processes used in modern industry with those you use in your own product development. Adapt your own procedures so that you can develop your own quality management system.

APPLYING BRITISH STANDARDS TO TEXTILES AND CLOTHING

Check it out! Anthropometrics and ergonomics Unit 3B D&T in Society page xx

Anthropometrics

Garment sizes are very important to everyone in the supply chain, from designers, manufacturers and retailers right to the end-users – consumers. Clothing sizes are standardised so that if they cannot be tried on at the time of purchase, consumers have a way of assessing which size they require. All the data relating to the size and shape of the human body is called anthropometrics. At the time of writing British Standards relating to sizing are under revision, because the sizing data has been around since the 1950s. The new standards will be based on surveys of body shapes currently being undertaken in the UK.

Average heights

Anthropometrical data needs to be representative of the greatest numbers of people, particularly in relation to garment size. The graph in Figure 4B.7 shows the frequency with which people of a specific height occur in the target population. The greatest height frequency is that of average (mean) height,

Figure 4B.7

Anthropometrics data uses measurements that are representative of the greatest numbers of people.

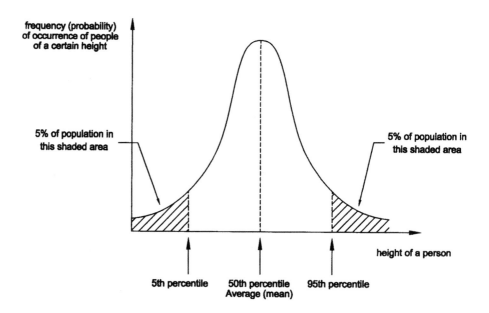

called the fiftieth percentile. The graph shows that 50 per cent of the population are taller and 50 per cent shorter than the mean. The fifth percentile represents the point at which one person in twenty (five per cent) is very short. The 95th percentile represents the point at which one person in twenty (five per cent) is very tall. Ninety per cent of the population falls between the between the 5th and 95th percentile.

Size charts

Size charts that are based on anthropometrical data should make it possible, therefore, to cater for 95 per cent of the population. Over the last few years, manufacturers have based their block patterns on their own ranges of standard sizes, depending on the target market. The increments between each size vary between manufacturers, which means that the same size from different manufacturers can vary. The table below shows increments of 5cm between sizes. You could try drawing a similar table, using increments of 4cm and 6cm. Do these increments provide more or less sizes in a range?

Table 4B.1

8	10	12	14	16	18
82	87	92	97	102	107

Another way that manufacturers calculate size ranges is to have batch sizes of small, medium, large and extra large, as shown in the table below.

Table 4B.2

8–10	12–14	16–18	20–22
82–87	92–97	102–107	112–117
S	M	L	XL

TASK

The use of standard sizes is fine for the 90 per cent of people who fall between the 5th and 95th percentile.

- Survey a sample of your peers to see how many fall between the 5th and 95th percentile.
- Discuss what problems very tall or short people might have in buying garments to fit.
- People today are taller and broader than in the past. Explain how changes in the sizes and shapes of people might affect the design of products.

Implementing British Standards (BS)

One example of the implementation of BS can be seen in the manufacture of children's nightwear. This nightwear is described as being made for children over the age of three months and under thirteen years of age.

* Children's nightwear includes night-dresses, dressing gowns and bathrobes, all of which must meet the requirements of BS 5722: 'Flammability performance of fabrics and fabric assemblies used in sleepwear and in dressing-gowns'.
* BS 5722 relates to the whole garment, threads, trimmings, decorations and labels.
* The test procedures for checking flammability have to comply with British Standards (BS) guidelines and must be carried out under controlled conditions.
* It is mandatory for all children's nightwear, baby garments, children's pyjamas and terry towelling bath robes made for sale, to carry a permanent label to show they meet the flammability standard.
* As a student in a school or college you need to be aware that the regulations must be followed when making any nightwear for young children or the elderly.

APPLYING BRITISH STANDARDS TO HAZARD IDENTIFICATION AND THE CONTROL OF RISKS

Under the Health and Safety at Work Act 1974, risk assessment is a legal requirement for all manufacturers in the UK. Its use is an essential part of any Quality Management System. In any designing and making process, therefore, it is the responsibility of the manufacturer (including a student) to ensure that hazards are controlled, both in manufacture and use of a product by a consumer.

Before deciding how risk can be controlled it is important to understand what is meant by the terms 'hazard' and 'risk'.

* A hazard is a source of potential harm or damage or a situation with potential for harm or damage.
* A risk combines the likelihood that a hazard might occur and the consequences of the hazard (i.e. and accident).

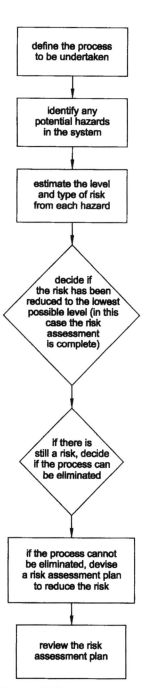

Figure 4B.8

How to identify and control hazards in a manufacturing process.

TASK

1 Draw up a checklist for each of the following:
- safety with people
- safety with materials
- safety with machinery.

2 Set up your own procedures for testing products, so that you can carry them out under controlled conditions. You need to take account of:
- how to run the test
- the criteria you will use to test the product
- how to record the results
- writing a test report.

3 Draw up a risk assessment plan for the processes involved in your own product manufacture.

RELEVANT LEGISLATION ON THE RIGHTS OF THE CONSUMER WHEN PURCHASING GOODS

Consumer rights are regulated and enforced by a range of consumer legislation. This means that whenever consumers buy or hire goods and services, a body of law called 'statutory rights' protects them. In the UK, such legislation includes:

- The Trade Descriptions Act (1988) – e.g. cannot say that products are waterproof, if they're not.
- The Textile Products (Indication of Fibre Content) Regulation (1986) – the fibre content must be indicated, although there is a tolerance of 3 per cent to 5 per cent other fibre.
- The Weights and Measures Acts (1985 & 1987) – sizing must be accurate.
- The Consumer Protection Act (1987) – if things go wrong, the onus of proof is on the consumer.
- The Sale of Goods Act (1979).

These Acts set out what consumers can reasonably expect when buying goods and services. In the textile and clothing industries there is also legislation and codes of practice relating to specific issues such as toxicity, metal contamination, flammability and children's clothing. A few examples of these regulations are shown below.

Toxicity
- after the year 2000 AZO dyestuffs are banned
- body piercing has increased intolerance to nickel – anything in contact with the body must be nickel-free.

Metal contamination

- contamination from pins and needles must be monitored in production
- machinists only have one needle in the machine at a time – supervisors dispose of broken needles
- there is a search for broken needles – if the bits are not found the product goes in a metal detector – if the bits are still not found the product does not enter the supply chain.

Flammability

- children's nightwear must comply with BS 5722.

Children's clothing

- cords and ribbons must not be accessible to the child's mouth – choking hazard
- no cords in hoods – there must be press studs to hold the hood at the front and a 90 Newton pull strength button on the back
- fastenings must not imitate food – for example, no strawberry shaped buttons
- no ties or zips for boys under five years old.

CONSUMERS' STATUTORY RIGHTS

Statutory rights apply regardless of where or how goods or services are bought. Consumers' 'reasonable expectations' are as applicable to someone:

- shopping at the corner shop or a department store
- buying by mail order, through advertisements or from door-to-door salesmen
- shopping on the Internet.

Naturally, consumers expect what they buy to perform satisfactorily. Even if consumers buy something in a sale, as a 'second' or as a 'shop soiled' item, the product must perform as they are told it will. In order to meet statutory requirements, products must:

- be of 'satisfactory quality', according to the sales description, cost and any other relevant factors. This covers appearance, safety and durability of the product. Items should be free from defects, except when openly sold as sub-standard such as 'shop soiled'.
- be 'fit for purpose' and perform as described. If a jacket is described as waterproof and it must be waterproof or you have every right to complain.
- be 'as described' on packaging, sales display or according to what the seller says. For example, a machine washable wool garment must not shrink when washed.

Making a complaint

If you buy a product after being shown a sample in a shop or market stall, you have every right to receive a product that is the same quality. If you need to complain, be clear about your rights.

Legally, you cannot expect a product sold as 'shop-soiled' to be as good as new. It may even be faulty, but you have no legal grounds for complaint if you:

- were told about the fault at the time of purchase
- examined the product and didn't see the fault
- damaged the item yourself
- bought it by mistake – maybe bought the wrong size by mistake
- changed your mind about the product.

However, sometimes all is not lost. In order to build customer loyalty, many retailers, including department stores often exchange products that are not faulty, provided you have proof of purchase. Many retailers will exchange goods that consumers decide are the wrong size, fit or colour.

Buying second-hand goods

Consumers buying second-hand goods can also claim their money back or for the cost of repairs if the goods are faulty provided the faults:

- are not due to the wear and tear expected on second-hand products
- were not pointed out at the time of sale
- were not obvious at the time of purchase.

Buying sale goods

In the rush of the January (or any other) sales, remember you have the same rights when buying marked-down goods as when buying new ones. Notices stating 'no refunds on sale goods' are illegal and local authorities can prosecute traders who try to avoid their responsibilities by displaying such notices.

TASK

Compare two fashion products that you bought recently. Answer the following questions about each product:
- Did you know what you wanted to buy before shopping?
- Did you buy the product because it's fashionable?
- Was it an impulse buy?
- Did you buy it in a sale?
- Were you influenced by the sales consultant or a friend?
- Did it cost more/less than you budgeted for?
- Did you pay by cash, credit or another way?
- Did you shop around before buying?
- Did you compare the prices in other shops?
- Did you buy it from a trader who is fair?
- Were you happy with it when you got home?

Include any other questions that are relevant. Write a report on the two products and compare your report with a peer.

Faulty products

A consumer who buys a faulty product should expect a refund. However, the retailer needs to be informed about the problem as soon as possible. Keeping a faulty product beyond a reasonable time without complaining, may lose any right to a refund.

- If it is impossible to return the product within a few days, a consumer should contact the retailer as soon as the fault is discovered, note the name of the person spoken to and keep a record of the conversation.
- A consumer should not hang on to faulty goods without complaining.
- The law says that sellers are responsible for the products they sell, so a consumer should not be fobbed off by a trader who says it's the manufacturer's fault.
- Losing the receipt does not mean a loss of statutory rights. There may be other evidence, such as credit card or bank statement.
- If, by chance, a faulty product should cause damage to another product (such as a faulty zip on jeans ruining a T-shirt), a consumer may be able to claim compensation.

If fault occurs in a product after you have had it for a reasonable time, or you have used it for some time, then you cannot have it replaced. You could, however, claim some compensation for the loss in value of the product or something towards the cost of repair or replacement.

Getting advice

Consumers sometimes need advice and guidance on everyday shopping problems. Local authority Trading Standards Officers and the Citizens Advice Bureau deal with all sorts of problems and complaints.

TASK

You recently bought a set of lambs' wool car seat covers that leave fluff all over the clothes of passengers in the car. How would you go about complaining about the product:

- in person
- by telephone
- in writing with a view to obtaining a replacement set of covers and the cost of dry cleaning an expensive dark suit affected by the fluff.

Chapter 3
Advertising and Marketing

ADVERTISING AND THE ROLE OF THE DESIGN AGENCY IN COMMUNICATING BETWEEN MANUFACTURERS AND CONSUMERS

The aim of all advertising, through any type of media communication, is to influence potential consumers to buy products.

For product manufacturers, the cost of advertising is a major but necessary expense in a competitive world. Advertising is often managed by specialist advertising agencies, each with its own distinctive approach. In spite of all the money spent on it, nobody can really say for certain how successful advertising works or what makes one advertising campaign memorable whilst another fails miserably. However there are said to be two approaches to advertising – the hard sell and the soft sell.

HARD SELL

A hard sell advertisement has a simple and direct message about the product's unique features and advantages over a competitor's products. This is called the product's Unique Selling Proposition (USP). The hard sell approach is sometimes used to advertise functional products. For example, advertisements in outdoor pursuits magazines for rucksacks, tents or climbing ropes often major on the functional and performance features that make the product superior to other similar products on the market. Most textile product advertising, however, also includes references to the look of the product, whether overtly or indirectly, since this can often differentiate one product from another.

Controversial advertising

The Italian company Benetton has long used controversial advertising in the form of shocking images to sell their clothes. Many people will remember seeing advertisements with the slogan 'United Colours of Benetton' alongside images such as an unwashed baby's first moments after its birth, a priest and a nun kissing, or a dying aids victim. Benetton claims that this style of advertising highlights social, moral or ethnic issues. This claim was substantiated in 1993 by Benetton's 'Empty your closets' campaign, which collected surplus clothing to be donated to Africa, Asia and the former Yugoslavia.

TASKS

1 It is widely accepted that values issues related to moral, social, cultural and environmental problems, influence the development of products. Explain why you think this is true.

2 Should advertising campaigns get involved with such issues? Using an advertisement of your choice, explain your views.

SOFT SELL

Most advertising related to textile products is associated with a softer approach, with which consumers can identify. Soft sell advertising promotes image and style and is often associated with brand advertising. This focuses on creating a positive product image, combined with the benefits it can bring to consumers. The aim is to promote brand loyalty, by creating positive emotional and psychological associations with the product.

Soft sell is often said to work best with expensive, high status products, such as designer clothing or luxury interiors products. It can, however, also be associated with frequently bought basic items such as men's underpants, which can be given a glamorous image! Think also of advertisements that use sports stars to promote products such as socks, trainers and sports equipment.

TASK

Look through newspapers or magazines to find examples of hard and soft sell advertisements.

• Identify the target market group for each advertisement.

• Suggest how you could make a hard sell advertisement softer.

• Explain how you could change a soft sell advertisement to make it harder.

Marketing fibres

Successful product marketing depends on creating demand in the first place, then developing new markets for the product. For fibre producers, this often means supporting the product in a number of different ways. This can be done through:

• developing websites where consumers can find out about the fibre and the products in which it's used

• working with fabric and product manufacturers to develop new end-uses

• using an advertising campaign that addresses consumers directly. This frequently includes the use of swing tickets and high profile press advertising.

The marketing of a new fibre needs to be a sustained activity, in order to build a successful brand. For example, the textile fibre Lycra has been around for 40 years and is still going strong! It was recently voted 14th out of 25 'Top Fashion Innovations of the 20th Century' by American consumers. Recent innovations in the marketing of Lycra include the concept of having garments bear the new 'Spirit of Lycra' logo. This is the first time the Lycra name will have been externally visible on products, rather than being inside on the label or on a swing ticket.

ADVERTISING STANDARDS AUTHORITY

In the UK, the Advertising Standards Authority (ASA) regulates all media advertising in non-broadcast media, such as newspapers or magazines. There is a code of practice, which states that advertisements should:

- be legal, decent, honest and truthful
- show responsibility to the consumer and to society
- follow business principles of 'fair' competition.

In Victorian times, many advertisements were downright untruthful. In the 1920s and 30s some advertisements claimed benefits for products that were questionable. Fortunately today, most of the 25 million advertisements created annually in the UK follow the ASA code of practice. One of the issues relating to society's acceptance of advertisements, though, is changing values.

TASK

Some of today's advertisements would not have been allowed in the past and some are even controversial in today's social climate. For example the recent advertisements for French Connection use a very controversial logo. Is this OK? Is it cool? Is it offensive to older people or for children to see? Explain your views.

THE ROLE OF THE MEDIA IN MARKETING PRODUCTS

The role of the media is to provide a channel through which consumer choice can be influenced in favour of a particular product. Media advertising can also be used to promote a good public image for a company. The choice of media depends on the type of product to be advertised. For example cinema advertising often promotes ice cream or sometimes the products or services of local companies. Why do you think this is?

When choosing advertising media, many companies subscribe to national surveys, such as the Target Group Index (TGI). The TGI is an important source of information about consumer consumption patterns – the type of products they buy and use, what television channels they watch, which newspapers they read and which radio stations they listen to. Using this kind of survey enables a marketing organisation to match a product's target market with the media it uses most. Table 4B.3 compares the average UK advertising expenditure for the press, television and radio, posters and billboards.

Media type	Advertising expenditure	Advantages of advertisements	Disadvantages of advertisements
Press	60%	• provides detailed product information • can use reply coupons for direct response	• need to be timed to match a marketing campaign • not always read by consumers
Television	33%	• large audiences, but spread over different channels • can show products being used	• limited by short time-span of commercials • viewers may not be in the target market
Posters and bill boards	4%	• cheap form of advertising • widely available	• low-impact form of advertising • seen as complicated to buy • liable to damage and defacement
Radio	3%	• can accurately target geographical areas	• low audience numbers compared to other media

Table 4B.3

Average UK expenditure on advertising in the media.

TASK

1 Undertake a survey of the following types of media advertising.
  • outdoor media – posters and bill boards
  • broadcast media – television and radio
  • the press – newspapers and magazines
  • electronic – the Internet.
Record and justify which media type is most frequently used for advertising fashion products, sports goods and household textiles.

2 Make a collection of press advertisements that target textile products. For each advertisement state the product type and explain:
  • the target market – based on demographics and lifestyle
  • if the approach is hard or soft sell
  • if there is any use of emotion, concern, compassion, persuasion or politics
  • any 'values' are attached to the product
  • if the advertisement is part of wider campaign – what other sort of media is used?

TASK

3 Plan a marketing strategy for your own course work product.
  - outline the buying behaviour and lifestyle of your target market group
  - describe the key characteristics and features of your product
  - justify the use of two different types of appropriate media
  - explain the strengths and weaknesses of using the Internet to advertise your product.

MARKET RESEARCH TECHNIQUES

Before making any decision about a product's design, manufacture, marketing and distribution, it is necessary to undertake marketing research in order to predict and target consumer needs. Using market research information enables manufacturers to develop products that people want to buy. This information is also used to improve existing products and to identify 'gaps' in the market. Market research identifies a wide range of information, such as:

- patterns and trends in the population and society, such as age, gender and income (demographics)
- trends in employment, interest rates and inflation
- the size, buying behaviour, lifestyle and preferences of target market groups and sub-groups (called market segments)
- styling trends, the colour palette and fabric trends for the season
- the required characteristics of new products – matched to target market needs
- pricing strategies – the effect of price increases on demand and sales, price comparisons with competitors' products, the price to set for new products
- the competition – and their strengths and weaknesses. This includes their pricing and marketing policies.

UNDERTAKING MARKETING RESEARCH

Marketing research is based on two sources of information, which are classified as primary and secondary.

- Primary sources of information come from original research, using shop and trade fair surveys, internal company data, questionnaires and consumer surveys.
- Secondary sources of information come from already published information from trade magazines, newspapers, trend forecasting companies, commercial reports, government statistics, computer databases and the Internet.

When undertaking primary marketing research, two types of data can be collected. These are called quantitative and qualitative data.

TASK

1 Collect textile product advertisements from magazines and try to identify the target market group they are selling to.
   • Explain why you think the product is aimed at a specific age group.
   • Describe the product image and consumer lifestyle that is being promoted.
   • Investigate the promotion of the product image at the point of sale.
2 A shop report can involve
   • window shopping
   • going into shops and stores to look for trends, themes, styling and colour ideas
   • going to art galleries and museums to look for ideas and design information.

Plan a shop report on ethnic-style interiors products. Use your research to match the design, style and price of the products to the needs of the target market group. Sketch the products and record the materials and fastenings used.

Quantitative research

Quantitative research is about *how many* people hold similar views or display similar characteristics – such as how many people watch sport on TV or how many belong to a sports club. This kind of research often uses surveys to collect data about the attitudes and opinions of a 'sample' (a small proportion) of a target market group. The responses from the sample are used to determine the views of the whole target market group. The techniques used to select the sample are similar to those used by pollsters asking voters who they intend to vote for in an election. Such research can be extremely accurate, with an error margin of only a few percentage points.

Qualitative research

Qualitative research is about *how people think and feel* about issues or *why they take certain decisions* – such as why people buy branded goods rather than own brand. This kind of research is usually conducted among a few individuals to explore in depth their behaviour. Further research can then be undertaken to see if the views of a few individuals are representative of the whole target market group.

Questionnaires

Questionnaires are useful for collecting primary research, but they need to be well designed so they provide relevant information that enables decisions to be made. It is important to test a questionnaire before using it. Generally shorter

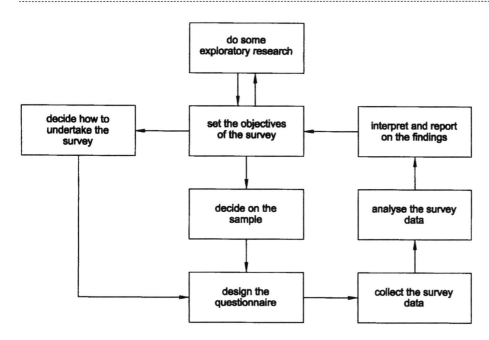

Figure 4B.9
The most effective way to conduct a survey is to follow a series of key activities.

questionnaires are better than long ones, because they are more focused. How the questions are worded is very important.

• Avoid long words, technical terms and jargon. Questions must be clear and easy to understand.
• Only include relevant questions that target the information required
• Use short questions of fewer than 20 words.
• Make sure that each question is precise and tackles one topic at a time.
• Avoid 'leading' questions that influence the answer.
• Take care with questions about age, social class, ethnicity and salary, so as not to cause offence. Use these types of question at the end.

Asking questions
Questions need to be focused and targeted to get the responses required.

1. Open-ended questions such as 'what is your opinion of stretch denim?' allow ambiguous answers that may be too wide to be very useful.
2. Closed questions are better because they provide a limited number of optional answers to choose from. They are easier to answer and are often used in surveys. For example:

   'What decoration would you prefer:
   (a)   a coloured strip around the bottom of the legs
   (b)   embroidery
   (c)   silver studs?'

Avoid offering two options such as yes/no because they are of limited use.

Figure 4B.10

Multiple-choice questions are often used in questionnaires.

To which age group do you belong? (tick one box only)

☐ 16-24   ☐ 25-34   ☐ 35-44   ☐ 45-54   ☐ 55-64   ☐ 65+

Which of the following factors influenced you to buy this product?

☐ Television advertisement
☐ Television programme
☐ Press advertisement
☐ Other (please specify)

Where did you buy this product?

☐ Supermarket
☐ Department store
☐ Mail order
☐ Other (please specify)

TASK

You are designing household textiles for use in loft apartments. Draw up a questionnaire to find out the needs of an appropriate target market group.

Product analysis

Check it out! Unit 1 Industrial and commercial products and practices page 6-8

Product analysis is an important primary research tool, because it enables the analysis of a competitor's product. This can provide a whole range of valuable information about materials, components, construction and assembly processes. It also helps in the development specifications for new products. Product analysis also provides valuable marketing information One method often used to is called SWOT – which involves the analysis the product's strengths, weaknesses, opportunities for market penetration and threats in terms of the competition it generates.

THE BASIC PRINCIPLES OF MARKETING

Check it out! Unit 1 Industrial and commercial products and practices pages 11
Unit 3B Design and technology in society pages 291

Marketing involves identifying a need and satisfying it. The aim of all marketing activities is therefore to satisfy consumer needs, generate product sales, increase market share and to ensure that a company remains profitable. Successful marketing can also include promoting a brand image and developing new markets for the product.

MARKETING PLAN

A successful marketing plan enables a company to develop a competitive edge. This means providing reliable, high quality products at a value-for-money price customers can afford – combined with the image they want the product to give them. In general a marketing plan involves:

- background and situation analysis, including SWOT
- analysing political, economic, social and technological issues (PEST) that may have an impact on marketing the product. For example, using concerns about the environment to promote an eco-friendly product
- collecting information on target markets, consumers and competitors
- developing an action plan and advertising strategies
- investigating and planning marketing costs
- planning the best time to market the product to an achievable timetable – for example pre-Christmas or pre-back-to-school shopping in late August
- developing a plan for monitoring the marketing campaign – using feedback to improve it.

Marketing a fibre brand name

In recent years, a limited number of new fibres have come onto the market – one example being the Tencel brand. Most fibre innovation has tended to take place in the development of blends that target specific end-uses or consumer needs. A key factor in the marketing of new fibres or fibre blends has been in supporting the product right down the supply chain from yarn, fabric and product, right to the customer. Many fibre companies develop strong marketing support for their fibre brands. This often includes some or all of the following:

- in-house development of colour and style trends to stimulate innovative fabric development
- designer/weaver/knitter partnerships to provide innovative design concepts
- promotion at international trade fairs, such as Premiere Vision in Paris
- workshops and presentations of fabric developments and trends to manufacturers and retailers

- the provision of trend information and fabric sourcing information to manufacturers
- joint partnerships with manufacturers to encourage product development
- high profile advertising and marketing to influence retail and consumer understanding of the fibre
- point of sale labelling to build consumers' quality and value awareness
- focused promotions at retail level
- website information about the fibre, its benefits to the consumer and its end-use in products.

TASK

Look out for advertisements for fibre brands in the press.
- What kind of image for the fibre is being promoted?
- What is the target market?
- How is the fibre supported by advertising in other media?
- Explore the fibre promotion at retail level.
- Further investigate the fibre through its website. Describe the benefits it brings to consumers and the competition from other fibres for the same target market.

TARGET MARKET GROUPS AND MARKET SEGMENTATION

A target market consists of all the customers of all the companies and organisations supplying a specific product, such as in the sportswear market or the interiors market. In the past companies identified and satisfied market needs through market research, which targeted a broad target market group. Targeting a broad group was not always successful – maybe the market was very large, geographically scattered, the competition too strong or the consumer needs too varied.

Market segments

The development of modern ideas about marketing has influenced companies to divide markets into separate consumer groups – called market segments. Many variables have been used to segment target markets, such as age, gender, disposable income, lifestyle, country or degree of fashion awareness. In the clothing industry manufacturers have traditionally targeted a segment of the market by:

- the range of clothes they made (menswear, womenswear or childrenswear)
- social class (through the product price)
- geographical areas (selling through a limited range of retailers).

Developing a marketing mix

These days, the driving force behind market segmentation is the need to develop marketing approaches for specific segments of the market, where their needs are not fully satisfied. For example in the shorts market, specific segments have been identified and you can now buy shorts for sunbathing, jogging, aerobics, cycling hiking or for playing football. The identification of market segments through market research has lead to the development of the concept of a marketing mix. This includes marketing a range of products using advertising, promotion and specially designed retail outlets. Many retail chains are designed to target segments that are differentiated by age, gender, buying behaviour, spending power and lifestyle.

CONSUMER DEMAND AND TECHNOLOGY PUSH

There are thought to be two main concepts relating to why and how products are developed: consumer demand (market pull) and technology push. Market pull refers to the requirements of the marketplace 'pulling' companies to produce what consumers want. Table 4B.4 gives examples of market pull and technology push in relation to textile products.

TASK

Identify two textile products that were developed through market pull and two that were developed through technology push. For each product explain the influences that contributed to its development.

TEST SELLING

The purpose of test selling is to find out consumer and retailer reactions to the product – is the product selling to the target market segment? What is their reaction to the product? Is the product selling successfully? Test selling enables forecasts to be made of future sales and profitability and enables production planning to take place.

LIFESTYLE MARKETING

Lifestyle is a well-established basis for targeting different market segments. It can be identified through investigating the geographic and demographic characteristics of the population. People with similar demographic characteristics often have similar lifestyles, live in similar types of houses and wear clothing to suit their lifestyle.

- One important lifestyle trend over the last generation is the movement to standardise the body to a slimmer shape by dieting and exercise.

Market pull	This may be explained through:	This may result in:
Market place demand creates a need for • higher quality products • value for money • new or modern styling	• a rise in consumer expectations, i.e. more money to spend • changes in lifestyle, i.e. an ageing population • the influence of the work of fashion designers, i.e. the need to be 'fashionable'	• updating existing products • creating new brands targeting specific market groups
Changing consumer attitudes creates a demand for • environmentally-friendly or recyclable products	• greater awareness of environmental, ethical or moral issues, i.e. global warming or the burning of the rain forests	• using different materials or processes to manufacture existing products • creating new 'eco' brands
Demographics creates a demand for • products with improved performance, function or appeal • bespoke garments	• changes in lifestyle, i.e. greater leisure time results in need for higher performance sportswear • an ageing population needs clothes with better fit, form and function	• updating existing products • using different or new materials or technology • creating new brands for sportswear • mass-produced bespoke garments

Technology push	This may be explained through:	This may result in:
New technologies used to develop new products	• developments in materials technology or processes, i.e. Tencel or Teflon coating • development of new technologies, i.e. using Bio-sensors in sportswear to monitor heart rate	• updating existing products or developing new ones • creating new 'smart' products
Using new styling to develop new products before old ones wear out	• the need to increase market share, i.e. creating the need to be 'modern' or 'fashionable'	• updating existing products through colour and styling • creating new 'modern' brands
Improving product quality through development of new materials or processes	• developments in fibres, i.e. Sportwool • developments in biotechnology, i.e. biopolishing cellulose fabrics to reduce 'pilling'	• updating existing products • creating new brands
New technologies used to develop new manufacturing systems or processes	• CADCAM enables faster time to market • ICT enables Quick Response manufacturing • Laser technology results in garment size measuring booths	• faster turn-round of fashionable styling • fast response to customer demand • mass-produced bespoke garments

Table 4B.4

- The demand for simpler styles of clothing that reflects working lives is another trend. For example many companies now have 'Dress down Fridays' when employees wear smart casual clothing rather than formal suits.
- The demand for clothing that is easier to maintain, by washing rather than dry-cleaning is another lifestyle trend that has had an enormous impact on product development.

TASK

A customer profile can provide details about the likes, dislikes and lifestyle of consumers. Designers, buyers and merchandisers often build up 'customer profiles' to help establish the characteristics of products that customers want. This information enables a company to target the right retail outlet with the right product, at the right price and at the right time.

A customer profile could include information about where the customer shops, their gender, age group, income bracket, level of disposable income, their brand loyalty, the newspaper and magazines they read, the music they like, TV programmes they watch, their interests and where they eat out.

Write a customer profile for the following products. In doing this you could think about customers' lifestyles, values and tastes.

- A cropped top for clubbing.
- A tweed jacket.
- Denim jeans.

BRAND LOYALTY

A 'brand' is a name or logo – a marketing identity – that sets a product apart from competitors' products. It protects and promotes the identity of the product. Branding is a key marketing tool because it promotes the concept of brand loyalty. Consumers buy the chosen brand, because it provides a perceived level of reliability, quality, special features or added value that makes it 'special' in the eyes of consumers.

Fibre branding

Fibre branding is extremely important because it:

- speeds up market acceptance of fibre innovation all the way through the value chain
- develops a reputation and image which increases its influence in the market
- provides an easy way for retailers to communicate excitement about hi-tech fibres and modernity in clothes
- is the focus for lots of information about product offerings and technical data
- is highly visible through promotion and advertising, point of sale material and swing tickets, seen by trade and consumers.

TASK

Brands are often developed to target specific market segments. The young sports and fashion market is a prime target for this type of marketing. There are many views about the morality of marketing fashion brands, because many young people are pulled in to a cycle of needing to be seen to be wearing the latest 'logo' or brand name. Other opinions say that fashion is fun and you're only young once. What do you think? Are young people under pressure to be seen in the latest styles? Is this kind of brand marketing ethical? Explain your views.

COMPETITIVE EDGE AND PRODUCT PROLIFERATION

Many companies produce similar products aimed at the same market segment for customers with similar needs. Apart from the obvious aesthetic characteristics – what the product looks like – the only other criterion upon which many consumers can base their buying decision is price. In theory, the most expensive brands would not sell, but this is rarely the case. For one thing, many consumers are not aware of every product and price on the market. Also, the pulling power of brands means that many consumers are prepared to pay the price for what they perceive to be a 'must have'.

Even so, many manufactures try to make their products different from the competition to ensure that their products have a successful market share. This may involve creating unique characteristics or using special or high-tech materials to give the product a 'competitive edge' or a different level of quality. Different price levels may then be set, which are often based on the value that consumers put on special features or qualities.

TASK

Identify a product which you think has a competitive edge over other similar products. Explain the benefits that this product brings in relation to its price.

PRICE AND MARKETING

Price is one of the most important aspects of marketing, because it affects the level of profit, the volume of manufacture, the market share and the image of the product. For example, is it high quality, high price or cheap and nasty?

When thinking about price it is important to distinguish between the retail price and the manufacturer's price – the difference being what is called 'mark up'. Whatever the mark up, everyone in the supply chain must make a profit. One aspect of pricing policy is to set a price that provides a satisfactory profit now and for the foreseeable future, rather than setting a higher price that produces a larger immediate profit. Another pricing policy might be market penetration, where the price is low enough to deter competition, but just high enough to make a profit.

The key to successful pricing is the attractiveness of the price to the consumer. For most consumers there is a fine line between the concept of price, value and quality. How much the consumer is prepared to pay for a product depends on how much the product is valued. A product may warrant a higher price if it:

- has extra features, special characteristics or innovative design
- is perceived as a quality product
- has an increased reputation through branding, advertising or promotion
- is possible to buy the product on credit
- if there is a guarantee of fast delivery, through mail order or the Internet.

MARKET SHARE AND PROMOTIONAL GIFTS

The aim of advertising and marketing is to increase market share. It is said that it is easier to increase the market share of a well-known brand than increasing the market share of a lesser known one. Various methods are used to increase market share, including:

- direct marketing by telephone or mailshot
- free 'gifts' or samples
- coupons that provide money off for the next purchase.

DISTRIBUTION

As recently as 10 years ago, products were stored in a warehouse before distribution. The storage, handling and preparation of products prior to customer despatch was 'the end of the line' in terms of manufacturing cost calculations.

In the last few years, however, the search for quality at the lowest cost has transformed distribution methods. The 'man, van and delivery sometime next week' has been displaced by the use of outsourcing to specialised expert organisations. The use of outsourcing is seen to be the most efficient route to the market. It makes use of flexible management systems and logistical expertise, supported by the use of computer systems that often interface with those of customers. The benefits of outsourcing distribution include efficiency, control, overheads reduction, security, flexibility and price. For example, Marks & Spencer have recently moved to outsourcing for all its general merchandising and transport in the UK and Ireland.

TASK

Advertising and distribution are important aspects of successful product marketing. Discuss how the use of specialist outside organisations can help manufacturers.

Chapter 4

Conservation and Resources

ENVIRONMENTAL IMPLICATIONS OF THE INDUSTRIAL AGE

One of the greatest problems faced by our modern industrial society is the consumption of non-renewable (finite) resources, such as coal, gas, oil and minerals. These will eventually run out, unless steps are taken to conserve and manage them. This will not be an easy task, because our modern lifestyle relies heavily on the benefits that coal, gas and oil in particular, can bring. Imagine, for example, a life without central heating, plastics or synthetic fibres!

PRODUCTS AND THE ENVIRONMENT

It is also difficult to imagine life without all the myriad of products in today's market place. Modern society has come to rely on what some people call a 'purchase-attraction' culture, in which we are encouraged and influenced to buy more and more products through advertising and marketing. This has resulted in the proliferation of products that we see in the market place today. In particular the manufacturing and marketing activities related to 'fashion' and 'fashionable products' provide us with innumerable opportunities to support the 'throw- away' society.

DESIGN AND THE ENVIRONMENT

Designing with the environment in mind will be one of the greatest problems confronting product designers in the future. One of the key questions is how design can influence the environmental impact of products. Other questions relating to product design that need to be answered are:

- What should be the aims of product design in the future?
- How can we convert the 'throw away' society into something more sustainable? Does this mean we will take the fun out of fashion?

Supporting longer term use

Designers and consumers in the future may need to develop a culture that supports longer-term use of products and a slowing down of 'fashion', resulting in the conservation of non-renewable resources. Such notions as 'shop 'til you drop', 'it's so last season I must have the latest one' and shopping as a hobby are all manifestations of the purchase-attraction culture, that encompasses all types of consumer goods. Altering this culture will be an enormous task, but inroads could be made by:

- switching the focus from 'buy because you want it' (purchase-attraction) to longer-term use – to 'buy because you need it'
- developing household goods that would not be bought, but that could be rented from the manufacturer
- paying for the use, servicing and repair of the product during its useful lifetime
- returning the product to the manufacturer for recycling and/or re-use.

It is plain to see that in order to ensure the future of the planet, it is up to everyone to find starting points for making changes to the culture of the throw away society. As we have seen, one starting point is to think about the ethics and morals attached to design – how good design can influence the environmental impact of products.

CONSERVATION AND THE ENVIRONMENT

On a grander scale, the conservation movement is also concerned with the future of the planet. Conservation is about the protection of the natural and urban environment for use by future generations. It is concerned with the management of existing resources and the reduction of the consumption of non-renewable ones, in favour of renewable energy sources such as hydro (water), solar and wind power.

Sustainable development

One aspect of conservation related to product design is the concept of sustainable development. This was defined by the 1987 Bruntland Report 'Our Common Future' (World Commission on Environment and Development) as: 'development that meets the needs of the present, without compromising the ability of future generations to meet their own needs.'

TASK

a Discuss the impact of a 'purchase-attraction' culture on the environment. Give examples of how you, your friends and family may be caught up in it.

b Changing consumers' attitudes to buying household goods, such as kettles or toasters, is one thing, but how can we change attitudes towards fashion products?

c In light of environmental concerns, explain your views for and against mass production and the marketing of products.

d Discuss how the renting of products rather than buying them could be applied to textile products.

THE USE OF NON-RENEWABLE RAW MATERIALS AND FOSSIL FUELS DURING THE MANUFACTURING PROCESS

Check it out! Environmental issues Unit 1 Industrial and commercial products and practices page 29

The manufacture of textiles and products is heavily dependant of the use of renewable and non-renewable resources and both use energy in the manufacturing process. Natural fibres come from renewable sources and regenerated fibres like lyocell are made from regenerated wood pulp from managed forests. However, synthetic fibres are made from non-renewable petrochemicals based on oil. The many innovative developments in synthetic fibres over the last few years, have led to an increase in their popularity. This has benefits for the environment as well as disadvantages. It is interesting to consider, for example, that:

- synthetic fibre manufacture uses a relatively low percentage of oil worldwide, in comparison with the percentage use of oil for fuel
- synthetics provide enhanced or 'engineered' properties, which can prolong the useful life of many technical, industrial, performance and fashion products
- it is possible to recycle synthetic fibres if they are used 100 per cent in products – fibre blends are a problem to recycle though.

The electricity used in product manufacture is derived from coal, gas, oil or nuclear power. Managing such finite resources is an increasing environmental responsibility and companies are required to take account of UK, European and international legislation when designing and manufacturing products. The efficient management of resources in manufacturing:

- reduces the quantity of materials used
- makes more efficient use of energy
- uses less wasteful production methods
- re-uses waste materials within the same manufacturing process
- recycles waste materials in a different manufacturing process
- designs for easy product aftercare, so less energy is required to maintain it
- designs products that can be fully or partially re-used or recycled.

TASK

We all have a part to play in protecting the planet. Explain your views on:
- what it means to 'tread lightly on the planet' as a consumer
- whether manufacturers need to continually produce new products
- how lifestyle marketing encourages consumerism
- buying cheaper 'fun' products, rather than more expensive but more 'classic' ones that last longer.
- throwing away products simply because they are old-fashioned
- recycling or re-using products.

RENEWABLE SOURCES OF ENERGY, ENERGY CONSERVATION AND THE USE OF EFFICIENT MANUFACTURING PROCESSES

Renewable sources of energy are defined as those that flow naturally from nature. The wind, tides, rivers, solar energy, geothermal and biomass are all renewable sources of energy. See Table 4B.5 Renewable resources are living things which can be regrown, such as forests, cotton and flax (linen). However, forests are termed renewable only if they are not used faster than they can be replaced. The indiscriminate destruction of the world's rainforests in recent years has led to a severe shortage of some tropical hardwoods, which are now extremely expensive. In order to conserve valuable hardwoods, manufacturers are encouraged to use only those grown on plantations or in managed forests. Cellulose, the raw material for textile fibres, such as Modal, viscose, Tencel and lyocell is obtained from softwoods from managed forests.

Energy source	Production	Benefits	Disadvantages
Wind	Wind turbines on wind farms.	Non-polluting. Low cost power. Accessible sites on hills or coast.	High set-up costs. Unsightly. Provides low percentage of energy needs.
Tides	Reversible turbines for twice daily tides in estuary location.	Non-polluting. Reliable and regular. Possible large-scale energy production.	Very high set-up cost. May restrict ship movements. May cause flooding and damage wildlife.
Water	Rivers turn turbines to generate hydro-electricity.	Non-polluting. 80-90% efficient.	High set-up cost. Remote sites. Provides low percentage of energy needs.
Solar	Solar panels generate hot water and electricity.	Non-polluting. Reliable. Possible to generate 50% of hot water for a typical house.	High cost of solar panels. Highest demand in winter.
Geothermal	Steam from deep holes in earth's crust generate electricity.	Non-polluting. Low cost energy.	Poor access where earth's crust is thin: e.g. New Zealand, Iceland.
Biomass	Wood, plants and waste burned to generate heat.	Environmental pollution. Low cost power.	Potential for deforestation. .

Table 4B.5

Renewable sources of energy.

MAKING MORE EFFICIENT USE OF ENERGY

The production of manufactured goods consumes large amounts of raw materials and energy. Manufacturers are therefore in a powerful position to contribute to sustainable development and to reduce energy costs by adopting more efficient manufacturing processes. These may result from redesigning the product itself or the production process.

Reducing costs

For many textile companies environmental legislation and rising water and other raw materials costs are of increasing importance. The efficient use of raw materials and improved production processing are therefore vital if a company is to remain competitive. One way of achieving this is to set up an environmental management system (EMS). The advantages of using an EMS are based around reducing waste and operating costs. The aim is to:

- reduce consumption of raw materials
- improve output
- reduce waste treatment and disposal costs.

Making cost savings

The Yorkshire fibre manufacturer Moorhouse & Brook recently discovered the benefits of implementing an EMS, even though it had always sought to be environmentally-friendly. The EMS enabled the company to take a fresh look at every aspect of its operations, from recycling raw materials packaging through to the disposal of toner cartridges from the office printers. Thread waste left over from the weaving process was one issue that attracted attention.

- The waste is now either recycled or sold as a raw material.
- Any remaining wool waste is ground up and used as a fertiliser in horticulture.
- Over 33,000 kg/year of waste from around the mill is now re-used on site or sold for recycling, producing significant cost savings for the company.

TASK

Identify a textile product that you think could be redesigned to improve its efficiency of manufacture. Can the design of the product be simplified? Can you use different processes to reduce waste? Use sketches and notes to explain your thinking.

NEW TECHNOLOGY AND ENVIRONMENTALLY FRIENDLY MANUFACTURING PROCESSES

Check it out! New materials, processes and technology Unit 3B D&T in Society pages 152

Redesigning a product or process is one way of achieving efficiency in manufacturing. For many companies this also improves their compliance with environmental legislation, improves their public image and helps them increase profits. As environmental awareness increases among consumers, especially the young, companies will increasingly promote their 'green' credentials as a positive selling point or marketing tool.

Lyocell

One recent example of the redesign of a manufacturing process can be seen in the development of the lyocell family of regenerated cellulose fibres. The traditional viscose process uses sodium hydroxide and other chemicals in a number of steps to dissolve the cellulose. The new lyocell process makes use of an organic non-toxic solvent (amine oxide) and water to dissolve the cellulose in a single step. Not only is the lyocell process simpler but it recycles the amine oxide which can then be reused. Lyocell can be recycled, incinerated, land-filled or digested in sewage. The fibre degrades completely in eight days to leave only water and carbondioxide, which can be used to power the sewage plant itself.

Figure 4B.11

The logo of 'envirowise'.

ENVIROWISE

Since 1995, Envirowise (www.envirowise.gov.uk) has been working with textile companies to help them address issues such as rising water costs, stricter effluent regulations and increasing waste disposal costs. The Envirowise programme is a joint initiative of the Department for Trade and Industry (DTI) and the Department of the Environment (DOE). It helps manufacturing companies improve their environmental performance and increase their competitiveness. Waste minimisation and cost-effective, cleaner technology are the Envirowise programme's main themes.

- Waste minimisation can often be a way of making valuable cost savings through the use of simple, no-cost or low-cost measures. It reduces the consumption of raw materials, water and energy and lowers costs for waste treatment and disposal.
- Cleaner technology means using equipment or processes that produce less waste or emissions than conventional methods.

Using cleaner technology

In 1990 the National Rivers Authority (now the Environment Agency) set colour standards for discharges from sewage treatment works. Local water companies imposed these requirements on dye houses. The deadline for achieving these limits was January 1996, after which time there would be a surcharge imposed on companies not meeting the requirements.

In response to the colour standards requirements, Courtaulds socks reviewed its dyeing processes. The company evaluated the cost-effectiveness of a number of technical options for on-site removal of colour from its dye house effluent. After successful trials, an innovative absorbent system, based on layers of synthetic inorganic clay particles was installed. The warm, colourless water produced by the effluent treatment plant is stored and used for scouring and other dye house processes. The synthetic clay system not only reduced operating costs (by around £54,000/year) but removed the threat of having to pay a surcharge to the water company.

(Sara Lee Courtaulds was created when the Sara Lee Corporation bought Courtaulds PLC in May 2000))

Cleaner design and life-cycle analysis

Check it out! Life cycle analysis Unit 1 Industrial and commercial products and practices page 49

Two important elements of cleaner technology are cleaner design and life-cycle analysis (LCA). They identify exactly where in the manufacturing process changes can be made in order to bring about environmental benefits and cost-savings.

- Cleaner design aims to reduce a product's environmental impact from 'cradle to the grave'.
- Life-cycle analysis evaluates the materials, energy and waste resulting from the design, manufacture, distribution, use and disposal, re-use or recycling of a product.

TASK

Select two different textile products, such as a nylon rucksack and a cotton/polyester blend jumper. Prepare a list of questions you could ask to assess the environmental impact of each of these products. Make sure you include questions about raw materials, manufacture, use and disposal.

THE IMPORTANCE OF USING SUSTAINABLE TECHNOLOGY

Manufacturing companies that use environmentally-friendly processes, such as minimising waste and using cleaner technology, are putting into practice aspects of sustainable development. This concept views the earth and all its resources as an asset, a stock of available wealth, which, if not managed carefully, will one day run out. Sustainable technology basically means conducting any economic activity, including manufacture, in such a way that it preserves the environment for future generations. Sustainable technology encompasses key issues such as:

- meeting essential human needs for work, energy, water and sanitation
- conserving resources
- linking environmental and economic issues in decision making
- ensuring a sustainable level of population
- making industrial development more inclusive
- giving priority to the essential needs of the world's poor.

Sustainable development is a concept that has engaged the attention of the entire world and many countries are actively involved in policies that promote it.

Many government programmes in the UK are geared towards sustainable development – Envirowise, for example. Bio-Wise is another government initiative that supports and advises companies and organisations in developing sustainable practices that make use of biotechnology. The Bio-Wise website is on www.dti.gov.uk/biowise. Information about biotechnology can be found in the next section.

TASK

1 Explain what is meant by sustainable technology.
2 Discuss the impact of sustainable development on jobs and manufacturing and what can be done to help people adapt to change.

MANAGEMENT OF WASTE, THE DISPOSAL OF PRODUCTS AND POLLUTION CONTROL

In the garment and household textiles sector large amounts of solid waste, such as fabric, threads, trimmings, yarn, plastic, cardboard and paper waste are generated.

- Fabric waste from garment cutting can amount to 10–20 per cent of fabric consumption.
- Waste in the knitwear sector is around 6 per cent for shaped knitwear.
- For cut and sew manufacture waste accounts for up to 20 per cent.
- Fabric waste in the household sector is between 4-10 per cent.

Reducing waste can therefore make a considerable difference to a company's profits and competitiveness. Where waste is unavoidable companies are encouraged to reduce, re-use and recycle. There are various markets for fabric waste, including the re-spinning of natural and some manufactured fibres, felt manufacture, household textiles and toys (i.e. wadding, dish-cloths, dusters, toy stuffing), fertiliser ('shoddy manure'), geotextiles and the car industry (i.e. upholstery made from recycled polyester).

THE DISPOSAL OF PRODUCTS AND POLLUTION CONTROL

Around 90 per cent of household rubbish in the UK is buried in landfill, five per cent is incinerated and only five per cent is recycled. Clearly, then, disposal of products when they have reached the end of their useful life is a major problem.

- Designing for recycling, designing durable products that will last and using products until they actually wear out, will all reduce the overall volume of rubbish to be disposed of.
- Changing the consumer culture, where goods are often replaced not because they have worn out but because a more fashionable item is on the market, will be no easy feat. Nor would it be pain free, as lower consumption means lower economic activity and possibly an economic downturn and lower levels of employment.

Skip and tip

For the disposal of industrial waste a simple solution is 'skip and tip' either to landfill or the sewers. Disposal by landfill has in the past been inexpensive and popular. Legislation is now enforcing change and the landfill tax has increased the cost of waste disposal for all companies.

In the UK, a variety of agencies are responsible for pollution control, enforcing the 1990 Environmental Protection Act (EPA). This act introduced wide-ranging legislation with tight controls on the discharge of waste into air, water and land. It also reinforced the policy of 'polluter pays'. The aim is to limit harmful materials entering the environment and to place greater responsibility on those generating, handling and treating wastes. Legislation is strictly enforced so that any company or organisation that causes pollution can be fined huge sums.

TASK

Today the concept of 'eco fashion' is seen as a niche market and there are few examples of 'ecological design' around. The fashion industry is caught in a difficult situation, where consumers are not prepared to pay the price for eco-fashion. Its price will only decrease when more manufacturers start producing it – but this is unlikely to happen until there is an increase in demand!

1 Discuss the issues related to eco-fashion.
2 Suggest ways that consumers can be encouraged to demand environmentally-friendly products.

THE IMPACT OF BIOTECHNOLOGY ON MANUFACTURE

Check it out! The impact of modern biotechnology on the development of new fibres Unit 4A page 246

Biotechnology involves the use of living proteins, called enzymes, to create industrial products and processes. These enzymes are the similar to the ones that help us digest food, compost garden rubbish and clean clothes. Biotechnology is not new and has been used for centuries to produce traditional products such as bread, cheese, wine and yoghurt. More recently technologists developed enzymes that could be added to detergents to improve their cleaning properties, resulting in 'biological' washing powders.

New processes

In textile processing the enzymatic removal of starch sizes from woven fabrics has been used for most of the last century and the fermentation vat is the one of the oldest known dyeing processes. Biotechnology also offers the potential for new industrial processes that require less energy and that use renewable raw materials. Newer biotechnological processes include:

- biostoning (to replace the stone-washing of denim)
- biopolishing (the removal of microfibre fibrils to make a fabric smoother, softer, improve drape and reduce pilling).

GENETIC DEVELOPMENTS

Compared to the more traditional methods, biotechnology can often produce better, faster, cleaner, cheaper and more efficient ways of doing things. In addition to the use of enzymes, genetic fingerprinting can be used to identify speciality fibres to prevent fraud, such as that associated with the labelling of cashmere. New bio-fibres produced by microbial fermentation of waste or low value materials such as straw and starch are also being developed. Other genetic developments include improved plant varieties used in the production of textile fibres and improvements in fibres derived from animals and in the health care of animals.

HELPING THE ENVIRONMENT

Biotechnology is also increasingly being used in industry to provide ecologically sound and economically efficient answers to complex environmental problems. For example, biotechnology plays a part in:

- colour and pesticide removal from effluent
- treating odours and emissions from industrial plants
- treating industrial, agricultural organic waste and domestic wastes through composting
- cleaning up contaminated land with bioremediation techniques.

Increasingly, whatever attention is paid to the moral and ethical dimensions of manufacturing processes and the reality of the new millennium is that many companies have no choice but to turn to biotechnology to increase their competitiveness in the face of ever-stricter environmental legislation.

THE ADVANTAGES AND DISADVANTAGES OF RECYCLING MATERIALS

Check it out! Recycling Unit 3B D&T in Society pages 153

ADVANTAGES

The recycling of textile materials is not new. Traditionally, textile merchants who trade in waste fibres and materials are known as 'shoddy' merchants, while 'reclaimers' recycle garments and other hard waste such as yarn. Reclaimers

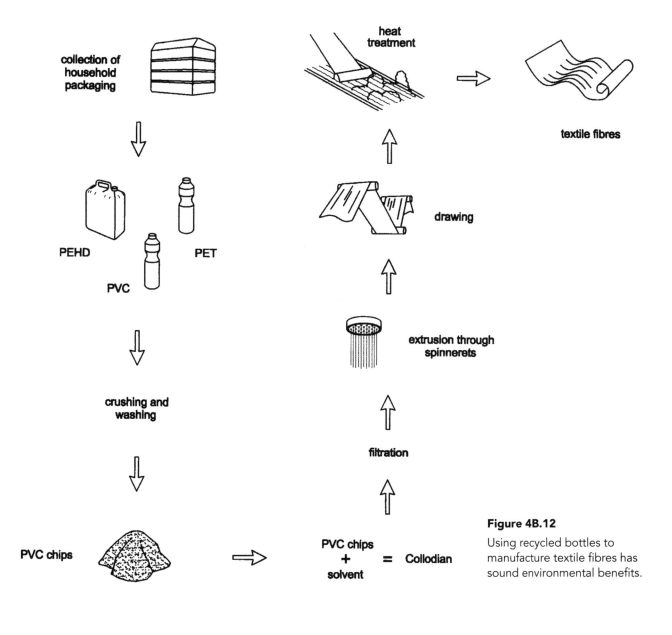

Figure 4B.12

Using recycled bottles to manufacture textile fibres has sound environmental benefits.

'pull' this waste to produce separate fibres, which are blended to produce flock. This is re-used for lower quality products such as some felts and blankets. Some reclaimers produce higher quality fibres where the natural and manufactured fibre content is tested and certified.

For manufacturers the advantages of recycling are cost-related. There are also numerous environmental advantages related to recycling, including:

- the conservation of non-renewable resources
- reduced energy consumption
- fewer greenhouse gas emissions
- cleaner air and waterways
- a decreased dependency on raw materials.

DISADVANTAGES

The main disadvantages of recycling are related to logistics – the time and effort it takes to adopt a structured recycling approach. The Envirowise programme supports companies in minimising waste and in finding opportunities for waste management. Another problem associated with recycling waste is the use of blended fibres, making the recycling of some products very expensive or impossible.

Recycling latex at Ulster carpet mills

There are many opportunities for recycling within manufacture. Ulster Carpet Mills Ltd, for example, developed a system of recycling latex. This is used to coat the back of carpets to retain the tuft. The latex is applied by passing the

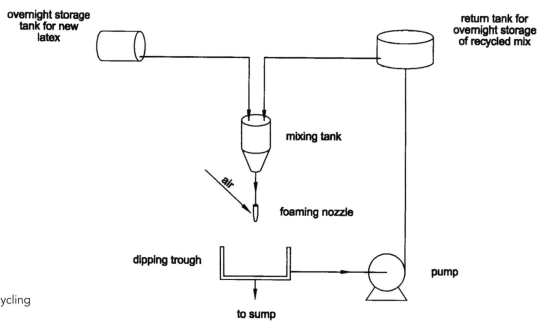

Figure 4B.13

The new latex recycling system.

carpet through a dipping trough containing a constant level of foamed latex mix, consisting of 30 per cent latex and 20 per cent limestone powder in water. At the end of each working day a full trough, equivalent to 5–10 per cent of daily use is left. Previously this mix was disposed of because it was too difficult to pump it to a storage tank. It couldn't be left in the dipping trough either, because a skin would form if left exposed to the air. Following an employee suggestion, the carpet company developed a system for pumping the leftover mix to an airtight overnight return tank. The leftover mix could then be recycled by mixing with the next day's latex mix, with the recycled mix representing around 9.6 per cent of the new combined batch.

The environmental and cost benefits of the latex recycling system include:

- cost savings of £13,000 in the first year
- an annual reduction in waste solids and wastewater to landfill of around 45 per cent
- a reduction of latex use by 5 per cent.

EXAM PRACTICE

The questions below are similar in style to the ones you will find in the examination paper for this unit. Before attempting to answer the questions read the relevant sections in the unit. Make note using key words or spider diagrams about the topic.

1 There are a number of economic factors related to the manufacture of products.

(a) Identify two economic factors and discuss their impact on the manufacture of mass produced products.

(6)

(b) Discuss the importance of accurate costing for one mass-produced product of your choice. (9)

2 British Standards has an important role to play in ensuring products fulfil consumer and environmental needs.

(a) Explain the role of British Standards. (9)

(b) With reference to relevant International Standards, discuss the importance of quality management systems in the design and manufacture of products. (6)

3 Advertising and marketing organisations spend huge amounts of money on influencing consumer choice.

(a) Discuss the role of the media in marketing products. (7)

(b) Explain, with the aid of product examples, the objectives of marketing and the importance of developing a competitive edge. (8)

4 Protecting the environment is a growing concern.

(a) Describe and explain the implications of using non-renewable resources for product manufacture. (7)

(b) Discuss the benefits of recycling for manufacturers and the environment. (8)

Preview

Unit	Level	Components	Areas of study
4	A2	Section B: Options	• Design and Technology in Society OR • CAD/CAM

Unit 4 Section B has two Options: Design and Technology in Society OR CAD/CAM. You must study the same ONE Option from Section B that you studied at AS.

WHAT YOU WILL LEARN IN THE UNIT

The content of the unit builds on what you studied at AS level and enables you to develop further your understanding of CAD/CAM. The work you undertake must include knowledge and understanding of the following areas:

Chapter 1 Computer-aided design, manufacture and testing (CADMAT)
- Computer-integrated manufacture (CIM)
- Flexible manufacturing systems.

Chapter 2 Robotics
- Industrial applications of robotics/control technology/automation
- Automated systems
- The use of block flow diagrams and flow process diagrams
- Advantages and disadvantages of automation.

Chapter 3 Uses of ICT in the manufacture of products
- The impact and disadvantages of ICT within the total manufacturing process.

WHAT YOU WILL DO IN THE UNIT

During the unit you should undertake a variety of activities to develop your understanding of the unit content. You may be asked to:

- work individually on some tasks – for example, when undertaking tasks to develop understanding of computer systems in industry
- work individually on some activities – for example, when using the Internet to research information about product marketing

- work collaboratively with others on some activities – for example, when developing understanding of the advantages and disadvantages of automation.

UNIT 4 ASSESSMENT

Unit 4 is externally assessed through a $1\frac{1}{2}$ hour written exam, which assesses your understanding of the unit subject content. There is one question paper, with two sections:

- Section A: Materials, Components and Systems
- Section B: Options

UNIT 4 SECTION B ASSESSMENT

The work that you do in this option will be externally assessed through Section B of the Unit 4 examination paper.

- There will be two compulsory long-answer questions, each worth 15 marks.
- Your answers should be from the viewpoint of Textiles Technology unless you are taught this option through another materials area.
- You are advised to spend 45 minutes on this section of the exam paper.
- This option, with Section A, is worth 15 per cent of the full Advanced GCE.

WHAT THE EXAMINER IS LOOKING FOR

The examination paper is designed to give you the opportunity to demonstrate your understanding of what you have learned in the option. Examiners are looking for longer, more in detailed answers that show a greater depth of knowledge and understanding at the Advanced GCE level.

EXAM TIPS

- Make brief notes about the topics covered in this unit.
- Summarise the key points on one or two sheets of paper.
- Learn these key points.
- Practise working through a complete exam so you will learn how to allocate the time available to you.
- In the exam read the questions through and then read them again to make sure you understand what you are being asked to do.
- Plan your answer briefly on paper then check the question again to make sure that you have covered it fully.
- Work through your answer making sure that you address each point in your plan.
- Use clearly written sentences and bullet points to make your answer clear.
- Use specialist technical terms and clear sketches to illustrate your answer where appropriate.
- Read through your answer, then move on to the next question.

Chapter 1

Computer-aided Design, Manufacture and Testing (CADMAT)

CADMAT

CADMAT is a term used to describe the integration of computer systems at every point in the manufacturing process. In addition to their use in CAD/CAM, computers play a major role in production planning, data control and the control of manufacturing systems. The use of computer systems has not only revolutionized the design and manufacture of products, but also enabled just in time, quick response and global manufacturing.

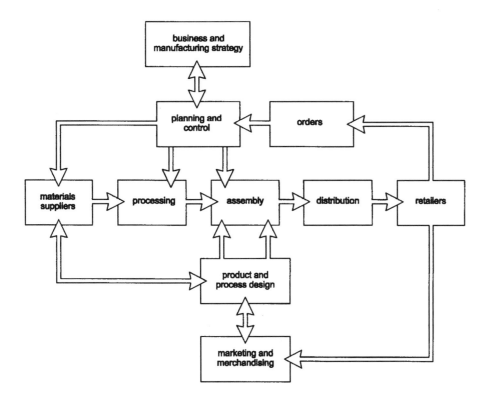

Figure 4B.14

Computer-intgrated manufacturing

Manufacturers use computer systems because they are adaptable and accurate. They provide easy access to data storage and cost-effective, fast, high quality production. The textile and product manufacturing industries uses computers for activities such as:

- creative and technical design
- modelling and testing before production
- communicating and sharing decisions about product design with clients, using electronic communications
- managing data about products, raw materials, components and stock.

Product data management (PDM) systems ensure the easy accessibility of data

- planning production and quality assurance, including costing, accounts and marketing
- controlling equipment and processes
- monitoring quality and safety
- control of manufacturing systems, including the management of business and manufacturing strategy and distribution logistics. This may include using graphs and spreadsheets to analyse orders data, scheduling processes, line balancing, planning machine maintenance or minimising the effects of training operators when changing over to new styles.

As with all systems, the efficiency of any computer system is determined by the sum of its parts – in other words the effectiveness of interrelated sub-systems. A failure in any one of the sub-systems – such as raw materials input – can lead to a production system that operates below capacity. For example, raw materials arriving at the wrong time or in the wrong quantities could mean interruptions to work in progress, thus damaging productivity and the ability to fulfil that vital order.

The ability to meet orders at the right time and cost is important for all manufacturers. An added pressure these days is the need to compete with low costs imports, to manage shorter production runs, a greater variety and number of product ranges and shorter delivery requirements. The control of manufacturing costs and the smooth running of the manufacturing system are key areas that rely on the accuracy and speed of processing electronic data. These days, many manufacturing systems are managed by computer software called 'product data management'. This kind of data management software makes use of the 'real time' processing of data.

Product data management (PDM) systems
PDM is a data management system that integrates all aspects of manufacturing, from product modelling to the management of manufacturing processes to the labelling and marketing of the product. PDM is an example of 'electronic product definition' (EPD) software, in which all the product and process data is generated once and stored electronically on a database. This evolves as the new product is developed, enabling manufacturers worldwide to manufacture products on a 'right first time' basis. The PDM software can organise and communicate accurate, up-to-date information in a database, monitor production and enable fast, efficient and cost-effective textiles manufacturing on a global scale.

PDM software enables instant communications, using ICT, between departments, manufacturers and retailers in the same or different city or country. This enables the design of products in one location and manufacture in another. For example, designers can research style information in one country and download from a laptop computer, via electronic links, to the central design office. Product development can begin immediately. The final product specification can be sent, electronically, to the manufacturing site in another country, where quality can be monitored on the production line, using digital cameras.

Real time processing

This kind of data management software makes use of the 'real time' processing of data, sometimes called 'telematics'. Real time in computer terminology is the updating of data at the time the event is happening. An every day example of real time is the use of a cash-dispensing machine – at the same time as withdrawing cash, the account is debited. Up-to-the-minute accurate information available from a real time production system includes information such as:

- work in progress – data about the contract, customer, style, order size, colour, bundle and delivery date.
- labour cost control – data about attended time, overtime, standard minutes earned, performance, efficiency, quantities produced, cost per unit, gross pay, average hourly rate

Advantages of real time processing

- increased productivity. This is mainly due to the increased motivation for operators, resulting from the immediate feedback of performance and wage information, such as efficiency and total pay earned today. Increased productivity also comes about through quality data related to balancing of work in progress
- improved quality control. This is due to the ability to identify where faults occur and to track reworking. Real time data shows how an operator's output drops while carrying out repairs and reinforces the message that it is more cost-effective to produce good work in the first place
- improved costing. Real time data enables actual product costs to be precisely calculated, which can be used as a basis for future costing
- reduced labour turnover. The use of feedback at workstation terminals enables operators to achieve higher performance and pay, enabling them to pace themselves throughout the day and reduce fatigue. More effective production control reduces labour turnover and absenteeism
- reduction in wage costs, possibly by one per cent. Real time enables pay to be automatically and accurately calculated, reducing wage costs in the wages office
- reduction in work in progress, bottlenecks, late deliveries and overtime. Up-to-date data can lead to increased flexibility, faster delivery, reduction in borrowing and space requirements and freight costs and higher profits.

The power of PDM to manage the product from receipt of the customer order to delivery is possible only through the use of real time data feedback. Production data can be analysed and merged with data relating to product demand and financial information.

- raw materials and components can be bought in as and when required. This results in improved financial efficiency, a reduction in stock levels and the requirements for storage capacity, reduced business overheads and increased profitability. This way of working is called 'just in time'.

TASK

1 Describe the benefits of using a product data management system.
2 Explain the term 'real-time' in relation to computer systems.
3 Use computer software to help your product development.
   - Design a pro-forma specification sheet that can be used to specify the requirements of the products you make.
   - Keep a file of all your product details to help you monitor your product development and quality.

QUICK RESPONSE (QR) AND JUST IN TIME (JIT)

The demands of quick response and more frequent style changes have encouraged industries to become much more flexible on the subject of working practices. One type of working practice, called 'just in time', has been applied in many industries around the world. JIT was first developed in the 1960s in the Toyota car manufacturing plants in Japan. Its aim was to meet customer orders quickly, at the required level of quality, in the right quantity and with minimum waste of raw materials, time and resources. In the clothing industry this system is known as 'the Toyota sewing system' and involves the use of just in time ordering of materials and team working (sometimes called 'modular manufacturing').

The use of computer systems and ICT enable JIT to function successfully – materials and components are ordered from the supplier and are delivered just before they are needed for production. JIT is used in combination with quick response manufacturing because it:

- reduces the need for raw materials stocks
- reduces the space requirement for keeping stock
- reduces the levels of finished goods kept in stock, waiting to be sold
- cuts the costs of tying up money in stock.

The principles of JIT

In JIT manufacturing the supplier can either provide the raw materials or manufactured components, such as buttons. The customer can either be a retailer that buys the final product, or another manufacturer that performs a continuing manufacturing process further down the production cycle.

JIT provides a systems approach to operating all the processes in a manufacturing system. It is so effective that it increases productivity, work performance, product quality and reduces costs. The use of software applications such as PDM has greatly enhanced the effectiveness of JIT, which relies on a continuous supply of information through the system. The underlying principles of JIT include:

- Use a multi-skilled flexible teams, that take responsibility for their own quality and output. This leads to higher productivity and increased job satisfaction.
- Reduce set up times, increase flexibility and the potential for producing cost-effective small batches.
- Ensure balanced operations to smooth the flow of products through the system and to prevent build-up of stock.
- Use a 'Kanban' approach to 'pull' products through the manufacturing system – use computer software to calculate resource requirements and schedule operations, so resources are at the right place at the right time
- Aim for continuous improvement (Kaizen) by limiting resources (such as time, people and equipment) and using less complicated production methods to prevent mistakes.
- Look for opportunities to provide machines, such as those used in fibre, yarn or fabric production that regulate their own production or that shut down if there is a problem.
- Ensure the factory layouts matches the production processes, to reduce the movement of materials and components.
- Eliminate waste by making to order, rationalising processes and product distribution, integrating processes, reducing stock levels and monitoring product quality to avoid faults.

The Toyota sewing system

In this system individuals are not stationed on a conventional production line. They work in small self-organised, multi-skilled, versatile teams of seven to nine, making joint decisions and sharing the responsibility for output in terms of quality and quantity.

- The teams stand to work and carry their garment pieces around a U-shaped group of machines.
- The ratio of machines to individuals in any team working system can be as high as three or four to one, although there has been a change in thinking towards smaller ratios based on more flexible and instantly re-programmable machines.
- The team works on one bundle at a time and there is no work in progress.
- The production manager provides continuous feedback to the team on their performance on an overhead display, showing target and actual output. The motivation of team members is very strong, absenteeism is low and the labour turnover considerably reduced.

Figure 4B.15

Schematic CIM system

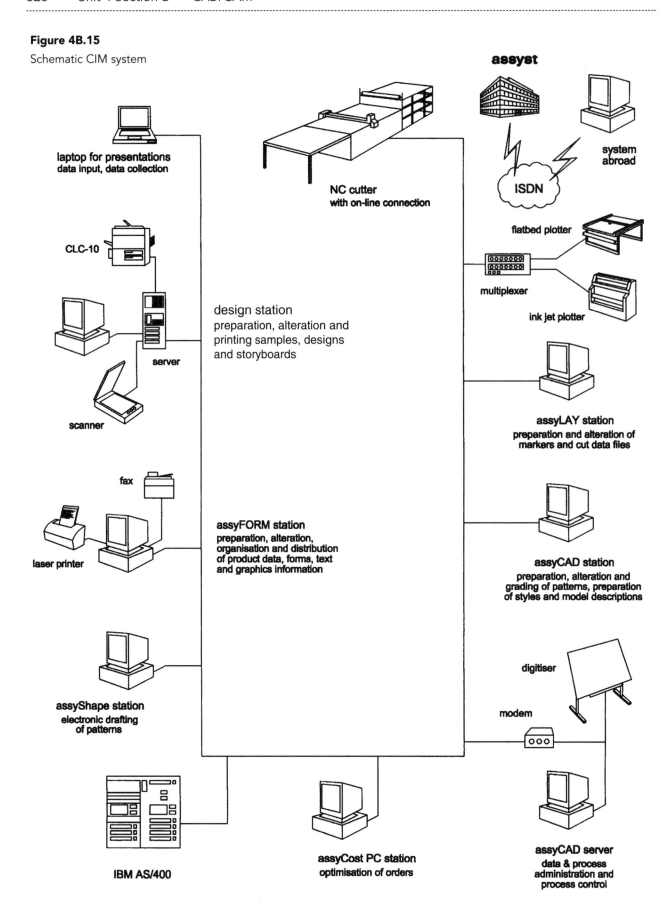

assyst

laptop for presentations
data input, data collection

CLC-10

server

scanner

NC cutter
with on-line connection

ISDN

system
abroad

flatbed plotter

multiplexer

ink jet plotter

design station
preparation, alteration and
printing samples, designs
and storyboards

assyLAY station
preparation and alteration of
markers and cut data files

fax

laser printer

assyFORM station
preparation, alteration,
organisation and distribution
of product data, forms, text
and graphics information

assyCAD station
preparation, alteration and
grading of patterns, preparation
of styles and model descriptions

digitiser

modem

assyShape station
electronic drafting
of patterns

IBM AS/400

assyCost PC station
optimisation of orders

assyCAD server
data & process
administration and
process control

TASK

1 Explain the role computers play in manufacturing operations.

2 Outline the key principles of JIT and its relationship with quick response manufacturing.

COMPUTER-INTEGRATED MANUFACTURING (CIM) AND FLEXIBLE MANUFACTURING SYSTEMS (FMS)

Check it out! Unit 3B Computer-integrated manufacture, page 179

Sophisticated and highly developed systems have an important role to play in the integration and control of manufacturing technologies. Computer-based ICT lies at the heart of many of these systems, but their scope is wider than just CIM, which ensures that all existing systems can talk to one another within both local and wider area networks. ICT also brings with it opportunities for developing flexible manufacturing systems which, since the 1960s, have been the main way of achieving competitive advantage. The following systems are examples of approaches to flexible manufacturing:

- Quick response is a system that incorporates a range of techniques to increase flexibility, shorten lead times, to keep stock levels low and to meet customer needs.
- Vertical partnerships between textile suppliers, product manufacturers and retailers have been used as an essential tool for the implementation of QR. The driving force, though, has usually been retailers. They are likely to benefit from increase in sales, reduction of stock levels and increase in stock turnover after the introduction of QR.
- Manufacturing resource planning (MRP) is a well-established management tool. It involves the use of a central computer and work station terminals to: collect real time data about current operator and machine allocations; track specific work through the production cycle; rebalance lines and teams and re-plan production in response to changing demand.

With the difficulties in achieving complete automation, the production of sewn goods products is likely to remain a labour-intensive operation. Developing flexible systems is therefore vitally important if the industry is to harness human resources to their maximum potential. Computers also play an important role in monitoring production and workflow in modular manufacturing and in line production.

CREATIVE AND TECHNICAL DESIGN

CAD is at the core of the integration of inter- and intra-business processes. Computer-aided design creates, designs and specifies the products to be produced and the technical information needed to manufacture them.

The success of CAD has been to drastically reduce design and development time. This reduction allows a company to develop products that are in direct response to market and consumer needs and to have a larger percentage of 'successful' products on the market. In addition, as the number of selling seasons increase, CAD tools can manage the increase in the number of new styles. Recent surveys have shown that the time required from ideas creation to the product in the market can vary from around 45 to 150 days. It's clear that any company that can sustain a design, develop, manufacture and distribution cycle of 45 days will be able to respond to the trends and demands of a fast changing marketplace.

MODELLING AND TESTING

The area of CAD that has been undergoing the fastest development in the last few years has been in 3D modelling and virtual modelling. The increased bandwidth now available in communications technology has also enabled the development of a number of web-based marketing initiatives.

- Virtual Reality Modelling Language (VRML), the 3D equivalent of HTML, is the tool by which 3D virtual products are displayed on the World Wide Web.
- Files written in VRML have a *wrl* extension (short for world).
- HTML files have the extension *html.*

VRML enables the production of a virtual world on the computer screen. In some environments the viewer can 'move' through the virtual world using the keyboard as an input device. Since the first VRML standards were only set in 1995, this technology is still in development, but it is set to become a powerful tool for the computer based modelling of products and their marketing.

TASK

Working with a colleague, investigate the use of virtual reality in e-marketing. Present your findings to the group.

PRODUCTION PLANNING, SCHEDULING AND CONTROL

Production planning translates sales orders and forecasts into deliveries to customers. It is the long- term view, based on marketing forecasts, about what is to be produced. Usually some of the products will be newly developed for the season, based on ideas from the design department. Quite often these new products will be marketed as a group.

Scheduling allocates work to the production capacity of the company, based on available machinery and labour capacity. Detailed production schedules are drafted. The progress of orders, timing and capacity utilisation are monitored throughout production. If delays occur or bottlenecks are found, action to balance production is taken – computer modelling is a key tool in achieving production control. Quality control data is monitored to ensure the minimum number of faulty products.

Seasonal calendar for Autumn/Winter

Activity	Ref	Week 1 (30 Nov)	2 (7 Dec)	3 (14 Dec)	4 (21 Dec)	5 (28 Dec)	6 (4 Jan)	7 (11 Jan)	8 (18 Jan)	9 (25 Jan)	10 (1 Feb)	11 (8 Feb)	12 (15 Feb)	13 (22 Feb)	14 (1 Mar)	15 (8 Mar)	16 (15 Mar)	17 (22 Mar)	18 (29 Mar)	19 (5 Apr)	20 (12 Apr)	21 (19 Apr)	22 (26 Apr)	23 (3 May)	24 (10 May)	25 (17 May)	26 (24 May)	27 (31 May)	28 (7 June)	29 (14 June)	30 (21 June)	31 (28 June)	32 (5 July)	33 (12 July)	34 (19 July)	35 (26 July)	36 (2 Aug)	37 (9 Aug)	38 (16 Aug)	39 (23 Aug)	40 (30 Aug)	41 (6 Sep)	42 (13 Sep)	43 (20 Sep)	44 (27 Sep)	45 (4 Oct)	46 (11 Oct)	47 (18 Oct)	48 (25 Oct)
Sample lengths ordered	(i)	X																																															
Samples made	(ii)		X	X	X	X	X	X	X	X	X																																						
Costings	(iii)										X	X	X																																				
Trade show	(iv)													X																																			
Private showings	(v)															X	X	X																															
Allocate work order	(vi)															X	X																																
Order fabric and trimmings	(vii)															X	X																																
Order extra fabric	(viii)																		X																														
Fabric delivered	(ix)																			X	X	X	X	X	X	X	X	X	X	X	X	X	X	X	X	X	X	X	X	X	X	X	X	X	X				
Pattern grading	(x)																	X	X	X	X	X	X	X	X	X	X	X	X	X	X	X	X	X	X	X	X	X	X	X	X	X	X	X	X	X	X	X	X
Production	(xi)																		X	X	X	X	X	X	X	X	X	X	X	X	X	X	X	X	X	X	X	X	X	X	X	X	X	X	X	X	X	X	X
Delivery	(xii)																				X	X	X	X	X	X	X	X	X	X	X	X	X	X	X	X	X	X	X	X	X	X	X	X	X	X	X	X	X

Figure 4B.16
Seasonal calendar

The control that makes or breaks a company schedule is the matching of fabric and components deliveries to available production capacity at the right time. Delivery on time is the most important service a company can offer its customers.

The production planning and control department provides information and documents to all the other departments in the company – design, marketing, buying, manufacturing and cost accounts. Production planning is responsible for:

- allocating work in the most profitable way
- providing information to other departments about the progress of orders
- adjusting production schedules to meet changing situations.

Production planning is therefore a complex activity and it is for this reason that planning and scheduling software is used to accommodate the different planning approaches used. Software such as PDM can manage and monitor all the information needed to manufacture the product. This information can be in the form of customer orders, costing sheets, cloth delivery control sheets, cloth record charts, specification sheets, work orders and style progress charts. The integration of PDM with electronic communications provides as essential tool for implementing flexible manufacturing systems such as quick response.

Scheduling

Scheduling is part of planning and control and its key features are to specify:

- the size of the work content – i.e. the scope and detail of the job
- the first start date
- the latest completion date
- the availability of specialist machinery and skills.

In most companies, the first step is to schedule the quantity of each product to be completed in each week over the short term. This involves using a database (such as those found in PDM software) to produce a master production schedule (MPS), which is formulated from known or forecast demand. The schedule, which can be accessed by different departments, allocates enough people to an order to ensure that it is completed on time. The work content of a sewn goods product can be estimated by comparing it to the time taken for other similar products – this information is accessed in the database library of previous styles. The PDM database can keep track of the status of hundreds of styles, what's late, what's on time, what's been changed or modified and what's been approved.

- Infinite capacity scheduling is a term used to describe the planning assumption is that there is always sufficient manufacturing capacity available.
- Resource scheduling (called finite scheduling) concentrates on scheduling enough resources required to manufacture the products.
- Scheduling also involves entering and invoicing orders (order processing), recording stock levels and cost accounting. It is essential that data be entered accurately into the database, since inaccurate data can cause multiple problems as products move through the production cycle.
- Constraint based scheduling aims to locate potential bottlenecks in production and ensure the synchronised flow of products through the system.

TASK

Describe the benefits of using computer systems to aid production planning and control. Suggest how you can use computer software to improve the efficiency of your own manufacture.

CONTROL OF EQUIPMENT, PROCESSES, QUALITY AND SAFETY

Control systems used for the control of equipment, processes, quality and safety can be electrical, electronic, mechanical and computer controlled. In textile and sewn goods products, control systems can include:

- computer control (CAD/CAM and CNC)
- integrated manufacturing systems (CIM, PDM software)
- quality control
- safety monitoring systems
- stock control systems.

The incorporation of feedback of information into control systems makes the process work more efficiently. Examples of control systems can be found in:

- Materials handling – i.e. moving fabric bundles around a garment factory, so they are in the right place at the right time.
- Processing of materials – i.e. automated manufacture of fibres, yarns and fabrics; using temperature control in pressing.

- Joining materials – i.e. stitching, bonding and heat-sealing, using electronic or computer control.
- Working out dye recipes, modelling textiles, drafting flat patterns, pattern grading, lay planning, fabric cutting – using CAD/CAM systems.
- Monitoring quality – i.e. using feedback from stitch control sensors to regulate a knitted fabric.
- ensuring safety – i.e. using feedback from electronic sensors to stop machinery if hands are in the way.

One of the most innovative recent manufacturing control systems is a software solution, which has modules that integrate different production functions. These include planning, costing, cut-planning, balancing and stock control modules. The different modules enable the real-time monitoring and output of operator, line, sectional and factory-efficient figures and work-in-progress reports. Easy-to-understand graphics and colour-coded highlights and warnings make it clear when production is not going to plan.

A real-time system by General Computers incorporates a graphical display that shows the floor-plan of the factory and which machines are being used at any one time. By placing the mouse over any workstation the output, efficiency and work status of each operator is seen. Time and attendance systems can be incorporated, together with machine-monitoring terminals and online machine maintenance follow-up. Big Brother is watching you!

The benefits related to the use of control systems include:

- providing feedback that makes processes more reliable and safe
- repeating processes easily to make identical products
- improving quality
- speeding up production
- automating tedious processes
- reducing waste.

Total quality

The ultimate aim of most companies is total quality, which is achieved through Total Quality Management (TQM). This concept extends the benefits of quality assurance to create a 'quality culture' in which quality is the responsibility of everyone in an organisation not just the quality control or inspection departments. The aim is to implement quality systems that provide continuing improvement for the complete life cycle of a product – always trying to make things better.

Computers are the enabling technology in the development of TQM and they are used at every stage of product development, together with providing training through the use of interactive learning methods and the use of computer-aided statistical tools and methods.

Monitoring quality

Despite the progress in designing for quality and incorporating quality into manufacturing processes, inspection still remains a necessary component of many quality assurance systems. The manual inspection or monitoring of any continuous process, such as in fabric manufacture, is commonly agreed to be inefficient. For a wide range of inspection tasks, detection proficiency is generally though to start at around 80-90 per cent detection rate. This can deteriorate rapidly after about half an hour, and the performance of a single inspector decreases with the number of faults to monitor.

Nowadays, artificial vision is a mature technology, which is well established in the electronics, automotive and pharmaceutical industries. It is gradually permeating the packaging, textiles, plastics and cosmetics sectors. Artificial vision applies digital image processing and analysis techniques to tackle quality problems in real-time conditions. It is a key tool in the manufacture and processing of woven textiles. For example, in the dry fabrics store each batch is inspected using optical quality control, followed by further inspection after washing, bleaching, dying and steam calendaring. Optical quality control offers a number of benefits, including:

- high-speed fault detection due to monitoring on the production line
- reduced labour requirement for quality inspection
- compliance with defined quality specifications
- real-time information from error graphics
- suitability for inspection of raw materials and finished goods
- simple installation and low running costs
- graphic user interface (GUI) can be tailored to user requirements.

TASK

1 For a product of your choice, identify the systems you could use to plan its manufacture.
2 Compile a flowchart to show the main stages of production and where inspection could be carried out.
3 Explain what and how you would check for quality.

Using computer software to analyse processes

Computers play an important role in representing and analysing processes and the causes and effects of different actions. For example Pareto charts used to compare different situations can help make production decisions. The Pareto principle has long been applied in stock control. It is sometimes known as the 80-20 rule – 80 per cent of the volume comes from only 20 per cent of the styles. Some companies establish a cut-off point and don't run styles that do not sell above a minimum quantity.

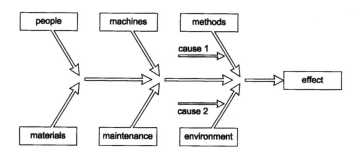

- Flow charts are useful for modelling processes, feedback and critical control points. They use symbols, text and arrows to the show direction of flow.
- Cause and effect or 'fishbone' diagrams provide a process or operation as a sequence. They provide a method for analysing processes to establish a cause and its effects.
- Bar graphs or histograms are used to analyse variations in data in graphic format. This makes it easier to 'see' graphical variations than it would be to read a table of numbers.
- Check sheets can be used to collect quantitative or qualitative data during production.

TASK

Investigate the potential for producing flow diagrams, fishbone diagrams or bar charts using the computer software available to you.

CONTROLLING COMPLEX MANUFACTURING PROCESSES

Computers are used in a variety of ways to model and control both products and manufacture. They can be used to describe the layout of equipment, the labour capacity and the scheduling of product manufacture. Computers also monitor the flow of information and work in progress through the whole production process and can control complex manufacturing processes. For example, the viability of manufacturing knitted fabrics may require information about stitch pattern, the colour and shape of the design, yarn requirements, the cost of materials and processes and lead times needed to manufacture the quantity required.

Digital stitch control

Knitting fabrics is a complex process and knitted forms, such as 3D knitted shapes, require a large number of needles to manage increases and decreases in the number of loops being knitted at any one time. The major development in flatbed 3D knitting has been the patented Shima Seiki Digital Stitch Control

System (DSCS). In this system each stitch (or loop) is treated as digital data. Once a loop length has been programmed, it is regulated by adjustments to the yarn feed and tension. The result is a consistent loop length every time and for every stitch, with a tolerance of +/- one per cent. This kind of quality control is impossible without digital control and is a crucial factor in producing:

- fully-fashioned knitted garments
- 3D whole garments
- consistent levels of quality in different batches and repeat orders.

Managing workflow

Production planning and control manages the input of fabric and components to the cutting and sewing departments and monitors output, labour costs, actual fabric usage and work in progress, which controls the work flow through the company. Production planning also controls order processing and ensures that products are made in the correct sequence to meet delivery dates. PDM software enables the processing and monitoring of information throughout this process. It also balances (levels) the different requirements of delivery and production – delivery is usually concentrated over short periods, whereas production is normally continuous throughout the year. For example winter coat delivery is at a maximum between September to November, so this is a time requiring high levels of labour. The company needs to manufacture different products at other times of the year in order to fill unused capacity and provide continuous employment for the workforce – otherwise skilled workers may go elsewhere. One way of maintaining a constant level of capacity is to produce the product early and hold the stock until the delivery time, although this method ties up capital in holding stock.

Bar coding

Data communication tags (bar codes) are an essential method of monitoring products through a system. Computer-controlled visual recognition systems recognise component parts, starting from raw materials and continuing through to cut fabric pieces and final products. Bar code readers are attached to individual work stations and not only monitor the product's progress but provide information about operator performance and the effectiveness of the manufacturing system. Laser scanners are often used to read bar codes (like in the supermarket!) – they are suited to applications requiring high reading performance, small size and low cost.

CONCURRENT MANUFACTURE
Linear or concurrent manufacture

The assessment criteria for your coursework product follow a linear approach to design and manufacture. In this approach the product passes through a series of stages and where and concepts are evaluated before moving on to the next stage. In commercial manufacturing situations this type of system would

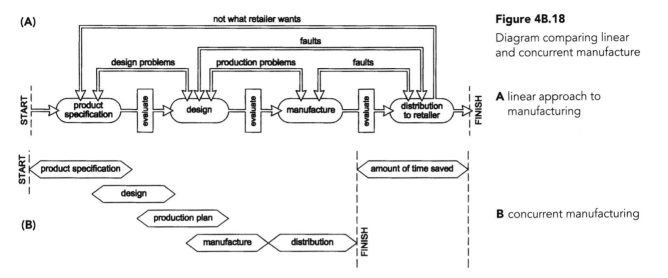

(A)

(B)

Figure 4B.18

Diagram comparing linear and concurrent manufacture

A linear approach to manufacturing

B concurrent manufacturing

be slow to respond to change, with longer lead times and may result in lower product quality because of the separation of design and manufacturing into discrete stages and the potential for costly re-design.

In practice when you design and manufacture your own product you often carry out a number of design and manufacturing stages at the same time – simultaneously. In the commercial world, concurrent manufacture is an effective manufacturing system. The key feature of concurrent or simultaneous manufacturing is a team-based approach to project management, so that the right people get together at the right time to identify and resolve design problems. (see Fig 4B.18)

Concurrent design and manufacture makes use of all the different functions of computers to enable fast, efficient and cost-effective product manufacture. It makes use of CAD/CAM/CIM, ICT, TQM and PDM systems to organise and communicate information between the product development team, manufacturers and retailers. Concurrent systems enable the use of just in time and quick response manufacturing, which reduce the product time to market.

Team working

In concurrent manufacturing, team working is a way of achieving more flexibility of production, improved motivation and a faster time to market. It has been defined by the Centre for Work and Technology as 'a flexible, quick response system, consisting of self-organised, self-motivated, multi-skilled, versatile personnel, who work collectively in teams, making joint decisions and sharing responsibility for output in terms of both quality and quantity.' Clearly then, there are benefits to both manufacturers and the workforce in adopting a team working approach.

The benefits to manufacturers of team working include:

- a flexible, multi-skilled workforce
- improved quality as a result of team responsibility

- higher productivity and efficiency
- retained orders from retailers, through meeting delivery dates
- reduced absenteeism, through greater commitment to work
- reduced labour turnover, through improved working conditions.

The benefits to the workforce of team working include:

- increased motivation, because workforce is multi-skilled
- opportunities for decision-making, to solve problems
- improved working conditions – greater variety, so less boredom
- opportunities for personal development
- increased average earnings
- improved relations with management.

Making the right decisions

A key objective of concurrent manufacture is to make the right decisions continuously through the product development cycle, in order to achieve quality products. This means setting appropriate specifications and 'quality indicators' to evaluate the both the design and intended manufacturing processes.

Many companies work closely in vertical partnerships with suppliers and retailers, in a 'value chain'. For this partnership to work effectively, information has to flow quickly between the partners. Increasingly this takes place electronically through Electronic Data Interchange (EDI) systems. (See page 358)

Computers are becoming increasingly useful in developing 'expert systems' or databases of best practice procedures such as on-line help files. Expert systems supplement human judgement and specialised knowledge in areas of complex decision-making in areas such as:

- selecting raw materials
- product design and application
- the optimisation of processes
- production planning and control
- quality assurance
- the monitoring and control of environmental impact
- health and safety
- financial analysis and control.

TASK

1 Explain why the use of ICT is such an important feature in controlling manufacturing systems.
2 For a product of your choice, explain the benefits of using a concurrent manufacturing system in comparison with a linear manufacturing system.
3 Discuss the importance of team working in concurrent manufacturing systems.

Chapter 2
Robotics

The textile industry, in its widest sense, is in a constant state of change, because of the availability of new technologies and changing consumer needs. In addition, the increasing older generation is set to demand products that will meet the problems of ageing. Looking into the future, it is possible that innovation may focus mainly on giving consumers exactly what they want in terms of style, colour and fit. This is likely to involve the further development of systems for in-store body measurement and for semi-bespoke manufacture. In turn, this may lead to an increase in small batch dyeing and printing. At the time of writing, digital printing is already starting to revolutionise many sectors of the clothing and furnishings industries. The Internet, too, will enable web-based business-to-business (B2B) and e-merchandising to flourish.

In the last section, we noted the increasing role of computers in developing 'expert systems' that supplement human judgement. Other key enabling technologies have also emerged, which are likely to have an important impact on future directions in industry organisation and competition. Apart from computers and electronics, these enabling technologies include anthropometrics, objective measurement, transport, packaging, anti-counterfeiting techniques and mechatronics. Some of these key enabling technologies apply to other industry sectors, as well as textiles and it is in this context that they are discussed in the next sections.

THE INDUSTRIAL APPLICATION OF ROBOTICS/CONTROL TECHNOLOGY AND THE DEVELOPMENT OF AUTOMATED PROCESSES

The term 'mechatronics' describes the multi-disciplinary application of mechanical, electronic, optical and computer engineering to the design of machinery and process feedback control. The term came originally from Japan and is indicative of that country's approach to the use of new technologies to create competitive advantage when developing new products.

Mechatronics integrates microelectronics and computer engineering into mechanical systems. It leads to a simplification of the mechanical parts, combined with greater operational precision and control. The Digital Stitch Control System developed by Shima Seiki for flat-bed 3D knitting is a good example of mechatronics. (See page 335-336).

Mechatronics also emphasises the development of processes and machinery based on systems thinking, flexibility, intelligence, reliability, self-adjustment, cost-effectiveness and safety. It is used in the development of multi-purpose user-friendly machinery that can be used for:

- the formation of shape weaving, knitting or braiding (i.e. 3D WholeGarment knits)
- automated and robotic testing and quality control
- fabric monitoring and process control
- robotic manipulation of fabric plies on the cutting table
- automated garment handling and part-assembly
- production of small batches.

AUTOMATION

The Jacquard loom was one of the first examples of automation and originally used a system of punched holes to control the pattern of a woven fabric. The term automation, then, describes the automatic operation and control of machinery without the interference of a human operator. Devices that can make adjustments and regulate the process in response to information from sensors often control modern automated machinery. This kind of adaptable automatic machine enables flexibility of manufacture, the fast repeat of repetitive processes and the production of cost-effective, high quality, reliable products. For example, automatic sock knitting machines are capable of knitting a sports sock in less than a minute!

Knitting machines are continually designed and improved to meet new situations. Machines with a mechanical patterning mechanism are suitable for manufacturers producing a small number of structures on a continuous basis, such as for packaging nets or pot scourers. Electronic patterning can be programmed via a PC to produce more complex and varied structures, such as those required for patterned stockings. A machine with a combination of electronic or mechanical patterning would therefore offer manufacturers great flexibility in producing a variety of products.

CNC machines

The electronic control of machines is by binary numbers in a sequence of instructions – this is called numerical control (NC). Changing the sequence of instructions alters the operation of the machine. Modern CNC machines are controlled through programs on a control computer, making the input of instructions much easier. Most modern systems can transfer CAD information from the designer's computer to a computer that controls the manufacturing machine. This process is called CAD/CAM. The combination of CAD/CAM with CNC now means that the computer in the design office and the manufacturing machine can be in completely different locations because the Internet is being used to send cutting patterns to factories in other countries.

TASK

Automation brings many benefits and some disadvantages. Discuss the pros and cons of automated manufacture in the textile industry.

ROBOTICS

CNC machines have been called the backbone of automation. This same CNC technology has been used to develop industrial robots – machines that can be programmed and re-programmed to perform routine tasks. Robots are electronic, computer controlled mechanical machines that enable the continuous operation of processes that can run concurrently, sequentially or in combination with other machines. Robotics is used in many different manufacturing processes, because it:

- helps improve product quality and minimise the waste caused by equipment malfunctions
- helps keep work environments safe – modern systems have sensors that shutdown the machine in cases of a hand in the way, for example.

Basic robotic machines were developed in the 1940s for use in atomic and hydrogen bomb manufacture. The industrial robots developed in the 1950s and 60s were more sophisticated and included sensors to provide feedback. Current robotic machines provide the flexibility required in manufacturing systems such as CIM and FMS. Future developments are expected to have more sophisticated sensory feedback systems that possess a degree of artificial intelligence (AI)

Computer control

All automated and robotic processes require a computer control system that can direct and control process operations. For example a PC that controls automatic machines knitting tights can memorise up to 50 styles with a very quick change over between each one. Such an automatic knitting system can sense and control the operation of processes by combining sub-systems of electrical, electronic, mechanical and pneumatic devices. In the case of tights manufacture, machines incorporate a variable profile system (VPS), which can identify and automatically program speed according to requirements for the part of the tights being knitted.

Automatic manufacturing systems

Manufacturing robotic devices are playing an increasing role in the development of industrial automation and CAM. They are computer-controlled machine tools that can be programmed to perform precise functions such as 'pick-and-place'. Their ability to make consistent repeated motions mean that robotic devices are used as part of an automated machine in a flexible manufacturing system.

Figure 4B.19

Diagram of automatic making-up line for tights

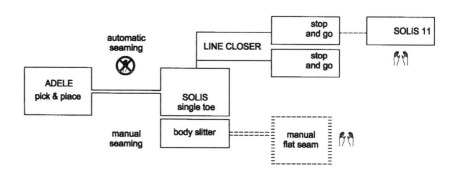

Figure 4B.19 shows a diagram of an automatic making-up line for tights. This consists of a robotic pick-and-place toe seaming plus seam closer system called 'Adele'. The machine has a robotic linkage between the toe-closer and seam closer, in which the product is turned through 90 degrees so that the toe is centralised with the body. The pick-and-place is able to re-set itself in case of an error occurring. This system enables the use of unskilled labour where there is a lack of skilled workers.

In another kind of knitting system, a master/slave relationship has been developed whereby only the master machine has an electronic unit, which tells the slave machine to knit the same product at the same time as the master. This type of system is cost-effective because only the master machine needs to have the expensive electronic unit installed.

Robotic devices

Most types of robotic devices are designed for manufacturing assembly or for materials handling, retrieval and storage. They cannot be used in all manufacturing situations – the greater the manufacturing complexity, the greater the complexity of calculations that need to be done before instructions can be given by the computer control system to the robot. Too complex a manufacturing process could slow down a robot's speed of action and therefore increase manufacturing time. This could be a no win situation, resulting in no manufacturing advantage – a human workforce could be more cost-effective.

Sensing, control and artificial intelligence (AI) technologies are continually evolving and there are expected to be significant increases in the processing power of computers in the future. The range and complexity of tasks that can be performed by manufacturing robots will therefore increase.

Working in hostile environments
As we have seen, the first robotic devices were developed for use in atomic and hydrogen bomb manufacture, where radioactivity would have been dangerous for human workers. These days, robotic devices are still used in hazardous manufacturing conditions, such as handling poisonous chemicals or toxic wastes in nuclear reprocessing plants. Of course, the people working in a nearby environment may also need to take advantage of protective clothing made from the wide range of available modern textiles. People working on the International Space Station, for example, not only need the help of robotic devices, but make use of survival clothing in one of the most hostile environments known.

TASK

Discuss the difference between automation and robotics, giving examples of their application in manufacturing.

Materials handling, retrieval and storage
Computer controlled systems are widely used to automate materials handling and the distribution of cut work in companies producing sewn goods products. The preparation of fabrics for sewing includes final inspection to eliminate faults and the application of finishes to improve later processes such as cutting, fusing, sewing, pressing and garment colouration. The processing of fabric, therefore, is a critical interface between textile and sewn goods manufacturers and an opportunity for the development of integrated manufacturing systems through the supply chain. This is becoming a reality, via electronic links and bar coding. This enables the processing and quality history of fabrics to increasingly follow them (and be updated) at each further processing stage.

Materials handling
Specialist manufacturers provide complete cutwork handling systems, such as computerised cutwork transporters. Computerised systems contain inform-ation about operators, processes they can do and their performance. Details of orders, style, sequence of operations and delivery date are fed into the system. The programme then finds the best route through the system for that order. Materials handling and cutting are the only operations within sewn goods manufacturing to have been fully automated.

- Advanced robotics is increasingly being used for retrieving fabric from store, loading it onto the fabric laying-up carriage and removing cut material pieces.

- In the cutting room, computers automate materials spreading and cutting, labelling each cut piece. An automated cut-piece pick-and-place device can be used to automatically off-load the cutting table, sort and shrink-wrap the cut piles ready for transport to the sewing room.

- Computer-controlled automatic overhead conveyor systems, such as the GERBERmover, monitor the movement of cut garment pieces around a factory. They provide the capability to locate and track individual pieces, as well as re-allocate work in the light of changing resources, styles and work content. The French company Technimanut has developed a new computerised Unit Production System (UPS) similar to the GERBERmover. This new system, already used in the car and laundry industries, allows bar-coded identification to be used to track products from the receipt of materials through to delivery, all the time providing real-time production information.

Hanging garment storage and distribution

Since the sewn goods industry is no longer localised and in order to compete in a global market, manufacturers have to meet demanding delivery schedules. Products must be available at the right time, in the right condition and in the right way. One of the implications of this in the garment industry is the move towards hanging garment storage and distribution. Look out for this kind of system used in a retail outlet like Next. Manufacturers delivering to such retail outlets need flexible handling solutions that deliver garments with speed and efficiency in a value-for-money way.

Fast track distribution systems are increasingly computerised, to match all aspects of customer requirements. Hanging storage is organised by overhead conveyor tracks to cater for changing stock mixes and seasonal variations. Conveyor tracks often follow U-path routes for stock loading and retrieval and some can process up to 340,000 different items for shipment to individual stores and retail outlets. To meet increasing demands from mail order and e-marketing, some distribution systems need to guarantee a 24-hour delivery for orders. Using a Windows-based PC system, barcode scanning and radio-data terminals, it is possible for only six or seven people to manage the distribution of something like 60,000 garments in around eight hours!

TASK

1 Describe the benefits that modern materials handling and distribution systems bring to manufacturers.
2 Investigate the storage systems in use in local retail outlets, to see the kind of systems they operate.
3 Distribution is a key logistical process for mail order and other companies. Using the Internet, investigate the guaranteed delivery schedules for different types of products.

Monitoring quality and safety

Automated and robotic devices are able to do repetitive tasks continuously, since machines, unlike humans, do not need rest breaks. This not only increases productivity, but also can be safer, because of the widespread use of electronic sensors that monitor different manufacturing processes. Safety of the consumer as well as the workforce is vitally important. For example, metal contamination can be a problem in sewn goods. To solve this problem, scanning devices are widely used to pinpoint any metal contamination in fabrics or end products before they get further down the supply chain or even to the consumer.

Optical devices are also used to monitor quality. For example, a company called Optotex has developed a Piezo digital ink-jet printing system, combined with a computer system, for printing lace strips. The lace pattern repeat is scanned into the system and the colouring design added, using Adobe Photoshop software. In production, the lace strip runs under a line-scan camera, which recognises the pattern and compares it with the memorised pattern repeat. The printer can then adapt the print to cater for any variations in the printed lace. This type of system can also be used to automatically adjust pattern pieces on a cutting table, for stripe and check fabrics.

COMPLEX AUTOMATED SYSTEMS USING ARTIFICIAL INTELLIGENCE AND NEW TECHNOLOGY

Artificial intelligence (AI) was defined in 1956 at the Massachusetts Institute of Technology (MIT) and describes a branch of computer science that is concerned with developing computers that think and act like human beings. AI covers a wide range of fields, such as optical and computer engineering, electronics and mechatronics, together with the use of 'expert' systems and 'enabling technologies', that supplement human judgement and specialised knowledge.

AI techniques have a major role to play in supplementing human expertise and in helping to solve complex problems. 'Super computers' nowadays are able to process large amounts of information both simultaneously and quickly in order to make rational, logical or expert judgements, although this ability does not make them 'intelligent'. One way of judging if a computer or machine is intelligent is to ask if it can deceive a human being into thinking that it was human. So far, this hasn't happened!

What is happening though, is that enabling technologies and AI are being used in developments such as:

- production planning and control, using computer-aided control systems
- techniques for judging the physical properties of flexible materials based on objective measurement data

- the redesign of manufacturing processes to meet health, safety and environmental concerns
- production line optical analysis of visual images for quality, safety and process control
- anthropometrics and body measurement systems for mass-customisation of garments
- distribution and bar-coding systems, using computerised warehouses and electronic links between suppliers and customers
- anti-counterfeiting devices, using new technology
- internet-based e-design, e-manufacturing, B2B and e-marketing.

OBJECTIVE MEASUREMENT DATA

Objective measurement of textiles, originally developed in Japan, aims to characterise their physical behaviour under conditions found in processing or wear. Reliable methods for measuring physical characteristics such as stiffness or handle and relating these to sewing and the end-use behaviour of garments were developed in an attempt to automate sewing processes. The automation of sewing processes has been found to be extremely difficult, because many sewn product processes involve the handling of the materials – picking up, turning, flattening, straightening, rather than simply sewing. Objective measurement is increasingly being used to scientifically match the design of fibres, yarns, fabric constructions and coatings to the needs of consumers for comfort, performance, 'touch' and visual aesthetics. This kind of data is useful for:

- using the evaluation of sewing characteristics of different fabrics and finishes to set pre-programmable and micro-processor machine controls
- evaluating tailoring, fusing and final pressing characteristics to set machine controls
- developing sophisticated CAD graphics programs, by numerically specifying fabric drape and folding characteristics
- communicating required standards for fabric handle to manufacturers, suppliers or retailers.

ANTHROPOMETRICS AND BODY MEASUREMENT SYSTEMS

Much of the currently used anthropometrical data is out of date and reflects a narrow cross-section of the population, such as members of the armed forces. Their measurements were closely measured because of the requirement for uniforms. Also average body sizes are changing due to better diets, changing lifestyles and less exercise. Consumers, particularly the increasing sector of the older generation, are more interested in garment fit, comfort and functionality. All of these related reasons, together with developments in CAD systems, have led to important new 3D virtual modelling techniques and in body scanning technology at point-of-sale or for feed back to bespoke garment manufacturing systems. Such systems have the possibility of combining CIM with computerised distribution systems, to provide mass customisation, mainly for the older market, which has an increasing spending power.

COMPUTERISED WAREHOUSING AND DISTRIBUTION

As we have seen earlier in this unit, there have been numerous developments in the use of computer systems in warehousing and distribution. For example Wincanton Logistics is providing manufacturers and retailers with a new 'Global Track and Trace' Internet-based software system. This will enable customers to track individual products from manufacture to the retail outlet. Manufacturers and retailers can check through the Internet to see if an order has left the factory in any part of the world, if it has been shipped and where it is at sea. Using network modelling within the system, it will be possible to build up a computer model of the whole supply chain, to see where bottlenecks occur and identify where costs can be reduced.

Another system involves the use of 'intelligent tags', using Radio Frequency Identification (RFID) tagging. This works by applying the tags to individual items at the warehouse. The tags are programmed with a unique ID, item description, time and date before being despatched to the store. The receipt of the item at the store becomes completely automated. A radio antenna reads the tags as the items arrive and the system automatically updates the store's computerised stock control system. The need for manual counting is eliminated. A second radio antenna monitors the movement of the item through the store and the tag is removed at the checkout for re-use.

ANTI-COUNTERFEITING DEVICES

In a world of global brands, the counterfeiting of branded garments is a serious problem. Various methods for identifying counterfeit goods have been developed, including DNA tagging, especially for expensive fibres. However, a new system has been developed, which uses what are called the 'Unique Identity' neck labels. These are made using a laser-etched Mylar thread running through the label, which includes the following information:

• the brand name
• a 2D data matrix number woven into it
• an individual product number
• a secret identity point, that can be accessed by a limited number of people.

All the information on the neck labels can be downloaded onto hand-held computers in the shop and any garment can be monitored anywhere in the world.

THE DEVELOPMENT OF ARTIFICIAL INTELLIGENCE

The development of AI is focusing on building responsive manufacturing systems that integrate the use of CAD modelling, AI, ICT and knowledge-based databases. Research areas currently include neural networks, voice recognition systems and natural language processing.

- A neural network is a computer system modelled on how the human brain and nervous system work. Whereas a computer manipulates data in zeros and ones, a neural network reproduces the types of processing connections (neurons) that occur in the human brain. This kind of neural network is effective for predicting events, when it has a large database of examples to draw on and is proving successful in systems used for voice recognition and language processing.

- A voice recognition system can recognise the spoken word and currently can take dictation but cannot understand what is being said. Since such systems are high cost and have operating limitations, they have only been used as an alternative to a computer keyboard. The main benefit is when working in a hostile environment, when an operator is disabled or the use of a keyboard is impracticable. It is hoped that in the future an operator will be able to talk directly to an expert system for guidance or instruction.

- The use of Natural Language Processing(NLP) is hoped will enable computers to understand human languages. This would allow people to interact with computers without the need for any specialised knowledge. Making this concept work had been more difficult than originally thought. At the moment, some rudimentary translation systems between human languages exist, but they are nowhere near as good as a human translator!

TASK

1 Explain and give examples of what is meant by an enabling system.
2 Discuss the role that enabling technologies play in the development of modern manufacturing systems.
3 Would you buy branded goods at markdown prices, knowing that they were probably counterfeit? Explain your views.

THE USE OF BLOCK FLOW DIAGRAMS AND FLOW PROCESS DIAGRAMS FOR REPRESENTING SIMPLE AND COMPLEX SYSTEMS

BLOCK FLOW DIAGRAMS

Systems thinking is evident all over the natural and manufactured world, in things like central heating systems, audio systems and in weather systems. In systems thinking, a system is a co-ordinated arrangement of activities working together in which inputs are processed into outputs.

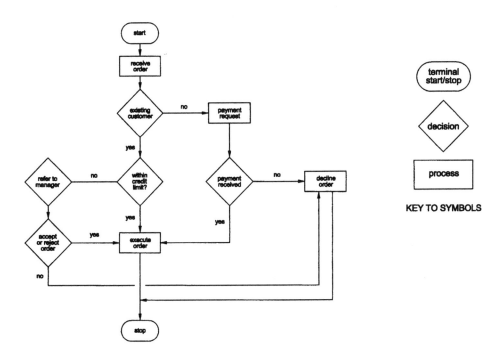

Figure 4B.20

'Block diagram symbols are used to identify activities within a system'

In a simple manufacturing system, for example, the input could be textile raw materials, the process is the product manufacture and the output is finished products delivered to customers. A systems diagram, such as a block flow diagram, explains how the activities that make up the system are organised and related to one another. They also explain the processes that change an input into an output.

FLOW PROCESS DIAGRAMS

All systems contain sub-systems that perform all the processes required to achieve the necessary output. Complex processes in any manufacturing system are modelled by breaking down the whole system into a series of sub-systems. Each of these has its own input and output.

In a production line, it is sometimes necessary to treat each processing sub-system as a system in its own right. This makes it possible to work out the

Figure 4B.21

A processing system for trousers.

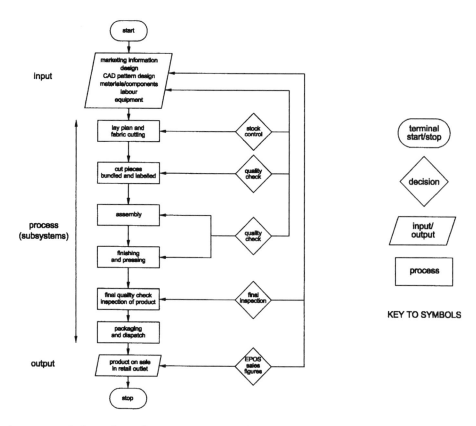

input needed so the sub-system can perform its output function in the whole production schedule.

OPEN AND CLOSED LOOP CONTROL SYSTEMS

A system that operates open-loop control has no feedback at all and continues to work without any interference from the control system. This can be a major disadvantage in an automated process, because there are no checks and balances if anything goes wrong. A system that operates a closed loop control can have two sorts of feedback: positive or negative, in which information is fed back and combined with the input in order to modify the output signal.

- Positive feedback in an automated process results in the system becoming unstable. The reason for this is that any increase in the output leads to an increase in the input. This, in turn, leads to an increase in the output, so the loop starts again.
- Negative feedback changes the input so that the output is decreased to provide stable operating conditions. This is why it is often used in automated control processes.
- In any system that has feedback, the error signal is the difference between the input signal and the feedback signal. The error signal's size determines how much the system output will need to be changed. A system in a near stable state will have an error signal of almost zero. For example, in a high volume garment company, an error signal would be generated if there were a difference between the projected sales figures and the actual ones. If sales were higher than expected, this would generate a positive error signal and

indicate the need to increase the level of production. If sales fell to below the projected level, this would generate negative error signal and indicate the need to reduce production.

- Hunting occurs when a system cannot reach a stable state. If in the high volume garment company, the production level were overcorrected, it would swing the error signal from positive to negative or vice-versa. Any production system, therefore, is continually searching to set the right production levels that will result in delivering goods on time, with no waste or problems.

- In any automated process or large-scale system, it takes time for the system to respond to the feedback signals it is getting. For example, a faulty batch of products that gets into the distribution chain may not be noticed until it gets to the retail outlet or the customers. The time delay before the system is able to respond is known as lag, which is a common feature in closed loop control systems. Manufacturers are using ICT systems to improve communications at all levels of the supply chain, in order to limit problems caused by lag. These systems include Electronic Data Interchange (EDI) and improved real-time sales data from Electronic Point of Sales (EPOS) systems.

TASK

Suggest where hunting and lag might occur and how they might affect an automated production system that you have studied. Explain the steps that can be taken to minimise the effect they have on the system.

AUTOMATED SYSTEMS USING CLOSED LOOP CONTROL SYSTEMS

Automated systems that use open loop control systems are at a disadvantage when controlling a device such as an electric motor on a conveyor belt. The motor may decrease in speed or stop completely if it is put under too great a load, resulting in overheating. One way of overcoming this is to use a closed loop system in which negative feedback provides proportional control of the

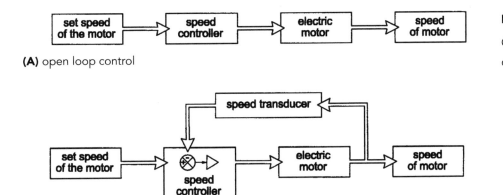

(A) open loop control

(B) closed loop control

Figure 4B.22

Open- and closed-loop control of an electric motor.

motor speed. If there is any difference between the required motor speed and its actual speed, an error signal is fed back to the speed controller, which adjusts the speed of the motor in order to stabilise the conveyor belt.

Sequential control programs

Sequential control programs, in which a series of actions take place one after another, are often used in robotic and automated processes. For example, in an automated fabric laying-up system, each action depends on the previous one having been carried out. If the laying-up system hasn't 'sensed' that the fabric to be loaded is ready waiting in position, the machine will not operate. It will wait until the sensor sends it the required signal to pick up the fabric.

Combinational logic used in the operational control

In situations where a series of conditions have to be met before an operation can take place, combinational logic is used. In the fabric laying-up machine, for example (see Figure 4B.23), all three of the inputs have to be 'on' for the machine to operate. The inputs are controlled by the logic gates AND / OR / NAND. Similar operations can be performed by PLCs.

Figure 4B.23

All of the three inputs have to be 'on' for the CNC fabric laying-up machine to work.

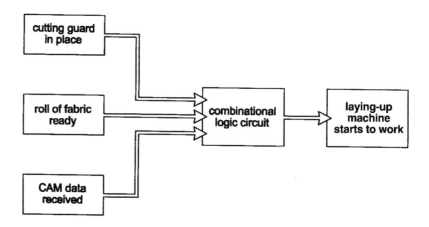

Fuzzy logic systems

Fuzzy logic systems are used in artificial intelligence applications, expert systems, database retrieval and engineering. They were developed in the 1960s, as a way of recognising more than just the straightforward true and false values based on 0s and 1s, that are used in the design of electronic systems. Fuzzy logic allows for the representation of degrees of true and false propositions. For example, the statement, 'today is sunny', could be 100 per cent true if there are no clouds at all, 70 per cent true if there are some clouds, 40 per cent true if it's a bit hazy and 0 per cent true if it rains all day long. Fuzzy logic, therefore, is an attempt to apply a more human-like way of thinking, by allowing for conditions such as 'quite warm' or 'somewhat cold' to be formulated mathematically and processed by computers.

Fuzzy controllers

Fuzzy controllers work differently from conventional systems controllers. They are the most important applications of fuzzy theory and use expert knowledge instead of equations to describe a system. This expert knowledge can be expressed using linguistic variables, which can be described by a fuzzy set – this is a collection of objects or entities without clear boundaries. Fuzzy control is used for:

- very complex processes, where there is no simple mathematical model
- non-linear processes
- the processing of (linguistically formulated) expert knowledge.

Fuzzy control is less useful when:

- conventional control theory provides a satisfying result
- a mathematical model already exists
- the problem cannot be solved.

HOW ROBOTS ARE CONFIGURED

Robots can be configured to move and work in a number of different ways. A robot can operate as a manipulator or can provide a load carrying function. The final configuration depends on the work volume and the area in which the end effector of the robot can be operated.

Degrees of freedom in a robotic system

The type of movements that a robot can provide is similar to the tool path motion of a CNC tool. The robot movements can include point to point motion, contouring or continuous path (linear, arcs or combination moves). Figure 4B.25 shows how the end effector on a jointed or articulated robot arm

Figure 4B.24 (left)
A robot arm.

Figure 4B.25 (right)
The six degrees of freedom on a jointed or articulated robotic arm.

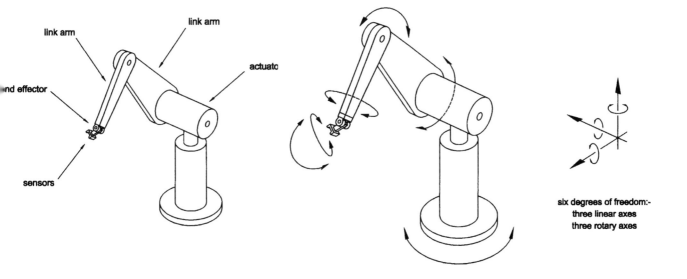

six degrees of freedom:-
three linear axes
three rotary axes

can be positioned to give five or six degrees of freedom within the work volume – three linear and three rotational. Usually three degrees of freedom are provided by the main operating mechanism, with the other two or three provided by the end effector, depending on how it is configured.

TASK

Explain how the different types of robotic movement described above can they be applied in an automated production process. Use diagrams to explain your answer.

METHODS OF PROVIDING FEEDBACK IN AN AUTOMATED PROCESS.

In automated processes, electronic switching and control circuits have three stages, input, processing and output. The sensors and switches used in the automated process are called input transducers, which are used to provide feedback information. A transducer allows electronic circuits to interface with the physical world. They provide either an analogue or a digital signal,

Figure 4B.26

Sensing and control in an automated system, using a robot.

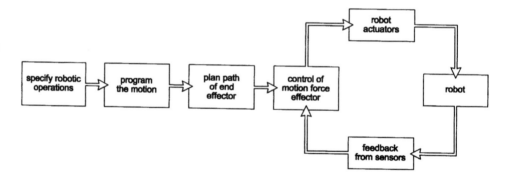

depending on how they operate. An analogue signal is:

- produced from a transducer device, such as a heat sensor used in a plastics production process. As the temperature increases, the signal produced by the heat sensor increases. As the temperature falls, the signal falls
- continuously varying, but it its action is to switch the heater on or off – which is a digital operation (on or off)
- one that has to be converted into a digital signal, so it can be processed by a computer-based control system. (All computers operate digitally, using on or off – 0s or 1s).

Analogue to digital conversion (A/D) is a critical process for providing feedback in computer control applications.

THE ADVANTAGES AND DISADVANTAGES OF AUTOMATION AND ITS IMPACT ON EMPLOYMENT, BOTH LOCAL AND GLOBAL

CREATING A COMPETITIVE ADVANTAGE

All manufacturing organisations need to develop production systems that respond to internal changes related to machinery or labour, as well as being able to respond to changes in the market place on a global scale. The global textile and sewn goods industry is increasingly likely to be dominated by large companies and by supply chain relationships. Two approaches appear to be dominant:

- newly industrialised countries (NICS) – where labour costs together with the latest production technology enable the manufacture of competitive, low-cost basic products
- the Japanese approach – where new technologies applied to fibres, fabrics, textile and product machinery are used to create competitive advantage through the use of superior production capabilities to produce innovative products.

LABOUR INTENSIVE PROCESSES OR NEW TECHNOLOGIES

Within manufacturing itself an increasing distinction has emerged between:

- different processes, such as design, fabric cutting and distribution, where large economies of scale and highly expensive technology are used
- the basic sewing and assembly operations, which are likely to remain labour intensive, though supported by ever more sophisticated, flexible and integrated technology.

The introduction of team working, Unit Production Systems (UPS) and CIM have transformed much in the way of organisation, skills and training requirements of the sewing room, but these changes are still unlikely to alter the labour-intensive nature of sewing. Lower labour costs, therefore are likely to continue to be the aim of most companies.

Automation and employment trends

Global competition also forces companies to compete on quality, delivery, flexibility, innovation, and service. The trend towards greater and more frequent product variety, smaller batch sizes, mass customisation and even more demanding delivery schedules is becoming the norm. One of the social impacts of all these changes and trends is the negative impact on local and global employment patterns. The other major impact that is likely, is that there will be a growing separation between centralised cutting operations and product assembly. This has already happened in Germany, where fully automated design, planning and cutting departments send cut work to low cost sewing companies in Eastern Europe. Made-up products are returned to computerised warehouses where they are prepared for delivery to retail outlets. Some of these distribution centres have the facility to press and finish the products.

Advantages of increased use of automation
- Large economies of scale in materials utilisation, cutting and distribution.
- Faster time to market though the use of flexible manufacturing systems, CAD/CAM and electronic communications.
- Greater potential for mass customisation through use of anthropometrics and body scanning.
- Increased levels of productivity through the use of CIM, PDM and computer systems for planning operations.
- Improved product quality through the use of computer systems and new technology for monitoring processes.

Disadvantages of automation
- The cost of buying and installing new technology.
- The cost of training personnel to use new technology.
- The cost of having to constantly keep up with new technology.
- Issues related to the over-production of non-essential goods.

The impact of automation on patterns of employment
People working in a manufacturing environment need to be flexible and adaptable to change, so that they can transfer their existing skills and experience to new situations. They need to continually develop their ICT skills and undertake education and training on a regular basis. In the UK, there is a shortage of people with technical skills wanting to work in the sewn product industry, particularly people trained in pattern cutting and those with engineering skills.

The increasing use of automation will impact upon all of us.

- One of its major impacts is related to the move to manufacturing in low-wage economies, in which there are winners and losers worldwide.
- The pattern in the reduction of available work, due to increased use of automation, may be repeated across the world.
- The control of CNC machines by robotic devices, rather than by human intervention can lead to poor job satisfaction.

Chapter 3

Uses of Information and Communications Technology (ICT) in the Manufacture of Products

THE IMPACT OF ICT WITHIN THE TOTAL MANUFACTURING PROCESS

Since the 1990s, some of the forces driving the sewn goods industry have included an increased emphasis on design, innovative fabrics, flexibility, quick response and quality. These may not be entirely new concepts, but they have been given a fresh stimulus by the changes in the structure of the supply chain worldwide and by the need to focus more on the requirements of the individual consumer. New technologies have grown up around these concepts, with computer systems at their centre. Key to the integration of all these new technologies is ICT, based on the development of Integrated Service Digital Networks (ISDN).

ELECTRONIC COMMUNICATIONS

ICT has revolutionised the way manufacturing industries work, enabling companies to communicate information quickly and to design and manufacture on a global scale. ICT integrates the use of computer systems and electronic links, enabling business partners to 'talk' to each other electronically. This cost-effective and efficient technology is gradually being adopted by many industries as an essential tool. We are witnessing the invention of many new terms: e-mail, e-design, e-manufacturing, e-business, e-commerce, e-distribution, e-marketing. (There will be many more!) All of these new e-terms (!) reflect the impact that the electronic revolution is having throughout the commercial and manufacturing world.

E-MAIL

This is still the simplest form of transferring data and file attachments with template documents. When using e-mail within a company for sending data to an individual or a work group, it has what is called a low level of 'reach' and 'range'.

- Reach refers to the possible level of communication with other users across a communications network.
- Range refers to the types of data transfer that can take place.

The key to efficiency when using e-mail is to automatically transfer data into

Figure 4B.27

Businesses need to have a strategy for developing e-commerce.

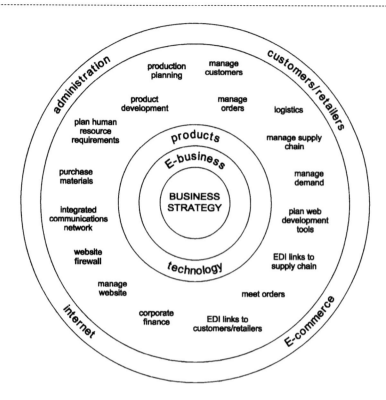

a company's administrative system. In a company with, say, 2,500 internal e-mail users, access to the Internet may be restricted to a minimum number of people who need to communicate with customers. This simplifies the control of the system and helps prevent 'hackers' and viruses getting into the company's internal system. Many companies maintain two 'firewalls' with virus-scanning software as protection.

When data can be shared electronically within a company, it puts in place the basic building block for the development of an effective computer-integrated manufacturing system that has extended reach and range. In order to achieve complete 'Electronic Data Interchange', a number of requirements need to be in place.

ELECTRONIC DATA INTERCHANGE (EDI)

EDI is defined as the transfer of structured data by agreed message standards, from one computer to another by electronic means. Full implementation of EDI requires the development of standards and systems for communication between trading partners in the supply chain. EDI has three basic requirements:

- a message standard – a standard way of representing the data to be transferred in a way that is recognisable to both computers.
- translation software – computer software that interfaces with in-house company systems, allowing it to be converted to the message standard and vice-versa.
- a method of transmitting standard data from one computer to another – across local, wide area and global networks.

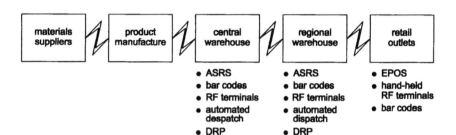

Satellite monitoring of distribution

KEY
ASRS automatic storage and retrieval system
RF   radio frequency
DRP distribution requirements planning

EDI has become an effective mechanism of communication for trading partners in the supply chain, from textile production, making-up and distribution to retailing. It has been instrumental in implementing manufacturing strategies such as Quick Response and Just in Time. Marks & Spencer have been using EDI since 1986, although Boots the chemist pioneered one of the first EDI services in the late 1970s.

Electronic Data Exchange (EDE)

One of the most important aspects of EDI is its ability to exchange technological data about products. The process of exchanging design and manufacturing data is called CDI (CAD/CAM Data Interchange). The system by which EDI and CDI are combined to provide automated transfer of data over a computer network is called EDE – Electronic Data Exchange. Various networks are available for implementing EDE systems, such as ISDN, LAN, WAN, Intranet, Extranet and global networks, such as the Internet.

INTEGRATED SERVICES DATA NETWORK (ISDN)

ISDN is an international communications standard that uses digital telephone lines to transfer data, images, voice and video along the whole supply chain from fibre manufacturer to point-of-sale. The data transfer rate (the throughput) is the speed with which data can be transmitted. ISDN provides high-speed data transfer rates more than three times faster than the fastest modems. This makes them ideal for transferring large data files such as CAD drawings. They offer the possibility of extending product visualisation right into the customer's home through the electronic equivalents of mail order and catalogue shopping – this kind of selling is called e-marketing.

TASK

1 Discuss the impact of the use of electronic communications on business worldwide.

2 Describe how changes communications systems have led to the development of ISDN.

Local Area Networks (LAN)

EDI enables the transfer of data using local area networks, which transmit data within a building. They are usually set up using systems that best meet a company's individual needs and restrict communications to the internal company networks, making them closed systems. These are usually protected by firewalls to keep the company business secure. A LAN can be used to communicate manufacturing data from the design office directly to CNC manufacturing equipment within the same building.

Wide Area Networks (WAN)

EDI enables the transfer of data using wide area networks (WAN), which transmit data from building to building, either next door, in different towns or in different countries. A WAN is a specially set up, controlled and managed cable, radio or digital telephone link between business and manufacturing centres. All WANs follow agreed standards and protocols to ensure compatibility between different computer systems. Many companies are now using the global network provided by the Internet.

Intranets

An Intranet is one company's own internal Internet, with web-type pages that are used to share departmental data and news. An Intranet can work within a building using a LAN or connect to other locations using a WAN. Access to an Intranet is controlled by username and password, so that only authorised company staff can use it and a firewall prevents unauthorised access from outsiders into the site.

Extranets

An Extranet is a group of business partners' own internal Internet, providing various levels of access between them. An Extranet connects the various partner buildings in a secure way, using a WAN and like Intranets, access is controlled by a username and password. The identity of the user will determine which parts of the network they can enter, with full access sometimes reserved for the most senior executives.

GLOBAL NETWORKS

EDI enables the transfer of data using global networks, such as the Internet, which uses cable, radio and satellite links to transmit data worldwide. The Internet, or World Wide Web (WWW) is a global network of millions of Internet servers. Web browsers, such as Netscape Navigator and Microsoft's Internet Explorer, make it easy to access the Internet. Each website on the Internet has its own address called an URL (Universal Resource Locator). A search engine, such as Yahoo collects together and lists URLs under subjects, to enable easy access to web pages. These are written in a language called **HTML** (HyperText Mark-up Language), which supports links to graphics, audio and video files. By clicking on 'hot spots' (Hyperlinks), you can easily jump from one website to another.

Benefits and disadvantages of the Internet

The Internet is an essential tool for those working in the supply chain, because it provides:

- an easy and relatively inexpensive way of sharing ideas
- a growing body of knowledge (remember, though, it has no 'quality control' and what appears on it may not be correct)

- a widely accessible medium for communicating with current and potential customers and for seeing what the competition doing
- a round the clock source of information about everything under the sun – ranging from product specifications to market trends to company values.

Although industrial espionage is a real problem in a paper-rich environment, computer systems can be even less secure. Computer viruses are another problem. There are various methods for improving security, such as passwords, data encryption techniques and firewalls. It is said that e-mail is the most insecure form of electronic communication – we have all heard stories of teenage hackers getting into highly secret or sensitive websites. The problem is that the more secure a system, the more difficult it becomes to use.

TASK

1 Explain the difference between a LAN, WAN and a global network.

2 Describe the benefits to designers and manufacturers of using the Internet.

3 It is easy to get sidetracked when accessing the WWW, so it is important to be clear about what you want to find out. Using a search engine of your choice, produce a list of websites that provide information about fibres and products. Put together a presentation, using a software package like PowerPoint, to share your information with your peers.

VIDEO CONFERENCING (VC)

Computers, electronic communications and video technologies have revolutionised the way people live and work today. The technique called video conferencing integrates these three technologies. It enhances communications, speeds up decision-making and eliminates the need for time-consuming travel to meetings, which may be across the other side of the world. VC allows two or more people at different locations to communicate visually and verbally through the use of computer networks that transmit audio and video data.

Until the mid-1990s, hardware costs made video conferencing too expensive for some companies, but falling prices now mean that VC is a rapidly growing ICT sector. Different forms of VC organisation include:

- Multi-point VC – this enables three or more people to sit in a 'virtual' conference room and conduct a meeting as if they were in the same room.
- Desktop video conferencing (DTVC) – this works like a video telephone between two people. Each person has a video camera, microphone and speakers attached to a desktop computer, equipped with a sound card. This means that each person can see and hear the other talk right on their desktop monitors.

Video conferencing technology

Typically, a desktop video conferencing (DTVC) set-up uses a board that digitises and compresses video data. This data is sent to the receiving computer terminal, where it is decompressed and reconstructed in the form of the original data. Compressing and decompressing DTVC data can be achieved using a CODEC (Compression – Decompression) system involving hardware or software. The more compressed the video data, the bigger and smoother the video images on the receiving computer terminal.

- For face-to-face VC, a miniature video camera is attached above a computer screen. Its narrow field of vision and relatively short depth of focus is not a problem if only one individual is using the system. A DTVC system also requires loudspeakers and a microphone, which can pick up a number of voices.
- For larger groups of people, conventional tripod-mounted camcorders are required. These enable all the individuals to speak and be seen, without the need to be constantly moving into a small video camera's line of vision. Several microphones are better for larger groups and they are usually controlled by a sound 'mixer'.

Using ISDN lines to send audio-visual data

It is relatively straightforward to send audio data over standard telephone lines, because these were originally intended for voice communications. However, standard telephone lines do not handle video data very well, because these contain much more information than audio. Sending complex audio-visual data, therefore requires a much greater information-carrying capability. This is provided by the use of ISDN lines which provide a wider 'bandwidth'. The use of limited bandwidth, maybe trying to send audio-visual by standard telephone lines, can result in VC problems, such as:

- video pictures that are jerky or 'choppy'
- the sound and picture being 'out of sync' – caused by synchronisation problems
- poor quality, fuzzy images.

The use of two-channel ISDN lines for VC and other applications is now commonplace. Two-channel lines are capable of handling a tremendous amount of information, ensuring a smooth, 'noise free' video signal and simultaneous file-transfers. For example, at the end of a video conferencing session, a CAD file may need to be sent to another office. The file can be transferred after the VC meeting has ended. However, if a two-channel ISDN line is available, the file can be sent in the background on one channel at the same time as audio-visual is being exchanged on the other channel. Wide-band ISDN lines are also useful for surfing the Internet at the same time as sending a fax or making a telephone call.

Using video conferencing
Videoconferencing can be used for various purposes, including:

1 Remote decision-making and diagnostics
VC is a useful tool for designers working with clients in different locations. For example CAD data can be sent electronically and then discussed between the designer and client in order for decisions to be taken. VC is also useful for quick virtual meetings between a flat pattern maker and the designer, when developing a pattern marker. For example, will the design still function as the designer

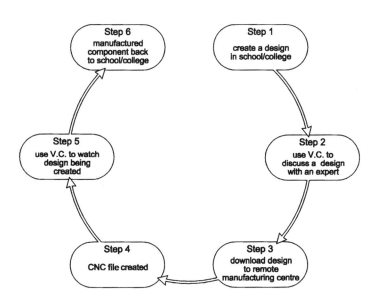

Figure 4B.29

Diagrammatic representation of how VC can be used.

intended, if 1cm is taken off part of the pattern? Both of these scenarios enable a problem to be solved quickly, ensuring a faster time-to-market.

2   Marketing presentations

A manufacturer and its chosen marketing organisation may not always operate in the one country. This can cause problems, as its important to keep track of how the marketing organisation intends to present the product and persuade people to buy it. VC can therefore be a useful tool for seeing a product presentation as it develops and to provide feedback on its effectiveness.

3   Corporate training

VC is used fairly extensively for staff training. It is cheaper and faster to work in this way, after the initial outlay of the costs of setting up the system.

4   Compatability

To date the issue of compatibility has been the biggest difficulty with video conferencing, because several organisations have their own 'standards' for VC hardware and software. Recently, however, the International Tele-communication Union (ITU) has approved a uniform standard as to how audio-visual data should be transmitted across networks. This standard aims to facilitate the use of different VC technologies by users participating in the same conference – in much the same way as IBM and Apple users can communicate via e-mail even though they use different GUIs.

5   Remote manfacturing

In the UK a company called Denford Ltd has developed an on-demand 'Remote Manufacturing' system, enabling staff and Resistant Materials students to use VC to talk to experts at a manufacturing centre and manufacture component parts at a distance in real time, using industry standard equipment and software. If you have the opportunity, try and see this Remote Manufacturing set-up in operation. The steps involved in using VC to facilitate Remote Manufacturing are as follows:

1 Create a design of a component part, using CAD/CAM software
2 Using VC, discuss the design of the component with an expert at the Remote Manufacturing Centre
3 Download the component design to the Remote Manufacturing Centre. Use VC to discuss and/or amend the design, where appropriate
4 Have a CNC file of the component design created at the Remote Manu-facturing Centre
5 Use VC to watch the component manufactured on a CNC machine
6 Using VC, evaluate the finished component. Wait for it to arrive by post back at school or college.

(See Figure 4B.29.)

TASK

1 Explain the technology that enables companies to use video conferencing.

2 Describe the benefits that video conferencing could bring to product design.

3 Suggest ways that VC could be used to aid the manufacture of a sewn goods product.

NEW COMMUNICATIONS TECHNOLOGY – ELECTRONIC WHITEBOARDS

Electronic whiteboard technology grew out of the fax machine and the photocopier, to develop what is sometimes called a 'smart board'. An electronic whiteboard is like an ordinary white board that incorporates the power of a computer. This makes it an interactive, flexible device for use at all stages of the design process, for recording data, developing specifications, giving presentations and many other uses.

Electronic whiteboards are portable devices, with approximately an AO-sized usable area, which is perfect for viewing by the whole team. The board can be stood side-by-side with other electronic whiteboards to give very large displays. Touching an electronic whiteboard provides access to:

- a sensitive writing surface that connects to a computer, a scanner and a thermal printer
- computer software such as Word, PowerPoint, spreadsheets and databases, for file manipulation and storage, printing or e-mailing
- data and video images, either stored or live from a camera or VCR
- live or stored data from the Internet
- automatic recordings of VC, which is available for playback and reference.

ELECTRONIC INFORMATION HANDLING

The flexible manufacturing system known as Quick Response (QR) was first put in place as a means of competing with low-cost labour economies. It is now clear that in a time of change and uncertainty, QR, together with the use of ICT, is a driving force in the move away from technology push to that of consumer pull – providing the market with what it wants. The use of electronic information handling systems is essential to the entire supply chain, because it enables the development of working partnership between suppliers, manufacturers and their customers, the retailers. In this sense, the sharing of information is the primary enabling resource and ICT is the enabling technology in the drive towards e-design, e-manufacturing, e-business, e-commerce, e-distribution and e-marketing. At the start of any design and manufacturing process, a range of computer based systems is available for collecting market information about consumer needs and wants.

COMPUTER-AIDED MARKET ANALYSIS (CAMA)

Market research involves the collection of data about colour and styling trends, consumer lifestyle and niche-markets and such like. The analysis of market research data is used to predict the future of a specific market trends. Many companies use the services of trend-forecasting organisations such as Promostyl or Peclers Paris. Other specialist market research companies can provide customised data related to demographics, business and finance, consumers or market segments.

CAMA enables the analysis of this kind of market research data, often managed most effectively through the use of a computerised relational database. Other market research involves the analysis of product sales data, collected through electronic point-of-sale tills. Many retail organisations use Enterprise Resource planning software (ERP) to manage this information, which defines their relationship with consumers and manufacturers. Information is compiled from sales, marketing and customer service activities and stored on a database. The database can be questioned in various ways, depending on the type of information required.

- Qualitative analysis provides information, such as who is buying a specific type of product and what consumers like or dislike about it.
- Quantitative analysis provides factual numerical information, such as where, when and how many of this type of product is bought.
- Trend analysis provides information, such as lifestyle requirements of differing market segments.

CAMA is useful for providing market research data for formulating e-business strategies and for supply chain planning. It enables access to up-to-date research, in-depth market analysis and industry-specific expertise. Using computer-based market analysis software can help manufacturers and retailers to:

- convert data into usable information, such as graphs and pie charts that aid marketing and planning decisions
- calculate accurate product demand and sales targets
- identify market segments and where potential consumers shop
- target market segment groups that have specific characteristics
- use focused strategies such as regional or mini product launches.

COMPUTER AIDED SPECIFICATION DEVELOPMENT (CASP)

Computer-aided specification development saves time and costs through basing new product specifications on those already held in a Product Data Management (PDM) system. The new specification is therefore a variation on an existing one. The integration of all aspects of design into an 'intelligent' database like a PDM system, enables the development of CAD data, a design library and a knowledge database.

- CAD data provides specific information about the aesthetic, technical and cost characteristics of each product – the product design and manufacturing specifications.
- The design library is a reference database that contains a history, together with manufacturing details of every product produced by a company.
- The knowledge database provides information about design and manufacturing methods.

The development of a PDM system enables a design team to manage the whole product development from conception to manufacture. One of its major benefits is that it incorporates a design team's 'expert' knowledge, which remains readily available, even when individual team members move on to another company.

TASK

1 During your product development you have developed your own 'expert' system of knowledge and understanding. Using this knowledge, list six design and six manufacturing strategies that you have applied. These could relate to raw materials, production planning, cost control, quality assurance, production processes, the monitoring and impact of environmental issues, health and safety.

2 Discuss how you could use a computer application to set up an expert system to aid product development and manufacture.

AUTOMATED STOCK CONTROL

Earlier in this unit we saw how the use of computer systems enable Just in Time – materials and components ordered just in time for production – to function successfully. A characteristic of JIT is that waste and resulting costs are reduced, through the availability of materials on demand in the right quantities. Automated stock control systems are supporting the move to bespoke or customised mass production and are integral to the process of line balancing, a scheduling technique that reduces waiting times caused by unbalanced production times.

PRODUCTION SCHEDULING AND PRODUCTION LOGISTICS

Computer-based scheduling and logistics systems ensure the implementation of a production plan, so that production is balanced to meet demand. This is achieved by the use of software such as PDM, which manages the allocation of work and the progress of orders against changing situations. The integration of all sides of a business, including planning, manufacturing, sales and marketing can be achieved through the use of Enterprise Resource Planning systems (ERP). The advantage of computer-based scheduling and logistics applications is that they are:

- flexible and adaptable to changes in the product range or size of order
- able to balance work in progress and reduce stock levels
- able to control the balance between the work stations in a production system
- able to increase productivity levels.

FLEXIBLE MANUFACTURING SYSTEMS

A flexible manufacturing system such as QR aims to minimise stock levels and cope with a greater number of buying seasons. This focuses on reducing product lead times and the batch production of products that target specific market segments at specific times of the year. For example, a manufacturer may produce a range of back-to-school wear aimed at the under-eleven market, to be marketed in late summer.

QR provides a faster time to market and 'real time' re-programming of manufacturing through Manufacturing Resource Planning (MRP) systems. MRP is a production management tool that offers the potential for enormous savings in both time to market and increased business efficiency. It involves the use of relatively low-cost data collection terminals, which can be installed at each work station, and materials control point. These terminals are able to provide a central computer with a complete real-time breakdown of operator and machine allocations, track specific work through the production cycle, dynamically rebalance production lines and teams, and re-plan production in response changing demand. Stock levels can be constantly re-evaluated as demand patterns change. The use of PDM software to facilitate MRP enables the impact of a change to the business or a manufacturing process, to be immediately available to every member of the team, anywhere in the world.

PRODUCTION CONTROL AND THE MONITORING OF QUALITY

The monitoring of quality involves the use of electronic sensors that use scanning and optical devices. Specialist electronic instruments companies supply a range of devices aimed at knitters, weavers, carpet tufters and yarn producers. These include devices such as:

- broken yarn detectors
- tension devices
- point of manufacture fabric inspection
- data gathering systems
- knitting machine controls
- yarn inspectors
- point of manufacture carpet inspection.

The main advantages of optical methods of monitoring quality are that there is no need for physical contact between the sensor and the product; the distance between the sensor and the product is not critical and there is a fast response time in quality monitoring. The visual monitoring of quality enables manufacturers to detect faults in products, monitor manufacturing processes and monitor product safety.

Using digital cameras

Inspection during the manufacturing process usually involves the selection of a random sample of products. If faults are found at this late stage, re-working is very expensive. It may result in a high level of 'seconds' or scrap. One way of overcoming this problem is the use of a digital camera on the production line. The benefits of kind of computer-based visual control system include the monitoring of work in progress and the tracking of stock used in automated stock control systems.

Advantages of using computer-aided monitoring of quality

Computer-aided systems for monitoring quality provide real time quality control throughout the manufacturing process. Any faults can be identified and analysed, so that changes can be made to optimise the manufacturing system, thus reducing costs. Quality-monitoring software can generate reports that are compliant with ISO9000 and can export the information for use in other applications.

TASK

Discuss the benefits that dedicated computer software can bring to activities like stock control, production scheduling, and management of quality.

PRODUCT MARKETING, DISTRIBUTION AND RETAILING

Product marketing, distribution and retailing are becoming more reliant on the use of integrated software systems to manage the business. In this business climate, terms such as e-commerce, e-distribution and e-marketing are becoming more widely used. Electronic point-of-sale lies at the heart of product marketing.

Electronic point-of-sale (EPOS)

EPOS and EDI are essential elements in the implementation of Quick Response and Just in Time manufacturing and distribution strategies. They speed up the flow of information between manufacturers and retailers, enabling them to keep stock levels to a minimum. The collection of up-to-date information about current sales patterns, directly from retail stores has usually been the first link in this chain to be established. Its more widespread introduction has since been made easier by the development of a common bar-code standard (the Universal Product Code) and by 'open' EDI standards and protocols throughout the textile and sewn product industries.

Figure 4B.30

Communication links in the
supply chain.

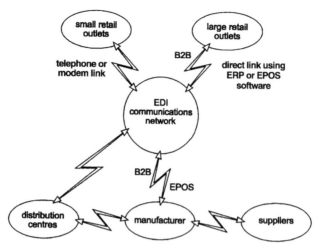

Using Enterprise Resource Planning (ERP)

A range of devices, such as fixed or hand-held bar code readers are used to record electronic information about the product, at the point-of-sale. Retailers use computer software to collect this sales information automatically or at scheduled times during the day, such as at close of business. A wide range of computer options is available for retailers wanting to integrate ICT into their businesses. One option is to rebuild the company's logistics system around Enterprise Resource Planning (ERP) software. This software links up all the activities of a retail business, from warehousing, to accounts, to store deliveries. ERP provides a retailer with greater knowledge about its business and can be a key tool in maximising the allocation of resources and the reduction of waste. Kookai and Bay Trading both use software systems to analyse stock sales data and make it available to buyers, designers, merchandisers and shop staff. This kind of system helps such companies react faster, which is critical in fashion, where ranges must change so frequently.

Business-to-business (B2B)

Not all retailers, however, are ready to invest in ERP systems. The Internet can be a more cost-effective e-commerce option, with facilities such as 24-hour stock ordering and access to accounts status details. Jigsaw, for example, has devised a system where 70 of its tills are linked to the Internet. The tills are continually exchanging sales information so that the consumer and product are united as quickly as possible. The concept of linking up a retailer with a manufacturer via the Internet is termed 'B2B'. This allows the retailer to order stock, check deliveries and view new product collections online, 24-hours a day. B2B is eventually expected to replace EDI as the main method of ordering stock.

e-distribution

Some retailers are using tried and tested e-distribution systems, some of which have been working for the last 15 years, especially those monitoring stock delivery. The childrenswear retailer, Adams, for example, knows exactly where its stock is all the way along the route it takes from Hong Kong to its arrival at its warehouse. New technology, however, has been introduced, mainly at store level, where it is used to check what stock is being bought, which products to re-order and which to drop from its inventory.

The benefits to manufacturers and retailers of EPOS, ERP and B2B

Manufacturers and retailers use electronic communications systems, because they make available:

- up-to-date detailed financial transactions related to specific products
- the data required for a sales/profit margin analysis, which can be exported into accounts management software using spreadsheets
- the monitoring of sales performance figures for all product lines, enabling fast reaction to demand variations
- accurate information about buying trends, which helps organisations make the most effective marketing choices
- a responsive stock control and distribution system covering logistics, stock delivery, transfer between warehouses and retail outlets, stock received and re-ordering.

Internet Marketing

The move to Internet marketing, e-commerce and e-business is a major strategic decision for any company. This major step alters relationships along the supply chain, between manufacturers, retailers and consumers and requires the restructuring of internal and external business processes. Such restructuring is expensive, time consuming and can be disruptive. For some companies, such a move involves greater upheaval than updating production to an automated system, or other ICT- based manufacturing process.

Products on the Web

Check it out! Unit 3B CAD/CAM Virtual merchandising and store layout systems; e-Merchandising; The virtual dressing room. Pages 194-196

For all businesses, the rush to develop Web sites and Internet marketing strategies is a costly activity. For some companies, despite investing heavily in putting their product catalogues on to the WWW, the response has been disappointing. However, the use of Internet-based communications along the supply chain can prove more cost-effective than integrating expensive software solutions. As we saw in Unit 3B CAD/CAM, developments in visual merchandising and e-merchandising, together with the virtual dressing room are set to revolutionise the way the manufacturers, retailers and consumers regard e-marketing.

The move towards using interactive 3D virtual products in e-marketing on the Web would seem to be a natural extension of modern marketing activities.

Manufacturers faced with even shorter product life cycles and increasing global competition, need to ensure that customers not only understand their products, but also have easy access to them. As we have seen with the concept of the virtual dressing room, this can mean enabling consumers to see how a particular garment will fit or which will be the best size to buy.

Some of the potential benefits of e-marketing include:

· instant global reach to new markets and an increased customer base
· the move to faster processing of orders and transactions, resulting in reduced overhead costs
· access to a detailed knowledge of user preferences, leading to improved customer relations
· development of mass customisation of bespoke products with a reduced time-to-market
· a higher company profile on a worldwide basis.

The future use of ICT
Advances in ICT are already providing manufacturing with the benefits a faster time-to-market and for instant viewing of virtual products on the Internet.

As desktop PC based systems become ever more powerful, product development teams can view the progress of a product at every stage of its life cycle, from anywhere in the world. The development of 'knowledge ware' or expert databases, targeted at the design and manufacturing processes can provide an instantly-accessible electronic product library of best practice information and procedures.

The streamlining of product development within manufacturing is likely to continue at an even faster pace. The development of mass-customisation, through the use of body scanning, will allow consumers to have direct access to the design process and product specification via the Internet. Already some Web sites, enable the customisation of products, such as trainers and jeans. The involvement of consumers in specifying their own products, is likely to create new pressures on manufacturers, to manage stock levels and predict product sales. One thing is certain, the integration of computer systems and ICT in e-design, e-manufacturing, e-commerce, e-business and e-marketing is set to continue if companies are to survive in a global economy.

TASK

Discuss the way manufacturing companies are doing business in the light of changing communications technologies. Use products from your chosen materials area, to exemplify your discussion.

EXAM PRACTICE

The questions below are similar in style to the ones you will find in the examination paper for this unit. Before attempting to answer the questions read the relevant sections in the unit. Make note using key words or spider diagrams about the topic.

1 Consumers have differing and ever changing needs that manufacturers try to satisfy with the development of innovative products. When this is combined with the use of new technologies, it increases the pressure on companies to improve the product time-to-market. With the aid of specific examples from your chosen materials area, describe how ICT can be used to develop quick response (QR) systems of manufacture to meet consumer demand.

(15)

2 a) The organisation and management of manufacturing has been completely changed by the use of computer systems. Explain the following terms related to computers used in manufacturing:

    i)   Computer-aided production planning. (2)
    i)   Computer-integrated manufacturing systems. (2)

  b) Describe how computer technology provides support for monitoring the quality of products.

(5)

  c) Using examples from your chosen materials area, evaluate the use of computers in a Flexible Manufacturing System (FMS)

(6)

3 Discuss the impact of the use of CNC machines in the design and manufacture of products within your chosen materials area.

(15)